MW01146651

Foreign in Two Homelands

What happens when migrants are rejected by the host society that first invited them? How do they return to a homeland that considers them outsiders? *Foreign in Two Homelands* explores the transnational history of Turkish migrants, Germany's largest ethnic minority, who arrived as "guest workers" (*Gastarbeiter*) between 1961 and 1973. By the 1980s, amid rising racism, neo-Nazis and ordinary Germans blamed Turks for unemployment, criticized their Muslim faith, and argued they could never integrate. In 1983, policymakers enacted a controversial law: paying Turks to leave. Thus commenced one of modern Europe's largest and fastest waves of remigration: within one year, 15 percent of the migrants – 250,000 men, women, and children – returned to Turkey. Their homeland, however, ostracized them as culturally estranged "Germanized Turks" (*Almancı*). Through archival research and oral history interviews in both countries and languages, Michelle Lynn Kahn highlights migrants' personal stories and reveals how many felt foreign in two homelands. This title is also available as Open Access on Cambridge Core.

Michelle Lynn Kahn is Associate Professor of Modern European History at the University of Richmond. Her research examines post-1945 Germany and Europe in a global and transnational frame, focusing on migration, racism, far-right extremism, gender, and sexuality. She was awarded the 2019 Fritz Stern Dissertation Prize of the German Historical Institute and the 2022 Chester Penn Higby Prize of the American Historical Association.

Publications of the German Historical Institute

Edited by
Simone Lässig
with the assistance of Kelly McCullough

The German Historical Institute (GHI) is a center for advanced study and research whose purpose is to facilitate dialogue and collaboration among historians across national and disciplinary boundaries. The GHI conducts, promotes, and supports research in three core fields: German/ European and Jewish history, the history of the Americas and transatlantic history, and global and transregional history. The GHI works closely with partner institutions and organizations to provide scholars from around the world with opportunities to extend their professional networks and build relationships across borders.

A full list of titles in the series can be found at:
www.cambridge.org/pghi

Foreign in Two Homelands

Racism, Return Migration, and Turkish-German History

MICHELLE LYNN KAHN
University of Richmond

German
Historical Institute
Washington

and

CAMBRIDGE
UNIVERSITY PRESS

CAMBRIDGE
UNIVERSITY PRESS

Shaftesbury Road, Cambridge CB2 8EA, United Kingdom

One Liberty Plaza, 20th Floor, New York, NY 10006, USA

477 Williamstown Road, Port Melbourne, VIC 3207, Australia

314–321, 3rd Floor, Plot 3, Splendor Forum, Jasola District Centre, New Delhi – 110025, India

103 Penang Road, #05–06/07, Visioncrest Commercial, Singapore 238467

Cambridge University Press is part of Cambridge University Press & Assessment, a department of the University of Cambridge.

We share the University's mission to contribute to society through the pursuit of education, learning and research at the highest international levels of excellence.

www.cambridge.org
Information on this title: www.cambridge.org/9781009486712

DOI: 10.1017/9781009486682

© Michelle Lynn Kahn 2024

This publication is in copyright. Subject to statutory exception and to the provisions of relevant collective licensing agreements, with the exception of the Creative Commons version the link for which is provided below, no reproduction of any part may take place without the written permission of Cambridge University Press & Assessment.

An online version of this work is published at doi.org/10.1017/9781009486682 under a Creative Commons Open Access license CC-BY-NC-ND 4.0 which permits re-use, distribution and reproduction in any medium for non-commercial purposes providing appropriate credit to the original work is given. You may not distribute derivative works without permission. To view a copy of this license, visit https://creativecommons.org/licenses/by-nc-nd/4.0

When citing this work, please include a reference to the DOI 10.1017/9781009486682

First published 2024

A catalogue record for this publication is available from the British Library

Library of Congress Cataloging-in-Publication Data
NAMES: Kahn, Michelle Lynn, author.
TITLE: Foreign in two homelands : racism, return migration, and Turkish-German history / Michelle Lynn Kahn, University of Richmond.
DESCRIPTION: Cambridge, United Kingdom ; New York, NY : Cambridge University Press, 2024. | Series: Publications of the German Historical Institute | Includes bibliographical references and index.
IDENTIFIERS: LCCN 2023057629 (print) | LCCN 2023057630 (ebook) | ISBN 9781009486712 (hardback) | ISBN 9781009486682 (ebook)
SUBJECTS: LCSH: Turks – Germany (West) – Social conditions. | Foreign workers – Germany (West) – Social conditions. | Racism – Germany (West) | Turks – Migrations. | Germany (West) – Ethnic relations. | Germany (West) – Race relations. | Germany (West) – Emigration and immigration | Turkey – Emigration and immigration – History – 20th century.
CLASSIFICATION: LCC DD78.T87 K346 2024 (print) | LCC DD78.T87 (ebook) | DDC 305.894/350430904–dc23/eng/20240327
LC record available at https://lccn.loc.gov/2023057629
LC ebook record available at https://lccn.loc.gov/2023057630

ISBN 978-1-009-48671-2 Hardback

Cambridge University Press & Assessment has no responsibility for the persistence or accuracy of URLs for external or third-party internet websites referred to in this publication and does not guarantee that any content on such websites is, or will remain, accurate or appropriate.

To

Lonna, Marvin, and Susan Kahn

My name is foreigner.
I work here,
I know how hard I work.
Do the Germans know it too?
My work is difficult,
My work is dirty.
I don't like it, I say.
If you don't like the work,
Go back to your homeland, they say.
...
But the blame doesn't lie with the Germans,
Nor with the Turks.
Turkey needs remittances,
Germany needs workers.
My country sold us to Germany,
Like stepchildren,
Like useless people.
But they still need remittances.
...
My name is foreigner.

> —"My Name is Foreigner" (Benim Adım Yabancı/
> Mein Name ist Ausländer, 1981), poem by Turkish-
> German anti-racism activist Semra Ertan[1]

---

[1] These lyrics and subsequent quotations (unless otherwise indicated) have been translated
from the Turkish or German by the author. Republished with permission.

The foreign land to which we sold our labor,
In which our sweat dripped onto machines,
In which we earned riches upon riches,
Is now telling us to go back.
...
The babies we birthed in the foreign land grew up
And we handed them over to schools.
Their language is not our language.
They don't know "Merhaba," they say "Guten Tag."
...
I go on vacation once per year,
Treading on the roads of Bulgaria and Yugoslavia,
Longing for Edirne and Ardahan.
My dear homeland calls us "Almancı."
                    —"Almancılar" (1987), song by Turkish
                      rock star Cem Karaca[2]

[2] Republished with permission.

Contents

ix

Figures

Acknowledgments

The spark of an idea for this book began over a decade ago in Vienna, Austria. With multiple zigzags and border crossings along the way, the idea traveled back and forth with me across continents, oceans, and cities near and far – from Los Angeles and Palo Alto, to Ankara and Istanbul, to Cologne and Berlin, and finally, to Richmond, Virginia. The idea and the book that emerged from it transformed along the way, as I wrote, revised, and revised again, each time incorporating new tidbits of information, grand ideas, and constructive feedback from colleagues and friends. This may be the "final" version, but, as this book ultimately concludes, the very concept of finality is itself elusive. After all, to paraphrase Jonathan Petropoulos, my mentor at Claremont McKenna College and the person who first inspired me to become a historian, "Our writing is never done. We just give up on it."

At Stanford University, I began putting this idea on paper. My doctoral advisor, Edith Sheffer, both grounded me and encouraged me to "chase rainbows," as I have often quipped. She infused this project with empathy and humanity, modeling how to center the history of everyday life and the power of ordinary people to shape geopolitical change. Ali Yaycıoğlu pushed me to tell a Turkish story, not only a German one, and to think in broader terms about space, place, landscapes, and journeys across layers of time. J. P. Daughton introduced me to transnational history, expanding my narrow idea of what "Europe" means, who "Europeans" are, and where the boundaries of "Europe" lie. Tara Zahra generously joined my committee from afar, helping me place my story within the larger histories of European migration, gender, sexuality, and the family.

Many others at Stanford pushed me to think across geographic, temporal, and disciplinary borders. In our quest to find new narratives for German history, our tight-knit cohort of Germanist doctoral students – Ian Beacock, Benjamin Hein, and Samuel Huneke – found intersections among topics as diverse as migration, sexuality, emotions, and capitalism. The History Department faculty – particularly Laura Stokes, Estelle Freedman, Ana Minian, and Steven Press – infused my work with insights from the Early Modern period to the present, and from Europe to the Middle East, Latin America, and the United States. Members of the European History Workshop, Gender History Workshop, Program in Feminist, Gender, and Sexuality Studies, and the Haas Center for Public Service offered feedback on the early stages of my writing and helped me conceive of this project within the broader scope of feminist and community-engaged scholarship.

Generous funding made this research possible. The Alexander von Humboldt Foundation, through its German Chancellor Fellowship Program, funded fifteen months of research in Germany. Grants from the Central European History Society, the Europe Center at Stanford University, and Stanford's Abbasi Program in Islamic Studies supported summer research and language training. The Beinecke Scholarship Program and the Stanford History Department provided financial support throughout my graduate career. For sabbatical-year support that allowed me to balance revisions to this manuscript with research on a new project, I thank the American Historical Association for awarding me a Bernadotte E. Schmitt Grant and the United States Holocaust Memorial Museum for granting me a visiting fellowship at the Jack, Joseph, and Morton Mandel Center.

Over the last decade, many colleagues have offered practical advice, read drafts, shared feedback at conferences, and even worked alongside me in the archives. I am especially appreciative of Frank Biess, Astrid M. Eckert, Esra Özyürek, and Edith Sheffer for participating in a manuscript workshop that fundamentally reshaped some of the core arguments of this book, helped me refine my interpretations, and sparked exciting new ideas. For their engagement with this book project at various stages, I thank Rita Chin, Christopher Ewing, Brian J. K. Miller, Jennifer A. Miller, Christopher Molnar, Lauren Stokes, Brian Van Wyck, and Sarah Thomsen Vierra. Participants in numerous conferences, workshops, and invited lectures have further shaped my work. Among them, I am grateful for Jeremy Best, Brandon Bloch, Gideon Botsch, Austin Clements, Jazmine Contreras, Anna Duensing, Jennifer Evans, Atina Grossmann,

Paige Newhouse, Gavriel Rosenfeld, Kira Thurman, Janet Ward, and Jonathan Wiesen. My colleagues at the Documentation Centre and Museum for Migration to Germany (DOMiD e.V.) in Cologne hosted me in-house for eighteen months during my field work. They welcomed me with open arms, invited me onto their team, provided me with my own office, and served as a surrogate family. For their research assistance, guidance, and companionship, I thank the whole DOMiD team: Robert Fuchs, Beate Rieple, Bettina Just, Bengü Kocatürk-Schuster, Timothy Tasch, Sandra Vacca, Fatma Uzun, Burkhard Eiden, and Arnd Kolb. I remain forever inspired by their tireless efforts to bring migration history and migrants' stories to light.

Countless others in Germany made this research possible. I especially thank the staff of the German Federal Archives in Koblenz, the Political Archive of the Foreign Office in Berlin, and the Friedrich Ebert Stiftung in Bonn. Professor Dr. Ralf Jessen hosted me as a guest scholar at the University of Cologne Historical Institute, and the members of the Kolloquium zur Neuren und Neusten Geschichte provided feedback on my early ideas. Steffi De Jong not only sharpened my intellectual ideas and helped me navigate German academia but also made Cologne special by sharing her friendship, laughter, long hikes, museum excursions, evening teas, and many homemade cakes.

In Turkey, many people helped me convey migrants' stories while navigating the limitations of official Turkish archives. The librarians at the Milli Kütüphanesi found documents when I thought none existed. My host mother in Ankara, Emine Zaman, cooked for me every day for six weeks and passed a dictionary across the kitchen table to teach me Turkish. Burcu Karahan, my Turkish language professor at Stanford, hosted me at her parents' home in the beach town of Şarköy during two summers of oral history interviews. She took me door-to-door to visit all the return migrants in her parents' neighborhood, sat in on hours-long interviews, and translated orally when needed. On my second visit to Şarköy, my bus arrived just three hours after Turkey's 2016 military coup, and the Karahan family took great care to make sure that I felt secure.

It became clear early on that Cambridge University Press, the German Historical Institute (GHI), Washington DC, and the Friends of the GHI would be strong partners in this project. Liz Friend-Smith at Cambridge guided me clearly and efficiently through the acquisition process. The GHI has supported this project since 2017, when I presented one of my first conference papers at the inaugural Bucerius Young Scholars Forum.

Two subsequent talks at the GHI elicited lively audience questions that enriched this book. One of those talks occurred in November 2019, when I was fortunate to be awarded the Fritz Stern Dissertation Prize of the Friends of the GHI. I thank the members of the prize committee and the Friends in general for their support for and endorsement of my work. David Lazar and Richard Wetzell first encouraged me to publish my book in the Publications of the GHI series. Simone Lässig and Kelly McCullough have been fantastic editors; their enthusiasm, intellectual engagement, clear communication, and logistical guidance have enriched the book itself and made the publication process smooth and enjoyable. I would also like to thank GHI intern Jacob Forbes and indexer Christine Brocks for their contributions.

Many individuals and institutions generously granted me permission to reprint photographs, cartoons, song lyrics, and text in this book. The second chapter is a revision of my previous article: "The Long Road Home: Vacations and the Making of the 'Germanized Turk' across Cold War Europe," *The Journal of Modern History* 93, no. 1 (2021): 109–49. Likewise, certain parts of this book contain text from another one of my previous articles: "Rethinking Central Europe as a Migration Space: From the Ottoman Empire through the Cold War and the Refugee Crisis," *Central European History* 55, no. 1 (2022): 118–37. I am grateful to *Central European History* editor Monica Black for encouraging me to write the latter article, which proved instrumental to my thinking as I revised this book.

The University of Richmond provided an ideal home as I completed my revisions. I am immeasurably grateful for the warm welcome, encouragement, and mentorship of my colleagues in the History Department. Across disciplines, colleagues in the Global Studies Program, German Studies Program, Jewish Studies Program, Faculty Learning Community on Migration, Humanities Connect Program, and Interim Jewish Life Advisory Committee have enriched my experience at the university. Completing these revisions while adjusting to a new campus would have been impossible without the administrative support of Debbie Govoruhk, Sabrina Anderson, Liza Carpenter, Nancy Probst, and Emily Woody Tarchokov.

Most rewardingly, I have had the privilege of working with many talented undergraduate students. Robert Bentley, Maggie Castelli, Simon Curry, Carly Kessler, Ian Levy, and Caroline Martin provided invaluable research assistance. Janis Parker read the entire final draft of this manuscript and provided sharp critique of both its ideas and style. Joe

Haines and Adelaide Tracey engaged astutely with my writing at numerous stages. Countless other students – especially Christopher Barry, Saige
Beatman, Courtney Ford, Kristin Joostema, and Rachel Matthews – supported my work with enthusiasm and provided much-appreciated moral
support as I balanced scholarship, teaching, and academic service.

I am likewise grateful for my strong network of friends. During our
writing retreats and strategy sessions, Mackenzie Cooley kept me on
pace, helped me think more expansively, and pushed me to achieve more
than I ever thought I could. Rebecca Gruskin not only deepened my
ideas but also encouraged me to treat myself kindly, know my limits,
and remind myself that "everyone is doing their best." The broader
graduate student community at Stanford provided support, stimulation,
and levity, especially Branden Adams, Lukas Dovern, Ali Karamustafa,
and Vladimir Hamed-Troyansky. Nisrine Rahal provided crucial guidance and friendship during the final stages of production. Special thanks
go to Samantha Goldman, Evan Faber, Samantha Wendler, Christopher
Lawyer, Maddie McElfresh, Kevin Clatterbuck, and all my fellow ath-
letes at the Weight Room.

My family endured their own "separation anxieties" while I was away
researching for months and years. Bettie and Gene Mathless have supported my education since childhood, and Lonna, Marvin, and Susan
Kahn opened their homes to me as a refuge. John, Sharon, Matthew,
Jennifer, and Ella Douglas warmly welcomed me into their family. My
brothers, Michael and Daniel Kahn, continually remind me that there is,
in fact, life beyond history. Michael has instilled in me crucial habits for
success, and Daniel has provided wisdom beyond his years. My parents,
Carole and Richard Kahn, have given me more than I can express in
words. With her biting wit, take-charge attitude, and relentless perse-
verance, my mother has ensured that I work hard, play hard, and never
give up. By inviting me to sit in on his classes when I was just a child,
my father inspired me to become a professor, and discussing our shared
profession has been among the greatest honors of my life.

Finally, maintaining work–life balance at the final stages of this
book – and at the height of the COVID-19 pandemic, no less – would
have been impossible without my wonderful husband, Andrew Douglas.
Not only is he the world champion of fixing the printer, but he is also the
sounding board for my ideas. He listened to me talk incessantly about
this book, from its major arguments to the very last image caption, and
he sat patiently as I read thousands of words aloud to him. Somehow, he
tolerated working from home together even as my excessively loud voice

echoed throughout the house during Zoom meetings. And he graciously spent six (or, if you ask him, ten) months doing the dishes and watering the vegetable garden – without me lifting a finger – so that I could focus on revisions. Perhaps my greatest thanks go to our three cats: Marty, Minnie, and Sherlock. Although their incessant meowing for food and sitting on the keyboard distracted me from my work, they more than made up for it with their love, warmth, and cuteness.

Abbreviations

AA	Auswärtiges Amt (Federal Foreign Office)
AdsD	Archiv der sozialen Demokratie (Archive of Social Democracy)
AKP	Adalet ve Kalkınma Partisi (Justice and Development Party)
BArch	Bundesarchiv (German Federal Archives)
BMA	Bundesministerium für Arbeit und Soziales (Federal Ministry for Labor and Social Affairs)
BMWi	Bundesministerium für Wirtschaft (Federal Ministry of Economics)
BMZ	Bundesministerium für wirtschaftliche Zusammenarbeit und Entwicklung (Federal Ministry for Economic Cooperation and Development)
BRD	Bundesrepublik Deutschland (Federal Republic of Germany [FRG]; West Germany, 1949–1990)
CDU	Christlich-Demokratische Union (Christian Democratic Union)
CSU	Christlich-Soziale Union (Christian Social Union)
DDR	Deutsche Demokratische Republik (German Democratic Republic [GDR]; East Germany, 1949–1990)
DGB	Deutscher Gewerkschaftsbund (German Confederation of Trade Unions)
DM	Deutsche Mark, Deutschmark
DOMiD	Dokumentationszentrum und Museum über die Migration in Deutschland e.V. (Documentation Centre and Museum of Migration to Germany e.V.)

EEC	European Economic Community
EU	European Union
FAZ	*Frankfurter Allgemeine Zeitung*
FDP	Freie Demokratische Partei (Free Democratic Party)
FEBAG	Federal Almanya Bedelli Askerlik Girişimleri; Bundesinitiative der Jugendlichen aus der Türkei im Wehrdienstalter (Federal Initiative of Military-Age Youth from Turkey)
FR	*Frankfurter Rundschau*
IG Metall	Industriegewerkschaft Metall (Industrial Union of Metalworkers)
IGBE	Industriegewerkschaft Bergbau und Energie (Industrial Union of Mining and Energy)
IMF	International Monetary Fund
KSA	*Kölner Stadt-Anzeiger*
NATO	North Atlantic Treaty Organization
NPD	Nationaldemokratische Partei Deutschlands (National Democratic Party of Germany)
NRW	Nordrhein-Westfalen (North Rhine-Westphalia)
OPEC	Organization of the Petroleum Exporting Countries
PAAA	Politisches Archiv des Auswärtigen Amts (Political Archive of the Federal Foreign Office)
PEGIDA	Patriotische Europäer gegen die Islamisierung des Abendlandes (Patriotic Europeans Against the Islamicization of the Occident)
RP	*Rheinische Post*
RückHG	Gesetz zur Förderung der Rückkehrbereitschaft von Ausländer; Rückkehrhilfegesetz; Rückkehrförderungsgesetz (Law for the Promotion of the Voluntary Return of Foreigners; Remigration Law)
SPD	Sozialdemokratische Partei Deutschlands (Social Democratic Party of Germany)
TL	Turkish Lira
TÜSTAV	Türkiye Sosyal Tarih Araştırma Vakfı (Social History Research Foundation of Turkey)
USD	US Dollars
WAZ	*Westdeutsche Allgemeine Zeitung*

Introduction

The Woman with the German House

During her thirty years in Şarköy, a quaint beach town about a four-hour drive west of Istanbul, an elderly lady named Gül, whose petite, five-foot frame can barely contain her exuberant personality, earned herself quite a reputation among her neighbors. When I visited her in 2014 and again in 2016, "Auntie Gül" or "Gül Teyze" (as neighbors called her deferentially) spoke loudly and excitedly, switching back and forth between Turkish and German. For vacationers and passersby, Gül's bursts of German must have seemed inconsonant with the picturesque local setting of Şarköy, which has remained untainted by the booming international tourism industry so evident elsewhere along the Turkish coast. Long-term residents, however, were accustomed to Gül's frequent use of German, and truth be told she was not the only local who did not quite fit in. In fact, within just a three-mile radius lived two dozen other so-called *Almancı*, as Turkish migrants in Germany and Western Europe are called derogatorily in Turkish. Like Gül, they too had returned to Şarköy only to become the targets of local gossip and speculation. Depending on whom I asked, these returnees were simultaneously outsiders and insiders, embraced and ostracized. They were both Turkish and German, neither Turkish nor German, or perhaps half-and-half.

Gül and the other returning migrants in Şarköy are just some of the millions of people who have journeyed back and forth between Turkey and Germany for the past sixty years, fundamentally reshaping both countries' politics, economics, cultures, and national identities in the process. Since the 1970s, Turks, 99 percent of whom are Muslim, have been Germany's largest and most contentious ethnic minority. Despite Germany's historical refusal to identify as a "country of immigration" (*Einwanderungsland*),

I

the reality is undeniable: today, people with Turkish heritage in Germany number at nearly 3 million, representing approximately 12 percent of the 23.8 million "people with migration backgrounds" (*Menschen mit Migrationshintergrund*) in a country where every fourth person is now ethnically "non-German."[1] Migration is also crucial to Turkey, not only in terms of the diaspora. Four million people living in Turkey are ethnic Turks who at some point remigrated after living in Germany. No longer can one speak only of a Turkish diaspora in Germany without considering what one might call a "German diaspora" in Turkey, comprised of return migrants.[2]

The eldest among these returnees, like Gül, now in their eighties, had been part of the first generation of Turks to migrate abroad as participants in West Germany and Turkey's bilateral guest worker program (*Gastarbeiterprogramm*), which lasted formally from 1961 to 1973. As young men and women, they had learned that the Federal Republic of Germany (FRG) suffered from a labor shortage and was recruiting foreign workers to revitalize its industry after the death and destruction of the National Socialist regime, World War II, and the Holocaust. They had also heard the plea from the Turkish government, which faced the opposite problem: too many workers and not enough jobs. Their backbreaking labor in German factories and mines would be a patriotic duty, the Turkish government insisted, as the workers would return with newfound technical knowledge and skills to spark their struggling homeland's internal industrialization.[3] For the migrants themselves, the goal was overwhelmingly financial. Racked by poverty and unemployment in Turkey, they believed that working in Germany would allow them to earn riches beyond their wildest dreams, secure a better life for their families, and retire comfortably upon their return (Figure I.1).[4]

---

[1] Bundeszentrale für politische Bildung, "Bevölkerung mit Migrationshintergrund," April 29, 2023, www.bpb.de/kurz-knapp/zahlen-und-fakten/soziale-situation-in-deutschland/61646/bevoelkerung-mit-migrationshintergrund/.

[2] Susan Beth Rottmann, *In Pursuit of Belonging: Forging an Ethical Life in European-Turkish Spaces* (New York: Berghahn, 2019), 15.

[3] On Turkey's motivation for modernization and development, see: Brian Joseph-Keysor Miller, "Reshaping the Turkish Nation-State: The Turkish-German Guest Worker Program and Planned Development, 1961–1985" (PhD diss., University of Iowa, 2015).

[4] On both countries' motivations and the recruitment process, see: Karin Hunn, *»Nächstes Jahr kehren wir zurück...« Die Geschichte der türkischen »Gastarbeiter« in der Bundesrepublik* (Göttingen: Wallstein, 2005); Ahmet Akgündüz, *Labour Migration from Turkey to Western Europe, 1960–1974: A Multidisciplinary Analysis* (Amsterdam: University of Amsterdam, 2008); Jennifer A. Miller, *Turkish Guest Workers in Germany: Hidden Lives and Contested Borders, 1960s–1980s* (Toronto: University of Toronto Press, 2018), 9–18, 31–56.

FIGURE I.1 Gül, age twenty-eight, waves the Turkish flag on a train from Istanbul to Göppingen, where she worked as a guest worker, mid-1960s. Family photograph, given to author with permission.

At first, Gül felt welcome in the Federal Republic, and that feeling remained with her for quite some time. By the early 1980s, however, she watched in horror as Turks became the primary targets of West German racism since the Holocaust. Amid the global economic recession and unemployment following the OPEC oil crisis of 1973, West Germans argued that guest workers had overstayed their welcome. In response, the West German government stopped recruiting guest workers in 1973 and encouraged existing guest workers to leave. Fearing further restrictions, however, guest workers navigated the situation by exploiting West Germany's lax family reunification policy (*Familiennachzug*) and bringing their spouses and children to the Federal Republic.[5] On the streets, neo-Nazis and right-wing extremists shouted "Turks out!" (*Türken raus!*), spray-painted swastikas and racist graffiti, and attacked migrants – sometimes fatally. Inside parliamentary chambers, politicians responded to popular racism by passing a law to persuade Turks to leave the country – or, as critics decried, to "kick out" the Turks. Based both on culture and biology, this racism was overlaid onto an archaic ethnoracial definition of citizenship that dated back to 1913. Rather than embracing guest workers' contributions to West Germany's famed "economic miracle" (*Wirtschaftswunder*), Germans blamed them for taking their jobs, perpetrating crimes, birthing too many babies, draining the social welfare system, and lowering the quality of German schools. They further justified their racism with an essentialist, Orientalist interpretation of Turkish migrants' culture and Islam that denigrated the migrants as "backward," "authoritarian," and "patriarchal."[6] The overall conclusion, many

---

[5] On family reunification, see: Lauren Stokes, *Fear of the Family: Guest Workers and Family Migration in the Federal Republic of Germany* (Oxford: Oxford University Press, 2022).

[6] On German controversies over Muslim migrants' gender relations, see: Susan B. Rottmann and Myra Marx Ferree, "Citizenship and Intersectionality: German Feminist Debates about Headscarf and Antidiscrimination Laws," *Social Politics* 15, no. 4 (2008): 481–513; Rita Chin, "Turkish Women, West German Feminists, and the Gendered Discourse on Muslim Cultural Difference," *Public Culture* 22, no. 3 (2010): 557–81; Katherine Pratt Ewing, *Stolen Honor: Stigmatizing Muslim Men in Berlin* (Stanford: Stanford University Press, 2008); Damani J. Partridge, *Hypersexuality and Headscarves: Race, Sex, and Citizenship in the New Germany* (Bloomington: Indiana University Press, 2012); Barbara M. Weber, *Violence and Gender in the "New" Europe: Islam in German Culture* (New York: Palgrave MacMillan, 2013); Anna C. Korteweg and Gökçe Yurdakul, *The Headscarf Debates: Conflicts of National Belonging* (Stanford: Stanford University Press, 2014). For the French case, see: Joan Wallach Scott, *The Politics of the Veil* (Princeton: Princeton University Press, 2010); Mehammed Amadeus Mack, *Sexagon: Muslims, France, and the Sexualization of National Culture* (New York: Fordham University Press, 2017).

Germans insisted, was clear: Turks could never integrate into German society, and they could never truly be considered German. It was amid this racist climate of the 1980s that hundreds of thousands of migrants like Gül left West Germany and returned to cities, towns, and villages throughout Turkey. Gül and the others who chose to settle in Şarköy did so deliberately, hoping to live out their twilight years as they pleased: drinking tea, chatting with neighbors, and lounging along the sapphire-blue Marmara Sea. Underlying their triumphant return, however, was a sense of unease. The foreignness that they experienced in Germany accompanied them back to Turkey – this time, in the eyes of their Turkish neighbors who had not migrated. Both to their faces and behind their backs, neighbors mocked them as *nouveau-riche*, culturally estranged, and no longer "fully Turkish." They insisted that the migrants had transformed into *Almancı* – the derogatory moniker that I translate as "Germanized Turk." For the home country, the problem was not that the migrants had *insufficiently* integrated into German society, but rather that they had *excessively* integrated into it.

For the migrants themselves, the term *Almancı* is a slur. Many regard it as the Turkish analog of *Ausländer*, the German word for foreigner, which is frequently deployed to derogatory effect. This sentiment is best encapsulated in the rhyming phrase "Almanya'da Yabancı, Türkiye'de *Almancı*" (Foreigner in Germany, *Almancı* in Turkey), which is the title of a 1995 anthology of essays and poems by migrants.[7] The cartoon on the book's cover conveys the message well (Figure I.2). A stereotypically portrayed guest worker – a man with working boots, a mustache, and a feathered fedora – stands between two signs pointing in opposite directions to "Deutschland" and "Türkei" and carries a red bindle adorned with the Turkish half-moon. On his buttocks is a footprint in the colors of the German flag, symbolizing that Germans have not only kicked him out of the country in response to rising racism but also that his time spent in Germany has left an indelible imprint on him that he can never erase.[8] But crucially, returning to Turkey is not a positive experience. His shoulders are hunched, his expression is somber, and tears stream down his face. As the anthology's writings convey, being labeled as an *Almancı* makes the migrants feel foreign even in their own homeland.

---

[7] *Almanya'da Yabancı, Türkiye'de Almancı. Türkiye ve Almanya'dan İlginç Yorumlar* (Ulm: Merhaba Yayınları, 1995).
[8] For the latter insight, I thank my student Hailey Faust.

ALMANYA'DA YABANCI
TÜRKİYE VE ALMANYA'DAN İLGİNÇ YORUMLAR
TÜRKİYE'DE ALMANCI

FIGURE I.2 Cartoon on the cover of the 1995 anthology *Almanya'da Yabancı, Türkiye'de Almancı* (Foreigner in Germany, *Almancı* in Turkey), illustrating the migrants' dual estrangement. Merhaba Yayınları, used with permission.

Of all the so-called *Almancı* in Şarköy, Gül stood out the most. She had even earned a special nickname: "The Woman with the German House." Apparently, as her neighbors told me, Gül loved Germany so much that she had attempted to transport her entire German life to Turkey when she moved back in the 1980s. Jaws open and ears abuzz, neighbors had gawked at Gül and her late husband's red station wagon, a German Volkswagen Passat, filled to the brim with construction materials lugged 3,000 kilometers from Germany. Everything in her two-story home – the appliances, light switches, doors, and windows – had been "Made in Germany." Gül confirmed the rumors. While giving me a tour, she pointed out German pots and pans, bedroom furniture, picture frames, vases, radios, televisions, and chandeliers. In her kitchen, she even had a German deli meat slicer, which, she whispered shamefully, she had often used to slice ham. "I miss pork!" she exclaimed and lamented having to keep her "yearning for beer and bratwurst" a secret.[9] If neighbors found out that she was violating Muslim dietary restrictions, they might call her not only an *Almancı* but also a *gâvur*, a derogatory word for non-Muslims.

Well aware that her private home had become the target of local gossip, Gül defended herself by dismissing her German possessions as "just things." To any outside observer, however, these objects clearly had emotional significance. Her middle-aged nephew, who accompanied us on the tour and had been threatening to clean the junk out of her house for years, likewise saw through Gül's attempts to distance herself from the term *Almancı*. "She doesn't know what she's talking about," he said, rolling his eyes. "Obviously she's obsessed with Germany, and she keeps these things around so that she never loses the connection."[10] His assessment rang true. Weary of travel in her old age, Gül had been visiting Germany less frequently. She had given up her German apartment, where she had often spent up to six months at a time, and now traveled there only once a year to visit her sister. Holding onto these objects and continuing to speak German helped preserve her emotional ties to the beloved "second homeland" that her body had long departed. Neither in her reputation nor her heart, could she escape her connection to Germany (Figure I.3).

Although each of the returning migrants in Şarköy had a different relationship to their *Almancı* identity, the pattern was the same for all – the label had been initially imposed upon them externally by individuals within Turkish society, by fellow Turks who had never been to

FIGURE I.3 Gül, then in her early 80s, welcomed the author in her "German house," 2016. In the background is one of Gül's most cherished possessions from Germany: a red radio. Author's personal collection.

Germany and had little direct knowledge of what life in Germany was like. Nevertheless, the nonmigrants were still able to judge from afar whom and what could be considered "German." Little by little, year after year, as guest workers like Gül returned to Turkey driving German cars, wearing German clothes, giving neighbors tastes of German chocolates, speaking German, and raising German-speaking children, Turks in their home country increasingly concluded that they had transgressed their national identity. Neither fully Turkish nor fully German to outside eyes, the migrants existed in a liminal space between rigidly constructed conceptions of Turkish and German national belonging that had come to assume new and contested undertones of fluidity. As physical estrangement evolved into emotional estrangement, the migrants became foreign in two homelands.

RETURN MIGRATION AND TRANSNATIONAL LIVES

This book tells the history of Turkish-German guest worker migration from a transnational perspective, focusing on the themes of return

migration, German racism, and the migrants' changing relationship to
their home country. It begins in 1961, when Turks first arrived in West
Germany as formally recruited "guest workers" (*Gastarbeiter*), and ends
in 1990, the year that marked both the reunification of divided Germany
and landmark revisions to German citizenship law.[11] Putting a human
face on migration, it tells the stories of guest workers and their families as they traveled back and forth between Germany and Turkey and
navigated their uncomfortable connections to both countries over three
decades. In so doing, it turns the concept of "integration" on its head:
while not nearly as egregious as the overt racism they faced in Germany,
many migrants encountered parallel difficulties *reintegrating* into their
own homeland. After years or decades of separation, their friends,
neighbors, and relatives met them not only with open arms, but also
with ostracization, scorn, and disavowal. Turkey's ambivalence toward
returning migrants complicates our understanding of German identity.
As much as Germans assailed Turks' alleged inability to integrate, they
had integrated enough for their own countrymen to criticize them as culturally estranged, "Germanized," and no longer "fully Turkish." Kicked
out of West Germany and estranged from Turkey, many migrants felt
foreign in both countries, with consequences that still drive a rift between
Germany, Turkey, and the diaspora today.

   By focusing not only on the migrants' arrival and integration but also
on their return and reintegration, this book adds complexity to a story
that has been typically told within German borders. Its narrative is – at
once – German, Turkish, European, transnational, and local. The chapters resemble the migrants' lives in that none is strictly delineated by the
rigid boundaries of a static "homeland" or "host country." Likewise,
none offers an exclusively "German" or exclusively "Turkish" perspective. Rather, the book and its various chapters take readers on a spatial
journey, following the migrants back and forth between West Germany
and Turkey, as well as along the 3,000-kilometer international highway
that lay between them, traversing Austria, Yugoslavia, and Bulgaria at the
height of the Cold War. Zooming in and out between domestic policies,

---

[11] The term "guest worker" (*Gastarbeiter*) is inherently problematic. The notion that the
migrants were guests who were only staying temporarily and were expected to return
home made it harder for Germans to accept them as permanent residents, long-term
immigrants, and citizens even decades later, and the word "worker" reduced them solely
to their economic function. In line with other scholars, I nevertheless use "guest worker"
because it was the primary term at the time, and because it identifies a particular group
of people who, while far from homogenous, shared a similar migration experience.

international affairs, public discourses, and the history of everyday life (*Alltagsgeschichte*), the story not only plays out in editorial offices, parliamentary chambers, and other public spaces, but also in more private settings where the migrants' personal agency and emotions take center stage.[12] To portray the richness of the migrants' transnational lives, the book brings together a kaleidoscope of sources collected in both countries and both languages, including government documents, newspaper articles, sociological studies, company records, handwritten letters, memoirs, films, novels, poems, songs, material objects, and two dozen oral history interviews that I conducted with former guest workers and their children.

Above all, this book rests on a fundamental premise: global migration and mobility are central to the history of modern Europe, and we cannot fully understand European history without placing migrants' transnational lives at the center of it.[13] To a certain extent, this premise might seem intuitive: after all, migration and mobility are core parts of human experiences across time and space. But placing migration at the center of European history is especially crucial, not least since Europeans have historically defined their national identities homogenously. While all European societies have struggled to come to terms with demographic shifts, the German experience has been peculiar due to the country's exclusive, ethnonationalist, and blood-based (*jus sanguinis*) definition of identity, which began to change only in the 1990s.[14] Such a narrow view of what it means to be "European," or what it means to be "German," obscures the reality that people in Europe have always been on the move. Europeans have traveled both within and beyond the constructed borders of empires, nation-states, and supranational institutions, crossing

---

[12] On the history of everyday life, see: Alf Lüdtke, ed., *Alltagsgeschichte. Zur Rekonstruktion historischer Erfahrungen und Lebensweisen* (Frankfurt am Main: Campus, 1989).

[13] For a historiographical overview of this argument and a call for further scholarship, see: Tara Zahra, "Migration, Mobility, and the Making of a Global Europe," *Contemporary European History* 31 (2022): 142–54.

[14] For theoretical discussions of the ethnoracial foundation of German identity in a comparative European framework, see: Rogers Brubaker, *Citizenship and Nationhood in France and Germany* (Cambridge, MA: Harvard University Press, 1992); Christian Joppke, "Immigration Challenges the Nation-State," in Joppke, ed., *Challenge to the Nation-State: Immigration in Western Europe and the United States* (Oxford: Oxford University Press, 1998), 5–46; Jan Palmowski, "In Search of the German Nation: Citizenship and the Challenge of Integration," *Citizenship Studies* 12, no. 6 (2008): 547–63; Dieter Gosewinkel, "Citizenship in Germany and France at the Turn of the Twentieth Century: Some New Observations on an Old Comparison," in Geoff Eley and Jan Palmowski, eds., *Citizenship and National Identity in Twentieth-Century Germany* (Stanford: Stanford University Press, 2008), 27–39.

landscapes and waterways near and far, and have often become immigrants themselves. Sometimes, such as during the ages of exploration and imperialism, they have twisted their outward mobility toward bloody and genocidal ends.[15] On the other hand, people from across the globe have traveled to Europe, increasingly settling there permanently. And in so doing, they have forever staked a claim as a part of European history, fundamentally reshaping both national and European identities.

Migration is not, however, always a one-directional process, whereby migrants leave a static "home country," arrive in a static "host country," and stay put. Rather, as scholars of transit migration have emphasized, migration is also circular and back and forth, marked by frequent twists, turns, and *returns* in "zigzag-like patterns" rather than straight lines.[16] Both temporarily and permanently, migrants often return to the places from which they came, encountering new and unexpected challenges while *reintegrating*.[17] Before they arrive at an intended destination, they

[15] Imperialism must be viewed as part of the longer history of European mobility. On German colonizers (and their brutality), see among others: Isabel V. Hull, *Absolute Destruction: Military Culture and the Practices of War in Imperial Germany* (Ithaca: Cornell University Press, 2006); David Olusoga and Casper W. Erichsen, *The Kaiser's Holocaust: Germany's Forgotten Genocide and the Colonial Roots of Nazism* (London: Faber and Faber, 2011); Jürgen Zimmerer, *Von Windhuk nach Auschwitz?: Beiträge zum Verhältnis von Kolonialismus und Holocaust* (Münster: Lit Verlag, 2011); Jeremy Best, *Heavenly Fatherland: German Missionary Culture and Globalization in the Age of Empire* (Toronto: University of Toronto Press, 2020); Steven Press, *Blood and Diamonds: Germany's Imperial Ambitions in Africa* (Cambridge, MA: Harvard University Press, 2021); Adam Blackler, *An Imperial Homeland: Forging German Identity in Southwest Africa* (University Park: Pennsylvania State University Press, 2022); Zoe Samudzi, "Capturing German South West Africa: Racial Production, Land Claims, and Belonging in the Afterlife of the Herero and Nama Genocide" (PhD diss., University of California San Francisco, 2021).

[16] Robert Donnelly, review of *Rethinking Transit Migration: Precarity, Mobility, and Self-Making in Mexico*, by T. Basok, D. Bélanger, M. L. Rojas Wiesner, and G. Candiz, *Population, Space and Place* 23 (2017). See also: Aspasia Papadopoulou-Kourkoula, *Transit Migration: The Missing Link Between Emigration and Settlement* (London: Palgrave MacMillan, 2008); Franck Düvell, Irina Molodikova, and Michael Collyer, eds., *Transit Migration in Europe* (Amsterdam: University of Amsterdam Press, 2014).

[17] For interdisciplinary studies of return migration in general, see: Takeyuki Tsuda, ed., *Diasporic Homecomings: Ethnic Return Migration in Comparative Perspective* (Stanford: Stanford University Press, 2009); Katie Kuschminder and Russell King, eds., *Handbook of Return Migration* (London: Routledge, 2022). Scholars of European history have often emphasized return migration from North America. Mark Wyman, *Round-Trip to America: The Immigrants Return to Europe, 1880–1930* (Ithaca: Cornell University Press, 1993); Mark I. Choate, *Emigrant Nation: The Making of Italy Abroad* (Cambridge, MA: Harvard University Press, 2008); Tara Zahra, *The Great Departure: Mass Migration from Eastern Europe and the Making of the Free World* (New York: W. W. Norton, 2016); Benjamin Peter Hein, "Emigration and the Industrial Revolution in German Europe, 1820–1900" (PhD diss., Stanford University, 2018); Grant W.

pass through multiple cities, countries, landscapes, seascapes, and airways. And they often go on to further journeys, some planned and some unexpected, turning former destinations into mere stops along the way. Just as migrants impact their points of departure and arrival, so, too, do they shape the spatial buffer zones that they pass through.[18] In this sense, the journeys themselves, not just the start or end points, are central to migrants' experiences, for they are the roads – both physical and psychological – on which migration *happens*. But, as the dark global history of slavery, imperialism, war, genocide, and displacement reminds us, their pathways are often precarious and involuntary. The policing of borders, whether through legislation, brutal force, or racial and socioeconomic exclusion, blurs the line between "voluntary" and "forced."[19] These themes – return migration, the policing of borders, and the journey itself – guide this book.

Within this vast history of mobility and migration, the period after the end of World War II stands out for the enormous challenge – and opportunity – that the unprecedented rise in mass migration posed to European demographics and national identities. Although Europeans had previously encountered so-called foreigners within their borders, postwar labor shortages and decolonization brought millions of migrants to European shores – in numbers like never before.[20] Countries with long

Grams, *Coming Home to the Third Reich: Return Migration of German Nationals from the United States and Canada, 1933–1941* (Jefferson, NC: McFarland and Company, 2021). See also, on the *longue durée* and the global British case: Marjory Harper, ed., *Emigrant Homecomings: The Return Movement of Emigrants, 1600–2000* (Manchester: Manchester University Press, 2005).

[18] On the "buffer zone," see: Claire Wallace, et al., "The Eastern Frontier of Western Europe: Mobility in the Buffer Zone," *Journal of Ethnic and Migration Studies* 22 (1996): 259–86; Claire Wallace, "The New Migration Space as a Buffer Zone," in Claire Wallace and Dariusz Stola, eds., *Patterns of Migration in Central Europe* (London: Palgrave, 2001), 72–83.

[19] I emphasize the blurriness between voluntary and forced migration, or what others have called "mixed migration," in my discussion of the 1983 remigration law in Chapters 4 and 5. See also: Nicholas Van Hear, Rebecca Brubaker, and Thais Bessa, "Managing Mobility for Human Development: The Growing Salience of Mixed Migration," MRPA paper, no. 19202 (Oxford: United Nations Development Reports, 2009); Marta Bivand Erdal and Ceri Oeppen, "Forced to Leave? The Discursive and Analytical Significance of Describing Migration as Forced and Voluntary," *Journal of Ethnic and Migration Studies* 44, no. 6 (2006): 981–98.

[20] Rita Chin, *The Crisis of Multiculturalism in Europe: A History* (Princeton: Princeton University Press, 2017). See also: Leo Lucassen, *The Immigrant Threat: The Integration of Old and New Migrants in Western Europe since 1850* (Champaign: University of Illinois Press, 2005); Elizabeth Buettner, *Europe after Empire: Decolonization, Society, and Culture* (Cambridge, UK: Cambridge University Press, 2016); Peter Gatrell, *The*

histories of brutal imperialism, like the United Kingdom and France, relied on migrants from their former colonies to revitalize their infrastructure.[21] The two halves of Cold War Germany, whose colonies had been stripped from them after World War I, sought laborers elsewhere.[22] Amid its 1955–1973 "guest worker" program, West Germany recruited workers from Italy beginning in 1955, Spain and Greece in 1960, Turkey in 1961, Morocco in 1963, Portugal in 1964, Tunisia in 1965, and Yugoslavia in 1968. Turkey, eager to export surplus laborers, sent workers to other countries as well: to Austria, Belgium, and the Netherlands in 1964, France in 1965, Sweden and Australia in 1967, Switzerland in 1971, Denmark in 1973, and Norway in 1981.[23] The history of labor migration is also inextricable from the history of Germany's Cold War division. Across the Iron Curtain, the German Democratic Republic (GDR), or East Germany, recruited "contract workers" (*Vertragsarbeiter*) from the socialist, communist, or nonaligned countries of North Vietnam, Cuba, Angola, and Mozambique.[24] And crucially, West Germany signed

Unsettling of Europe: How Migration Reshaped a Continent (New York: Basic Books, 2019). On Europeans who returned from the colonies after 1945, see: Andrea L. Smith, *Europe's Invisible Migrants* (Amsterdam: Amsterdam University Press, 2003); Amy L. Hubbell, *Remembering French Algeria: Pieds-Noir, Identity, and Exile* (Lincoln: University of Nebraska Press, 2015).

[21] On the impact of postcolonial migration in Britain, see among others: Paul Gilroy, *There Ain't No Black in the Union Jack: The Cultural Politics of Race and Nation* (Chicago: University of Chicago Press, 1987); Jordanna Bailkin, *The Afterlife of Empire* (Berkeley: University of California Press, 2012); Clair Wills, *Lovers and Strangers: An Immigrant History of Post-War Britain* (London: Penguin UK, 2017). On France: Paul A. Silverstein, *Algeria in France: Transpolitics, Race, and Nation* (Bloomington: Indiana University Press, 2004); Todd Shepard, *The Invention of Decolonization: The Algerian War and the Remaking of France* (Ithaca: Cornell University Press, 2006); Amelia H. Lyons, *The Civilizing Mission in the Metropole: Algerian Families and the French Welfare State during Decolonization* (Stanford: Stanford University Press, 2013).

[22] For a comprehensive account of postwar German migration history, see: Jan Plamper, *Das neue Wir: Warum Migration dazugehört: Eine andere Geschichte der Deutschen* (Frankfurt am Main: S. Fischer Verlag, 2019).

[23] Outside continental Europe, Turkey also signed recruitment agreements with the United Kingdom in 1961 and Australia in 1967. Ahmet İçduygu, "International Migration and Human Development in Turkey," United Nations Development Program Human Development Research Paper, no. 52.

[24] On migration, racialization, and foreignness in the GDR, see: Jan C. Behrends, Thomas Lindenberger, and Patrice G. Poutrus, eds., *Fremde und Fremd-Sein in der DDR. Zu historischen Ursachen der Fremdenfeindlichkeit in Ostdeutschland* (Berlin: Metropol, 2003); Quinn Slobodian, ed., *Comrades of Color: East Germany in the Cold War World* (New York: Berghahn Books, 2015). On Vietnamese migrants, see: Pipo Bui, *Envisioning Vietnamese Migrants in Germany: Ethnic Stigma, Immigrant Origin Narratives, and Partial Masking* (Münster: Lit Verlag,

the 1961 recruitment agreement with Turkey just two months after the GDR began constructing the Berlin Wall, thereby cutting off the steady stream of East German day laborers. Highlighting the West German case is important because, as Emmanuel Comte has argued, the Federal Republic developed a "strategic hegemony" over European migration policy and European integration, shaping them in a way that favored its long-term geopolitical and economic interests.[25]

Return migration was embedded into the logic of the Turkish-German guest worker program, but both the perceptions and reality of return fluctuated greatly from 1961 to 1990. Despite rampant discrimination even in the 1960s, West Germans initially welcomed guest workers as crucial to the economy.[26] This idea manifested in the choice of the problematic term "guest worker" itself, whose hospitable connotation distanced it from forced labor (*Zwangsarbeit*) under Nazism.[27] Also embedded in

2003); Karin Weiss and Mike Dennis, eds., *Erfolg in der Nische? Die Vietnamesen in der DDR und in Ostdeutschland* (Münster: Lit Verlag, 2005); Bengü Kocatürk-Schuster, Arnd Kolb, Thanh Long, Günther Schultze, and Sascha Wölk, eds., *Unsichtbar. Vietnamesisch-Deutsche Wirklichkeiten*, vol. 3 of *edition-DOMiD* (Cologne: DOMiD, 2017); Phi Hong Su, *The Border Within: Vietnamese Migrants Transforming Ethnic Nationalism in Berlin* (Stanford: Stanford University Press, 2022); Paige Newhouse, forthcoming PhD dissertation at University of Michigan, Ann Arbor. On Mozambicans and Angolans, see: Ulrich van der Heyden, Wolfgang Semmel, and Ralf Straßburg, eds., *Mosambikanische Vertragsarbeiter in der DDR-Wirtschaft: Hintergrund – Vorlauf – Folgen* (Berlin: Lit Verlag, 2014); Marcia C. Schenck, *Remembering African Labor Migration to the Second World: Socialist Mobilities between Angola, Mozambique, and East Germany* (New York: Palgrave Macmillan, 2023). On Africans who came to the GDR as students, see: Sara Pugach, *African Students in East Germany, 1949–1975* (Ann Arbor: University of Michigan Press, 2022).

[25] Emmanuel Comte, *The History of the European Migration Regime: Germany's Strategic Hegemony* (London: Routledge, 2018).

[26] On the perception of the 1960s as both an economic and a cultural miracle, see: Hanna Schissler, ed., *The Miracle Years: A Cultural History of West Germany, 1949–1968* (Princeton: Princeton University Press, 2001).

[27] *Gastarbeiter* was the term chosen from 2,000 submissions to a West German radio contest, with other proposed names including "loyal helpers" (*treue Helfer*) and, sarcastically, "Euro-slaves" (*Eurosklaven*). Ernst Klee, ed., *Gastarbeiter: Analyse und Berichte* (Frankfurt: Suhrkamp, 1972), 149–57, quoted in Chin, *The Guest Worker Question*. On Nazi forced labor, see: Ulrich Herbert, *Hitler's Foreign Workers: Enforced Foreign Labor in Germany under the Third Reich*, trans. William Templer (Cambridge, UK: Cambridge University Press, 1997); Alexander von Plato, Almut Leh, and Christoph Thonfeld, eds., *Hitler's Slaves: Life Stories of Forced Labourers in Nazi-Occupied Europe* (New York: Berghahn Books, 2010); Marc Buggeln, *Slave Labor in Nazi Concentration Camps*, trans. Paul Cohen (Oxford: Oxford University Press, 2014).

the word "guest" was the assumption that the migrants' stays would be temporary. Per the recruitment agreement's "rotation principle" (*Rotationsprinzip*), they were only supposed to stay for two years, after which time they would be rotated out and replaced by new workers. The Turkish government, too, initially welcomed the guest workers' return on the grounds that they would bring the knowledge and skills needed to modernize their home country's struggling economy. In reality, the rotation principle was minimally heeded, since guest workers wished to keep earning money in Germany, and employers considered it too cumbersome to train new workers. Beyond economics, political optics also played an important role in West Germany's failure to adhere to the rotation principle: just decades after the atrocities of Nazism, forcibly moving labor migrants, as Adolf Hitler had done earlier in the twentieth century, was simply not an option.[28] Numerically, the turning point was the 1973 recruitment stop, after which half a million guest workers – 20 percent – left West Germany within three years.[29] Still, the number of Turkish citizens who left was outweighed by those who arrived through family migration in the 1970s.

By the early 1980s, the very idea that Turks had *failed* – or even *refused* – to go home became a dangerous weapon in Germans' racist arsenal: if only Turks had returned as planned, many Germans insisted, these massive demographic changes and the perceived threat of Islam might have been avoided.[30] Such rhetoric feeds into what I call the "myth of non-return": the idea that Turks' return migration was a mere "illusion" or "unrealized dream" that failed to materialize.

[28] Triadafilos Triadafilopoulos and Karen Schönwälder, "How the Federal Republic Became an Immigration Country: Norms, Politics, and the Failure of West Germany's Guest Worker System," *German Politics and Society* 24, no. 3 (2006): 1–19.

[29] Comte, *The History of the European Migration Regime*, 111. On the recruitment stop, see: Marcel Berlinghoff, *Das Ende der »Gastarbeit«. Europäische Anwerbestopps 1970–1974* (Paderborn: Ferdinand Schöningh, 2013).

[30] Scholars have offered varying interpretations of when Turkish guest workers became seen first and foremost as Muslims. Historians have generally emphasized the 1980s as the turning point, while Gökçe Yurdakul and others have highlighted the importance of the September 11, 2001, terror attacks. Brian Van Wyck has added importantly that being labeled as Muslim "had quite different stakes depending on who was making it." Gökçe Yurdakul, *From Guest Workers into Muslims: The Transformation of Turkish Immigrant Associations in Germany* (Newcastle upon Tyne: Cambridge Scholars, 2009); Brian Van Wyck, "Turkish Teachers and Imams and the Making of Turkish German Difference" (PhD diss., Michigan State University, 2019), 205. On the longer history of postwar Muslim migration, see: Elizabeth Howell, forthcoming PhD dissertation at Northwestern University.

Because of its prevalence, this myth has influenced the writing of his-tory.[31] Historians have generally treated Turkish-German migration as a one-directional process, whereby the migrants left Turkey, arrived in Germany, and did not return. Early studies situated the guest worker program within the longer history of labor migration and Germans' experiences with ethnic minorities.[32] Thanks to more recent histories by Karin Hunn, Rita Chin, Sarah Hackett, Brittany Lehman, Jennifer Miller, Sarah Thomsen Vierra, Lauren Stokes, and Stefan Zeppenfeld, we now know much about West German migration policies and chang-ing attitudes toward Turkish migrants, how the tensions of integra-tion played out on the ground, how migrants experienced their daily lives, and how they negotiated their belonging with nuanced attention to gender and generational divides.[33] Brian J. K. Miller and Brian Van

---

[31] Nonetheless, the importance of return migration at the time is evidenced by the numerous sociological studies from the 1970s through the 1990s that took it as their subject. Ethnographic interviews included in these studies appear throughout this book, and their findings inform my work more generally. Among others, see: Nermin Abadan-Unat, et al., *Göç ve Gelişme: Uluslararası İşgücü Göçünün Boğazlıyan İlçesi Üzerindeki Etkilerine İlişkin Bir Araştırma* (Ankara: Ajans-Türk Matbaacılık Sanayii, 1976); Werner Schiffauer, *Die Migranten aus Subay: Türken in Deutschland: Eine Ethnographie* (Stuttgart: Ernst Klett Verlag, 1991); Barbara Wolbert, *Der getötete Paß. Rückkehr in die Türkei. Eine ethnologische Migrationsstudie* (Berlin: Akademie Verlag, 1995). Moreover, countless studies in disciplines outside history have testified to the value of transnational approaches to Turkish-German migration. Betigül Ercan Argun, *Turkey in Germany: The Transnational Sphere of Deutschkei* (New York: Routledge, 2003); Eva Østergaard-Nielsen, *Transnational Politics: Turks and Kurds in Germany* (London: Routledge, 2003); Martin Sökefeld, *Struggling for Recognition: The Alevi Movement in Germany and in Transnational Space* (New York: Berghahn Books, 2008); Barbara Pusch, ed., *Transnationale Migration am Beispiel Deutschland und Türkei* (Wiesbaden: Springer, 2012); Bahar Başer and Paul T. Levin, *Migration from Turkey to Sweden: Integration, Belonging, and Transnational Community* (London: I. B. Tauris, 2017); Ayhan Kaya, *Turkish Origin Migrants and their Descendants: Hyphenated Identities in Transnational Space* (Wiesbaden: Springer, 2018).

[32] Klaus Bade, ed., *Auswanderer – Wanderarbeiter – Gastarbeiter. Bevölkerung, Arbeitsmarkt und Wanderung in Deutschland seit der Mitte des 19. Jahrhunderts* (Ostfildern: Scripta Mercaturae, 1984); Ulrich Herbert, *A History of Foreign Labor in Germany, 1880–1980: Seasonal Workers/Forced Laborers/Guest Workers*, trans. William Templer (Ann Arbor: University of Michigan Press, 1990); Panikos Panayi, *Ethnic Minorities in Nineteenth and Twentieth Century Germany: Jews, Gypsies, Poles, Turks and Others* (Harlow: Pearson, 2000).

[33] Hunn, *»Nächstes Jahr kehren wir zurück...«*; Chin, *The Guest Worker Question*; Sarah E. Hackett, *Foreigners, Minorities, and Integration: The Muslim Immigrant Experience in Britain and Germany* (Manchester: Manchester University Press, 2013); Brittany Lehman, *Teaching Migrant Children in West Germany and Europe, 1949–1992* (New York: Palgrave Macmillan, 2018); J. Miller, *Turkish Guest Workers in Germany*; Sarah

Wyck have illuminated the Turkish government's motivations and its role in shaping the migrants' lives in Germany.[34] Overall, however, the Turkish and German sides of the story – at least within the discipline of history – have largely been viewed as separate rather than inextricably linked.[35]

In this book, I bridge this divide by taking readers on a back-and-forth transnational journey between Turkey and Germany, revealing that Turkish-German migration history is far more vibrant and dynamic than typically told. The core argument is the following: return migration was *not* an illusion or an unrealized dream but rather a core component of all migrants' lives, and Turkish-German migration was *never* a one-directional process, but rather a transnational process of reciprocal exchange that fundamentally reshaped both countries' politics, societies, economies, and cultures. We cannot understand how the labor migration impacted Germany without understanding how it impacted Turkey. We cannot understand German migration policy without understanding Turkish policy and how the two were constituted mutually. And we

Thomsen Vierra, *Turkish Germans in the Federal Republic of Germany: Immigration, Space, and Belonging, 1961–1990* (Cambridge, UK: Cambridge University Press, 2019); Stefan Zeppenfeld, *Vom Gast zum Gastwirt? Türkische Arbeitswelten in West-Berlin* (Göttingen: Wallstein, 2021); Lauren Stokes, *Fear of the Family: Guest Workers and Family Migration in the Federal Republic of Germany* (Oxford: Oxford University Press, 2022).

34 B. Miller, "Reshaping the Turkish Nation-State"; Van Wyck, "Turkish Teachers and Imams." For other interdisciplinary accounts of the Turkish side, see: Levent Soysal, "The Migration Story of Turks in Germany: From the Beginning to the End," in Reşat Kasaba, ed., *Turkey in the World*, Vol. 4 of *The Cambridge History of Turkey* (Cambridge, UK: Cambridge University Press, 2006), 199–225; Ahmet Akgündüz, *Labour Migration from Turkey to Western Europe, 1960–1974: A Multidisciplinary Analysis* (Burlington: Ashgate, 2008).

35 Return migration, while minimally discussed in the historical scholarship on Turkish-German migration, has been the focus of important studies of other cases of migration across the globe. The case of Mexican labor migration to the United States, which became institutionalized with the 1942–1964 *Bracero* program, bears an especially fruitful point of comparison and has been instrumental to my thinking. See, among others: Francisco E. Balerrama and Raymond Rodríguez, *Decade of Betrayal: Mexican Repatriation in the 1930s*, revised ed. (Albuquerque: University of New Mexico Press, 2006); Deborah Cohen, *Braceros: Migrant Citizens and Transnational Subjects in the Postwar United States and Mexico* (Chapel Hill: The University of North Carolina Press, 2011); Ana Elizabeth Rosas, *Abrazando El Espíritu: Bracero Families Confront the U.S.-Mexico Border* (Berkeley: University of California Press, 2014); Sarah Lynn Lopez, *The Remittance Landscape: Spaces of Migration in Rural Mexico and Urban USA* (Chicago: University of Chicago Press, 2015); Ana Raquel Minian, *Undocumented Lives: The Untold Story of Mexican Migration* (Cambridge, MA: Harvard University Press, 2018).

cannot understand the migrants' experiences *integrating* in Germany without understanding their experiences *reintegrating* in Turkey. By unifying these two histories, this book expands our definition of "Europe" to include Turkey, provides a fuller understanding of migrants' lives, and shows how migration – and migrants themselves – transformed both countries.

Far from oppressed industrial cogs tethered to their workplaces and factory dormitories, guest workers and their families were highly mobile border crossers. They did not stay put in West Germany but rather returned both temporarily and permanently to Turkey. They took advantage of affordable sightseeing opportunities throughout Western Europe, and each year many vacationed back in Turkey, typically traveling there by car on a 3,000-kilometer international highway that traversed the Cold War border checkpoints of Austria, Yugoslavia, and Bulgaria. Once they arrived, they reunited with friends, relatives, and neighbors, built houses, invested money in their homeland, and shared stories of life in Germany. Hundreds of thousands, moreover, packed their bags, relinquished their West German residence permits, and remigrated to Turkey permanently, making their long deferred "final return" (in Turkish *kesin dönüş*, and in German *endgültige Rückkehr*). Around 500,000 of the 867,000 Turkish citizens who migrated to Germany between 1961 and 1973 eventually returned as expected, as did tens of thousands more who arrived in the 1970s through family reunification.[36] Returning to Turkey, and their journeys of return, were just as important to guest workers and their families as their time in West Germany (Figure I.4).

Guest workers' decisions to stay or leave were also shaped by pressures from above. Both countries' governments were deeply invested – both metaphorically and financially – in the question of the migrants' return. Crucially, however, their goals differed: whereas West Germany strove to *promote* the migrants' return, Turkey strove to *prevent* it. Racked by skyrocketing unemployment, hyperinflation, and foreign debt in the 1970s, the Turkish government changed its previously enthusiastic stance toward return migration, fearing that a mass return of guest workers would overburden the labor market and cut off the stream of remittance payments. Bilateral tensions climaxed when West Germany passed a controversial 1983 law that paid guest workers and their family

---

[36] Bundeszentrale für politische Bildung, "Die Anwerbung türkischer Arbeitnehmer und ihre Folgen," August 5, 2014, www.bpb.de/internationales/europa/tuerkei/184981/gastarbeit.

FIGURE I.4 Vacationing guest workers wait at the Düsseldorf airport for their flight back to Istanbul, 1970. © dpa picture alliance/Alamy Stock Foto, used with permission.

members to leave immediately. The result of this law, which critics in both countries decried as a blatant attempt to "kick out the Turks" and "violate their human rights," was one of the largest and fastest remigrations in modern European history. In 1984, within just ten months, 15 percent of the Turkish migrant population – 250,000 men, women, and children – packed their bags, crammed into cars and airplanes, and journeyed across Cold War Europe back to Turkey, with their residence permits stamped "invalid" at the border.

Crucial to this transnational story is the fraught, elusive, and highly politicized concept of "integration." Beginning in the mid-1970s, Germans used "integration" (*Integration* or *Eingliederung*) to describe a linear process by which migrants should become part of German society by abandoning the features that make them different.[37] All three major political parties distinguished "integration" from another loaded term – "assimilation" (*Assimilation*) – on the grounds that the latter could slip into "forced Germanization" (*Zwangsgermanisierung*), a term that recalled the Nazis' brutal "Germanization" of 200,000 Polish children

[37] Vierra, *Turkish Germans in the Federal Republic of Germany*, 11.

by ripping them from their homes and giving them to German families on the basis that they had blonde hair and blue eyes and were thus "racially valuable."[38] By contrast, postwar Germans considered "integration" more palatable because, at least in theory, it implied a "give-or-take process" in which both the migrants and Germans shared responsibility.[39] In practice, however, the rhetoric of integration gave rise to the expectation of assimilation: Germans blamed Turks for not "integrating" rather than acknowledging that they had done little to "integrate" them.

Viewed in a transnational frame, debates about "integration" were also fundamentally tied to return migration and to Turkish expectations about the role of the migrants in relation to their home country. One of the German conservatives' arguments against "Germanization" was that it would be detrimental to the migrants – and to West German efforts to kick them out – as it would erase their Turkish cultural identities and thereby impede them from "reintegrating" upon their return. And, in fact, that turned out to be the case. Turks in the home country, as this book reveals, invoked the language of "Germanization" to express their concerns about the opposite problem: excessive integration into West Germany and the loss of Turkish identity. The transnational history of return migration thus shows how the migrants were caught not only between two countries but also between two opposing sets of multifaceted, shifting, and unachievable expectations about who they were at their very core: how they were supposed to act, what clothes they were supposed to wear, how much money they were supposed to spend, whom they were supposed to have sex with, what their moral and religious values were supposed to be, and ultimately where they belonged.

Placing the migrants at the center of this story, this book highlights their agency as they navigated both countries' attempts to police their mobility, define their identities, and embrace or exclude them over three decades. It also reveals, however, that the very act of returning "home" was not always the joyous occasion that they had dreamed of. Instead of enjoying a happy homecoming, many found themselves socially ostracized and economically worse off than they had been in West Germany.

---

[38] Catherine Epstein, *Model Nazi: Arthur Greiser and the Occupation of Western Poland* (Oxford: Oxford University Press, 2010); Bradley Jared Nichols, "The Hunt for Lost Blood: Nazi Germanization Policy in Occupied Europe" (PhD diss., University of Tennessee at Knoxville, 2016); Janina Kostkiewicz, *Crime Without Punishment: The Extermination and Suffering of Polish Children During the German Occupation, 1939–1945* (Krakow: Jagiellonian University Press, 2021).

[39] Chin, *The Guest Worker Question*, 99.

In this sense, physically traveling to Turkey was not always a *return* to a static homeland but rather a journey to a place that had transformed in their absence and from which, over years and decades, they had become gradually estranged. For them, the challenge became not only how to *integrate* into Germany but also how to *reintegrate* into Turkey.

GRADUAL ESTRANGEMENT FROM "HOME"

Focusing on return migration not only highlights the migrants' agency but also shows how migration shaped the lives of ordinary people in Turkey. When we think of migration only in terms of the people on the move, we tend to overlook a crucial reality: for every guest worker who went to Germany, there were dozens of friends, neighbors, and family members who stayed behind in Turkey. Even though many of them would never set foot in Germany, individuals in the homeland also had a stake in the guest worker program. Placing their hopes and dreams in the guest workers' hands, they sent them off with not only physical but also emotional baggage. The expectations were clear: work hard, send money home, keep in touch, and return quickly. But the reality was complicated. Migration fundamentally disrupted the lives of those left behind, from their day-to-day activities and financial security to their relationships with relatives near and far. Just as the migrants had to adjust to their new lives in Germany, so too did individuals in Turkey have to adjust to their absence. Rethinking migration from their point of view underscores the inescapable dualities. Arrival meant departure. Immigration meant emigration. Presence meant absence.

Part I of the book, "Separation Anxieties," shows how, through the everyday act of repeatedly crossing the two countries' borders, guest workers and their children transformed their home country and destabilized dominant understandings of German, Turkish, and European identities from the 1960s through the 1990s. During this period, migrants became targets and carriers of difference and ambivalence in Turkish understandings of identity, as both the migrants themselves and observers in Turkey struggled to rethink their relationship to their homeland (*vatan*) while they lived, at least temporarily, 3,000 kilometers away.[40] While most guest workers yearned to return to the *vatan*, their children

---

[40] On the idea of the *vatan* and the territoriality of modern Turkish identity, see: Behlül Özkan, *From the Abode of Islam to the Turkish Vatan: The Making of a National Homeland in Turkey* (New Haven: Yale University Press, 2012), 1–11.

born or raised in Germany frequently questioned whether the *vatan* was truly their homeland or rather just a faraway place they knew from their vacations and their parents' stories. Although they always remained an extension of the nation, they gradually became estranged from it as the discomfort surrounding them grew.[41] And because migration was circular, marked by frequent returns to Turkey for both short and longer periods of time, the distinction between "migrants" and "nonmigrants" also blurred. All at once, a person could feel – and be treated as – both uprooted and left behind.

The history of Turkish migrants' dual estrangement is in many respects the history of emotions.[42] Anger, sadness, fear, joy, envy – all of these are fundamental parts of the human story told in this book. Emotions are socially constructed and dynamic, changing over time in response to circumstances and expectations. Still, understanding the migrants' emotions does not always require reading between the lines. Instead, migrants explicitly expressed their emotions in the countless sources they produced: oral histories, handwritten letters, poetry, folk songs, love ballads, memoirs, novels, films, interviews with journalists, and petitions to government officials. They did so not only to express themselves, but also to gain sympathy, effect change, and achieve certain strategic aims in the process. At times, they also performed their emotions, attempting to appear happier or sadder than they actually were.[43] One guest worker staged happy photographs to send to worried loved ones, even though she felt miserable and homesick. Another pretended to cry on the train to Germany just to fit in with her fellow passengers, even though she was delighted to leave Turkey. Moreover, observers in both countries leveraged the migrants' emotions toward political goals. Lamenting the sorrow of guest workers' children became an especially powerful tool for opponents of immigration restrictions to express their discontent – albeit

---

[41] I am particularly inspired here by Werner Schiffauer's ethnography of returning guest workers in the early 1990s. Schiffauer, *Die Migranten aus Subay.*

[42] On theorizing the history of emotions, see among others: Ute Frevert, "Angst vor Gefühlen? Die Geschichtsmächtigkeit von Emotionen im 20. Jahrhundert," in Paul Nolte, Manfred Hettling, Frank-Michael Kuhlemann, Hans-Walter Schmuhl, eds., *Perspektiven der Gesellschaftsgeschichte* (Munich: C. H. Beck, 2000), 95–111; William M. Reddy, *The Navigation of Feeling: A Framework for the History of Emotions* (New York: Columbia University Press, 2001); Barbara H. Rosenwein, "Worrying about Emotions in History," *American Historical Review* 107, no. 3 (2002): 821–45.

[43] This performance of emotions recalls the conflict between the expected "emotional regime" (the expectation that a person is normatively supposed to display) versus the actual emotional experience.

in ways that sometimes inadvertently diminished the migrants' agency and perpetuated discrimination. The migrants' emotions, in this sense, became a tool for reinforcing uneven power dynamics. Turkish guest workers and their children were not a homogenous population, even though both countries largely tended to treat them as such. Although guest workers overwhelmingly came from rural parts of Anatolia, most of the early migrants came from major cities such as Istanbul. While guest workers have been stereotyped as male, women accounted for 8 percent in 1961, tripling to 24 percent in 1975 – a statistic reflecting firms' desire to employ women, whose smaller hands made them better suited for delicate piecework.[44] Women who migrated formally as guest workers had different experiences than those who migrated through family reunification, as did children who spent most of their lives in Turkey versus children born and raised primarily in West Germany. Nor was the guest worker population ethnically, religiously, or politically homogenous. While Turkish guest workers were primarily Sunni Muslim, they also included internal minorities such as Kurds, Alevis, and Armenians, all of whom suffered a long history of persecution under Ottoman and Turkish rule.[45] Labor migration also overlapped with other forms of migrations, since applying for the guest worker program became a pathway for political dissidents and ethnic minorities to flee Turkey.[46] After the 1980 military coup, as the Turkish government perpetrated rampant human rights violations, the demographics of West Germany's Turkish population further transformed,

---

[44] On female guest workers, see: Monika Mattes, »Gastarbeiterinnen« in der Bundesrepublik: Anwerbepolitik, Migration und Geschlecht in den 50er bis 70er Jahren (Frankfurt am Main: Campus Verlag, 2005).

[45] There remains much historical work to be done on the unique experiences of Kurdish, Alevi, and Armenian guest workers. Other disciplines, however, have produced many important studies on these groups, particularly in the context of asylum-seeker migration since the 2000s. See, among others: Argun, Turkey in Germany; Østergaard-Nielsen, Transnational Politics; İbrahim Sirkeci, The Environment of Insecurity in Turkey and the Emigration of Turkish Kurds to Germany (Lewiston, NY: Edwin Mellen Press, 2006); Sökefeld, Struggling for Recognition; Ararat Göçmen, "Hay, Yabancı, Mensch: National Difference and Multinational Society in the Political Thought of Armenian Workers from Turkey in Postwar Germany" (MA thesis, Queen Mary University of London, 2021).

[46] In his study of Yugoslav migration to West Germany, Christopher Molnar exemplifies new thinking about the "blurred borders" across multiple "waves of migration": displaced persons, asylum seekers, labor migrants, and refugees. Christopher A. Molnar, Memory, Politics, and Yugoslav Migrations to Postwar Germany (Bloomington: Indiana University Press, 2018). See also: Brigitte Le Normand, Citizens Without Borders: Yugoslavia and its Migrant Workers in Western Europe (Toronto: University of Toronto Press, 2021).

leading to contestations among Turkish nationalists, Kurds, and leftists that played out on West German soil. By the early 1980s, the backlash against Kurdish asylum seekers amplified the existing criticism of Turkish guest workers, becoming another potent weapon in the arsenal of those who wanted to "kick out" the Turks.

Each time guest workers and their children journeyed back to Turkey, they encountered a "homeland" that was not static but rather ever-changing. With the fall of the Ottoman Empire and the establishment of the Republic of Turkey in 1923, founder Mustafa Kemal Atatürk sought to build a new identity for Turkey that was rooted in modernization and "Turkishness." The 1924 constitution bestowed citizenship to individuals born in Turkey regardless of their religion and race if they embraced Turkish culture and language.[47] Yet the Kemalist utopia of a singular Turkish nation belied the reality that Turkey remained politically, socially, and culturally fragmented and racked by economic turmoil. During the period covered by this book, Turkey experienced three military coups: in 1960 (just one year before the first guest workers arrived in West Germany), 1971, and – most crucially for this book's narrative – 1980. Struggling to position Turkey in the increasingly neoliberal global economy, policymakers found themselves in a virtually perpetual state of economic crisis that intensified amid the global recession of the 1970s. Especially central to the migrants' experiences – and to transnational attitudes about them – was the continued social, economic, and cultural gap between Turkish cities and the countryside.[48]

Rather than passively responding to these vast changes, guest workers and their children played active roles in accelerating them.[49] Alongside

---

[47] The government enacted this cultural homogeneity often violently through state-sponsored forced assimilation of ethnic and religious minority groups – a process that, as an intriguing counterpoint to discourses surrounding migrants' "Germanization," was called "Turkification" (*Turkleştirme*). *The New Constitution of Turkey (1924)*, Art. 88, www.worldstatesmen.org/Turkeyconstitution1924.pdf.; Amy Mills, *Streets of Memory: Landscape, Tolerance, and National Identity in Istanbul* (Athens: University of Georgia Press, 2010); Ayhan Aktar, *Nationalism and Non-Muslim Minorities in Turkey, 1915–1950* (London: Transnational Press, 2021).

[48] On the rural-urban divide as a post-Ottoman legacy, see: Şerif Mardin, *Religion and Social Change in Modern Turkey: The Case of Bediüzzaman Said Nursi* (Albany: State University of New York Press, 1989); Michael Meeker, *A Nation of Empire: The Ottoman Legacy of Turkish Modernity* (Berkeley: University of California Press, 2002).

[49] Nermin Abadan-Unat, "Impact of External Migration on Rural Turkey," in Paul Stirling, ed., *Culture and Economy: Changes in Turkish Villages* (Cambridgeshire: The Eothen Press, 1993), 201–15; quoted in Argun, *Turkey in Germany*, 59.

guest workers' contributions to Turkey's economy, society, culture, and identities, this book examines the historical process by which guest workers and their children introduced new categories of ambivalence and exclusion in Turkey. To anchor this analysis, the book traces the origins of the most contentious Turkish term for classifying the migrants: *Almancı*. Crucially, the term has not been used to describe all Turks living in Germany, a group that even before the 1960s included diplomats, students, and white-collar professionals. Rather, it initially emerged as a more particular reflection of Turkish ideas about guest workers, class, and socioeconomic difference. The economic connotations of the term, which does not translate smoothly into English, are evident in its etymology. *Almancı* combines the Turkish adjective *Alman* (German) with the suffix "*-cı*." Most akin to the English "-er" or "-ist," this suffix typically creates a noun identifying a person by their professional occupation or how they make a living (a basketball player is a *basketbolcu*, a taxi driver is a *taksici*, an antiques dealer is an *antikacı*).[50] By this logic, an *Almancı* is simply a person who makes a living out of Germany. But the meaning of the term – often interchanged with *Almanyalı* and *Alamancı* – is complex. Noting the term's derogatory connotation, Ruth Mandel has defined it as "German-like," while Susan Rottmann has interpreted it as "becoming a 'professional German' and thus faking or putting-on German-ness."[51]

In this book, I deliberately define *Almancı* as "Germanized Turk," and I investigate from a historical perspective how the term and its associated stereotypes developed from 1961 to 1990. Given its derogatory connotation, I do not use the word when referring to the migrants, but rather place it in quotation marks when discussing the home country's explicit or implied perceptions of them. Though contested in both countries, the word "Germanized" is more suitable for this book than "German-like" because it underscores Turks' concerns at the time that the migrants were undergoing a process of gradual estrangement – that

---

[50] Gerjan van Schaaik, *The Oxford Turkish Grammar* (Oxford: Oxford University Press, 2020), 457.

[51] Ruth Mandel, *Cosmopolitan Anxieties: Turkish Challenges to Citizenship and Belonging in Germany* (Durham: Duke University Press, 2008), 57; Rottmann, *Forging an Ethical Life*, 15. See also: Kevin Robins and David Morley, "Almancı, Yabancı," *Cultural Studies* 10, no. 2 (2006): 248–54; Barbara Pusch and Julia Splitt, "Binding the *Almancı* to the 'Homeland' – Notes from Turkey," *Perceptions* 18, no. 3 (2013): 129–66; Filiz Kunuroğlu, Kutlay Yağmur, Fons J. R. van de Vijver, and Sjaak Kroon, "Consequences of Turkish Return Migration from Western Europe," *International Journal of Intercultural Relations* 49 (2015): 198–211.

they were transforming, to a certain extent, from Turks into Germans.[52] The emphasis on the historical process of *becoming* an *Almancı* reflects the dual character of discourses surrounding the contentious concept of "integration." Whereas West Germans complained about Turkish migrants' *insufficient* integration, the Turkish government, media, and population worried about *excessive* integration – that long-term exposure to West Germany had estranged the migrants from Turkey, making them unable to *reintegrate*. In its most virulent uses, the term *Almancı* blamed the migrants for their own estrangement: not only had the migrants absorbed German culture through osmosis, but they had also made an active choice – a choice for Germany over Turkey, and a choice for abandoning those at home.

Whether out of hostility or jest, the term *Almancı* also projected Turks' anxieties about the country's external and internal transformations in a globalizing Cold War world, particularly regarding "Westernization" and urbanization. This point recalls Ayşe Kadıroğlu's suggestion that "the Turkish psyche has been burdened with the difficult task of achieving a balance between the Western civilization and the Turkish culture."[53] In this sense, when viewed in a geopolitical frame, concerns about the migrants' "Germanization" and loss of Turkish identity reflected Turks' broader ambivalence about their own country's "Westernization," "modernization," and "Europeanization" during the 1960s through the 1980s.[54] But these tensions also reflected ambivalence about Turkey's rural–urban divide, especially amid the internal seasonal labor migration that both preceded and overlapped with guest worker migration abroad.[55] When

---

[52] Several other scholars of Turkish-German migration have used the term "Germanization." Patricia Ehrkamp, "'We Turks are no Germans': Assimilation Discourses and the Dialectical Construction of Identities in Germany," *Environment and Planning A* 38 (2006): 1673–92; Susan Beth Rottmann, "Negotiating Modernity and Europeanness in the Germany-Turkey Transnational Social Field," *Insight Turkey* 16, no. 4 (2014): 143–58; Aylın Yıldırım Tschoepe, "Locating the German-Turks: Transnational Migration to Turkey and Constructions of Identity and Space," in M. Ersoy and E. Özyürek, eds., *Contemporary Turkey at a Glance II: Turkey Transformed? Power, History, Culture* (Wiesbaden: Springer VS, 2017), 113–30.

[53] Ayşe Kadıroğlu, "The Paradox of Turkish Nationalism and the Construction of Official Identity," *Middle Eastern Studies* 32, no. 2 (1996): 177–93.

[54] In many respects, "Germanized Turk" was really a proxy for "Europeanized Turk." Although variations of the term existed – such as *Hollandcı* for those in the Netherlands, or *Fransızcı* for those in France – *Almancı* was a catch-all term indiscriminately applied to all guest workers in Europe.

[55] Kemal Karpat, *The Gecekondu: Rural Migration and Urbanization* (Cambridge, UK: Cambridge University Press, 1976).

Turkish urbanites denigrated *Almancı*, they often recycled stereotypes about the rural labor migrants they encountered in Turkish cities, whom they – like Germans – disparaged as poor, backwards, and traditional. For villagers, by contrast, "Germanization" was a proxy for urbanization. Having already observed changes in the behaviors of seasonal migrants who returned from Turkish cities, villagers worried that migrants in West Germany would succumb to the seedy underbelly of urban life, drink alcohol, engage in sex and adultery, and abandon Islam.[56] As psychologist Gündüz Vassaf observed in his 1983 book on guest workers' children, Turks' previous experience with internal migration had already bred concerns that Anatolians were "Istanbulizing" (*İstanbullarırken*) and that Istanbulites were "Anatolianizing" (*Anadolululaşıyor*).

These separation anxieties, I argue, were inextricably linked to return migration, for it was during vacations and permanent remigration that guest workers reunited face-to-face with those in Turkey. Within the scope of transnational mobility, numerous crosscutting themes – at the levels of the family, community, and nation – all contributed to the development of the idea that the migrants had "Germanized" and become culturally estranged. Chapter 1, "Sex, Lies, and Abandoned Families," traces the process of gradual estrangement in the migrants' intimate and emotional lives, viewing them not as nameless, faceless proletarian workers but rather as spouses, parents, children, lovers, and friends. In the formal recruitment years of the 1960s and 1970s, guest workers tried to maintain close contact with their loved ones at home. Still, homesickness and fears of abandonment spread across borders. Amid West Germany's sexual revolution, rumors about male guest workers having sex with buxom blonde German women, cheating on their wives, and abandoning their children spread like wildfire throughout Turkey, becoming core themes in Turkish media, films, and folkloric songs. Amid the rising family migration of the 1970s, guest workers' children came to be seen in both countries as at once victims and threats. While Germans complained about migrant children as "illiterate in two languages," Turks in the home country worried that they had excessively "Germanized." These "*Almancı* children" (*Almancı çocukları*) were stereotyped as dressing and acting like Western Europeans, abandoning their Muslim faith, and barely speaking the Turkish language. Far more so than their parents, these children faced harsher social difficulties *reintegrating* into Turkey upon their return.

[56] Gündüz Vassaf, *Daha Sesimizi Duyurmadık: Avrupa'da Türk İşçi Çocukları*, 2nd ed. (Istanbul: Istanbul Bilgi Üniversitesi Yayınları, 2010[1983]), 207.

Ironically, the migrants' growing emotional estrangement from their friends, neighbors, and relatives at home was largely attributable to the times when they physically reunited face-to-face. Chapter 2, "Vacations across Cold War Europe," examines the significance of the seemingly mundane act of temporarily returning "home." Every year, as a small seasonal remigration, guest workers embarked upon a three-day, 3,000-kilometer road trip from West Germany to Turkey, passing through Austria, Yugoslavia, and Bulgaria at the height of the Cold War. Their unsavory experiences driving through Yugoslavia and Bulgaria reinforced their disdain for life east of the Iron Curtain and solidified their self-identification with the modernity and prosperity of Germany and "the West." Moreover, the cars and consumer goods they brought from West Germany on their vacations played a significant role in external processes of identity formation. By the 1970s, those in the home country came to view guest workers as a *nouveau-riche* class of gaudy, superfluous spenders, or "little capitalists," who neglected the financial needs of struggling local economies and had adopted the habit of conspicuous consumption – a trait that villagers associated with West Germany and Western Europe at the time.[57]

Crucially, guest workers were one of the strongest backbones of the Turkish economy at a time of great economic crisis. Chapter 3, "Remittance Machines," investigates how the growing rift between guest workers and their home country was tied up in the transnational circulation of finances amid an increasingly globalizing neoliberal economy. Government officials and journalists regularly referred to guest workers as "Turks working/living in Germany" (*Almanya'da çalışan/yaşayan Türkler*) and "our workers in Germany" (*Almanya'daki işçimiz*), the latter of which reflected the importance of guest workers' economic contributions – not only to their own wallets but also to the entire nation. Each Turk working abroad, after all, was one less person to tally as unemployed. Likewise important were their remittance payments: cash transfers from West Germany to Turkey in Deutschmarks, a much more valuable currency than the hyperinflated Turkish lira. Guest workers sent remittances to their families on a regular basis, and tens of thousands invested in factories to be built in Turkey, often in their home regions. But, as this chapter reveals, Turkey's dependence on – and cultural obsession with – guest workers' Deutschmarks created a conflict between self

[57] On consumption in West and East Germany, see: David F. Crew, ed., *Consuming Germany in the Cold War* (Oxford: Berg, 2003).

and nation, especially regarding return migration.[58] The Turkish government was so desperate for remittance payments that it began to oppose the migrants' return, even when it countered their best interests. Many migrants thus felt like "remittance machines," unwanted not only in West Germany but also by their own government.

Although the *Almancı* label is primarily defined externally and used derogatorily, and largely based on stereotypes, the Turkish discourse about the migrants' "Germanization" reveals an important point: whereas Germans have historically harbored anxieties about migrants' inability to "integrate," members of societies with high rates of outward migration, like Turkey, have developed fears of the opposite – and have responded with nationalist discourses according to which emigrants betray some or all of their identity by leaving their country of origin, choosing to remain abroad, and assimilating excessively. The very notion of "Germanization" casts migrants not as isolated "foreigners" (*Ausländer*), but as fundamentally German actors, exposing the reality that nineteenth-century notions of blood-based German citizenship no longer fit the dynamics of a migratory postwar world. In this way, the term "Germanization" itself suggests that Germans have not had a singular claim to delineating the contours of what it means to be German. Rather, both the Turkish migrants themselves and the populations of their home country, from the government and media to even the poorest of villagers, have been able to influence debates about German national belonging and the disputed role of Turkey in "Europe."

Likewise, the idea of the *Almancı* encourages us to destabilize the directional categories we use to discuss migration. When they traveled back to Turkey for their so-called "permanent return," they could be considered not as *immigrants to* but rather as *emigrants from* Germany. Although this interpretation falls shorter for guest workers and their children who were born in Turkey, it does apply to the experiences of thousands of children who were born or raised primarily abroad, and who knew Turkey only as a vacation destination or from their parents' stories. One of my interview partners, Murad B., who was born in

---

[58] In his 1991 ethnography, German anthropologist Werner Schiffauer also emphasized the conflict between self and nation (represented by the metaphorical son and father) as central to the migrants' relationship to their home country. Schiffauer, *Die Migranten aus Subay*. See my analysis of this theme in Schiffauer's work: Michelle Lynn Kahn, "Rebels against the Homeland: Turkish Guest Workers in 1980s West German Anthropology," *Migrant Knowledge*, October 23, 2019, migrantknowledge .org/2019/10/23/rebels-against-the-homeland/.

Germany, and whose parents shuttled him back and forth between the two countries before finally sending him to live with his grandparents in Istanbul, expressed this sentiment eloquently: "I think the term 'going back' to Turkey is so inappropriate, because I was never *there* to be back there ... It's not a 'going *back*' to somewhere. It's a 'going *to*' somewhere that was completely strange."[59]

RACISM AND THE HISTORY OF 1980S WEST GERMANY

Part II of this book, "Kicking out the Turks," writes the history of racism into the history of West Germany. Whereas the entire book spans 1961 to 1990, the second part focuses exclusively on the 1980s, a decade about which histories are still begging to be written. Thematically, Part II explores the nexus between return migration and what I call West Germany's "racial reckoning" of the 1980s: a turning point at which Germans, Turkish migrants, and individuals in the migrants' home country grappled, in both public and private, sometimes self-consciously, and sometimes not, with the very existence and nature of West German racism itself and especially the continuities between anti-Turkish racism and the Nazi past. This racial reckoning was motivated by a confluence of factors. As the demand "Turks out!" was amplified in the early 1980s, popular racism exploded with an intensity unprecedented in the Federal Republic's history, second only to the surge in neo-Nazi violence in the early 1990s.[60] At precisely the same moment, West German intellectuals began publicly debating the role of the Third Reich and the Holocaust in German historiography and identity, sparking what became known as the "historians' dispute" (*Historikerstreit*) of the 1980s.[61] As rising anti-Turkish racism was mapped onto the growing public attention to Holocaust memory, it became a tense part of Germans' process of coming to terms with the past (*Vergangenheitsbewältigung*).

Racism is not static across time and space. Rather, the historian's task is to examine how racism has manifested in different contexts – how racist discourses, targets of racism, and experiences of racism have evolved over time. For historians of postwar Germany, this task is especially

---

[59] Murad B., interview by author, Cologne, February 11, 2017.

[60] Christopher A. Molnar, "Asylum Seekers, Antiforeigner Violence, and Coming to Terms with the Past after German Reunification," *The Journal of Modern History* 94, no. 1 (2022): 86–126.

[61] Charles Maier, *The Unmasterable Past: History, Holocaust, and German National Identity* (Cambridge, MA: Harvard University Press, 1988).

challenging due to the prominence of the Holocaust in German understandings of racism. The emphasis on the singularity of the Holocaust, which was reaffirmed in the 1980s at the exact same time that Germans were debating how to kick out the Turks, inadvertently bolstered postwar Germans' reluctance to acknowledge the varying forms of racism that have existed both before and after Hitler.[62] Moreover, the prominence of Holocaust education and memorial sites in Germany from the 1990s onward has made it easier to celebrate Germany as a success story when compared to other countries, particularly the United States, that have long repressed histories of imperialism, enslavement, and genocide.[63] But, as this book shows, the intensification of both state-sponsored and everyday racism in the 1980s, as well as the prevalence of overt Holocaust comparisons in public discourse, challenges the portrayal of the Federal Republic as a success story and questions the image of the 1980s as the decade during which West Germany stabilized, turned toward postnationalism, and acknowledged its collective guilt for the Holocaust.[64] West Germany was not only the liberal democratic precursor to reunified Germany in 1990; it was also a country of great darkness, fear, extremism, and racism, whose history could have turned out quite differently (Figure I.5).

Engaging further with the history of emotions, this book shows how both racism and migrants' experiences of racism were both fundamentally connected to fears of the future and memories of the past. Its interpretation thus reinforces Frank Biess's and Monica Black's respective conclusions that West Germany was riddled with "German *Angst*," during

---

[62] This point relates to one of the most recent historiographical debates among Germanists, the "Historikerstreit 2.0" or "Catechism Debate" sparked by Dirk Moses's controversial essay: "The German Catechism," *Geschichte der Gegenwart*, May 23, 2021, www.geschichtedergegenwart.ch/the-german-catechism/. In the summer of 2021, *The New Fascism Syllabus* solicited and published a series of essays by scholars of twentieth-century Germany, Black Studies, critical theory, and the history of empire in direct response to Moses: Jennifer V. Evans and Brian J. Griffith, eds., "The Catechism Debate," *The New Fascism Syllabus*, 2021, www.newfascismsyllabus.com/category/opinions/the-catechism-debate/.

[63] This interpretation is most strongly argued in: Susan Neiman, *Learning from the Germans: Race and the Memory of Evil* (New York: Farrar, Straus and Giroux, 2019). The comparison between the memory politics of the Holocaust and American slavery is also made in: Michael Rothberg, *Multidirectional Memory: Remembering the Holocaust in the Age of Decolonization* (Stanford: Stanford University Press, 2009).

[64] On the call to push beyond this success-story narrative, see: Frank Biess and Astrid M. Eckert, "Introduction: Why Do We Need New Narratives for the History of the Federal Republic?" *Central European History* 52, no. 1 (2019): 1–18.

FIGURE I.5 A West German neo-Nazi performs the Hitler salute, 1987.
His shirt depicts Hitler and a swastika with the accompanying English-
language text: "No remorse" and "The world will know Hitler was
right." © picture alliance/dpa, used with permission.

which the "ghosts of the past" conjured existential fears about the stability of democracy itself.[65] As Biess explains, the key questions here are not
only "how did West Germans make sense of the past?" but also "how
did West German memories of their past inform anticipations of the
future?"[66] Amid the Cold War, contemporary West Germans feared not
only left-wing communism but also the resurgence of right-wing extremism and the possible coming of a Fourth Reich. Moreover, when West
Germans expressed existential fears of migrants taking over German society and committing a "genocide" against the German *Volk*, they placed
their anxieties about the future in relation to their memory and forgetting

[65] Frank Biess, *German Angst: Fear and Democracy in the Federal Republic of Germany*
(Oxford: Oxford University Press, 2020); Monica Black, *A Demon-Haunted Land:
Witches, Wonder Doctors, and the Ghosts of the Past in Post-WWII Germany* (New
York: Metropolitan Books, 2020).
[66] Biess, *German Angst*, 14.

of the Holocaust. Migrants, too, must be included in the entangled histories of fear and racism. By the early 1980s, guest workers and their children increasingly feared that they would be fired from their jobs, evicted from their apartments, deported, or separated from their families. They feared that they would become the targets of verbal and physical violence, explicitly contextualizing West German racism as a continuity of the Nazis' treatment of Jews. Return migration, too, provoked fear, as Turkish guest workers wondered what would happen to them if they returned to a homeland racked by a military coup and an economic crisis.

The dominant idea of the Federal Republic as a success story was rooted both in Cold War posturing and in postwar Germans' efforts to distance themselves from the Nazi past.[67] Per this mythology, the stroke of midnight on May 8, 1945, the formal end of World War II, marked a "zero hour" (*Stunde Null*) at which Nazism disappeared and Germany was reborn. From 1945 to 1949, the Allied occupation governments reinforced this myth by overpraising their denazification programs.[68] The limited number of high-ranking Nazis indicted and sentenced in the 1945–1946 Nuremberg Trials, moreover, seemed to absolve ordinary Germans of guilt and to portray them as victims of Hitler and his henchmen. This victimhood myth was reinforced by ordinary Germans' real trauma immediately after the war. Millions of German men were dead, in prisoner-of-war camps, or unaccounted for, and returning soldiers suffered physical and psychological scars.[69] Until the 1948 currency stabilization, Germans hungered on meager rations and resorted to trading on the black market.[70] The underground bomb shelters remained, in Jennifer Evans's words, places of "predation, crisis, death, and decay."[71] Up to two million women were raped by the "liberating" Soviet Red Army, while the iconic "rubble women" (*Trümmerfrauen*) searched through the ashes of their

---

[67] In Anglo-American discourse, among the main proponents of this narrative were Dennis Bark and David Gress, who insisted that "shadows no longer haunt Germany" and dismissed any criticism of Nazi continuities as the ramblings of disaffected "leftists." Dennis L. Bark and David R. Gress, *A History of West Germany, Volume 1: From Shadow to Substance, 1945–1963*, 2nd ed. (Cambridge, MA: Blackwell, 1993), lvi.

[68] Mikkel Dack, *Everyday Denazification in Postwar Germany: The Fragebogen and Political Screening during the Allied Occupation* (Cambridge, UK: Cambridge University Press, 2023).

[69] Frank Biess, *Homecomings: Returning POWs and the Legacies of Defeat in Postwar Germany* (Princeton: Princeton University Press, 2006).

[70] Paul Steege, *Black Market, Cold War: Everyday Life in Berlin, 1946–1949* (Cambridge, UK: Cambridge University Press, 2007).

[71] Jennifer V. Evans, *Life among the Ruins: Cityscape and Sexuality in Cold War Berlin* (Basingstoke: Palgrave Macmillan, 2011), 45.

homes, rebuilding Germany stone by stone.[72] Millions of ethnic German expellees (*Heimatvertriebene*) from Eastern Europe hurried across German borders, fleeing territories under Soviet control.[73] The thousands of Black "occupation babies" born to German women and African American soldiers in the U.S. occupation zone became the targets of a new iteration of centuries-long anxiety about "race-mixing" (*Rassenschande*) that the Nazis had taken to a genocidal extreme.[74] The division of Germany into two separate countries in 1949 provided further fodder for narratives of victimhood, as the new border walls physically bifurcated communities and separated family members from one another.[75] Well into the postwar period, Germans clung to these "war stories," as Robert Moeller has called them, to reject the accusation of collective guilt.[76]

As Germans attempted to "recivilize" themselves after Nazism, memories of the Third Reich and the immediate postwar period shaped the way that Germans viewed guest workers and the ways in which they articulated their racism.[77] Rita Chin and Heide Fehrenbach have criticized

---

[72] Atina Grossmann, "A Question of Silence: The Rape of German Women by Occupation Soldiers," *October* 72 (Spring 1995): 43–63; Elizabeth Heineman, "The Hour of the Woman: Memories of Germany's 'Crisis Years' and West German National Identity," in Hanna Schissler, ed., *The Miracle Years: A Cultural History of West Germany, 1949–1968* (Princeton: Princeton University Press, 2001), 21–56; Petra Goedde, *GIs and Germans: Culture, Gender, and Foreign Relations, 1945–1949* (New Haven: Yale University Press, 2003); Leonie Treber, *Mythos Trümmerfrauen: Vor der Trümmerbeseitigung in der Kriegs- und Nachkriegszeit und der Entstehung eines deutschen Erinnerungsortes* (Essen: Klartext, 2014).

[73] Andrew Demshuk, *The Lost German East: Forced Migration and the Politics of Memory, 1945–1970* (Cambridge, UK: Cambridge University Press, 2012); Peter Gengler, "'New Citizens' or 'Community of Fate'? Early Discourses and Policies on 'Flight and Expulsion' in the Two Postwar Germanies," *Central European History* 53, no. 2 (August 2020): 314–34.

[74] Heide Fehrenbach, *Race after Hitler: Black Occupation Children in Postwar Germany and America* (Princeton: Princeton University Press, 2005); Julia Roos, "The Race to Forget? Bi-Racial Descendants of the First Rhineland Occupation in 1950s West German Debates about the Children of African American GIs," *German History* 37, no. 4 (2019): 517–39.

[75] Edith Sheffer, *Burned Bridge: How East and West Germans Made the Iron Curtain* (Oxford: Oxford University Press, 2011); Astrid M. Eckert, *West Germany and the Iron Curtain: Environment, Economy, and Culture in the Borderlands* (Oxford: Oxford University Press, 2019); Demshuk, *The Lost German East*.

[76] Robert G. Moeller, *War Stories: The Search for a Usable Past in the Federal Republic of Germany* (Berkeley: University of California Press, 2001); Bill Niven, ed., *Germans and Victims: Remembering the Past in Contemporary Germany* (New York: Palgrave Macmillan, 2006).

[77] Konrad Jarausch, *After Hitler: Recivilizing Germans, 1945–1995*, trans. Brandon Hunziker (New York: Oxford University Press, 2006); Paul Betts, *Ruin and Renewal: Civilizing Europe after World War II* (New York: Basic Books, 2020).

postwar German historians' reluctance to critically engage with the categories of "race" (*Rasse*) and "racism" (*Rassismus*), which had become taboo and silenced after the biologically based racism of the Nazis.[78] Postwar Germans, they emphasized, overwhelmingly eschewed the term *Rassismus*, which connotated discrimination based on biological race, and instead favored *Ausländerfeindlichkeit*, literally "anti-foreigner sentiment" or "hostility against foreigners," sometimes translated as "xenophobia."[79] Though a contentious term itself, *Ausländerfeindlichkeit* appeared more palatable than *Rassismus* because it implied a "legitimate" or "rational" criticism of foreigners grounded in socioeconomic problems and "cultural difference" (*kulturelle Unterschiede*) rather than biological or racial inferiority. This condemnation of migrants on the basis of culture rather than biology was part of a broader trend emerging across Western Europe in the 1980s, which scholars have called a "new racism," "neo-racism," "cultural racism," and "racism without races."[80] Many have provided strong theorizations of this development in the German case, with Maria Alexopoulou, in particular, arguing that the word *Ausländer* (foreigner) itself was racialized: after all, *Ausländerfeindlichkeit* is not used to target White migrants from countries like Sweden, Switzerland, or Australia.[81] Michael Meng, Christopher Molnar, and Lauren Stokes have further

---

[78] Rita Chin and Heide Fehrenbach, "Introduction: What's Race Got to Do With It? Postwar German History in Context," in Rita Chin, Heide Fehrenbach, Geoff Eley, and Atina Grossmann, *After the Nazi Racial State: Difference and Democracy in Germany and Europe* (Ann Arbor: University of Michigan Press, 2009), 1–29; Rita Chin, "Thinking Difference in Postwar Germany: Some Epistemological Obstacles around 'Race,'" in Cornelia Wilhelm, ed., *Migration, Memory, and Diversity: Germany from 1945 to the Present* (New York: Berghahn Books, 2017), 206–32.

[79] Because this term is so contentious and does not translate smoothly, I leave it in the original German throughout this book.

[80] Martin Barker, *The New Racism: Conservatives and the Ideology of the Tribe* (London: Junction, 1981); Étienne Balibar, "Is There a 'Neo-Racism'?" in Étienne Balibar and Immanuel Maurice Wallerstein, *Race, Nation, Class: Ambiguous Identities*, trans. Chris Turner (London: Verso, 1991 [1988]), 17–28.

[81] Maria Alexopoulou, "'Ausländer' – A Racialized Concept? 'Race' as an Analytical Concept in Contemporary German Immigration History," in Mahmoud Arghavan et al., eds., *Who Can Speak and Who Is Heard/Hurt? Facing Problems of Race, Racism, and Ethnic Diversity in the Humanities in Germany* (Bielefeld: Transcript, 2019), 45–67; Maria Alexopoulou, *Deutschland und die Migration. Geschichte einer Einwanderungsgesellschaft wider Willen* (Ditzingen: Reclam, 2020). For other critiques of racism and racialization in the Federal Republic by German scholars and journalists, see: Alex Demirović and Manuela Bojadžijev, eds., *Konjunkturen des Rassismus* (Münster: Westfälisches Dampfboot, 2002); Christine Morgenstern, *Rassismus – Konturen einer Ideologie. Einwanderung im politischen Diskurs der Bundesrepublik Deutschland* (Hamburg: Argument Verlag, 2002); Maureen Maisha Eggers, Grada Kilomba, Peggy Piesche, and Susan Arndt, eds., *Mythen, Masken und Subjekte. Kristische Weißseinsforschung in Deutschland*, 4th ed. (Münster: UNRAST, 2020 [2005]);

illuminated how anti-Turkish racism was central to the Federal Republic's history both before and after reunification, describing the nuances with which Germans expressed racism in both cultural and biological terms.[82] The growing emphasis on excavating racism from the migrants' perspectives speaks to the broader postcolonial imperative to decolonize European history and owes much to the work of scholars of Black German Studies.[83]

Building on their work, this book highlights the prevalence not only of cultural but also biological racism in discussions in the early 1980s about whether and how West Germany could convince the Turks to "get out!" and "go home!" In Chapter 4, "Racism in Hitler's Shadow," the book traces the historical genealogy of the terms that West Germans used to discuss racism, citing the early 1980s as the critical moment at which *Ausländerfeindlichkeit,* previously virtually nonexistent in the German lexicon, came to dominate public discussions of racism. But, as much as they tried to deny and deflect the terms *Rasse* and *Rassismus,* both right-wing extremists and ordinary Germans alike continued to condemn Turks, Black Germans, asylum seekers, and other groups of "foreigners" by using the language of biology, skin color, and genetic inferiority.[84] While only a minority of Germans expressed overtly biological racism, the prevalence of such rhetoric alongside the rising neo-Nazi violence forced West Germans

---

Noah Sow, *Deutschland Schwarz Weiß: Der alltägliche Rassismus* (Munich: Bertelsmann, 2008); Fatima El-Tayeb, *Undeutsch: Die Konstruktion des Anderen in der postmigrantischen Gesellschaft* (Bielefeld: Transcript, 2016); Fatma Aydemir and Hengameh Yaghoobifarah, eds., *Eure Heimat ist unser Albtraum* (Berlin: Ullstein, 2019); Vojin Saša Vukadinović, ed., *Rassismus: Von der frühen Bundesrepublik bis zur Gegenwart* (Berlin: De Gruyter, 2022). On race and whiteness throughout Europe, see: Hans Kundnani, *Eurowhiteness: Culture, Empire and Race in the European Project* (London: Hurst, 2023).

[82] Michael Meng, "Silences about Sarrazin's Racism in Contemporary Germany," *The Journal of Modern History* 87, no. 1 (2015): 102–35; Christopher Molnar, "'Greetings from the Apocalypse': Race, Migration, and Fear after German Reunification," *Central European History* 54, no. 3 (2021): 491–515; Stokes, *Fear of the Family.*

[83] On postcolonial approaches to Europe, see: Salman Sayyid, *A Fundamental Fear: Eurocentrism and the Emergence of Islamism* (New York: Zed Books, 1997); Dipesh Chakrabarty, *Provincializing Europe: Postcolonial Thought and Historical Difference* (Princeton: Princeton University Press, 2000); Fatima El-Tayeb, *European Others: Queering Ethnicity in Postnational Europe* (Minneapolis: University of Minnesota Press, 2011). On Black German studies, see: Patricia Mazón and Reinhild Steingröver, eds., *Not so Plain as Black and White: Afro-German Culture and History* (Rochester: University of Rochester, 2005); Tiffany N. Florvil and Vanessa Plumly, eds., *Rethinking Black German Studies: Approaches, Interventions, and Histories* (Oxford: Peter Lang, 2018).

[84] On right-wing extremism in the Federal Republic, see among many others: Gideon Botsch, *Die extreme Rechte in der Bundesrepublik Deutschland: 1949 bis heute* (Bonn: wbg academic, 2012); Norbert Frei, Christina Morina, Franka Maubach, and Maik Tändler, *Zur rechten Zeit: Wider die Rückkehr des Nationalismus* (Berlin: Ullstein Verlag, 2019).

to reckon with the very existence and nature of racism itself in a country that praised itself as liberal, democratic, and committed to human rights.[85] This racial reckoning also reverberated transnationally, even creating conflict in official international affairs. Despite harboring their own ambivalent views toward the migrants, Turks in their home country exposed the hypocrisy of West German liberalism by accusing West Germans of abusing Turks, just as they had done to the Jews in the 1930s, and by comparing various West German chancellors to Adolf Hitler.[86] In line with Michael Rothberg's concept of "multidirectional memory," the Holocaust became a usable past that Turks could use to fight German racism in the present.[87]

Anxieties about Nazi continuities were not only abstract, but also had real policy implications when it came to the legal enactment of state-sanctioned racism. The centerpiece of Chapter 5, "The Mass Exodus," is the November 28, 1983, Law for the Promotion of the Voluntary Return of Foreigners (*Rückkehrförderungsgesetz*) – or the remigration law, as I call it. Initially developed during the late 1970s by the center-left Social Democratic Party (SPD), the law did not become a reality until after October 1982, when the conservative Christian Democratic Union (CDU) took the reins of government. The CDU made "promoting return migration" (*Rückkehrförderung*) a core plank of its platform, and newly elected chancellor Helmut Kohl secretly expressed his desire to reduce the Turkish population by 50 percent. To fend off allegations of racism, the government's solution was to apply what political scientists have called "checkbook diplomacy" to domestic policy.[88]

[85] On human rights, see: Lora Wildenthal, *The Language of Human Rights in West Germany* (Philadelphia: University of Pennsylvania Press, 2012); Ned Richardson-Little, *The Human Rights Dictatorship: Socialism, Global Solidarity, and Revolution in East Germany* (Cambridge, UK: Cambridge University Press, 2020).

[86] Gökçe Yurdakul has examined how German Turks have employed the "German Jewish trope" as a discursive analogy since the September 11, 2001, terrorist attacks: Gökçe Yurdakul, "'We Don't Want To Be the Jews of Tomorrow': Jews and Turks in Germany after 9/11," *German Politics and Society* 24, no. 2 (2006): 44–67. On Muslims and Holocaust memory, see: Esra Özyürek, "Rethinking Empathy: Emotions Triggered by the Holocaust among the Muslim-Minority in Germany," *Anthropological Theory* 18, no. 4 (2018): 456–77 and "Muslim Minorities as Germany's Past Future: Islam Critics, Holocaust Memory, and Immigrant Integration," *Memory Studies* 15, no. 1 (2019): 139–54. See also: Mandel, *Cosmopolitan Anxieties*, chapter 4.

[87] Although Rothberg writes about Holocaust memory and decolonization, his interpretation can be applied to migration as well. Rothberg, *Multidirectional Memory*.

[88] The concept of "checkbook diplomacy" is typically applied to Germany's approach to the 1991 Gulf War, but it had already been a common feature of the 1980s under Chancellor Helmut Kohl. Eric Langenbacher, for example, has called checkbook diplomacy "a German specialty." Eric Langenbacher, *The German Polity*, 12th ed. (Lanham: Rowman and Littlefield, 2021), 346.

Building on earlier failed attempts to financially incentivize return migration through the provision of bilateral development aid to Turkey, the 1983 remigration law unilaterally offered unemployed former guest workers a so-called remigration premium (*Rückkehrprämie*) of 10,500 DM, plus 1,500 for every child under age eighteen, to voluntarily leave the country by a strict deadline: ten months later. Although the law failed to achieve Kohl's goal of repatriating half the Turks, it did lead to the mass exodus of 15 percent of the Turkish migrant population – 250,000 men, women, and children – in 1984 alone. Many who left amid this mass exodus, however, soon ended up regretting their decision. After years of ostracization as *Almancı* – and with no hope of assistance from the Turkish government, which had long opposed their return – they encountered both social and financial difficulties *reintegrating* into Turkey.

Far more so than their parents, children who returned amid the mass exodus of 1984 faced difficulties reintegrating into Turkey and became political tools in West German efforts to deny and deflect their racism. Stressing the importance of generational difference, Chapter 6, "Unhappy in the Homeland," examines guest workers' children who returned to Turkey in the 1980s, in many cases against their will, when their parents decided to leave. As the Turkish Education Ministry scrambled to "re-Turkify" these so-called "return children" (*Rückkehrkinder*) or "*Almancı* children" in special "re-adaptation courses," the West German government, press, and population watched closely. Widespread reports of the children's struggles reintegrating into their authoritarian homeland after the 1980 military coup contributed strongly to West Germans' negative perceptions of Turkish guest worker families. By 1990, sympathy for the children's plight compelled a rare relaxation of West German immigration policy. Just seven years after kicking them out, the government made a landmark revision to its citizenship law and allowed the children to return once again – this time to West Germany, the country that many called home. By deflecting the children's problems onto Turkey and portraying themselves as the children's savior, West Germans further obfuscated their own racism and reinforced their self-definition as liberal and democratic at the very moment that the Cold War ended, East Germany dissolved, and the reunified Federal Republic emerged.

Ultimately, by rethinking the early 1980s in terms of a racial reckoning, this book further challenges our idea of German identity itself. Amid the *Historikerstreit* of the 1980s, the renowned West German philosopher Jürgen Habermas argued that West Germans needed to further embrace what he called "postnationalism" and "constitutional patriotism": an attachment to a country grounded not in a sense of ethnic or cultural identity, but rather in an appreciation for liberal democracy and the constitution itself.[89] This basis for national identity, he maintained, would make German society more politically inclusive and tie it closer to European supranational institutions. Despite backlash, the idea of a "postnational" Germany gained traction, especially among migration scholars who have cited the liberalization of Germany's blood-based citizenship law in the 1990s and 2000s as evidence that Germany had, in fact, turned toward postnationalism.[90] But, as this book reminds us, the 1980s were not the 2000s. Amid the racial reckoning of the early 1980s, West Germans clung so ardently to their national and ethnoracial identity that they weaponized it – both rhetorically and violently – against the guest workers whom they had welcomed just two decades before. Back then, the debate centered not on whether to grant migrants citizenship, but rather – as embodied in the 1983 remigration law – on how to kick them out.

This reality also forces us to revise our interpretation of the onslaught of rightwing violence and far-right politics in more recent German history. One of the founding myths of the post-reunification Federal Republic is that racism was an East German import, whereby upon the fall of the Berlin Wall in 1989, socioeconomically downtrodden former East Germans rushed across the border, turned toward neo-Nazism, and enacted their revenge against foreigners.[91] While this interpretation holds true in certain respects, dismissing racism, right-wing extremism, and anti-migrant violence as East German imports points to an outdated Cold War mindset that views East Germans as "backward" in comparison to "liberal" West Germans and perpetuates the longstanding West German pattern of

---

[89] Among his many writings on the subject, see: Jürgen Habermas, *Die postnationale Konstellation: Politische Essays* (Frankfurt am Main: Suhrkamp Verlag, 2001). On "constitutional patriotism," see: Jan-Werner Müller, *Constitutional Patriotism* (Princeton: Princeton University Press, 2007).

[90] Yasemin Nuhoğlu Sosyal, *Limits of Citizenship: Migrants and Postnational Membership in Europe* (Chicago: University of Chicago Press, 1994). Critiquing Sosyal, see: Christian Joppke, "From Postnational Membership to Citizenship: Germany," in *Immigration and the Nation-State: The United States, Germany, and Great Britain* (Oxford: Oxford University Press, 1999): 186–222. For a broader critique of postnationalism, see: El-Tayeb, *Undeutsch*.

[91] On the memory of the post-reunification violence, see: Esther Adaire, "'This Other Germany, the Dark One': Post-Wall Memory Politics Surrounding the Neo-Nazi Riots in Rostock and Hoyerswerda," *German Politics and Society* 37, no. 4 (2019): 43–57; Molnar, "Asylum Seekers."

denying and deflecting racism. By complicating the post–Cold War transition, this book thus joins Jennifer Allen's recent work in showing that, just like the mythical "zero hour" in 1945, the "fetishized" fall of the Berlin Wall and reunification in 1989 and 1990, respectively, marked not only a new era of history but also a continuity.[92] The new iteration of the Federal Republic inherited not only democracy but also the inescapable shadow of darkness, racism, and fear that had plagued West Germany for decades. And even if West Germans were not willing to admit it, Turkish migrants and their home country had been exposing this fact all along.

MUSLIMS, TURKS, AND THE BOUNDARIES OF "EUROPE"

Finally, by tying Germany and Turkey together, this book contributes to the postcolonial project of decentering Europe and expanding its imagined boundaries.[93] It shows how studying migrants' fluid identities can change our conception of both countries' geographic space. Here, the home country's assertion that the migrants had transformed into "Germanized Turks," or *Almancı*, is crucial. If we consider Turkish migrants as German actors (either self-identifying as German or being externally identified as *Almancı*), then we can broaden our scope of Germany to include Turkey. Turkey, after all, was the site of the migrants' lives before they joined the guest worker program, as well as the place where the migrants – once they had already begun to be viewed as "Germanized" – traveled upon their temporary or permanent returns. Moreover, following the migrants on the journey itself also encourages us to consider the geographic space *between* Turkey and Germany as part of the two countries' shared geography and history.[94] As they traveled on cars, trains, and airplanes across Austria, Bulgaria, and Yugoslavia during the Cold War, the migrants transformed a series of seemingly distinct border checkpoints into a unified migration space, where contestations over their mobility both reinforced and eroded imagined divides.

Including Muslims and Turks as part of European history addresses what Mark Mazower has called the "basic historiographical question": how to integrate the Ottoman Empire and its legacy into the broader

---

[92] Jennifer L. Allen, "Against the 1989–1990 Ending Myth," *Central European History* 52, no. 1 (2019): 125–47.

[93] Chakrabarty, *Provincializing Europe*.

[94] I elaborate on this argument in a previous article: Michelle Lynn Kahn, "Rethinking Central Europe as a Migration Space: From the Ottoman Empire through the Cold War and the Refugee Crisis," *Central European History* 55, no. 1 (2022): 118–37.

narrative of European history.[95] In this task, the book speaks to scholars beyond migration studies who, amid the rise of global history, have contributed substantially to the revision of Eurocentrism by highlighting Ottoman and Turkish ties to Germany and Europe.[96] Stefan Ihrig, for one, has traced the centuries-long history of Turkish-German affairs from ancient times to the present day, while Emily Greble has argued more broadly that Islam was "indigenous" to Europe and that Muslims were crucial to "the making of modern Europe."[97] Building on these contributions and more, this book further shows that Turkey was likewise crucial to the making of modern Germany – and vice versa.[98] The guest worker program, which sparked an unprecedented movement of people between the two countries, was pivotal to this relationship. While migration inextricably tied the two countries closer together, it also pulled them apart. As the migrants' integration into West Germany became a proxy for Turkey's integration into European supranational institutions, both Germans and Turks questioned where the physical and imagined boundaries of "Europe" lay and how malleable they could – and should – be.

The year 1961, which marked the signing of the recruitment agreement, was neither the start of migration between the two countries nor of Turkish-German entangled history. Rather, it emerged from centuries of diplomatic, intellectual, commercial, and cultural exchange. In the seventeenth century, when the Ottoman Empire was at its height, it ruled over a quarter of the European continent and was multiethnic, multilingual, multiracial, and multireligious.[99] In the eighteenth century, Ottomans

---

[95] Mark Mazower, *The Balkans: A Short History* (New York: Random House, 2007), xl.
[96] See among others: Molly Greene, *A Shared World: Christians and Muslims in the Early Modern Mediterranean* (Princeton: Princeton University Press, 2000); Walter G. Andrews and Mehmet Kalpakli, *The Age of Beloveds: Love and the Beloved in Early Modern Ottoman and European Culture* (Durham: Duke University Press, 2005); Giancarlo Casale, *The Ottoman Age of Exploration* (Oxford: Oxford University Press, 2011); Sibel Zandi-Sayek, *Ottoman Izmir: The Rise of a Cosmopolitan Port, 1840–1880* (Minneapolis: University of Minnesota Press, 2012); Halil İnalcık, *The Ottoman Empire and Europe: The Ottoman Empire and Its Place in European History* (Istanbul: Kronik, 2017); Gábor Ágoston, *The Last Muslim Conquest: The Ottoman Empire and Its Wars in Europe* (Princeton: Princeton University Press, 2021).
[97] Emily Greble, *Muslims and the Making of Modern Europe* (Oxford: Oxford University Press, 2021).
[98] I am also inspired by the growing scholarship on Ottoman migration history. For one important recent study, see: Vladimir Hamed-Troyansky, *Empire of Refugees: North Caucasian Muslims and the Late Ottoman State* (Stanford: Stanford University Press, 2024).
[99] Marc David Baer, *The Ottomans: Khans, Caesars, and Caliphs* (New York: Basic Books, 2021), 3.

were crucial actors in the Enlightenment, the Age of Revolutions, and the development of modern science.[100] Intellectual and ideological entanglements intensified during the Tanzimat period (1839–1876), when Ottoman administrators sought to centralize power and "modernize" and "westernize" the state by implementing reforms heavily influenced by European ideas and international pressure.[101] Yet overwhelmingly, Europeans came to homogenize Ottomans into a Muslim, Turkish "other," or even worse into "Oriental despots" and "bloodthirsty Turks."[102] These tensions were heightened by the brutal Habsburg-Ottoman wars and nineteenth-century Balkan nationalist movements that sought to break free from the so-called "Ottoman yoke."[103]

Despite these Europe-wide tensions, the particular relationship between Turks and Germans has often been described with fondness and cordiality – so much so that individuals in both countries at the time praised the guest worker program as the outgrowth of a centuries-long history of friendship.[104] This rhetorical trope of "friendship" was grounded in a long history of Germans' extensive military, economic, and diplomatic ties to the Ottoman Empire and the Turkish Republic, which complicates Edward Said's assertion that Germans did not have a "protracted sustained national interest" in the "Orient."[105] In 1835, Prussian officers

---

[100] Miri Shefer-Mossensohn, *Science among the Ottomans: The Cultural Creation and Exchange of Knowledge* (Austin: University of Texas Press, 2015); Ali Yaycıoğlu, *Partners of the Empire: The Crisis of the Ottoman Order in the Age of Revolutions* (Stanford: Stanford University Press, 2016); Christopher de Bellaigue, *The Islamic Enlightenment: The Modern Struggle Between Faith and Reason* (New York: Random House, 2017); Alexander Bevilacqua, *The Republic of Arabic Letters: Islam and the European Enlightenment* (Cambridge, MA: Harvard University Press, 2018); Duygu Yıldırım, "The Age of the Perplexed: Translating Nature and Bodies between the Ottoman Empire and Europe, 1650–1730" (PhD diss., Stanford University, 2021).

[101] M. Şükrü Hanioğlu, *A Brief History of the Late Ottoman Empire* (Princeton: Princeton University Press, 2008), 72–108; Yonca Köksal, *The Ottoman Empire in the Tanzimat Era: Provincial Perspectives from Ankara to Edirne* (New York: Routledge, 2019).

[102] Božidar Jezernik, ed., *Imagining "The Turk"* (Newcastle upon Tyne: Cambridge Scholars Publishing, 2010).

[103] Vera Mutafchieva, "The Notion of the 'Other' in Bulgaria: The Turks. A Historical Study," *Anthropological Journal of European Cultures* 4, no. 2 (1995): 53–74; Maria Todorova, *Imagining the Balkans* (Oxford: Oxford University Press, 1996); Edin Hajdarpašić, "Out of the Ruins of the Ottoman Empire: Reflections on the Ottoman Legacy in South-eastern Europe," *Middle Eastern Studies* 40, no. 5 (2008): 715–34.

[104] The concept of Turkish-German "friendship," or rather "limited friendship," is emphasized in: Sabine Mangold-Will, *Begrenzte Freundschaft. Deutschland und die Türkei 1918–1933* (Göttingen: Wallstein, 2013).

[105] Edward W. Said, *Orientalism* (New York: Pantheon Books, 1978).

began traveling to Istanbul to help "reform" the Ottoman army.[106] During the long nineteenth century, German intellectuals in the academic discipline of Oriental Studies (*Orientalistik*) harbored a curious fascination with Ottomans.[107] The Berlin–Baghdad railway, whose construction began in 1903, further tied Ottomans and Germans together commercially.[108] After the demise of the Ottoman Empire in 1923, Turkish Republican founder Mustafa Kemal Atatürk, who had trained under Prussian military officers in the Ottoman army's military academy, drew inspiration from Germany and Europe and channeled it into his top-down "modernization" campaigns.[109] The two countries also shared a long history of migration even before the guest worker program: since the nineteenth century, Ottomans and Turks had been a sizeable presence in Prussia and Germany, coming to Berlin in particular as diplomats, politicians, military officers, academics, journalists, and artists.[110]

But this history of "friendship" was tainted with collaborations that ended in violence and genocide. During World War I, the Ottomans swiftly allied with Germany under the command of Enver Pasha, a leading perpetrator of the 1915–1916 Armenian Genocide, whom one Turkish scholar later referred to as an *Almancı* due to his close ties to German diplomats and intellectuals.[111] Many Germans, moreover, sympathized with the Armenian Genocide, denigrating Armenians as the "Jews of Europe."[112] Prussian companies and military officials were even complicit

[106] Gerhard Grüßhaber, *The "German Spirit" in the Ottoman and Turkish Army, 1908–1938: A History of Military Knowledge Transfer* (Oldenbourg: De Gruyter, 2018).
[107] Suzanne L. Marchand, *German Orientalism in the Age of Empire: Race, Religion, and Scholarship* (Cambridge, UK: Cambridge University Press, 2009); Ursula Wokoeck, *German Orientalism: The Study of the Middle East and Islam from 1800 to 1945* (London: Routledge, 2009). In the field of literature, see: Todd Kontje, *German Orientalisms* (Ann Arbor: University of Michigan Press, 2004).
[108] Sean McMeekin, *The Berlin-Baghdad Express: The Ottoman Empire and Germany's Bid for World Power* (Cambridge, MA: Belknap, Harvard University Press, 2010); Murat Özyüksel, *The Berlin-Baghdad Railway and the Ottoman Empire: Industrialization, Imperial Germany, and the Middle East* (London: I. B. Tauris, 2016).
[109] M. Şükrü Hanioğlu, "*Das Volk in Waffen*: The Formation of an Ottoman Officer," in *Atatürk: An Intellectual Biography* (Princeton: Princeton University Press, 2011), 31–47.
[110] Ingeborg Böer, Ruth Haerkötter, and Petra Kappert, eds., *Türken in Berlin 1871–1945. Eine Metropole in den Erinnerungen osmanischer und türkischer Zeitzeugen* (Berlin: De Gruyter, 2002).
[111] Mustafa Müftüoğlu, *Yalan Söyleyen Tarih Utansın* (Istanbul: Çile, 1977), 175.
[112] Stefan Ihrig, *Justifying Genocide: Germany and the Armenians from Bismarck to Hitler* (Cambridge, MA: Harvard University Press, 2016). On Armenian Genocide denial, see: Taner Akçam, *Killing Orders: Talat Pasha's Telegrams and the Armenian Genocide*

by providing guns and, in rare cases, participating in or witnessing the shootings.[113] Moreover, as Stefan Ihrig has shown, Atatürk was praised in the "Nazi imagination" – and even served as an inspiration for Hitler – for his bold leadership in fostering Turkish nationalism and ethnic exclusivity through ruthlessly suppressing minority groups.[114] During the Third Reich, German intellectuals fleeing Nazism found a welcome refuge in Turkey, where many continued to study eugenics and "race science" alongside Turkish professors.[115] Turkey maintained neutrality during World War II until, upon the certainty of German defeat, it joined the side of the Allies in February 1945. Although Turkey had no official antisemitic policies, and despite rescuing some European Holocaust refugees, Turkey still persecuted the 75,000 Jews within its borders.[116] Both the memory of Ottoman atrocities and Turkey's relationship to Nazi Germany shaped the way that observers in both countries in the 1980s discussed Germans' anti-Turkish racism and return migration policies. This shared history of genocide became a political tool that could be condemned, whitewashed, denied, and deflected – all in the service of debating migration.

The Cold War was the key backdrop for the guest worker program, as it ushered in a new era of especially close ties between Turkey, West

(New York: Palgrave Macmillan, 2018); Marc David Baer, *Sultanic Saviors and Tolerant Turks: Writing Ottoman Jewish History, Denying the Armenian Genocide* (Bloomington: Indiana University Press, 2020).

[113] The anti-arms trade organization Global Net produced this widely publicized report. See: Ben Knight, "New Report Details Germany's Role in Armenian Genocide," *Deutsche Welle* (*DW*), April 5, 2018, www.dw.com/en/new-report-details-germanys-role-in-armenian-genocide/a-43268266.

[114] Stefan Ihrig, *Atatürk in the Nazi Imagination* (Cambridge, MA: Harvard University Press, 2014).

[115] Murat Ergin, *"Is the Turk a White Man?": Race and Modernity in the Making of Turkish Identity* (Leiden: Brill, 2017); Horst Widmann, *Exil und Bildungshilfe. Die deutschsprächige akademische Emigration in die Türken nach 1933* (Frankfurt am Main: Peter Lang, 1973).

[116] Corry Guttstadt, *Turkey, the Jews, and the Holocaust,* trans. Kathleen M. Dell'Orto, Sabine Bartel, and Michelle Miles (Cambridge, UK: Cambridge University Press, 2013); İ. İzzet Bahar, *Turkey and the Rescue of European Jews* (London: Routledge, 2015); Marc David Baer, "Turk and Jew in Berlin: The First Turkish Migration to Germany and the Shoah," *Comparative Studies in Society and History* 55, no. 2 (2013): 330–55. These works contradict the much rosier – and verging on apologetic – argument of Stanford Shaw, who has come under fire for denying the Armenian Genocide and exhibiting a pro-Turkish bias. Stanford J. Shaw, *Turkey and the Holocaust: Turkey's Role in Rescuing Turkish and European Jewry from Nazi Persecution, 1933–1945* (New York: Palgrave Macmillan, 1993). On Turks living in Nazi Germany, see: Marc David Baer, "Mistaken for Jews: Turkish PhD Students in Nazi Germany," *German Studies Review* 41, no. 1 (2018): 19–39.

Germany, and Western Europe as a whole.[117] Rather than being a peripheral actor in the grand narrative of Cold War Europe, Turkey was a crucial Western ally and bulwark against communism, as it shared land borders with the Soviet Union and the oil-rich Middle East. Turkey joined the Council of Europe in 1950, the North Atlantic Treaty Organization (NATO) in 1952, and the European Economic Community (EEC) as an associate member in 1963.[118] Although it never materialized, the prospect of Turkey's becoming an EEC member state remained very real until the late 1980s, with freedom of movement between the two countries being planned for 1986 but never implemented. Throughout the Cold War, moreover, Turkey increasingly relied on European and American loans and development aid to mitigate its economic crisis. By 1980, West Germany was Turkey's largest trading partner, which became especially important amid the "Third World" debt crisis that devastated the Turkish economy. Although Turks often viewed these European and American ties with skepticism and debated the merits of "Westernization" and the peculiar nature of Turkish "modernity," the overall trend was a deepening relationship throughout much of the late twentieth century.[119] Significantly, in dictating the contours of this relationship, Turkey was neither submissive nor passive. Rather, Turkish officials exerted their interests so strongly – especially their opposition to return migration – that their West German counterparts were left frustrated, frazzled, tongue-tied, and scrambling to keep up.

Ultimately, this history of "friendship" soured during the 1980s, due partly, as this book argues, to the dual swords of racism and return migration. Especially important is that West Germany passed the remigration law just three years after Turkey's September 12, 1980, military coup, as the military dictatorship was committing rampant human rights violations against political leftists, Kurds, and other internal ethnic minorities. While historical examinations of this watershed moment largely remain to be written, this book centers the 1980 coup in nearly every chapter as a fundamental but underacknowledged part of

---

[117] On the Cold War context's significance for migration to West Germany, see: Alexander Clarkson, *Fragmented Fatherland: Immigration and Cold War Conflict in the Federal Republic of Germany, 1945–1980* (Oxford: Oxford University Press, 2013).

[118] Şaban Halis Çaliş, *Turkey's Cold War: Foreign Policy and Western Alignment in the Modern Republic* (London: I. B. Taurus, 2017).

[119] Mehmet Döşemeci, *Debating Turkish Modernity: Civilization, Nationalism, and the EEC* (Cambridge, UK: Cambridge University Press, 2013).

Turkish-German migration history and transnational European history writ large.[120] Even from afar, the postcoup regime impacted migrants' lives and return migration decisions, especially when it came to matters of education and mandatory military service for guest workers' children. Geopolitically, tensions about the coup also trickled down into the newly overlapping contestations about return migration and asylum policies, forcing West Germany onto a shaky diplomatic tightrope. As the Turkish government assailed West German racism and strove to prevent return migration at all costs, West German officials had to balance their domestic and international interests: kicking out Turkish guest workers and preventing an influx of asylum seekers, while simultaneously appeasing a military dictatorship that, despite its human rights violations, was crucial to its Cold War geopolitical goals. As the battle over racism and return migration evolved into a battle over human rights, democracy, and authoritarianism, debates about the migrants' integration in Germany became inextricably linked to debates about Turkey's integration into European institutions and the ever-changing idea of "Europe" itself.

* * * * *

Migration is, in many respects, a universal story. For thousands of years, human beings have been on the move, encountering new places, peoples, ecologies, and cultures. Amid the heightened globalization of the twentieth century, the increased access to trains, planes, and automobiles made crossing national borders a core aspect of modern life. Even today, the lines between voluntary and forced migration are often blurred, as individuals make their decisions to leave – and to return to – their homes amid uncontrollable pressures from above: global capitalism, government policies, wars, genocides, and, increasingly, environmental catastrophes. So, too, has the very idea of "home" become murky. Even as new technologies provide opportunities for bridging physical distance, emotional

---

[120] A valuable historical account of the 1980 coup in relation to West German affairs is: Tim Szatkowski, *Die Bundesrepublik Deutschland und die Türkei 1978–1983* (Berlin: De Gruyter, 2016). On the collective memory of the coup, see: Elifcan Karacan, *Remembering the 1980 Turkish Military Coup d'État: Memory, Violence, and Trauma* (Wiesbaden: Springer, 2015); Göze Orhon, *The Weight of the Past: Memory and Turkey's 12 September Coup* (Newcastle upon Tyne: Cambridge Scholars Publishing, 2015). On coups in Turkish history, see: Ümit Cizre, "Ideology, Context and Interest: The Turkish Military," in Reşat Kasaba, ed., *Turkey in the Modern World*, vol. 4 of *The Cambridge History of Turkey* (Cambridge, UK: Cambridge University Press, 2008), 301–31.

distance can widen, and migrants' relationships to themselves, their new milieus, and the people they leave behind remain ever-changing. Within this particular story about Turkish migration to Germany, readers may thus find parallels to other cases of migration across time and space, or perhaps to their own experiences or deeper family histories. While appreciating the uniqueness of every individual's migration story, I encourage readers to contemplate and sit with these parallels long after turning this book's final page.

Above all, this book is fundamentally influenced by how the migrants themselves have told and preserved their own stories – not only during our oral history interviews but also in the very structure of archives themselves. Alongside government and private archives, I conducted most of the research for this book at Germany's migration museum, DOMiD e.V., which was founded in 1990 by a group of Turkish guest workers who wished to preserve their own history. At first just scraps of paper and objects collected from neighbors and friends, DOMiD is now home to hundreds of thousands of sources that counter the myth of non-return and other top-down narratives of the guest worker program. The very structure of the DOMiD archive – which includes categories like "Connections to the Homeland," "Vacations," and "Return Migration" – reflects the continued presence of the Turkish *vatan* in their lives. Turkey was a place that they always returned to, not only with their hearts and minds but also with their physical bodies. It is my hope that this book honors them, gives them voice and agency, and does justice to what truly are transnational lives.

PART I

SEPARATION ANXIETIES

I

Sex, Lies, and Abandoned Families

The moment when guest workers departed Turkey was one of great rupture – not only for the guest workers themselves but also for the families they left behind. In all corners of Turkey's vast landscape, from major cities and the Anatolian countryside, the news of West Germany's urgent need for laborers had spread. Seeking to escape unemployment, gain wealth, or simply have an adventure, hundreds of thousands of young men and women flocked to the West German government's recruitment offices. The largest one was in Istanbul, where 200,000 prospective workers applied each week.[1] Weary and hopeful, they filled out extensive paperwork, underwent humiliating medical examinations, and waited seemingly interminably for the result. Would they be accepted? Or would they be rejected on the grounds that they were too young, old, sickly, or disabled? Especially for those from rural Anatolia, the stakes of rejection were high. Having "scrambled together" thousands of lira, or even sold their fields and animals to afford the two-day car or bus ride to Istanbul, they feared returning empty-handed, to be greeted with disdain, disappointment, and a loss of prestige. "Not passing would have been a catastrophe for us," one guest worker explained years later. "Those who did not pass cried like children." They considered it a "matter of honor" and "did not have the courage to return to their villages."[2]

---

[1] Karin Hunn, "'Irgendwann kam das Deutschlandfieber auch in unsere Gegend...' Türkische 'Gastarbeiter' in der Bundesrepublik Deutschland – von der Anwerbung bis zur Rückkehrförderung," in Jan Motte and Rainer Ohliger, eds., *Geschichte und Gedächtnis in der Einwanderungsgesellschaft. Migration zwischen historischer Rekonstruktion und Erinnerungspolitik* (Essen: Klartext, 2004), 78.

[2] Metin Gür, *Meine Fremde Heimat. Türkische Arbeiterfamilien in der BRD* (Cologne: Weltkreis, 1987), 130.

FIGURE I.I With mixed emotions, family members watch guest workers
depart for Germany at Istanbul's Sirkeci Train Station, 1964. © Hans Rudolf
Uthoff, used with permission.

For those who survived the arduous recruitment process, then came
the scene of departure, full of tearful goodbyes at Istanbul's Sirkeci Train
Station (Figure I.I). Friends, parents, aunts, uncles, spouses, and children all crowded together, reaching over the wooden gates for one last
hug and kiss. "We'll miss you! Send us a color photo from Germany!"
they shouted.[3] Only those from Istanbul enjoyed the luxury of being
present on the platform. Others, from all throughout the vast country,
had already said their goodbyes. As the train door shut, they strained
their necks to look upward at the windows, catching a final glimpse
before the departure. Some embarking on the journey waved excitedly
back, while others stared wistfully into the distance, wondering if they
would soon regret their decision. The stay in Germany was only supposed to last two years, but neither the guest workers nor their loved
ones knew when they would be reunited. They hoped that the happy
day would come soon.

---

[3] Ali Başar, "'Mit den Peitschenstriemen der Armut kam ich hierher.' Im Ruhrgebiet zu
Hause," in Jeannette Goddar and Dorte Huneke, eds., *Auf Zeit. Für immer. Zuwanderer
aus der Türkei erinnern sich* (Cologne: Kiepenheuer & Witsch, 2011), 43.

Migration, as this chapter shows, was not only an individual experience but also a familial and communal one. Guest workers' departure fundamentally disrupted the lives of the family members, neighbors, and friends they left behind. Economically, it drained village economies of able-bodied young men and women, leading to gendered and generational shifts in the division of labor that created new burdens and opportunities. It was the social destabilization, however, that left the most lasting mark on Turkish attitudes toward the guest worker program. Although parents and spouses often encouraged guest workers to travel abroad, tensions emerged due to conflicts between expectations and reality: whether guest workers were sending enough money home, writing enough letters to their loved ones, or – crucially – returning frequently enough (or at all). As time passed, and as emotional distance grew to match physical distance, the perceived abandonment of the family came to represent the abandonment of the nation.

Not all families shared the same experiences, of course, and the perception of abandoned families changed over time. During the formal recruitment years of 1961 to 1973, most guest workers traveled to West Germany alone, leaving husbands, wives, children, and parents behind. Guest workers' spouses and children did not begin migrating in large numbers until after the 1973 recruitment stop, strategically navigating West Germany's lax (though complex) policy of family reunification.[4] But even during the 1970s, not all families reunified. Some who reunified did not reunify entirely, and others moved back and forth between the two countries as "suitcase children" (*Kofferkinder*) in a seemingly perpetual state of transience.

Despite efforts to overcome the physical distance, fears of abandonment were inescapable on both sides. Struggling with homesickness and living in isolated factory dormitories, guest workers developed multiple strategies to avoid isolation and maintain contact with home. But letters, phone calls, and even cassette recordings of their voices were not enough, and families struggled to adapt to the absence of a husband, wife, parent, child, or breadwinner. Rumors reverberated in the echo chamber of village chatter, newspapers, films, and folklore. Bombarded with horror stories about male guest workers lavishing themselves in West Germany's sexually promiscuous culture, wives grew increasingly concerned about their husbands' whereabouts. They worried that guest workers were running off with blonde German women, and fears of adultery spread. Children left behind in villages with grandparents or shuttled between the two countries became viewed as orphaned and uprooted victims of

---

[4] On family reunification, see: Stokes, *Fear of the Family.*

parental neglect, while those born in Germany, or whose parents brought them there amid the family reunifications of the 1970s, were seen as caught between two cultures, unable to speak the Turkish language, and dressing and behaving like Germans. These concerns, despite emerging within families and local communities in Turkey, spread throughout both countries and became frequent themes in news reports, novels, and films.

In West Germany, guest workers' family relations and sexualities were crucial to their racialization. Guest workers' arrival in the 1960s and early 1970s coincided with West Germany's sexual revolution, a time when concerns about promiscuity, immorality, and the breakup of the family pervaded German public discourse. As Lauren Stokes has shown, Germans condemned the "Mediterranean family," "Southern family," and "foreign family" as a backward and oppressive institution that allegedly clashed with West Germany's self-definition as a liberal democracy.[5] Guest workers' sex with German women also dominated headlines, perpetuating stereotypes of violence, patriarchy, and the transgression of national and racial borders. When Turks became the largest ethnic minority in the late 1970s, feminists in the nascent German women's movement increasingly applied these racializing tropes to the "Turkish family" or "Muslim family" as a litmus test for their inability to integrate.[6] In both countries, therefore, concerns about the family became enduring tropes in the migrants' sense of dual estrangement.

COPING WITH HOMESICKNESS

Of all the hardships guest workers faced in Germany, from the back-breaking work in factories and mines to the everyday discrimination by Germans, homesickness and fears of abandonment were among the harshest. Would their parents, husbands, and wives cry every night missing them? Would their young children be able to recognize them upon their return? How would they stay connected to their families at home, and to their homeland as a whole? Where would they get news from Turkey? How could they start new lives without abandoning – or feeling abandoned by – home? To quell these anxieties, guest workers developed numerous strategies – from sending letters, postcards, and photographs, to making friends with other Turks who functioned as surrogate families

---

[5] Stokes, *Fear of the Family*, 8–10.
[6] Rita Chin, "Turkish Women, West German Feminists, and the Gendered Discourse on Muslim Cultural Difference," *Public Culture* 22, no. 3 (2010): 557–81.

and support systems, to decorating their bedrooms with Turkish half-moon flags and other nationalist symbols. All worked to ease, but never cure, the pangs of homesickness, and to compress, but never fully close, the growing emotional distance.

These anxieties began even before guest workers set foot in Germany, on the initial train ride.[7] Not only did the trains lack food, water, and adequate seating (with one West German transportation planner admitting that they were "unacceptable from a humanitarian perspective"), but the idle time also forced guest workers to process their emotions.[8] The Turkish singer Ferdi Tayfur captured these emotions in his renowned 1977 arabesque ballad "Almanya Treni" (Germany Train). As his train leaves the platform, the singer is overwhelmed with sweet memories of time spent at home with his lover, from whom he will now be separated by thousands of miles. "Do not cry, do not hurt, my rose," he comforts her, imploring her to remain faithful. "Germany is very far," he sings. "Do not abandon me. Do not leave me in Germany without a letter."[9]

One former guest worker, Filiz, explained that the reactions of the women on her train varied based on marital and maternal status. While the younger, single women delighted in imagining the exciting life that awaited them abroad, the wives and mothers of the group appeared "mournful." One woman "wailed and wept" because she had left her three children behind.[10] Displays of sadness were so common that one departing woman, Cemile, felt excluded from the collective experience. Assuming that she would cry upon her departure, her brother-in-law had given her a pill that would supposedly subdue her tears. In reality, as she remarked years later, she was not sad at all, because departing her village "freed" her from her despised mother-in-law, who had "oppressed and bullied" her. To bond with her fellow passengers, she performed the expected emotion of sadness by smearing spit into her eye and pretending to cry.[11]

These reactions reflect the wide variance in guest workers' relationships to their families. A 1964 study reported that 56 percent of all Turkish workers in Germany were married, while a Turkish State Planning

[7] On the train ride, see: J. Miller, *Turkish Guest Workers in Germany*, 57–77.
[8] BAVAV, VAm Krusch, "Bericht über die Dienstreise nach Belgrad zwecks Beobachtung eines Sammeltransports Istanbul-München," September 1966, BArch, B 119/4036.
[9] Ferdi Tayfur, "Almanya Treni," track 5 on *Huzurum Kalmadı*, Elenor Müzik, 1977, audio cassette.
[10] Filiz Y., quoted in Hannelore Schäfer, "Ich bleibe hier. Eine Türkin in West Berlin," Norddeutscher Rundfunk, 1983.
[11] "Cemile S," in Ergün Tepecik, *Die Situation der ersten Generation der Türken in der multikulturellen Gesellschaft* (Frankfurt am Main: IKO-Verlag, 2002), 94.

Organization report ten years later showed that the number had climbed to 80 percent.[12] This increase reflected the West German government's evolving recruitment strategy, which first centered on cities with higher numbers of single young adults but later expanded to rural regions with higher marriage rates.[13] While some married migrants appreciated the liberation from overbearing in-laws or abusive spouses, they were overall more likely to mourn the distance from their families, especially if they had young children. Single men and women, on the other hand, missed their parents, siblings, and lovers, but tended to be more willing to embrace Germany as an exciting opportunity. For rural women, as sociologist Nermin Abadan-Unat has explained, migration resulted in a "pseudo-emancipation," offering them the chance to escape gender constraints and develop new power over family spending and decision-making.[14]

But no matter how excited, sorrowful, or bittersweet they felt, homesickness and fears of abandonment loomed large, and employers, organizations, and the West German and Turkish governments sought to ease the difficult transition to life abroad. In 1963, the Workers' Welfare Organization (Arbeiterwohlfahrt, AWO) in Cologne established a Center for Turkish Workers, nicknamed the "Turkish library," which featured daily Turkish newspapers and books sent by the Turkish Ministry of Culture. While enjoying Turkish coffee or tea, guest workers could chat about gossip from home, watch Turkish films, and play table tennis in the basement recreation room. Reflecting the importance of the center to the Turkish government, Ambassador Mehmet Baydur presented the workers with a gift emblematic of national pride: a bust of Mustafa Kemal Atatürk, the founder of the Turkish Republic. Appreciating the comfort and community, one guest worker who attended the opening called Cologne his "second homeland."[15] Yet the Center was exceptional, as cultural venues in most cities and smaller towns were slim to none.

[12] Nermin Abadan-Unat, *Batı Almanya'daki Türk İşçileri ve Sorunları* (Ankara: T. C. Devlet Planlama Teşkilâtı Yayınları, 1964), 64; T. C. Başbakanlık Devlet Planlama Teşkilâtı, *Yurt Dışından Dönen İşçilerin Sosyo-Ekonomik Eğilimleri Üzerine Bir Çalışma*, report no. 264 (Ankara, 1974), table 4.

[13] Mübeccel B. Kıray, "The Family of the Immigrant Worker," in Nermin Abadan-Unat, *Turkish Workers in Europe 1960–1975: A Socioeconomic Reappraisal* (Leiden: Brill, 1976), 215.

[14] Nermin-Abadan Unat, "Implications of Migration on Emancipation and Pseudo-Emancipation of Turkish Women," *The International Migration Review* 11, no. 1 (1977): 31–57.

[15] "Türken fühlen sich bei uns wie zu Hause," *Kölner Stadt-Anzeiger (KSA)*, December 11, 1963; Erdoğan Olacayto, "Köln Türk kütüphanesi işçilerin buluşma ve sohbet yeri oldu," *Anadolu Gazetesi*, January 1964, 4.

Employers, too, sometimes created spaces to accommodate Turkish workers. The focus was on their Muslim faith, which West Germans considered the most significant marker of cultural difference. Management at the Sterkrade coalmine in Oberhausen, which in the early 1960s employed primarily Turkish workers, boasted that their dining halls never served pork and that their facility featured a prayer room with a rug facing Mecca.[16] Others came up with creative solutions. The Hanover branch of the German Federal Railways turned two empty train cars into makeshift prayer rooms, which guest workers affectionately called "mobile mosques" or "mosques on wheels."[17] As in the case of cultural centers, however, the provision of prayer rooms was a rarity. A 1971 study revealed that only 8 percent of firms with predominantly Turkish workers in the State of North Rhine-Westphalia offered prayer rooms.[18]

Absent designated spaces, guest workers created their own. Local train stations, so characteristic of guest workers' transient experiences, soon became among their most frequent meeting points. The eleventh platform of the Central Train Station in Munich, where most guest workers had first arrived in Germany, held special nostalgia, with Mahir, one of the earliest Turks to come to Germany, calling it the "gate to the homeland" (*Tor zur Heimat*).[19] On their days off each Sunday and on Christian holidays, dozens of usually male Turkish workers congregated in the station's halls, reading newspapers aloud, catching up on Turkish politics, and sharing advice on how to solve conflicts with German employers (Figure 1.2).[20] These gatherings, however, made Germans uneasy. Repeating unfounded tropes of Turkish men's criminality, one German newspaper asked in 1972: "The guest workers in the Munich Central Train Station – are they really so dangerous or do they only look like it?"[21] With few exceptions, however, guest workers were not engaging in crime and would have preferred to meet elsewhere. But, at

---

[16] "Foruk meinte: 'Sterkrade serr gutt,'" *General-Anzeiger*, December 6, 1965.
[17] "İşçilerimiz için yürüyen camiler," *Anadolu Gazetesi*, February 1964, 4.
[18] Ernst Zieris et al., *Betriebsunterkünfte für ausländische Mitbürger. Bericht zur Situation in Betriebsunterkünften für ausländische Arbeitnehmer in Nordrhein-Westfalen* (Düsseldorf: Minister für Arbeit, Gesundheit und Soziales des Landes Nordrhein-Westfalen, 1972), 77.
[19] Mahir Zeytinoğlu, "'Atatürk, Ludwig, Goethe und ich – wir gehören zusammen!' Der bunte Hund des Münchner Bahnhofsviertels," in Goddar and Huneke, eds., *Auf Zeit. Für immer*, 132–33.
[20] Max von der Grün, *Leben im gelobten Land. Gastarbeiterportraits* (Darmstadt: Hermann Luchterhand, 1975), 11.
[21] Zeytinoğlu, "'Atatürk, Ludwig, Goethe und ich,'" 132–33.

FIGURE 1.2 Guest workers read the Turkish newspaper *Hürriyet* at a train station in Hanover, 1974. © picture alliance/dpa, used with permission.

a time before the proliferation of Turkish coffee houses opened by guest workers seeking self-sufficiency, train stations were a last resort. Back then, Mahir explained, "We had no other places."[22]

In the private sphere, as Jennifer Miller and Sarah Thomsen Vierra have illuminated, no space was as central to guest workers' lives as their factory dormitories.[23] Before the 1973 recruitment stop and rise in family migration, housing guest workers collectively in dormitories was not only an efficient and cost-effective way for firms to keep workers close to their jobs but also

---

[22] On coffee houses, see: Rauf Ceylan, *Ethnische Kolonien. Entstehung, Funktion und Wandel am Beispiel türkischer Moscheen und Cafés* (Wiesbaden: Verlag für Sozialwissenschaften, 2006); Mustafa Acar, *Türkische Kaffeehäuser in Deutschland. Ein Integrationshindernis für die Türken in der deutschen Gesellschaft* (Saarbrücken: VDM Verlag, 2007).

[23] J. Miller, *Turkish Guest Workers in Germany*; Thomsen Vierra, *Turkish Germans in the Federal Republic of Germany*. See also: Anne von Oswald and Barbara Schmidt, "'Nach Schichtende sind sie immer in ihr Lager zurückgekehrt...' Leben in 'Gastarbeiter'-Unterkünften in den sechziger und siebziger Jahren," in Jan Motte, Rainer Ohliger, and Anne von Oswald, eds., *50 Jahre Bundesrepublik – 50 Jahre Einwanderung. Nachkriegsgeschichte als Migrationsgeschichte* (Frankfurt: Campus, 1999).

a means of social control. These dormitories accommodated mostly Turkish workers but were also home to guest workers from other countries that had signed labor recruitment agreements with the Federal Republic. With all guest workers residing in the same location, factory personnel could monitor their whereabouts and ensure that their focus was, in fact, their work. The carefully crafted dynamics of the dormitories ensured that social interactions typically occurred along gender and national lines. Men and women lived in separate buildings, and workers of the same nationality shared rooms. Those seeking to interact with local Germans or other guest workers of the opposite gender generally had to venture outside their residences. Segregating guest workers in these dormitories had the lasting effect of impeding their social interactions with Germans from the very beginning, serving as evidence of the West German government's failure to make efforts to integrate them even though Turks were often blamed for failing to integrate.

The ability to forge friendships in factory dormitories depended not only on gender and nationality but also on the cleavages and prejudices of class, rural versus urban origin, and religiosity. Many guest workers of urban origin – especially those who came from middle-class families in Istanbul and other major cities on the geographically western side of Turkey – considered themselves "modern," "cosmopolitan," and "European" and found more commonality with Germans than they did the pejoratively named "village Turks" (*Dorftürken*) from Anatolia.[24] Muazzez, who worked at the Blaupunkt factory in Hildesheim, summarized these prejudices and the name-calling among the women in her dormitory: the "modern" women were "prostitutes," and the "traditional," "religious" women were "stupid bumpkins."[25] Photographs from Polaroid cameras – one of the first purchases guest workers made to document their new lives in West Germany – portray these divides. In some photographs, smiling guest workers drink beer, play cards, watch television, listen to music, and sit on bunk beds – all segregated by gender.[26] One photograph shows cliques of urban-looking women dressed in accordance with the fashion magazines to which they would have had access in Turkish cities, wearing colorful tank tops, miniskirts, and tight jeans.[27] Another photograph,

---

[24] Tanju Ü, interview by author, Şarköy, July 20, 2014.
[25] Hasan Topraklar, *Zur Situation türkischer Rückkehrfamilien. Ursachen, Folgen, Probleme* (West Berlin: Fachhochschule für Sozialarbeit und Sozialpädagogik Berlin, 1986), 70.
[26] Photographs in DOMiD-Archiv, BT 0315,0000; BT 0603,0003; E 1090,0016; BT 0806,0000; BT 0648,0000; BT 0813,0000; BT 0603,0003; BT 0163,0001; BT 0163,0005.
[27] Photograph, October 19, 1969, DOMiD-Archiv, BT 0675,0002-3.

however, shows several women wearing headscarves and the long skirts typical of the countryside as they sit on the floor, cleaning their shoes and cracking nuts – activities that the German archive housing these photographs tellingly refers to as "village traditions."[28]

Beyond everyday social interaction, friendships forged in factory dormitories also served as crucial support networks, or surrogate families, which sustained them in times of crisis or uncertainty. Halil, who worked at a cotton mill in Neuhof along with 230 other Turkish men, explained how his friends supported each other both emotionally and financially. They stood in line to visit sick colleagues in the hospital and even pooled their paychecks when one of them urgently needed to travel to Turkey to care for a sick family member. Even in less dire circumstances, such as when a colleague wanted to purchase a house in Turkey or invest in a Turkish company, they handed him some cash and wished him the best of luck.[29] By the late 1960s, guest workers institutionalized informal meetings between friends and colleagues into cultural, religious, economic, and political immigrant associations.[30] And by the 1970s, male guest workers in particular began assuming leadership positions in trade unions.

The downside to the formation of new communities along gender, national, and rural–urban lines was that they often spun into a downward spiral of collective commiseration. Necan, a guest worker at the Siemens factory in Berlin, recalled that she and her roommates tended to discuss only Turkey – or, more specifically, only Istanbul, as many urbanites considered their home city representative of the entire country. "We had no other topic," she explained. "What else could we have talked about? Economics or politics? The entire topic was our homeland."[31] The situation was similar for Nuriye, who left her husband behind in 1965 to work at a factory in Bielefeld. "It was terrible being alone in this foreign country," she recalled. "At the beginning we sat together every evening, listened to Turkish music, and cried."[32]

With socializing a powerful yet inadequate antidote, guest workers also quelled their homesickness through material objects, decorating their

---

[28] Photograph, 1965, DOMiD-Archiv, BT 0867,0007-8.

[29] Halil Güven, "Wir haben immer Ja gesagt," in Beate Franck and Aytunç Kılıçsoy, eds., *Sehnsucht nach Heimat. Hofer Gastarbeiter aus der Türkei erzählen aus ihrem Leben* (Hof: Hoermann, 2006), 12.

[30] On Turkish migrants' associations, see: Yurdakul, *From Guest Workers into Muslims*.

[31] Necan, quoted in Schäfer, "Ich bleibe hier."

[32] Nuriye M., quoted in Dieter Sauter, dir., "Die vergessene Generation. Von 'Gastarbeitern' der ersten Stunde," in *In der Fremde zu Hause. Deutsche und Türken*, Bayerischer Rundfunk, 1990, VHS, DOMiD-Archiv, Cologne, VI 0090.

bedroom walls with items that reminded them of home (Figure 1.3).[33] These objects were often symbols of nationalism, such as Turkish flags, portraits of political figures (including a popular wall tapestry of Atatürk, in full military garb, standing next to the Turkish flag), images of scenic Turkish landscapes and maps, and even magazine covers depicting famous Turkish wrestlers.[34] Workers from Turkish cities, where cameras were available for purchase, also adorned their walls with photographs of family members or even pets left behind.[35] Not all decorations, however, were connected to Turkey. Some male workers hung up photographs of scantily clad women cut out from magazines.[36]

Of course, staring wistfully at nationalistic decorations on walls and chatting about the homeland with new Turkish friends were no substitute for communication with loved ones at home. Over the years, guest workers developed multiple strategies for keeping in touch with their families. Not only did they fulfill their financial obligations by sending their families substantial portions of their paychecks, but they also regularly sent (and received) letters, postcards, and even cassette recordings of their voices. Yet communication between the two countries was hindered not only by slow postal systems and letters getting lost in the mail but also by guest workers' and their families' varying socioeconomic statuses, literacy rates, and rural versus urban origins. The necessity of relying on other guest workers, or other neighbors in villages, as translators or intermediaries made communication between the two countries not only an individual or intrafamilial but also a communal experience. Even if they did not have relatives working in Germany, friends and neighbors in Turkey, too, heard stories – both real and fabricated – about the migrants' lives and the riches they had earned. These stories shaped perceptions of guest workers in the homeland and tended to encourage future migration.

Sending money home was the most important factor driving guest workers' individual decisions to migrate, as well as the Turkish government's decision to send workers abroad. They did so through remittance

---

[33] Photographs in DOMiD-Archiv, E 1216,0058; E 1090,0004; BT 0386,0001; BT 0546,0000; E 0365,0001; BT 0318,0000; BT 0012,0000; BT 0502,0000.

[34] In the 1980s and 1990s, nationalist imagery of Atatürk became commodified and sold as nostalgia for Turkey's early republican period. Esra Özyürek, *Nostalgia for the Modern: State Secularism and Everyday Politics in Turkey* (Durham: Duke University Press, 2006), 95–124.

[35] Photograph, 1965, DOMiD-Archiv, E 0365,0001.

[36] Photographs in DOMiD-Archiv, E 0773,0001; E 1216,0058; BT 0547,0001; BT 0546,0000.

FIGURE 1.3 Ömer displays his bedroom decorations at his factory dormitory
in Hanau, 1966. Among them are the Turkish flag, a portrait of Mustafa
Kemal Atatürk, and scenic images of Turkey – all reminders of home.
© DOMiD-Archiv, Cologne, used with permission.

payments: one-time cash transfers from their bank accounts in West Germany to their relatives' accounts in Turkey. Guest workers' families prized remittances not only for the lump sum itself but also for the substantially higher value of the West German Deutschmark compared to the Turkish lira. In 1961, at the start of the guest worker recruitment, the Deutschmark was worth triple the lira and, ten years later, quadruple.[37] "I get four liras for one mark," Hasan explained. "If I send 200 marks home, then the family gets 800 liras for it," he said, adding that he lived frugally and sent his parents in Istanbul 100–150 DM monthly.[38]

Although guest workers were certainly not living luxuriously, the notion that they had "pockets full of Deutschmarks" shaped Turkish perceptions of them. Family members' expectations of receiving remittances were no secret. Özgür, the father of a guest worker, repeatedly sent letters from the Turkish coal-mining town Zonguldak to his German daughter-in-law, Charlotte, in Cologne, inquiring about his son's finances behind his back. "It has been three years since Metin went to Germany," he wrote in 1964. "Since then, those who went to Germany from Turkey have made big money. How much money does Metin have in the bank now?"[39] When Charlotte complained about Metin's excessive spending habits, Özgür suggested that the couple move back to Zonguldak and live with him. Grossly exaggerating the exchange rate, he noted that Deutschmarks were worth twenty-five to thirty lira. "You would not need to pay rent, a kilogram of water costs six lira, and vegetables and fruits are inexpensive."[40]

As the case of Özgür, Metin, and Charlotte reveals, the other most important forms of communication between the two countries were letters, postcards, and packages. Like the migrants themselves, correspondence from parents, spouses, and children journeyed from Turkey to Germany – but, unlike the guest workers' three-day train ride, could often take weeks, if not months, to arrive. After waiting seemingly interminably for a response, receiving a letter was such a cause for excitement that guest workers regularly photographed themselves sitting in their dormitory rooms reading mail. In one photograph, Filiz lies on her bed with a pen and paper in hand, likely responding to one of the many postcards she received from her friends and family in Istanbul, which tended to feature landscapes

---

[37] Rodney Evanson, "Historical Currency Converter," www.historicalstatistics.org/Currencyconverter.html.
[38] Hasan K., quoted. in Horst Kammrad, »*Gast«-Arbeiter-Report* (Munich: Piper, 1971), 51–55.
[39] Özgür to Charlotte (pseudonyms), September 14, 1964, DOMiD-Archiv, ED 0168.
[40] Although the measurement for water should be "liter," Özgür wrote "kilogram."

of the city's most beloved tourist sites, such as the Bosphorus Bridge, the Emirgan Forest, and the neighborhood of Eminönü.[41] In another, a male guest worker sits at a small side table covered in an embroidered tablecloth (presumably brought from the home country) and opens a letter, while one of his roommates stands beside him, eager to hear any news from home.[42]

In their handwritten letters home, guest workers described their living situations – the good and the bad – and expressed somber emotions of longing and homesickness. In the winter of 1966, a young married couple named Hatice and Zoltan wrote to Zoltan's parents, airing their grievances. Although they lived on their own rather than in a factory dormitory, their apartment was cramped and cold, and long work hours and minimal contact with locals left them struggling to learn German.[43] "Despite having seen you four months ago, I miss you now more than ever before," Zoltan confessed. "I am homesick."[44] The couple's letters also reveal that guest workers' family members often sent packages in the mail. Hatice asked his parents to send him some wool gloves, long underwear, and cotton briefs from Çift Kaplan, a popular store headquartered in Istanbul. "It is quite cold here," Hatice wrote, and "things made of cotton are expensive here," alluding to Turkey's postwar role as a major exporter of cotton.[45] Yet packages also carried symbolic meaning. Relics of their homeland, the objects sent in packages were physically touched by Turkish textile workers, purchased at favorite Turkish stores, and packed by their loved ones.

The ability to send letters, however, depended on rural–urban origin, socioeconomic status, and education level. Communicating in writing was the privilege of a few, largely confined to individuals from urban centers or the highest echelons of rural societies. Having grown up and been educated in Istanbul, Hatice and Zoltan wrote well, with the exception of minor grammatical errors. By contrast, guest workers of rural origin left fewer letters in the archives because they and their family members were more likely to be illiterate. When reading letters or newspapers in factory dormitories, guest workers from rural regions regularly relied on social networks, asking their urban counterparts to read and write their letters. Literate neighbors and friends in villages – typically men – performed this act of translation at

---

[41] Postcards to Filiz Y. in DOMiD-Archiv, December 28, 1966, BT 0552,7; February 3, 1964, BT 0552,15.

[42] Photograph, 1973, DOMiD-Archiv, BT 0546,0001.

[43] Hatice to Zoltan's parents (pseudonyms), January 13, 1966, DOMiD-Archiv, E 1301,2.

[44] Zoltan to parents, January 13, 1966, DOMiD-Archiv, E 1301,3.

[45] Ibid. On cotton production, see: Çağlar Keyder and Zafer Yenal, "Agrarian Change Under Globalization: Markets and Insecurity in Turkish Agriculture," *Journal of Agrarian Change* 11, no. 1 (2011): 60–86.

home.[46] The communal experience of letter writing meant that knowledge of guest workers' lives in Germany spread broadly throughout home communities, even among those who did not have relatives abroad.

Telephone communication, too, reflected both Turkey's rural–urban divide and the communal experience of circulating knowledge about guest workers. In the formal recruitment years of the 1960s and early 1970s, telephone connections were not yet installed in most rural regions of Turkey. But even in large cities, not everyone owned a telephone, and even for those who did, expensive international fees made phone calls to West Germany a rarity, often reserved for special occasions such as birthdays.[47] Owning a telephone thus imbued a family with not only social status but also a newfound responsibility to serve as an intermediary between guest workers in Germany and their families at home. Fatma, whose family came from a small village near Trabzon, recalled this frequent experience in the 1980s: "Individuals from neighboring villages – or the relatives of those in Germany – would call us and say, 'We would like to talk to so and so. Is he there?' And then we set the phone down, ran over, and shouted, 'Telephone for you!' and they came over to our house and spoke on the phone, of course."[48]

To bypass the complications of telephone calls, guest workers and their loved ones at home developed another strategy: sending audio recordings of their voices.[49] The mechanism was the creative repurposing of battery-operated cassette players, a new technology that guest workers frequently purchased in Germany to listen to Turkish music. The process was complex. After recording their voice messages on a blank tape, the senders located fellow guest workers who were planning to travel home to a neighboring city or village and who would be willing to transport the cassette player, along with some extra blank tapes, to the recipients. After listening to the voice message, the recipients would then record their own responses on the blank tapes and send the cassette player back to Germany through the same or another liaison. As with letters and telephone calls, social networks were crucial to carrying out this process. The

---

[46] Fevziye Sayılan and Ahmet Yıldız, "The Historical and Political Context of Adult Literacy in Turkey," *International Journal of Lifelong Education* 28, no. 6 (2009): 735–49.
[47] Bengü K., interview by author, Cologne, September 6, 2017.
[48] Fatma U., interview by author, Cologne, September 12, 2017.
[49] See the many cassette players held in DOMiD-Archiv. Sending audio recordings on cassette tapes was also a strategy used among migrants elsewhere across the globe at the time. Mirca Madianou and Daniel Miller, "Crafting Love: Letters and Cassette Tapes in Transnational Filipino Family Communication," *South East Asia Research* 19, no. 2 (2011): 249–72.

Sunday meetings at the train stations, for example, were spaces where cassette players exchanged hands.

Not all guest workers, however, conveyed truthful accounts. Instead, they sometimes performed emotions that they believed were expected of them. Filiz and her long-term best friend Necan admitted that they had staged the happy photographs they had sent to Filiz's parents in Istanbul. Upon first glance, the photographs show exciting lives filled with music, parties, and window shopping through the streets of West Berlin.[50] Although they truly enjoyed these experiences, the two women deliberately downplayed their malaise and exhaustion from hard work. To avoid worrying Filiz's parents, they dressed up in fancy clothing, made their room look nicer than it was – "We even purchased flowers!" – and smiled extra widely.[51] The staging of these photographs calls into question the veracity of the stories guest workers told to loved ones at home. Other guest workers, too, may have fabricated or exaggerated their quality of life, as well as the wealth they acquired in Germany, to offer reassuring accounts of their happiness and success.

Despite possible fabrications, those in the home country – whether family members, neighbors, friends, or community members – generally took guest workers' stories at face value and saw within them a glimmer of hope for themselves to forge a better life.[52] These stories thus served as a pull factor that convinced others to work in Germany via chain migration.[53] One guest worker named Osman, for example, attributed his migration decision to his uncle, who wrote letters from Germany boasting that "he was full of meat and vegetables every day."[54] Osman's uncle then "invited" him to come to Germany by securing a work permit for him not through the formal channel of the governmental recruitment program, but rather through his employer – a common practice at the time for circumventing the bureaucracy, the seemingly interminable waiting period, and humiliating medical examinations at the official recruitment offices.

Above all, the best antidote to homesickness was the ability to have one's family in Germany (Figure 1.4). By 1968, already 58 percent of

---

[50] Photograph, January 20, 1966, DOMiD-Archiv, BT 0163,0005; Photograph, March 6, 1966, DOMiD-Archiv, BT 0165,0002.

[51] Filiz Y. and Necan, quoted in Schäfer, "Ich bleibe hier."

[52] "Mehmet Adalya," in Tufan Kıroğlu, ed., *Die ersten Türken von Neumünster. 12 Lebensgeschichten* (Berlin: epubli, 2011), 58.

[53] B. S. Waldorf, A. Esparza, and J. O. Huff, "A Behavioral Model of International Labor and Nonlabor Migration: The Case of Turkish Movements to West Germany, 1960–1986," *Environment and Planning A* 22 (1989): 961–73.

[54] Von der Grün, *Leben im gelobten Land*, 11.

FIGURE 1.4 Members of the Dağdeviren family, who were able to migrate through West Germany's family reunification policy, smile from their apartment window in Munich, 1969. © Süddeutsche Zeitung Photo/Alamy Stock Foto, used with permission.

married male guest workers of all nationalities had brought their wives to Germany, typically within one year of their departure. By 1971, over half of the guest workers had brought at least one of their children to Germany. These numbers increased markedly throughout the 1970s upon the surge in family migration, and by 1980 over 90 percent of guest workers moved out of their factory dormitories and into their own apartments.[55] But eliminating physical distance did not mean that emotional distance disappeared. No amount of money, letters, post-cards, or voice recordings could substitute for the absence of a loved one, and even the happiest of reunions after years apart were often tinged with remorse.

ADULTEROUS HUSBANDS AND SCORNED WIVES

Although guest workers generally endeavored to maintain close commu-nication with Turkey, long distances and a slow postal system left many families worrying about the workers' fates. Nightmare scenarios played out in their heads, fueled by rumors and stereotypes about the unscru-pulous behaviors to which guest workers might adapt in a West German society that villagers often imagined as promiscuous and immoral. Sexually charged, gendered, and racialized, these rumors were grounded in true, yet isolated, cases of male workers cheating on their wives with busty, blonde German women – or worse, abandoning their wives and children entirely. These rumors were not confined to men. The imagined sexual proclivities of female guest workers, who were living in Germany alone and were no longer bound to the watchful eye of traditional family structures, became the focus of concern as well. By the mid-1970s, the trope of the sexually promiscuous – or worse, adulterous – guest worker had reached urban milieus and had crystallized into music, film, litera-ture, and other forms of popular culture. By transgressing both family and nation and fueling feelings of abandonment, sex between Turks and Germans was one of the earliest indications that Turks had purportedly "Germanized" and lost their Turkish identity

Even before guest worker migration to Germany, Turkish villag-ers already associated migration with the vices of urban life. From the 1930s to the 1950s, millions of villagers migrated as seasonal work-ers to Turkish cities, particularly to Istanbul's notorious shantytowns

---

55 Cord Pagenstecher, "Die 'Illusion' der Rückkehr: Zur Mentalitätsgeschichte von 'Gastarbeit' und Einwanderung," *Soziale Welt* 41, no. 2 (1996): 153.

(*gecekondu*), and returned with shocking tales of corruption and sexual depravity.[56] The perceived immorality of cities threatened the stability of rural gender relations and family life, which were already in flux. Since the 1923 founding of the Turkish Republic under Atatürk, Turkish policymakers had embarked upon a mission to secularize, "modernize," and "civilize" the countryside, in part by promoting greater autonomy for rural women, whom urbanites viewed as submissive victims of Islamic law.[57] While these reforms succeeded in improving women's legal position in relation to their husbands (particularly regarding divorce), customary family structures remained largely in place.[58] Once women reached adulthood and marriage, they typically wore headscarves, long skirts, and long-sleeved shirts – a far cry from the miniskirts, spaghetti straps, and high heels popular in both German and Turkish cities at the time. Premarital sex, adultery, and promiscuity were serious taboos, and rumors about deviance often spread like wildfire.

More so than internal migration from the Turkish countryside to cities, migration abroad to West Germany posed a special threat to gender and sexual norms. Despite Germany's own rural–urban divides, Turkish villagers imagined the country (and Western Europe as a whole) as a monolithic urban space – made more fearsome due to religious differences. Villagers feared that guest workers would eat pork, worship in Christian churches, have extramarital sex, and turn into *gâvur*, the derogatory Turkish word for non-Muslims, which implied that one was an infidel or traitor to the faith.[59] These concerns were decidedly gendered. Men might eagerly indulge in the seedy yet tantalizing offerings of the underbelly of German cities, such as bars, brothels, prostitution, and late-night hookups.[60] Women wandering alone and unprotected in German cities might provoke unwanted sexual attention. "As soon as you get off the train, German men will kiss you!" one woman was warned.[61] "Thank God!" she recalled years later, "No one kissed us, and no one tried to make a pass at us." So, too, were these discourses

[56] Kemal Karpat, *The Gecekondu: Rural Migration and Urbanization* (Cambridge, UK: Cambridge University Press, 1976).

[57] Nilüfer Göle, *The Forbidden Modern: Civilization and Veiling* (Ann Arbor: University of Michigan Press, 1996), 63–71.

[58] June Starr, "The Role of Turkish Secular Law in Changing the Lives of Rural Muslim Women, 1950–1970," *Law and Society Review* 23, no. 3 (1989): 497–523.

[59] Schiffauer, *Die Migranten aus Subay*, 95.

[60] Seyfettin Turhan, "Almanya'da Türk İşçileri X: Kadın işçilerin durumu," *Ulus*, September 11, 1963, 3, quoted in B. Miller, "Reshaping the Turkish Nation-State," 104–5.

[61] "Cemile S," in Tepecik, *Die Situation der ersten Generation*, 94.

overwhelmingly heteronormative. Sources testifying to homosexuality among guest workers in the early 1960s, particularly those produced by guest workers themselves or those in their home country, are comparably scant – reflective largely of the stigmatization and silences surrounding homosexuality at the time.[62]

Although villagers' concerns predated guest worker migration, they were amplified amid vast transformations in gender and sexuality within West Germany itself. Germany's loss in 1945 represented a national emasculation, whereby German men – prized for their strength and vigor during the Third Reich – experienced a collective crisis of masculinity.[63] Moreover, in 1961, the same year that Turkish guest workers first began arriving in Germany, the contraceptive pill burst onto German markets, giving women newfound control over their bodies and reproductive choices and ushering in the sexual revolution, second-wave feminism, and gay liberation movements.[64] Despite this transformation of sexuality

[62] Although I have been unable to locate sources about homosexuality among Turkish guest workers in the 1960s, this subject is an imperative future research avenue, especially when considering factory dormitories as homosocial (and perhaps homoerotic) spaces. The most compelling historical study of the intersection between migration and queerness in 1970s West Germany is: Christopher Ewing, *The Color of Desire: The Queer Politics of Race in the Federal Republic of Germany after 1970* (Ithaca: Cornell University Press, 2023). Another essential book, on the case of Arab postcolonial migrants in France, is: Todd Shepard, *Sex, France, and Arab Men, 1962–1979* (Chicago: University of Chicago Press, 2021).

[63] Robert G. Moeller, "The Remasculinization of Germany in the 1950s: Introduction," *Signs* 24, no. 1 (1998): 101–6.

[64] On Turkish women and the contraceptive pill in the 1980s, see: Claudia Roesch, "Of Turkish Women and Other Foreigners: Family Planning and Guest Workers in 1980s West Germany," in Eva-Sabine Zehelein, Andrea Carosso, and Aida Rosende-Pérez, eds., *Family in Crisis?: Crossing Borders, Crossing Narratives* (Bielefeld: Transcript, 2020), 193–204. On the sexual revolution and second-wave feminism in West Germany, see: Kristina Schulz, *Der lange Atem der Provokation: Die Frauenbewegung in der Bundesrepublik Deutschland und in Frankreich, 1968–1976* (Frankfurt am Main: Campus, 2002); Eva-Maria Silies, "Taking the Pill after the 'Sexual Revolution': Female Contraceptive Decisions in England and West Germany in the 1970s," *European Review of History* 22, no. 1 (2015): 41–59; Jane Freeland, *Feminist Transformations and Domestic Violence in Divided Berlin, 1968–2002* (Oxford: Oxford University Press, 2022); Alexandria Ruble, *Entangled Emancipation: Women's Rights in Cold War Germany* (Toronto: University of Toronto Press, 2023). On gay liberation movements, see: Craig Griffiths, *The Ambivalence of Gay Liberation: Homosexual Politics in 1970s West Germany* (Oxford: Oxford University Press, 2021); Samuel Clowes Huneke, *States of Liberation: Gay Men between Dictatorship and Democracy in Cold War Germany* (Toronto: University of Toronto Press, 2022); Jake W. Newsome, *Pink Triangle Legacies: Coming Out in the Shadow of the Holocaust* (Ithaca: Cornell University Press, 2022); Jennifer V. Evans, *The Queer Art of History: Queer Kinship After Fascism* (Durham: Duke University Press, 2023); Ewing, *The Color of Desire*; Sébastien Tremblay, *A Badge of Injury: The Pink Triangle as Global Symbol of Memory* (Berlin: De Gruyter, 2023).

in the public sphere, the 1950s conservative emphasis on the stability of the family did not disappear, and many Germans, particularly the aging postwar generation, associated promiscuity and pornography with the moral corruption of youth and, by proxy, of the nation.[65] Contestations over gender and sexuality impacted Germans' and Turks' attitudes about each other, becoming a litmus test for cultural compatibility. By the late 1970s, as Rita Chin has shown, white mainstream West German feminists committed to the emancipatory potential of sexuality inadvertently fueled racism by decrying Turkish and Muslim gender relations as "backward," "patriarchal," and incompatible with a post-fascist and Cold War society that defined itself as liberal, democratic, and free.[66] Moreover, German women's decisions to have sex with Turkish men rather than (or in addition to) German men enflamed preexisting tensions about "race-mixing" (*Rassenschande*) and contributed to German men's crisis of masculinity.[67]

Sex across borders had a racialized component (Figure 1.5). German women's blonde hair and blue eyes were repeatedly mentioned in Turkish newspapers, folklore, and films from the 1960s through the 1980s, while Germans reiterated Orientalist tropes by racializing migrants from the Mediterranean and the Middle East as "dark-skinned" and "exotic." Even in the 1980s, West German feminists invoked this racialized view as they struggled to wrap their heads around what they perceived as the curious phenomenon of sex across borders. "Why do Arab men love blonde women and German men love black women? Is it the exoticism, the dark skin, the erotic voice, the swaying gait, or are they simply more charming, natural, sensual, more of a man, more of a woman? Is it the other language, the simultaneously different emotions or caresses that hide within them?" Perhaps, they wondered, the "search for the unknown" was a projection of one's inner psychological struggles – "an attempt to break through one's own cultural limitations or imaginative horizon, to intellectually and emotionally conquer something new for oneself?"[68]

[65] Robert G. Moeller, *Protecting Motherhood: Women and the Family in the Politics of Postwar West Germany* (Berkeley: University of California Press, 1993); Dagmar Herzog, *Sex after Fascism: Memory and Morality in Twentieth-Century Germany* (Princeton: Princeton University Press, 2005); Elizabeth Heineman, *Before Porn Was Legal: The Erotica Empire of Beate Uhse* (Chicago: University of Chicago Press, 2011).

[66] Chin, "Turkish Women, West German Feminists."

[67] I thank my student Janis Parker for the latter point.

[68] Karin König and Hanne Straube, *Kalte Heimat. Junge Ausländer in der Bundesrepublik* (Reinbek bei Hamburg: Rowohlt, 1984), 81.

FIGURE 1.5 Male guest workers walk past a blonde German woman with a short skirt upon their arrival in Dortmund, 1964. © Hans Rudolf Uthoff, used with permission.

Beyond the transnational discourses, concerns about sex were central to guest workers' everyday lives. Alongside homesickness and isolation, male guest workers often complained about sexual malaise, with one man calling himself "psychologically ill" due to the lack of physical and emotional intimacy.[69] Another young guest worker was so starved for sex that he admitted having to restrain himself from touching a German woman on a streetcar, confessing that she was so "beautiful" and "free" and "smell[ed] so good."[70] Married guest workers were further constrained by their vows, as well as Turkish law, which expressly forbid adultery. Not until the rise of family reunification in the 1970s, when guest workers increasingly brought their spouses to Germany, could they have sex within marriage on a regular basis. If a guest worker alone in Germany wished to have sex with their spouse, they would have to wait until they traveled back to Turkey on vacation, which usually took place just once per year. In 1975, a Turkish midwife in the small village of Çalapverdi explained that the ability to have sex only during their summer vacations drastically impacted birthrates in guest workers' home

[69] Schiffauer, *Die Migranten aus Subay*, 170.
[70] Von der Grün, *Leben im gelobten Land*, 21.

villages: while the village typically had only one or two births per months, about thirty women expected babies during the month of March, which was precisely nine months after vacationing guest workers returned to the village in July.[71]

For single guest workers, the lack of sexual gratification owed in many respects to employers' restrictions on their private lives. As dormitory personnel restricted visitors, especially overnight guests, guest workers seeking satisfaction needed to leave their dormitories.[72] Female guest workers recalled that their male counterparts often waited outside their dormitories, hoping to take them out on dates.[73] Frequently, groups of male guest workers also went out on the town to meet German women at bars. Certainly, not all guest workers were interested in German women. Searching for love, a thirty-three-year-old car mechanic who had been living in West Berlin for three years placed a personal advertisement in *Anadolu Gazetesi,* a newspaper produced by the Turkish government for guest workers: "I have not warmed up to German girls. I prefer Turkish girls," he wrote, describing himself as 1.7 meters tall, 72 kilograms, with auburn hair, hazel eyes, and even his own apartment (a rarity for a guest worker at the time).[74] But to his dismay, his dating pool, so to speak, was limited, as male guest workers far outnumbered female guest workers.

Largely due to the racialization of Turks, male guest workers' attempts to meet German women, either for one-time sexual encounters or long-term romance, often proved frustrating. One guest worker insisted that German women "run after the Italians and Spaniards, and even the Greeks, but ... say that they are afraid of us Turks" and "do not want anything to do with us."[75] The popular Turkish folkloric singer Ankaralı Turgut captured this frustration in his hit song "Alman Kızları" (German Girls), in which the narrator fantasizes about young German women with "blonde hair" who go out to bars to "chase love" with "handsome young men." "Turks cannot live without you German girls," he admits, but laments that they "do not like migrants because they are Turkish."[76]

---

[71] Abadan-Unat, "Implications of Migration," 48.
[72] Informations-Plakat, DOMiD-Archiv, E 0991,1113; Von Oswald and Schmidt, "'Nach Schichtende sind sie immer in ihr Lager zurückgekehrt...,'" 201.
[73] Thomsen Vierra, *Turkish Germans in the Federal Republic of Germany,* 68.
[74] "Okuyucu mektupları. Eş arıyorum," *Anadolu Gazetesi,* December 1963, 4.
[75] Anonymous ("Turk"), in Von der Grün, *Leben im gelobten Land,* 16.
[76] Ankaralı Turgut, "Alman Kızları" (sometimes titled "Alman Güzelleri"), track b5 on *Ne Yersin?,* Emir Müzik, 1990s, audio cassette.

German women's distaste for Turkish men stemmed partly from the sensationalist media coverage of guest workers' criminality and sexual violence.[77] As early as the 1960s, German media warned against the wildly tempting "Mediterranean temperament" of dark-skinned, dark-haired men – a racialized category that included not only Turkish but also Italian, Greek, Spanish, Portuguese, and Moroccan guest workers – which allegedly made them prone to violating defenseless German women.[78] A Hamburg news report on a Turkish guest worker who had strangled his German wife included a remark from a male neighbor, who boasted, "If Helga were mine, she would still be alive."[79] Concerns about Turkish men as hypermasculine, virile, and dangerous also regurgitated centuries-long Orientalist tropes about polygamous orgies in the harems of the Ottoman Empire. The same newspaper denounced a Turkish man for entering a local bar with eight headscarf-clad belly dancers and threatening the German owner. Although the real threat was the owner – who had drunk "at least thirty whiskeys" and pulled out a pistol from behind the bar – the newspaper blamed "the Mohammedan," or "the man from the Orient."[80]

When a German woman did accept a guest worker's invitation for a night out on the town, the awkwardness of the first date was often compounded by racist prejudices and logistical issues. Osman Gürlük recounted a horrible series of dates he had with a seventeen-year-old German girl soon after arriving in Dortmund to work as a railroad constructor.[81] Osman was nervous for the date even before he arrived, since he had no car and "German girls are not interested in men without cars." But the real problems started as soon as they arrived at the movie theater for their first date, when the girl began disparaging his minimal German language skills. After a few dates, when the girl invited him home, her parents made it clear that "they did not want a Turk." Unable to have sex at her parents' house because the girl worried that she would moan too loudly, they were left with limited options. Osman did not have the privacy

[77] On media coverage of Turkish-German sexual relationships, see: Julia Woesthoff, "Ambiguities of Anti-Racism: Representations of Foreign Laborers and the West German Media" (PhD diss., Michigan State University, 2004), 100–8.

[78] Chin, *The Guest Worker Question*, 55; Stokes, *Fear of the Family*.

[79] "Nach der Bluttat brachte er die Kinder zur Wache. Eifersuchtsdrama im Soziallager: Türke erwürgte Ehefrau," *Hamburger Abendblatt*, March 31, 1969, 5.

[80] Hildegard Dambow, "Der Türke und seine acht Bauchtänzerinnen fielen unter den Tisch," *Hamburger Abendblatt*, June 1, 1969, 4.

[81] Von der Grün, *Leben im gelobten Land*, 21–22.

of a car, and sneaking her into his factory dormitory would have been too risky, since the dormitory personnel were always keeping watch – not to mention that he slept in a bunkbed with multiple other guest workers in the room. After searching around the city for a dark alley, the couple finally had sex – but the relationship ended soon thereafter.

Confirming the fears that circulated throughout Turkish villages, male guest workers sometimes did in fact resort to brothels. The Italian author and literary scholar Gino Chiellino, who lived in Germany and studied migrants' experiences, expressed guest workers' mixed feelings about cheating on their wives with prostitutes in a poem aptly titled "Loyalty."[82] Yearning sexually for his wife thousands of kilometers away, the poem's narrator visits a prostitute. He justifies this "dangerous breaking of the vow" by envisioning his wife cheating on him as well. Surely, he wonders, his wife must also feel "horny" (*geil*), as men in the village gaze at her licentiously during his absence. Having sex with random German women, however, could also lead to troubling encounters. Rumors circulated about unscrupulous German women who got guest workers drunk and stole their money. In one retelling of this tragic fate, a Turkish guest worker picked up a German woman at a bar and took her to a hotel. When he awoke with a hangover despite only drinking two glasses of schnapps, all his money was missing. "We made fun of him," one of his colleagues recalled. "He was furious at the German girl, and he told us they were all trash."[83]

Amid the Cold War context, as Jennifer Miller has revealed, male Turkish guest workers also crossed the border into East Germany to meet, have sex with, and even marry East German women.[84] These intimate relationships across the inter-German border represented a paradox: while West Germans viewed Turks as "eastern," East Germans viewed them as representatives of the "West." One Turkish man recalled that East German women dancing in nightclubs viewed Turks as sexually virile and were easily tantalized by the gifts they brought from West Berlin. These relationships, however, brought Turks under state surveillance, as the East German secret police (*Stasi*) suspected that they were Western spies attempting to subvert the state.[85]

---

[82] Gino Chiellino, "Treue," in Werkkreis Literatur der Arbeitswelt, ed., *Sehnsucht im Koffer*, 80.

[83] Hasan K., quoted in Kammrad, *»Gast«-Arbeiter-Report*, 58.

[84] J. Miller, *Turkish Guest Workers*, ch. 4.

[85] Samuel Huneke has revealed a similar pattern of *Stasi* espionage regarding gay men who crossed the inter-German border. Huneke, *States of Liberation*.

Popular culture in both West Germany and Turkey captured anxieties about sex across borders. In German director Rainer Werner Fassbinder's acclaimed 1974 film *Angst essen Seele auf* (Ali: Fear Eats the Soul), a German widow is ostracized, and even called a "whore" by her grown children, for falling in love with a dashing young Moroccan guest worker. The Turkish film *Almanyalı Yarim* (My German Lover), released the same year, tells a similarly tragic story of a Turkish guest worker and a wealthy blonde German woman named Maria (portrayed by a Turkish actress), who infuriates her father – a former German military officer during World War II – by moving to Turkey, converting to Islam, and changing her name to the Turkish "Meral." Like Fassbinder's, this film uses the trope of female victimization to critique anti-Turkish racism in Germany and – through the father's portrayal as an unrepentant Nazi – exposes the persistence of racialized thinking well after the fall of Nazism.

Though exaggerated in films, German women did face prejudices for engaging in relationships, and marriages, with Turkish men. In 1972, the Association for German Women Married to Foreigners (Interessengemeinschaft der mit Ausländern verheirateten Frauen, IAF) was formed to fight against their social and legal discrimination. Although the organization was originally founded by educated women married to foreign students, it expanded to include women married to guest workers. On an everyday level, the organization provided a forum for German women to raise consciousness, share their stories, and feel solidarity.[86] Within ten years, the IAF grew its membership to 28,000, became affiliated with the United Nations and the European Economic Community, and established partnerships with cities throughout the world. Yet the IAF, like many white feminist organizations at the time, was not immune from criticism for inadvertently perpetuating racism. Men affiliated with the IAF complained that the women were seeking to transform their "exotic" husbands into "regular German" men, and when the IAF finally began rallying on behalf of migrant women, their emphasis on migrant women's victimization at the hands of their excessively patriarchal husbands reinforced racialized stereotypes about the dangerous male foreigners.[87]

---

[86] "Wer ist die IAF – Was tut die IAF?" Hoover Archives, German Subject Collection, Box 95.

[87] Julia Woesthoff, "'Foreigners and Women Have the Same Problems': Binational Marriages, Women's Grassroots Organizing, and the Quest for Legal Equality in Post-1968 Germany," *Journal of Family History* 38, no. 4 (October 2013): 429–32. Also on the IAF: Stokes, *Fear of the Family*, chapter 6.

The West German government, too, worried about binational relationships. Some foreigners, especially following the 1973 moratorium on guest worker recruitment, engaged in fake marriages (*Scheinehen*) with German women to secure work and residency permits. In the late 1970s, the West German government threatened to deport a man who had divorced his Turkish wife, married a German woman to secure residency status, divorced the German wife, and married another Turkish woman.[88] Following Turkey's September 12, 1980, military coup, fake marriages became entangled with concerns about fake asylum seekers (*Scheinasylanten*). The state government of West Berlin, for example, blamed the surprising tripling of Turkish-German marriages on the asylum crisis, which officials in turn attributed to underground fake marriage syndicates. Officials were particularly alarmed by an outlying case in which an eighteen-year-old Turkish man married an eighty-two-year-old German woman.[89]

In Turkey, reactions to sex and marriage across borders were likewise complex. Some Turkish parents were delighted to know that their sons had found love abroad. Such was the case with Charlotte and Metin, whose father, Özgür, regularly inquired about his finances. When Metin wrote to his parents in Zonguldak informing them of his intention to marry Charlotte, Özgür gave the couple his enthusiastic blessing in a letter addressed directly to Charlotte.[90] "Our son is single," Özgür wrote. "We would like [him] to marry a good German girl," and "You bring our son much happiness." Özgür implored the couple to "get engaged in Germany, but marry in TURKEY," writing in capital letters for emphasis. By signing the letter with "best wishes from us, your parents," he welcomed Charlotte into the family even before the couple's engagement.[91]

Unlike West German news outlets, Turkish newspapers of the 1960s often portrayed binational marriages positively, using them to espouse nationalist narratives in which "young and beautiful" German girls cherished their Muslim Turkish husbands.[92] Yet within Turkish media

---

[88] Angelika Stepken, "Ehe mit Deutscher gescheitert – Zweck des Aufenthalts erfüllt," *Volksblatt Berlin*, January 19, 1982.
[89] "Wie man für 200 DM in der Bundesrepublik Asyl erhält," unnamed newspaper and undated (early 1980s), mentioned in: "Betr.: Einmalig unverfrorener Bericht einer großen türkischen Zeitung, der offenbart, daß die Türken unsere Politiker und Behörden nicht für liberal halten, sondern für dämlich," 1982, PAAA, B 82/1345.
[90] Özgür to Charlotte (pseudonyms), August 27, 1963, DOMiD-Archiv, ED 0181.
[91] Ibid.; Özgür to Charlotte (psueudonyms), September 14, 1964, DOMiD-Archiv, ED 0168.
[92] "Bir Alman kızı Türkiye köylerini inceliyor," *Milliyet*, June 1, 1964, 3.

discourse, wives' conversion to Islam was crucial.[93] During the 1960s, *Milliyet* published countless two-sentence reports often headlined "A German Woman Has Become a Muslim" that specified the woman's age, maiden name, and new surname.[94] Entire columns were devoted to especially intriguing cases. In 1964, a German woman was allegedly thrown out of the Catholic Church for her decision to marry her Muslim boyfriend, and the couple encountered difficulty finding a mosque and imam willing to perform their engagement ceremony until she converted to Islam and expressed her excitement for reading a German translation of the Koran.[95] By enthusiastically embracing Islam, German women could defy national boundaries and say with pride: "Now I, too, am a Turk."[96] The possibility that German women might be included in the Turkish national community, at least as implied in the Turkish urban press of the 1960s, stood in stark contrast to Germans' overwhelmingly racist hostility toward Turkish-German marriages.

The reception of sex across borders differed entirely, however, when it involved the adulterous affairs of guest workers who were already married. Adultery was by far the most pernicious threat involving guest workers' sexuality and, while overwhelmingly fabricated, rumors circulated widely. A woman from Bolu who later joined her husband in Hanover summarized the wives' "anxious and uneasy feelings" upon their husbands' departure: "We heard rumors that Turkish men would marry other wives here, without being divorced."[97] To a certain extent, these rumors were true. Lamenting his sexual frustration in the factory dormitory, one man estimated (likely an exaggeration) that 60 percent of his fellow guest workers cheated on their wives.[98] Frequent reports in Turkish newspapers in the 1960s supported these fears: a Munich judge had "permitted a harem" by allowing a guest worker to legally marry a German woman without divorcing the Turkish wife that he left behind; another migrant had married a German woman and left his four children at home.[99] In such cases, many abandoned wives in the countryside lived

93 On Germans converting to Islam, see: Esra Özyürek, *Being German, Becoming Muslim, Race, Religion, and Conversion in the New Europe* (Princeton: Princeton University Press, 2015).

94 "Bir Alman kızı, Müslüman oldu," *Milliyet*, November 25, 1962, 7.

95 "Almanya'dan dini nikâh neden olmasın?" *Milliyet*, June 11, 1964.

96 "Türk'le evlenen Alman kızı Müslüman oldu," *Anadolu Gazetesi*, February 1964, 4.

97 "Fidan B.," in Tepecik, *Die Situation der ersten Generation*, 166.

98 Schiffauer, *Die Migranten aus Subay*, 170.

99 "Alman yargıç bir Türkün iki evliliğini kabul etti," *Milliyet*, June 15, 1967, 1; "Evli odacı Almanya'da tekrar evlenince eski karısına 'beni boşa' dedi," *Milliyet*, March 5, 1966, 1.

as "married widows," perpetually mourning the loss of their husbands and enduring ostracization.[100]

In rare situations, adulterous male guest workers brought their new German wives back to their Turkish villages, even though Turkey had criminalized polygamy fifty years prior. A West German magazine reported on the disturbing case of Ali Yalçın who had returned to his Turkish wife and children with his new "blonde wife," Erika, in tow.[101] Immediately upon arriving, Erika laid down in their marital bed and demanded that Ali's Turkish wife serve her breakfast. The drama lasted only several days, however, until Erika realized that Ali had blatantly lied to her about the village's amenities. Furious that the village had neither electricity nor a hair salon, Erika stormed out of the house and traveled back to Germany, leaving Ali with a broken heart.

In at least one case, adultery occurred across the Iron Curtain. In 1980, a Turkish guest worker living in West Berlin appealed directly to West German Prime Minister Willy Brandt for help in a tricky situation. Two years before, he had divorced his wife in Turkey and – with the permission of East German authorities – married an East German woman. The marriage ceremony, which took place in Turkey, went smoothly, until the man reentered West German borders with his East German wife. Suspecting him of being an East German spy, the West German police came knocking on his door, searched through his bag, and interrogated him. Fearing imprisonment, the man spent a year hiding at a friend's house in Duisburg and was planning to relocate to a new hideout in Frankfurt. Whether or not the man was one of the Stasi's up to 189,000 "unofficial collaborators" (*inoffizielle Mitarbeiter*) is unknown, for the archival trail ends there. The staffer responsible for opening the prime minister's mail apparently rerouted it to the headquarters of the Workers' Welfare Organization in Cologne, where it sat in a box for decades before being donated to Germany's migration museum.[102]

Though usually directed at men, Turkish anxieties about adultery were also staged on women's bodies.[103] One female guest worker from

---

[100] Ali Gitmez, "Einwanderer aus der Türkei in Europa. Erfahrungen und Erinnerungen im Spiegel der Literatur," in Jan Motte and Rainer Ohliger, eds., *Geschichte und Gedächtnis in der Einwanderungsgesellschaft. Migration zwischen historischer Rekonstruktion und Erinnerungspolitik* (Essen: Klartext, 2004), 60.

[101] Oswald von Nagy, "Was Türken aus ihrer Mark machen," *Quick*, September 9, 1979.

[102] Z. C. to Willy Brandt, March 11, 1980, DOMiD-Archiv, ED 1035.

[103] On Turkish concerns about female guest workers' sexuality (particularly their alleged prostitution), see the forthcoming doctoral dissertation by Elisabeth Kimmerle at University of Potsdam.

Kastamonu was warned that she might "forget" her husband. "You'll have a man on every finger of your hand," her husband's uncle told her, and "you'll divorce your husband." She later interpreted these concerns as rooted in her fellow villagers' "stupid" fear that women would cheat on their husbands if they worked outside the home. "I went [to Germany] nonetheless and proved them wrong," she boasted.[104] Concerns also abounded about the infidelity of guest workers' wives who remained in Turkey. One male villager warned that "rather than having sex in Germany," a guest worker must "respect his wife and think about her pleasure," otherwise "the time will come when she sleeps with another man."[105] Such cases, while generally less common, did exist. In 1966, *Cumhuriyet* reported that the mother of a guest worker had stalked her daughter-in-law and caught her "red-handed" cohabitating with another man. After being found guilty of adultery – a crime under Turkish law until 1996 – the young woman violently attacked her mother-in-law outside of Istanbul's Criminal Court.[106]

Suspicious of their wives' infidelity, male guest workers often placed them under the watchful eye of relatives. This practice was far more common in Turkish villages, where migration's destabilizing effect on family structures was especially pronounced. In the village of Boğazlıyan, 56 percent of wives left behind lived alone with their children, whereas 29 percent lived with members of their husbands' families.[107] The mother-in-law of one twenty-one-year-old woman slept by her side every night during her husband's absence and, in another case, a fourteen-year-old brother-in-law kept watch.[108] While guest workers justified this supervision as crucial to "protecting" their wives against the dangers of living alone and the unwanted advances of other men, many women felt that their freedom was being constrained. Fatma, whose father departed for Germany in 1972, explained that her mother was forced to spend a year living with her "very hierarchal" in-laws, where she feared contradicting their authority and was "not allowed" to eat at their table. Estranged from her own parents due to their disapproval of her "poorer" husband,

---

[104] Schiffauer, *Die Migranten aus Subay*, 202.
[105] Ibid., 45.
[106] "Genç bir kadın Adliyede kaynanasını boğmak istedi," *Cumhuriyet*, May 3, 1966.
[107] Abadan-Unat, "Implications of Migration on Emancipation and Pseudo-Emancipation of Turkish Women," 47.
[108] Nermin Abadan-Unat et al., *Göç ve Gelişme: Uluslararası İşgücü Göçünün Boğazlıyan İlçesi Üzerindeki Etkilerine İlişkin Bir Araştırma* (Ankara: Ajans-Türk Matbaacılık Sanayii, 1976), 329–47.

Fatma's mother's only solace was the comfort of female friends, several of whom were in similar situations.[109]

However unfounded, the hot topic of guest workers' adultery circulated throughout Turkish popular culture during the 1970s – from folkloric village songs to novels and films produced in cities. In one popular song, "Almanya Dönüşü" (Return from Germany), a wife is furious when her husband appears at her doorstep after having cheated on her with a blonde German "slut."[110] To make matters worse, he had broken his promise to send her money: "Where are those bundles of money you used to dream about? Where is that multi-storied home? Where are those cars?" Likewise, in the iconic Black Sea region folksong "Almanya Acı Vatan" (Germany, Bitter Homeland), a wife condemns her husband for remarrying in Germany, failing to return after five years, and not sending a single letter. "What good is this money?" the singer asks. "Your family with five children, all of them miss you ... You have made your home worse. Worse thanks to you."[111] This ballad became so ingrained in Turkish culture that director Şerif Gören chose *Almanya Acı Vatan* as the title of his 1979 feature film, whose poster depicts a mustachioed guest worker surrounded by two beautiful blonde women drinking beer.[112]

These themes appear in other Turkish films of the time.[113] In Türkân Şoray's 1972 film *Dönüş* (The Return), a woman named Gülcan learns to read and write for the sole purpose of sending her husband letters, but he never responds, and a prominent elderly villager sexually assaults her. When her husband finally returns, he brings a German wife and baby, whom Gülcan must care for after he dies in an accident.[114] Released just two years later, Orhan Elmas's 1974 film *El Kapısı* (Foreign Door) centers on a female guest worker named Elvan who takes off her headscarf, wears sleeveless dresses, sings in a nightclub, and engages in sex

[109] Fatma U., interview.

[110] Zehra Sabah, "Almanya Dönüşü," Türküola, 1975, track 8 on *Songs of Gastarbeiter Vol. 1*, Trikont, 2014, CD.

[111] Ruhi Su, "Almanya Acı Vatan," track b2 on *El Kapıları*, İmece Plakları, 1976, vinyl.

[112] Şerif Gören, dir., *Almanya Acı Vatan*, Gülşah Film, 1979. For an analysis of this film, see: Can Sungu, "'Wenn wir nicht aufstehen, endet unser Elend nicht.' Gesellschaftskritik im türkischen Migrationskino: Baba (1971), Almanya Acı Vatan (1979) und Kara Kafa (1979)," in Ömer Alkın, ed., *Deutsch-Türkische Filmkultur im Migrationskontext* (Berlin: Springer, 2017), 73–91.

[113] On the portrayal of guest workers in Turkish films, see: Deniz Güneş Yardımcı, "The Representation of Turkish Immigration to Germany in German, Turkish German and Turkish Cinema" (PhD diss., Royal Holloway, University of London, 2017).

[114] Türkăn Şoray, dir., *Dönüş*, Akün Film, 1972.

work. After rumors circulate in her home village, her husband travels to Munich and fatally stabs her to protect his honor. The portrayal of both Gülcan and Elvan as victims of their husbands further reflects the importance of Turkey's rural–urban divide: produced in cities, the films' critique of gender relations in the countryside substantially overlaps with West Germans' stereotypes about Turkish "village culture" that were instrumentalized to foster racism and tropes of cultural incompatibility.

The widespread reach of these tragic songs and films likely influenced Gülten Dayıoğlu's 1975 book of short stories *Geride Kalanlar* (Those Who Stayed Behind). The cover art, which depicts five somber village women, sets the tone visually. In the book's opening vignette, a thirty-year-old woman travels to a city to visit a doctor but has difficulties articulating why she feels unwell. When the doctor asks whether she is married, she responds with an ambiguous "Eh." She has a husband, she says, but she has not seen him for seven years. Although she is comforted by the knowledge that German women have little fondness for "men with black hair, black eyes, and black mustaches," she has heard rumors that her husband has remarried and conceived a son with a woman with "blonde hair" and "sky-blue eyes." At first denying the accusation, the husband spreads rumors that she is "crazy," making her question her own sanity.[115]

Although some adulterous husbands returned to Turkey after steamy affairs abroad, the subject largely remained an unknown, or a deliberately repressed, taboo within families. Even fifty years after the incident, Yaşar hesitated to answer questions about his adultery, while his neighbors eagerly gossiped about the scandal.[116] Nowhere are the enduring emotional scars clearer, however, than in Marcus Attila Vetter's 2006 autobiographical documentary film *Mein Vater, der Türke* (My Father, the Turk), which traces Vetter's journey from Germany to a small Anatolian village to meet his biological father, who had abandoned his German mother upon hearing of the pregnancy.[117] When Vetter meets his long-lost family, including his half-siblings and his father's Turkish wife, a tearful reunion ensues. The documentary won Europe-wide acclaim and the award for best long-form documentary at the 2007 San Francisco International Film Festival. The festival's website puts it best: Vetter's story, representative of so many

[115] Gülten Dayıoğlu, *Geride Kalanlar* (Ankara: Bilgi Yayınevi, 1975), 9–23.
[116] Yaşar E., interview by author, Şarköy, July 19, 2014.
[117] Marcus Atilla Vetter, dir., *Mein Vater, der Türke*, Südwestrundfunk, 2006.

other guest worker families, shows "how one man's actions changed the course of an entire family" and unearths "more than thirty years of pent-up feelings and questions."[118]

CHILDREN AS VICTIMS AND THREATS

The other core component of the breakup and abandonment of the family was the situation of guest worker children (*Gastarbeiterkinder*), whom Turks and Germans alike viewed as both victims and threats. The perception of guest worker children as a threat was particularly pronounced in Germany, fueling racist tropes that emphasized Turks' inability to "integrate" into German society. The opposite threat, however, prevailed in Turkey: *excessive* integration. Turks in the homeland denigrated guest worker children, even more so than their parents, for having undergone a process of Germanization whereby they adopted German mannerisms and fashions, had premarital sex, lost their Muslim faith, and – most egregiously – spoke German better than Turkish. The very possibility that Turks, and particularly Turkish children, could become culturally German was vital: not only did it contradict German discourses about migrants' failed integration, but it also exposed the fluidity of Germany's rigid blood-based identity.

The experiences of guest workers' children varied greatly and changed over time – so much so that it is impossible to speak about a singular "second generation." Especially amid the family migration of the 1970s, many children were born or raised primarily in Germany (Figure 1.6). Yet the overwhelming emphasis on children on German soil obscures the reality that many children remained in Turkey and never set foot in Germany, while up to 700,000 others – colloquially called "suitcase children" (*Kofferkinder*) – regularly traveled back and forth. Reflecting the broader destabilization of family life, children left behind in Turkey lived with a single parent (usually their mothers) or, in cases when both parents worked abroad, with grandparents and other relatives. The perception that these children were victims or "orphans" who suffered because of their parents' abandonment or repeated uprooting fed into exclusionary tropes in both countries that blamed guest workers for the breakup of family life. Yet victimization tropes did not reflect the reality

---

[118] Brendan Peterson, "My Father the Turk," San Francisco International Film Festival, history.sffs.org/films/film_details.php?id=5869&search_by%5B6%5D=6&search_by%5B2%5D=2&searchfield=My%20Father%20the%20Turk/.

FIGURE 1.6 Turkish children outside a West German elementary school
in Duisburg-Hamborn. © Süddeutsche Zeitung Photo/Alamy Stock
Foto, used with permission.

of all children left behind, as many found advantages, and even power,
in their situations.[119]

In Turkey, children left behind were often victimized as "orphans"
who were emotionally distressed and poorly raised. This depiction
was especially true in cases of absent fathers in villages, who typically,
due to gendered social conventions, were the primary breadwinners,
had been granted more extensive education than their wives, and han-
dled disciplinary matters within the family. One teacher in a Turkish
village worried about the fifty "half-orphans" in his classroom being
raised by mothers and grandmothers who could "not even write their
own names." These children, many of whom apparently also lacked
discipline and diligence, "pay for the economic survival of their families with their own futures."[120] While this denigration of female
caretakers reinforced gendered tropes about male supremacy in the
household, it also reflected many mothers' real struggles during their

[119] For the main study emphasizing the victimization of suitcase children, see: Gülçin
Wilhelm, *Generation Koffer. Die zurückgelassenen Kinder* (Berlin: Orlanda, 2011).
[120] Michael Holzach and Tim Rautert, "Ahmets Heimkehr," *Zeit-Magazin* 41, no. 1
(October 1976): 28–45.

husbands' absences. In Nermin Abadan-Unat's 1976 study of 373 wives left behind in the province of Boğazlıyan, nearly half reported that they assumed greater responsibility for tasks otherwise completed by men, such as shopping for major purchases, borrowing money, and collecting debts, and one quarter expressed difficulties "establishing authority and discipline."[121]

For many children left behind, being separated from their parents was a painful experience. When she was just in the fifth grade, Alev Demir wrote a series of poems capturing this sense of estrangement. In a poem called "Yearning," she lamented: "I am distant from my mother and father. I do not know what to do because I am alone. I cannot laugh. I cannot cry. I do not like yearning."[122] Similarly powerful is Murat Çobanoğlu's popular 1970s folksong "Oğulun Babaya Mektubu" (A Son's Letter to His Father), in which a teenage son condemns his "cruel" father for breaking his promise to "return quickly" and having become "attached" to Germany. Eleven years have passed, and the family's situation has become "terrible": their house is "in ruins," they cannot afford to eat warm food, and their neighbors have "stigmatized" and "turned against" them. Although the son has assumed his father's care-taker role, he will soon leave for military service and will be unable to provide for the family. In a subsequent song, the father admits to crying upon reading the letter and, again, promises that he will return – but he never does.[123]

Some children, however, recalled the shift in family relations fondly. Yusuf K. from the village of Buldan described the absence of "fatherly authority" as a "nice time." His mother was not as "strict or authoritar-ian," and she let him play outside for hours without a curfew. Whereas he found it difficult to bond emotionally with his father, "I could tell my mother all my desires without being embarrassed."[124] In cases of the extended absence of mothers and fathers, some children felt even more comfortable with their surrogate parents. "I considered my grandmother my actual mother," Ebru T. explained, noting that, despite her parents visiting her village of Eskişehir only once per year, she did not miss them. When her parents finally brought her to Germany at age eight, she found

---

[121] Abadan-Unat et al., *Göç ve Gelişme*, 329–47.
[122] Alev Demir, "Özlem," in Alev Demir, *Zaman İçinde Değişim* (West Berlin: Yabanel Yayınları, 1987).
[123] Murat Çobanoğlu, "Oğulun Babaya Mektubu" and "Babanın Oğula Mektubu," Yavuz Plak, 1970s, vinyl.
[124] "Yusuf Kaya," in Tepecik, *Die Situation der ersten Generation*, 181.

it difficult to relate to them. To her, they were "foreign people" who barely existed.[125] Reiterating the notion of parents becoming "foreign," another child happily recalled that her grandparents "treated me like a queen" and "gave me everything I wanted," and that she was "ambivalent" about her parents.[126] Saddened by this estrangement, some parents regretted their decisions to leave their children behind, with one admitting that she was not a "good mother."[127]

But not all children left behind stayed in Turkey permanently. Especially central to transnational tropes of victimization were the "suitcase children," a term that evoked their never-ending transience, requiring them to keep their suitcases both literally and metaphorically packed. In the decades since, the situation of the suitcase children has been called one of Turkish-German migration history's "most difficult and painful" taboos, riddled with "unspoken trauma" in which parents violated their children's basic trust and fostered lifelong misconceptions that they were worthless and unlovable. The prominent Turkish-German politician Cem Özdemir, who grew up in Germany, even recalled years later that he had suffered a recurring childhood "nightmare" that he, too, would be abandoned by his parents and sent back to Turkey.[128]

Despite the subsequent repression of suitcase children's psychological trauma, the phenomenon was no secret at the time. Rather, the plight of suitcase children was a regular theme in both Turkish and German discourses about migrants. An animated short film produced in 1983 as part of a pedagogical West German cassette series aimed toward Turkish guest worker families depicts a young boy named Ali who travels to Munich to reunite with his parents after living with his grandparents in the village of Gülbahar.[129] Symbolic of Ali's physical and psychological burden, he stands with a suitcase grasped tightly in his hand, an enormous bindle slung behind his shoulder, and another bag jammed in the crook of his elbow. After jumping into his mother's arms upon his arrival, his enthusiasm for Germany soon deteriorates. Homesick for his village, he misses his best friends (who, in a commentary on guest workers' rural origins,

---

[125] "Ebru Tepecik," ibid., 197.
[126] Aynur G., "Mein Leben," in Werkkreis Literatur der Arbeitswelt, ed., *Sehnsucht im Koffer*, 51.
[127] "Nazife (Sancak) Aydemir," in Tepecik, *Die Situation der ersten Generation*, 136.
[128] Wilhelm, *Generation Koffer*, 15, 29, 33–35.
[129] Oğuz Peker and Thomas Plonsker, dirs., *Ali* (Munich: Kassettenprogramme für ausländische Mitbürger e.V., 1983) VHS, DOMiD-Archiv E 980,211.

are a rooster and a donkey) and spends his free time watching Turkish movies. Within a month, the situation turns brighter as he begins to integrate into German society, learn German, make friends, and dream of becoming an engineer. Yet the happy tale sours again when his father sends him back to Turkey. In the ominous closing scene, Ali – sitting at a desk with a notepad, protractor, and abacus – realizes that "there are, of course, no engineering schools in the village." The film enjoyed a positive reception in Germany, as its didactic message helped Turkish and German children develop intercultural sympathy based on their shared struggles with making new friends.[130] The film also offered room for other interpretations by emphasizing the victimization of Turkish children at the hands of their parents, and by implying the superiority of life in West Germany's urban and "modern" milieu.

A similar narrative, though with a different conclusion, appears in Turkish author Gülten Dayıoğlu's 1980 novel *Yurdumu Özledim* (I Miss My Homeland). When a young boy named Atil learns that his parents will take him to Munich, his teacher hands him a Turkish flag and photograph of Atatürk and pontificates about Atil's need to retain his national pride: "You are the child of an exalted and noble country with a glorious past that has lasted many thousands of years. You must be proud that you are a Turk and you may not feel inferior. Beware of disgracing your land and your people ... Never forget that you are a Turk!"[131] Influenced by his teacher's advice, Atil approaches life in Germany critically. Feeling like "a bird in a cage," he rants that he would "rather eat dry bread and walk around in dirty clothes at home" than stay in Germany any longer. To Atil's delight, his outburst helps his parents recognize their own homesickness, and the family returns to Turkey, with the novel ending happily.

Although the fictional stories of Ali and Atil portray their rural origins as central to their culture shock, many suitcase children came from cities and had a higher socioeconomic status. Born in Ankara in 1972, Bengü spent the first year of her life in Munich with her parents, both guest workers, who despite having white-collar jobs in Turkey opted to work in German factories for higher wages. Because they worked long hours, they placed Bengü under the daily care of a "German grandma" (*Deutsche Oma*) – an experience shared by many other guest worker

---

[130] I thank the film's director, Thomas Plonsker, for providing this information.
[131] Gülten Dayıoğlu, *Atil hat Heimweh [Yurdumu Özledim]*, trans. Feridun Altuna (Berlin: ikoo Verlag, 1985).

children – until they discovered her husband's borderline alcoholism.[132] Absent suitable childcare, they sent one-year-old Bengü back to Ankara to live with her grandparents. Over the next years, they sent her back and forth – at age two to Germany, at age five to Turkey, where she stayed until completing high school. During this time, her parents sent her regular letters and postcards and, like many other guest workers, recorded their voice messages on cassette tapes. Bengü's younger sister, who lived with their parents in Germany, sent her colorful drawings. In one drawing, which aptly reflects the emotional experience of family separation, a house stands between Bengü on one side and her parents and sister on the other. After twelve years apart, Bengü ultimately chose to reunite with her parents and sister and studied English at a German university.

Murad, another suitcase child, experienced a similar situation. Born in 1973 in the West German city of Witten, he was sent to Istanbul to stay with his grandparents due to insufficient childcare. After just six months, his parents missed him so much that they brought him back to Germany. Eight years later, they sent him back to Istanbul so that he could become accustomed to Turkish schools in anticipation of the family's planned remigration. Like so many other guest workers, however, they just "played with the idea of going back" and "never fully committed."[133] Waiting for a return migration that never materialized, Murad thus spent his teenage years separated from his parents and younger sister until, like Bengü, he returned to Germany for university. Decades later, at age forty, Murad expressed pride in his identity as a suitcase child and emphatically rejected the notion that he was a "victim." Instead, his experiences made him a "special kid" and "improved [his] personality" by exposing him to multiple perspectives. Murad did, however, experience long-term conflicts within his family. His relationship with his younger sister remained strained and distant throughout his life, as they did not grow up together and had vastly different childhoods. And his mother, the true "victim," in his words, remained racked with guilt her entire life, missing the lost years she could have spent with her son.

As the transience of the suitcase children reveals, the categories of "children left behind" and "children born or raised in Germany" were not mutually exclusive. Common to their experiences, however, was the feeling that they were caught between two cultures, questioning their own identities. These concerns, though ubiquitous in sources

---

[132] Fakir Baykurt, *Alman Oma. Deutsche Oma* (Duisburg: RAA Duisburg, 1984).
[133] Murad B., interview.

on Turkish-German migration history, are particularly well expressed in a 1980 volume of Turkish children's poems and short stories titled *Täglich eine Reise von der Türkei nach Deutschland* (Everyday a Journey from Turkey to Germany), whose German editors sought to give voice to youths "without a homeland." One boy described the title's meaning as a public–private spatial dichotomy: "When I leave my parents' house in the morning, I leave Turkey. I then go to my job or to my friends and am in Germany. In the evenings, I return to my parents' house and am back in Turkey." More common than the spatial dichotomy, however, was the opposition of cultural and national identities. In one poem, a boy named Mehmet wrote, "I stand between two cultures / the Turkish and the German / I swing back and forth / and thus live in two worlds."[134] This constant "swinging" fostered internal confusion. As another boy, Türkan, questioned: "Some say: 'You are a German.' Others say: 'You are a German Turk.' ... My Turkish friends call me a German! ... But what am I really?"[135] Reprinted verbatim in the *Kölner Stadt-Anzeiger*, the children's writings conjured broader German sympathy for their plight.[136]

Yet, overwhelmingly, Germans viewed Turkish children less as victims of confused identities and more as threats. They condemned their "illiteracy in two languages" as a burden on the education system that not only diminished the quality of German students' education but also, according to more explicitly racializing rhetoric, portended Germany's genetic and intellectual decline.[137] These concerns coincided with Germans' reckoning with the broader transformation of urban space with the rise of family migration. As migrant families moved out of factory dormitories and into apartments, Germans fled to "nicer" parts of the city and decried the emergence of "Turkish ghettos" (like the iconic "Little Istanbul" in West Berlin's Kreuzberg district) that seemingly testified to Turks' unwillingness to integrate.[138] These "parallel societies," as Germans often called

---

[134] Förderzentrum Jugend Schreibt, *Täglich eine Reise von der Türkei nach Deutschland. Texte der zweiten türkischen Generation in der Bundesrepublik* (Fischerhude: Verlag Atelier im Bauernhaus, 1980), 18–19, 37, 53.

[135] Ibid.

[136] Heinz Verfürth, "Das Dilemma der zweiten Generation. 'Warum bin ich nicht als Deutscher geboren?'" *KSA*, November 9, 1982, 4–5.

[137] See chapter 4 for details on this racializing and eugenic rhetoric in the early 1980s. *Analphabeten in zwei Sprachen* (Illiterate in Two Languages) is the title of a 1975 West German documentary by director Mehrangis Montazami-Dabui on guest worker families. The phrase has since found widespread use.

[138] "'Die Türken kommen – rette sich, wer kann!'" *Der Spiegel*, July 29, 1973.

them, were envisioned as particular sites of criminality and unrest, in which rowdy Turkish teenagers skipped class, loitered at parks, sold drugs, sexually assaulted German girls, and shouted insults like "German pig!" at elderly women.[139]

Fears of Turkish children were exacerbated by migrants' higher birthrates, with Turkish women derided as having their "wombs always full."[140] German birthrates, by contrast, had declined due to the release of the birth control pill in 1961, the legalization of abortion in 1973, and the growing number of women working outside the home. This imbalance stoked existential fears, widely reported in the media and repeatedly discussed among policymakers, that Turks would numerically overtake Germans within a matter of decades.[141] Especially infuriating was guest workers' alleged abuse of the social welfare system's child allowance (*Kindergeld*), whereby residents received a monthly lump sum per child even if the child did not live in Germany. One newspaper reported on the case of a Turkish guest worker in Heidelberg who apparently had twenty-three children between his two wives in Turkey and earned an impressive 1,440 Deutschmarks in child allowances monthly, which far exceeded the amount of his salary.[142] As criticism of "welfare migrants" mounted, West Germany reformed its *Kindergeld* policy in 1974, offering less money for children who lived outside the European Economic Community.[143]

Turks in the homeland, too, expressed an intense curiosity and mixed attitudes about guest worker children living abroad. While they sympathized with the children's identity crises and discrimination, they also viewed them as threats to Turkish national identity. By the late 1970s, the notion that guest worker children were losing their Turkishness and turning into Germans had become ubiquitous, resulting in the proliferation of the colloquial term *Almancı*, or "Germanized Turk." Although terms like "to become foreignized" (*yabancılaşmak*) or "to become *Almancı*" (*Almancılaşmak*), or the passive "to have been made foreign" or "to have been made *Almancı*" had already been applied to their parents, the use of

[139] Irmgard Recke to Karl Carstens, September 17, 1980, BArch, B 122/23886.
[140] E. Mizdriol to Karl Carstens, May 10, 1982, BArch, B 122/23885.
[141] "Ausländer: 'Schmerzhafte Grenze gezogen,'" *Der Spiegel*, November 6, 1981; "Was tun mit den Türken?" *Die Zeit*, May 31, 1982.
[142] "Das 24. Kind wird erwartet," *Hamburger Abendblatt*, July 24, 1963, 1.
[143] Lauren Stokes, "'An Invasion of Guest Worker Children': Welfare Reform and the Stigmatisation of Family Migration in West Germany," *Contemporary European History* 28, no. 3 (2019): 372–89.

"*Almancı* children" (*Almancı çocukları*) and "*Almancı* youths" (*Almancı gençleri*) reinforced the second generation's particular challenge.[144] Turkish journalists regularly expounded on the problems of *Almancı* children. In his 1975 book on his travels to Germany, Nevzat Üstün compared guest workers' children to children living in Turkish villages. Replicating longstanding tropes of rural backwardness, he condemned the "pathetic" situation of "the Anatolian child," who "has no school" and "does not know what sugar is, what honey is, what a toy is." Although those in Germany appeared to live in better conditions "from a distance," their situation was even more deplorable. "The only thing I know is that these children cannot learn their mother tongue, that they do not integrate into the society in which they are living, and that they are foreignized and corrupted."[145] Daily news articles went as far as to demonize the children as "a social time bomb" and "cocky, rowdy, and un-Turkish."[146] Yet the question of whom to blame for the children's Germanization was debated. A 1976 *Cumhuriyet* article reporting general "News from Germany" blamed the Turkish nation as a whole, noting that "we have abandoned hundreds of thousands of our young people," who are "adrift and alone."[147]

New forms of media, such as televised talk shows that reached elite city dwellers, transmitted audiovisual portrayals of *Almancı* children. Following a 1977 Turkish television interview, Erhan Önal, a guest worker's son who had gained international acclaim as a star player on Germany's Bayern-München soccer team, made headlines for demonstrating poor Turkish language skills and, by extension, for losing his Turkish identity. Yet, contrary to reports blaming Önal or his parents, one journalist leapt to his defense. "Certainly," he wrote, "this young countryman of ours is not to be condemned or blamed. We left him alone to his fate and, ultimately, Erhan Önal is one person among a generation of children and youths who can be neither Germans nor Turks."[148] Despite concerns about his cultural estrangement, in 1982 Önal moved to

---

[144] "Almancılar uyum sağlayamadı," *Milliyet*, May 14, 1985; Halim Demirci, *Almancıların Çocukları* (Berlin: Halim Demirci Yayınları, 1997).

[145] Nevzat Üstün, *Almanya Beyleri ile Portekiz'in Bahçeleri* (Istanbul: Çağdaş, 1975), 31–32.

[146] Hasan Pulur, *Hürriyet*, March 29, 1982, in German Embassy in Ankara to AA, "Betr.: Deutschlandbild in der türkischen Presse; hier: Leitartikel von Hans Pulur in 'Hürriyet' 29.03.1982," March 30, 1982, PAAA, B 85/1611; Hans-Ulrich Dillmann, "Dort Türkin – Hier Deutsche," *Die Tageszeitung*, April 30, 1985, 14–15.

[147] Oktay Akbal, "Almanya'dan Haberler," *Cumhuriyet*, May 17, 1976, 2.

[148] Ali Sirmen, "Ayıp," *Cumhuriyet*, February 18, 1977.

Turkey to play on the Turkish team Fenerbahçe (and later Galatasaray). Decades later, Turkish soccer fans continued to describe him as "one of our first emigrant (*gurbetçi*) football players," often used interchangeably with "*Almancı* football players."[149]

While often exaggerated, the frequent references to Germanized children in Turkish media and popular culture reflected real anxieties held by their parents. A 1983 sociological study of Turkish housewives in West Germany reported that "women find it very problematic when the children orient themselves to the norms and values of their German environment. They observe this development with great worry." Several mothers complained that their children's exposure to German society had diminished both their parental authority and their children's national and religious identities. "Outside, the children learn independence. At home, they don't take me seriously anymore," one mother complained. "They unlearn the Turkish language and no longer know our holidays," and "They learn to kiss on the street," others added.[150]

The 1984 book *Kalte Heimat* (Cold Homeland) fictionalized these concerns based on German social workers' observations of Turkish mothers during their therapy sessions. In one story, a mother named Fatma laments that her teenage children "have become like Germans." She casts this Germanization in terms of rowdiness, laziness, and promiscuity, which contrasts with her unspoken perception of Turks' superior discipline and morality. Not only do her children drink alcohol, smoke cigarettes, and listen to American music, but her "egotistical" son drops out of school, refuses to get a job, just "screws around," and "always wants money from me." Her daughter "dresses like a hippie," majors in German Studies, and takes contraceptive pills. "What will happen with our honor, our good reputation?" Fatma cries. "If word gets around, we won't be able to be seen anywhere."[151]

Fatma's woes about her daughter's use of contraception reflect broader concerns about *Almancı* children's sexuality. As in the case of the guest workers themselves, premarital sex and marriage with Germans were of particular concern. But, amid ongoing fears of their children's

---

[149] "İlk gurbetçi futbolcularımız," *FourFourTwo*, August 9, 2015, www.fourfourtwo.com .tr/ilk-gurbetci-futbolcularimiz/.

[150] Martina Kirschke, "'Hier ist alles nicht streng genug!'" *Frankfurter Rundschau (FR)*, January 14, 1984.

[151] Fatma, "Meine Kinder sind wie Deutsche geworden," in König and Straube, *Kalte Heimat*, 66.

Germanization, the intensity shifted, and the gendered script flipped: rather than male guest workers' sex with German women, the target became Turkish girls' sex with German boys. Upon reaching adulthood, some daughters of guest workers expressed a clear preference for marrying outside their nationality. "I would never marry a Turkish man," one young woman asserted. Echoing tropes about Turkish men's patriarchy – the very same tropes that Germans invoked in the service of racism – she complained that Turkish men "are far too authoritarian," whereas German men "take better care of their wives" and are "more liberal" and "good natured."[152] Many were concerned about their family's reaction. One woman recalled keeping her relationship a secret, while another feared her brothers would "kill" her if they found out.[153]

Yet, overwhelmingly, there was not much that was particularly "German" about parents' ideas about what it meant to "Germanize" (aside from the language). Rather, the term referred to the children's embrace of much larger trends common throughout European and American youth cultures at the time, such as fashion, music, and sexual freedom. Ironically, these were the same corrupting influences that many Germans, particularly those of the conversative 1950s postwar generation, also decried.[154] Neither was Turkey itself immune to the truancy, unemployment, partying, drug use, and sexual promiscuity that were prominent in cities across the globe. In this sense, Turkish parents' fears were not necessarily of "Germanization" but rather of urbanization – that the children were falling victim to the corrupting influences of city life.

While this fallacy was lost on Turkish parents, it does not invalidate the gravity of their concerns (as well as broader Turkish national concerns) about guest workers' children. From mohawks and leather jackets to cigarettes and contraception, material symbols of Germanization were mere proxies for the much larger sense of cultural abandonment. For the parents of guest worker children, this abandonment primarily threatened the breakdown of the family. But for Turks observing the migrants from abroad, this abandonment threatened the breakdown of the Turkish nation. Alongside physical distance and sexual transgression, the situation of *Almancı* children was among the most important factors

---

[152] "Türkisch-deutsche Ehen," *Bizim Almanca – Unser Deutsch,* August 1986, 10–11.
[153] Ibid.
[154] Ute G. Poiger, *Jazz, Rock, and Rebels: Cold War Politics and American Culture in a Divided Germany* (Berkeley: University of California Press, 2000).

that tested the boundaries of national identity and heightened wariness about migrants in both Germany and their homeland.

* * * * *

In 1990, three decades after the start of the guest worker program, a German television station broadcasted the performance of a Turkish arabesque band singing a mournful folksong with the simple title: "Almanya" or "Germany." Capturing the guest workers' collective memory, the ballad goes: "From all corners of our homeland we were brought together and packed onto the train at Sirkeci Station ... Those who remained waved to us with tearful eyes. How is one supposed to remain silent? Almanya, you have separated us from our loved ones."[155]

The idea that an all-powerful "Almanya" was to blame for the plight of guest workers and their families is both deceptive and inaccurate, for it perpetuates the notion that guest workers were powerless pawns with no decision-making ability of their own. In reality, the dynamics were different: Germany, of course, needed guest workers, but the guest workers also needed (or at least desired) Germany. Their decision to venture forth into the unknown points to their strength, courage, and initiative. It was their conscious quest to improve their lives that compelled them to navigate complex political, economic, and social structures in two countries and to grapple with forces beyond their control. From forging new friendships to maintaining connections to home, to having sex with Germans or abandoning their spouses and children altogether – all of these were active, rational, and emotional choices.

Why, then, blame "Almanya"? Working through decades of emotional baggage is no easy task, especially when that baggage has been repeatedly lugged back and forth between two countries 3,000 kilometers apart. Blaming "Almanya" thus became a useful strategy for deflecting discomfort and bottling up bad feelings. For the most part, contradicting the song lyrics, guest workers did take ownership of their actions, from their triumphs to their missteps. Some openly mourned the lost time of missed birthdays, holidays, major life events, and everyday companionship. Others, however, kept the pangs of remorse as a dark secret.

Cutting deeper than individuals and families, the scars of abandonment became crucial to how both Germans and Turks in the homeland

---

[155] Excerpt from song "Alamanya," performed by İşhanı and Cihan on guitar and lyre. For footage of this performance, view: Sauter, dir., "Die vergessene Generation."

perceived migrants. For Germans, the perception of guest workers' homesickness and yearning for companionship operated alongside racist and Orientalist tropes of violence, criminality, and hypersexuality by which fears of rapacious dark-skinned Turks sexually violating blonde-haired, blue-eyed German women stood as a proxy for the violation of German borders by racial others. For the homeland, largely unsubstantiated rumors of adultery portrayed guest workers as destroying not only marital bonds but also the stability of village and communal life. And children – whether left in Turkey, brought to Germany, or shuttled back and forth – were viewed in both countries as victims and threats. Symbols of migrants' insufficient integration or – in the eyes of the homeland – excessive "Germanization," they transgressed not only borders but also national identities.

2

Vacations across Cold War Europe

In the mid-1970s, the Frankfurt branch of the Turkish bank Türkiye İş Bankası distributed a roadmap to Turkish guest workers.[1] Hoping to wrest this hotly desired customer base from the clutches of leading West German competitors such as Deutsche Bank and Sparkasse, Türkiye İş Bankası – like many Turkish firms of the time – appealed to the guest workers' nostalgia for home. The front cover depicts a quaint Bavarian scene, with a cheerful blonde man in full Lederhosen and a traditional feathered cap, grinning as he drinks from a foamy beer stein. In stark contrast, the back cover features a modernizing, industrial Turkey, with a skyscraper looming behind a Turkish half-moon flag. The message is clear: in the years since the migrants had left the poverty and dilapidation of their home villages in the hopes of amassing great wealth, Turkey, too, had begun to industrialize. Investing their Deutschmarks in Turkish banks would not only be as lucrative as investing in West German ones but would also support the economy of their homeland – and, accordingly, the well-being of the families they left behind.[2]

More striking than the roadmap's advertising strategy are its contents once unfolded.[3] The map does not depict the municipal street plan of

---

[1] Türkiye İş Bankası, roadmap from West Germany to Turkey, DOMiD-Archiv, E 0046,05.
[2] This chapter first appeared as an article: Michelle Lynn Kahn, "The Long Road Home: Vacations and the Making of the 'Germanized Turk' across Cold War Europe," *The Journal of Modern History* 93, no. 1 (2021): 109–49. © 2021 by The University of Chicago. All rights reserved. Reprinted/Adapted/modified with the permission of the University of Chicago Press.
[3] An early 1980s study of Turkish workers in Duisburg revealed that 83.5 percent of their deposits were in Turkish banks. Ali Nejat Ölçen, *Türken und Rückkehr. Eine*

Frankfurt, where the would-be customers lived, but rather a much broader system of international highways, centered around Europastraße 5 (E-5), or Europe Street 5, which stretched from West Germany by way of Munich through Austria, Yugoslavia, and Bulgaria to Istanbul.[4] At the height of the Cold War, the road featured on the map traversed the entire Central European continent, providing a clear-cut path across the imagined boundary of the Iron Curtain. Given that guest workers had been recruited to work and live within the spatial confines of West Germany, the map's expansive reach is puzzling. If guest workers lived right in the bank's own backyard, why would they need a map of Cold War European highways? Would it not have been more pertinent to provide a map of Frankfurt's own roadways, which the guest workers could have used to find their way from their homes to the bank branch?

The map of Cold War Europe's international highways was in fact a crucial tool for Turkish guest workers in West Germany. At least once per year, they revved the engines of their (usually) pre-owned Mercedes-Benzes and Fords – for many, the products of the factories at which they worked – and set off on a three-day car ride on Europastraße 5 en route to Turkey. Perhaps best conceived as small seasonal remigrations, or even pilgrimages, vacations to the home country were widespread activities, occurring during the summer months and less commonly during Christmas time. While the West German government and media tended to use the German word *Heimaturlaube*, or "vacations to the homeland," the guest workers themselves, as well as those in the home country, typically used the Turkish word *izin*, which translates literally to "permission" or "leave." As Ruth Mandel has noted, the concept of "leaving" or "taking leave" was in reality more of an "undertaking," since the car ride involved not only substantial planning and capital expense but also long travel times, dangerous roads, emotional energy, and physical exhaustion.[5]

While financial expenditure sometimes prohibited guest workers from taking the trip every year, they generally made it a priority. Far more so than letters, postcards, phone calls, and cassette recordings, physically traveling to Turkey assuaged homesickness and fears of abandonment because it allowed guest workers and their families to reunite face-to-face. In the 1960s, when single guest workers yearned for their spouses,

Untersuchung in Duisburg über die Rückkehrneigung türkischer Arbeitnehmer als Funktion ökonomischer und sozialer Faktoren (Frankfurt am Main: Dağyeli, 1986), 90.
4 See other roadmaps in DOMiD-Archiv, PL 1913 and E 1015,129.
5 Mandel, *Cosmopolitan Anxieties*, 235.

FIGURE 2.1 A quintessential portrayal of an *Almancı*, whom Turks
in the home country denigrated as superfluous spenders, flaunting
his Deutschmarks and posing proudly in front of his loaded-up car,
1984. © akg-images/Guenay Ulutuncok, used with permission.

children, parents, and lovers left behind, vacations gave them the sole opportunity to hug, kiss, and spend time together. With the rise in family migration of the 1970s, vacations assumed new meaning as a crucial tactic for preserving "Germanized" children's connection to Turkey. For children who grew up primarily in Turkey, vacations were generally joyous occasions to spend time with dearly missed friends. For children born or raised in West Germany, vacations familiarized them with a faraway "homeland" that they might otherwise have known only from their parents' stories.

But the seemingly mundane act of taking vacations, as this chapter reveals, held much more significance: the road trip across the Iron Curtain, as well as the reunions upon arrival, not only tied the migrants closer to their friends, family, and neighbors at home, but also pushed them farther apart. The migrants' unsavory experiences traveling through socialist Yugoslavia and communist Bulgaria on the E-5 confirmed their affiliation with the democratic, capitalist "West," encouraging them to transmute their disdain for the Cold War "East" onto the perceived underdevelopment of Turkish villages. And more so than the rumors of abandonment, face-to-face contact provided firsthand impressions of how, year after year, guest workers and their children increasingly transformed into *Almancı*, or Germanized Turks. This sense of cultural estrangement involved not only mannerisms and language skills but also material objects. Even though in reality most struggled financially, guest workers used their vacations as an opportunity to perform their wealth and status as evidence of their success – that they had "made it" in Germany. Envious of the cars and consumer goods that guest workers flaunted upon their return, those in the homeland began to perceive the migrants as a *nouveau-riche* class of superfluous spenders who were out of touch with Turkish values and had adopted the habit of conspicuous consumption – a trait that many Turks associated with West Germany at the time (Figure 2.1). By using their Deutschmarks selfishly rather than for the good of impoverished village communities, they had stabbed their own nation in the back.

TRAVELERS, TOURISTS, BORDER CROSSERS

Despite spending long hours performing what West Germans called "dirty work" (*Drecksarbeit*) in factories and mines, Turkish guest workers were by no means an oppressed, nameless, faceless proletariat exploited by their employers and tied to their places of work as immobile peons. They experienced vibrant lives and social interactions centered not only in the space of the company-sponsored dormitory but also throughout West German cityscapes – participating to varying degrees in the world around them through everyday activities such as eating at restaurants, drinking at bars, attending cultural events, and shopping.[6] Yet guest workers and their family members in Germany did not spend their leisure time only in the cities surrounding their workplaces. Nor did their excursions take place only after work hours and on weekends. Rather, the migrants were highly mobile border crossers, who took vacations to other European countries during their holiday breaks from work and, at least once per year, traveled back to Turkey to visit their families, neighbors, and friends. The ability to take lengthy vacations of up to four weeks at a time, given West Germans' generous paid leave policy, was not only central to their personal migration experiences but also created much broader tensions. Employers imposed harsh disciplinary measures, including firing, on guest workers who failed to return to work on time, and the West German and Turkish governments – along with corporations – jockeyed to control and profit from guest workers' travel.

Effective trade unions, a powerful component of political life in the West German social welfare state since the establishment of the Federal Republic in 1949, ensured that guest workers received time off from their jobs – particularly during Christmas and summertime, when their children were out of school. Although guest workers' relationships with the trade unions were strained by discrimination and mistrust, trade unions upheld West Germany's "right to vacation" (*Urlaubsrecht*), which was codified in 1963, just two years after the signing of the guest worker recruitment agreement with Turkey.[7] The Federal Vacation Law (*Bundesurlaubsgesetz*), which applied also to guest workers, required employers to provide a minimum of twenty-four days, or roughly five weeks, of paid vacation per year.[8] Accompanying the legally codified right

[6] J. Miller, *Turkish Guest Workers in Germany*, 96–104.

[7] On the relationship between trade unions and guest workers, see: Oliver Trede, *Zwischen Misstrauen, Regulation und Integration: Gewerkschaften und Arbeitsmigration in der Bundesrepublik und Großbritannien in den 1960er und 70er Jahren* (Paderborn: Schöningh, 2015); Simon Goeke, *»Wir sind alle Fremdarbeiter!«. Gewerkschaften, migrantische Kämpfe und soziale Bewegungen in Westdeutschland 1960–1980* (Paderborn: Schöningh, 2020); Lena Foerster, *Hochofen, Maloche und "Gastarbeiter": Ausländerbeschäftigung in Unternehmen der Eisen- und Stahlindustrie des Ruhrgebiets in den 1950er bis 1980er Jahren* (Wiesbaden: Franz Steiner Verlag, 2021).

[8] *Mindesturlaubsgesetz für Arbeitnehmer (Bundesurlaubsgesetz, BUrlG)*, January 1, 1963, www.gesetze-im-internet.de/burlg/BUrlG.pdf.

to vacations was another perk: guest workers' work and residence permits, which afforded them the opportunity to travel freely throughout other European Economic Community member states – a privilege extended to other Turkish citizens only when in possession of tourist visas.

While the most common form of travel was the *Heimaturlaub* or *izin* vacation to Turkey, many others went sightseeing in nearby Western European countries. Family photographs depict groups of primarily male guest workers tanning on beaches in Cannes and posing in front of the Seine River in Paris, the narrow alleys of Venice, and the many fountains of Amsterdam – all the while smiling with cameras hanging around their necks.[9] Those who lived in West Berlin regularly took day trips (*Tagesausflüge*) to East Germany, since unlike West Germans, Turkish guest workers were permitted to cross the Berlin Wall with foreign tourist visas, as long as they returned by midnight.[10] Taking these trips, especially those to Western Europe, was a matter of privilege, however. Despite affordable bus and train travel to neighboring countries, even a short weekend trip still entailed great financial expense. Guest workers therefore needed to calculate whether they had sufficient funds left over for a short getaway after paying for rent, food, and other basic necessities and sending remittances to their families in Turkey.

Guest workers generally recalled their vacations to Western Europe fondly. Yaşar, the self-appointed "social organizer" of a local music club in Göppingen, enjoyed planning semiannual affordable bus tours of neighboring countries for around fifty of his German and Turkish friends and their family members.[11] He and his wife also took frequent weekend trips to nearby Switzerland, where they stocked up on the famed Swiss chocolate to bring back to Turkey as gifts. London, with its bright red double-decker buses, proved especially exciting. But France was his favorite country, because a friendly Parisian woman had once offered him assistance when he was lost. While his trips to Italy were "not as nice," he delighted in the scenic beauty of Venice. Though based on limited experiences and anecdotal encounters, Yaşar's pleasant experiences during these travels shaped his identity. While he felt adamantly Turkish, he insisted that he "lived like a European" – despite having to decline pork while trying national cuisines.

---

[9] Photographs in DOMiD-Archiv, BT 0812,0002; BT 0713,0001; E 0187,4; E 0031,0046; and E 1216,0026.

[10] On Turkish guest workers' encounters with East Germans, see: J. Miller, *Turkish Guest Workers in Germany*, 107–34.

[11] Yaşar E., interview.

Gül, whom neighbors in Şarköy called "the woman with the German house," fondly recounted visiting Istanbul for her sister's engagement party in 1965 – a trip that surprisingly led to a marvelous vacation in Vienna. Always eager to chat, the then twenty-nine-year-old seamstress struck up a conversation with a middle-aged Austrian couple who were traveling on the same train as tourists to Istanbul. The couple invited Gül and her sister to visit them at their posh home in Vienna. After a week of drinking Viennese coffee and sightseeing, most memorably at the stunning Schönbrunn Palace, the sisters took a train to Gül's home near her textile factory in Göppingen. The journey allowed Gül not only to experience life in Vienna but also to help her sister enter West Germany as a tourist and work "quietly" (*in Ruhe*) – a euphemistic term that Gül used to describe her sister's illegal employment.[12] Like Yaşar, Gül developed a positive impression of Western Europe, associating it with friendliness, beauty, consumption, and luxury even decades later.

Despite the prevalence of touristic travel throughout Western Europe, most guest workers took their annual leave all at once and used it during the summer for a one-month stay with their relatives at home. This pattern resulted in a massive summertime increase in travel between the two countries. Despite Turkey's status as a NATO member state, it was still relatively low on Germans' list of vacation destinations during the 1960s, not least because of the distance, the language barrier, and long-standing tropes about Muslim cultural difference. When Germans did travel to Turkey, they typically expressed a sort of Orientalist curiosity about the exotic "East." As one 1962 travel guide described it, "the land between Europe and the Orient" was so tantalizing that German visitors "never packed enough film for their cameras" and "one always hears the joyful cries: 'Oh, these colors, this vibrancy, this diversity!'"[13] Travel from Turkey to West Germany was also relatively limited. In 1963, the Turkish newspaper *Cumhuriyet* advertised a company called Bosphorus Tourism that offered bus tours from Istanbul to Rome, Paris, London, and Hamburg, with stops along the international highway Europastraße 5 in Sofia, Belgrade, Vienna, and Munich.[14] But affording these lavish

---

[12] Gülmisâl E., interview, 2014. On the longer history of "illegal migration" in the Federal Republic, see: Serhat Karakayali, *Gespenster der Migration. Zur Genealogie illegaler Einwanderung in der Bundesrepublik Deutschland* (Bielefeld: Transcript, 2015).

[13] Hans Edgar Jahn, *Türkei. Mit Stadtführer Istanbul, Ankara und Reiserouten* (Buchenhain outside Munich: Verlag 'Volks und Heimat,' 1962), 9–10.

[14] Advertisement for Bosfur Turizm, *Cumhuriyet*, November 14, 1963.

tours, especially given the high currency exchange rate, was a privilege available only to elite, wealthy, urbanites.

Yet the existing tourism offerings were no match for the guest-worker-fueled boom in travel between the two countries in the 1960s. To accommodate vacationing guest workers, the West German government, railway system, and individual firms all organized special travel options. In 1963, the Ford factory in Cologne granted Turkish guest workers an additional three weeks of vacation time and contracted special trains for them, with discounted roundtrip tickets.[15] During the 1972 Christmas season, the German Federal Railways (Deutsche Bundesbahn) commissioned special half-priced charter trains to the home countries of all guest worker nationalities.[16] Political events also put officials on alert for a surge in guest worker travel. In anticipation of the June 5, 1977, parliamentary elections in Turkey, for which voting by mail was not an option, the Federal Railways once again organized charter trains from Frankfurt and Munich to Istanbul.[17]

Guest workers' vacations were also a matter of international importance, creating conflict between the West German and Turkish governments when it came to air travel. Though flying was far less common than driving in the 1960s and 1970s, airlines competed over guest workers as customers. In April 1970, representatives from both countries' governments and airlines signed a "pool agreement" between Turkey's publicly owned Turkish Airlines and the West German private companies Lufthansa, Atlantis, Condor, Bavaria, GermanAir, and PanInternational.[18] Aiming to even the playing field, the pool agreement fixed prices between Istanbul and ten German cities and required guest workers' air travel to be split 50–50 between the two countries. West German firms, however, complained that Turkish Airlines (and hence the Turkish government) was breaching the agreement. Turkish Airlines' monopoly in Turkey due to the ban on private companies serving Turkish airports meant that it could offer a much more flexible schedule, whereas competition among West Germany's private airlines required

---

[15] "2 Bin Türk İşçisi Yurda İzinli Olarak Gidiyor," *Anadolu Gazetesi*, August 1963, 4.
[16] Referat E7, "Betr.: Gastarbeiterverkehr der Deutschen Bundesbahn (DB); hier: Interview von Herrn PSts im Deutschlandfunk," October 23, 1972, BArch, B 108/37406.
[17] Hermann Buschfort to Bundesminister für Verkehr und für das Post- und Fernmeldewesen Kurt Gscheidle, April 28, 1977, BArch, B 108/37406; Abteilung Eisenbahnen, "Betr.: Maßnahmen im Verkehrsbereich zur Unterstützung der bevorstehenden Parlamentswahlen in der Türkei," May 9, 1977, BArch, B 108/37406.
[18] "Pool Agreement (Draft)," February 17, 1970, BArch, B 108/48642.

dividing the number of flights among them. West German flights were permitted to land only in Istanbul, whereas Turkish Airlines could serve all the country's airports. Rumor also had it that Turkish Airlines tickets were available on the black market for cheap and that passing through customs in Turkey was much easier if a guest worker traveled on Turkish Airlines.[19]

Amid the Cold War context of Germany's internal division, tensions over guest workers' travels also strained relations between East and West Germany. In the 1960s, guest workers living in West Berlin flew to Turkey without exception through West Berlin's Tegel Airport. Problems began in 1973, however, when Turkish Airlines began offering flights through East Berlin's Schönefeld Airport. Given the cheaper prices and Schönefeld's closer proximity to the heavily Turkish neighborhoods of Kreuzberg and Neukölln, guest workers increasingly opted to cross the Berlin Wall and fly out of East Berlin. The situation intensified in 1977, when East Germany's budget airline Interflug commenced flights to Turkey, attracting 45 percent of guest workers. Concerned about the detrimental economic effect, the West German government repeatedly implored the Turkish government to reduce the number of Turkish Airlines flights through Schönefeld and to pressure Interflug to adhere to the fixed prices.[20] Yet little changed. In 1981, in an expression of Cold War paranoia, the West German newspaper *Die Zeit* attributed the "unfair competition" to a Moscow-led conspiracy to destroy the West German economy.[21]

In terms of everyday life, guest workers' vacations often caused conflicts with employers. Despite the legal right to vacation, their work and residence permits were beholden to the whims of floor managers, foremen, and other higher-ups prone to discriminating against Turkish employees, and a tardy return made a convenient excuse for firing them. Rumors about these firings became especially worrisome after the 1973 OPEC oil crisis, the associated economic downturn, and the subsequent moratorium on guest worker recruitment, when criticisms of Turkish workers "taking the jobs of native Germans" increased. The metalworkers' trade union IG Metall spoke out against an "immoral" trend whereby some employers handed out termination-of-contract notices

---

[19] Referat L 3, August 15, 1973, BArch, B 108/46565.
[20] "Betr.: Gastarbeiterflüge zwischen Berlin-Schönfeld und der Türkei," May 5, 1978, PAAA, B 26/115913.
[21] Joachim Nawrocki, "Tegel kontra Schönefeld," *Die Zeit*, November 13, 1981.

before the holiday season and then promised the workers their jobs back if they returned early enough.[22] Such clever though nefarious policies forced guest workers to choose between losing their jobs or sacrificing the opportunity to travel home. Although these discriminatory policies were rare, the rumors influenced guest workers' decisions. A representative of the German Confederation of Trade Unions noted a marked decline in the number of Turkish guest workers who booked trips home via the German Federal Railways, which she attributed to their fear of being fired even though these concerns were "mostly unfounded."[23]

Termination due to late return from vacation was most publicized during the August 1973 "wildcat strike" (*wilder Streik*) at the Ford automotive factory in Cologne, during which as many as 10,000 Turkish guest workers went on strike for multiple days alongside their German colleagues.[24] The Ford strike marked a turning point in Turkish-German migration history: taking place just months before the recruitment stop, it was a crucial moment of Turkish activism, resistance, and agency in which migrants demanded their rights and proved that they were not an easily disposable labor source.[25] In a transnational frame, the Ford workers were also inspired by the hundreds of organized strikes by trade unions in Turkey, which contributed to Turkey's 1971 and 1980 military coups and stoked fears that guest workers would import Turkish leftist radicalism into West Germany amid the Cold War.[26] Despite protesting

---

[22] Franz Westing, "'Völkerwanderung' zu Weihnachten rückläufig," *Berlinische Morgenpost*, December 13, 1975.

[23] Ibid.

[24] On the Ford strike, see: "Einwanderung und Selbstbewusstsein: Der Fordstreik, 1973," in Jan Motte and Rainer Ohliger, *Geschichte und Gedächtnis in der Einwanderungsgesellschaft: Migration zwischen historischer Rekonstruktion und Erinnerungspolitik* (Essen: Klartext Verlag, 2004), 237–323; Hunn, *»Nächstes Jahr kehren wir zurück...«*, 243–61; Jörg Huwer, "*Gastarbeiter" im Streik. Die Arbeitsniederlegung bei Ford Köln im August 1973* (Cologne: Verlag edition DOMiD, 2013); Lena Foerster, "Zwischen Integration und Rückkehrförderung – türkische Arbeitnehmer bei den Kölner Ford-Werken 1961 bis 1983," *Geschichte in Köln* 62, no. 1 (2015): 237–70.

[25] Jennifer Miller has illuminated the prevalence of labor strikes among female Turkish guest workers, particularly the 1973 strike at the Pierburg autoparts factory in Neuss. She has also noted that vacation time was a common reason for guest workers to strike across Germany, including Portuguese workers at the Karmann automotive factory in Osnabrück and Spanish workers in Wiesloch. Jennifer Miller, "Her Fight is Your Fight: 'Guest Worker' Labor Activism in the Early 1970s West Germany," *International Labor and Working-Class History* 84 (2013): 226–47; J. Miller, *Turkish Guest Workers in Germany*, 230, n. 58.

[26] On Turkish labor strikes, see: Brian Mello, "Political Process and the Development of Labor Insurgency in Turkey, 1945–1980s," *Social Movement Studies* 6, no. 3 (2007): 207–25.

labor conditions broadly, the immediate trigger of the Ford strike was the firing of 300 Turks who returned late from their summer vacations.[27] Süleyman Baba Targün, one of the strike's leaders, had missed the deadline to extend his work permit because of car trouble while driving along the Europastraße 5. Although Targün's work permit had expired just days prior to his reentry into West Germany, the Foreigner Office (Ausländeramt) of Cologne classified him as "illegal." Partly as payback for his leadership role in the Ford strike, his appeal to the federal government to extend his residence permit was rejected. By Christmas, Targün was set for deportation to Turkey, where, to compound his problems, he faced a prison sentence for anti-government political activity.[28]

Despite such high-profile cases, most guest workers took comfort in knowing that their right to vacation remained "just as firm" as it did for Germans – as long as they returned punctually.[29] Still, when threatened with travel delays, they often went to great lengths to avoid being fired. In 1963, one guest worker asked a Turkish Railways station director to send his boss a telegram testifying that his tardy return owed to a heavy snowfall that had prevented trains from traveling between Edirne and Istanbul.[30] In 1975, in a far more tumultuous and widely publicized situation, a Turkish Airlines flight from Yeşilköy to Düsseldorf carrying 345 Turkish passengers returning from their summer vacations made headlines when a twenty-four-hour delay caused massive unrest. Infuriated passengers ran onto the runway and attempted to storm the aircraft, shouting "Why are you treating us like slaves?" and "Rights that are not given must be taken!" To suppress the insurrection, airport security officials blocked the protestors with tanks. Several passengers were injured, and a father traveling with his young son was rushed to the hospital after fainting due to poor ventilation in the terminal.[31] To avoid

---

[27] "Gegen die Spaltung!" *Rote Fahne*, August 29, 1973. Scholars have cited the Ford strike as evidence that guest workers were not passive objects of racism but rather fought against it in various ways. Manuela Bojadžijev, *Die windige Internationale. Rassismus und Kämpfe der Migration* (Münster: Dampfboot, 2008), 157–62.

[28] Gerd-Ulrich Brandenburg, "Keine Aufenthaltserlaubnis erteilt. Türke Targün muß das Land verlassen," *Neue Ruhr Zeitung*, December 27, 1973. See also: Friedrich K. Kurylo, "Die Türken probten den Aufstand," *Die Zeit*, September 7, 1973; "Faden gerissen," *Der Spiegel*, September 9, 1973.

[29] Westing, "'Völkerwanderung' zu Weihnachten rückläufig."

[30] Telegram from Esref G., Turkish State Railways Station Director, February 1963, DOMiD-Archiv, E 1175,5.

[31] "Yeşilköy'de 24 saat bekletilen işçiler, uçak işgaline kalkıştı," *Milliyet*, September 2, 1975.

such situations, guest workers adjusted their travel plans accordingly. Following this incident, Yılmaz avoided Turkish Airlines and opted for the reputed "German punctuality" of Lufthansa.[32]

Guest workers' job security was also jeopardized by shady Turkish travel agents, who exploited them by forging tickets and selling far more seats than were available. One guest worker collaborated with GermanAir as co-plaintiffs in a lawsuit against a travel agency that had overbooked a flight from Istanbul to Düsseldorf, resulting in his tardy return.[33] The problem was more systemic, however. In 1970, officials at the Düsseldorf Airport complained to the West German transportation ministry about a nightmarish day, with one problem after the other – all caused by Turkish travel agencies.[34] Anticipating an influx of Turkish travelers, the airport had not only commissioned additional border officials for passport checks, but had also set up a 4,000 square-foot tent outdoors, with makeshift check-in counters, luggage carts, chairs, lighting, loudspeakers, toilets, and even a refreshment stand. But even more travelers arrived than had been expected, and by noon it became clear that hundreds held fraudulent tickets. In one of many such incidents, 110 passengers were stranded for three days because their travel agency had sold enough tickets for two flights even though only one had been scheduled. Expressing no sympathy, some blamed the "chaos" not on the travel agencies, but on the travelers. The next day, *Neue Rhein Zeitung* reported that "hordes" of "men of the Bosphorus" from the "land under the half-moon" had been "shoving themselves" through the airport and having "temper tantrums." "But what's the point?" the article quipped: "After all, for 450 DM to Istanbul and back, you can't expect first class service."[35]

As this racist and Orientalist rhetoric suggests, many West Germans exploited guest workers' right to vacation as another weapon in their arsenal of discrimination. Not only did employers use a tardy return as an excuse to fire unwanted workers, but the overwhelmingly negative portrayal of guest workers' travel reinforced stereotypes of Turkish criminality and backwardness that cast Turks as shady, deceitful, and dangerous. German airline firms blamed both Turkish Airlines and the Turkish

---

[32] Yılmaz Y., interview by author, Düsseldorf, 2016.
[33] Landgericht Düsseldorf, Judgment in the Case of Osmar Erdem and GermanAir against Asi Airlines Service GmbH, February 3, 1971, BArch, B 108/63800.
[34] Flughafen Düsseldorf, "Betr.: Abwicklung der Gastarbeiterflüge in die Türkei; hier: Ereignisse am 24.7.1970," July 27, 1970, BArch, B 108/63800.
[35] Karl-Ludolf Hubener, "Türken wurden verschaukelt," *Neue Rhein Zeitung*, July 28, 1970.

government for violating international agreements. Airport officials lambasted Turkish travel agencies' shady business practices and emphasized the overall chaos of being overrun by Turkish passengers. And, even though the guest workers were the real victims in these situations, the German media portrayed them as temperamental, violent aggressors who threatened the stability of air travel. Guest workers' vacations were thus not only a private but also a public matter: their mobility could also be mobilized against them.

ON THE "ROAD OF DEATH" THROUGH THE BALKANS

Far more than trains, buses, and airplanes, most guest workers vacationed to Turkey by car. Cars not only permitted autonomy and flexibility, but also served as a means of transporting large quantities of consumer goods from West Germany to Turkey and of securing heightened social status among friends and relatives. In the 1960s and 1970s, the only major route from West Germany to Turkey was the Europastraße 5 (Europe Street 5, or the E-5), the 3,000-kilometer international highway that spanned eastward across Central Europe and the Balkans through neutral Austria, socialist Yugoslavia, and communist Bulgaria, passing through Munich, Salzburg, Graz, Zagreb, Belgrade, Sofia, and Edirne. An alternative sub-route, which bypassed Bulgaria and went through Greece and the Yugoslav–Greek border at Evzonoi, posed too lengthy a detour. And while some Turks in West Berlin opted for a different route through East Germany, Slovakia, Hungary, Romania, and Bulgaria, the E-5 was by far the most common.

The journey across Cold War Europe was not easy. Traumatizing for some, adventurous for others, the drive from Munich to Istanbul alone lasted a minimum of two days and two nights, assuming the driver sped through, and much longer if they stopped along the way to catch much-needed shut-eye at a local roadside hotel. Yet, even as the migrants sighed with relief and kissed the ground as they crossed the Bulgarian-Turkish border at Kapıkule, the journey was not over. Considering that most Turkish travelers were journeying to Anatolian hometowns and villages much farther than Istanbul, such as the eastern provinces of Kars and Erzurum, the journey could take three or four days. Aside from the tediousness, the car ride also posed numerous dangers because of poor infrastructure, as well as traffic and weather conditions. Unpaved roads, seemingly endless lines of vehicles steered by overtired drivers, bribe-hungry border guards, fears of theft and vandalism, sleeping in cars, eating and urinating along the road – all remain vividly etched in both personal memory and popular culture. Reminiscing about both the hardship and the emotional significance of the journey, one Turkish migrant wrote in a poem: "Between Cologne and Ankara / One must speed through to arrive. / In between lie three thousand kilometers. / Who would drive it if he were not homesick?"[36]

Turks were not the only guest workers who made the arduous annual trek along the E-5. The geography of the European continent meant that Yugoslavs and Greeks took the same route. Given that Yugoslavia was geographically closer to West Germany, Yugoslavs' journey was a day shorter. Greeks, rather than passing through Bulgaria like Turks did, veered rightward at the Yugoslav city of Niš, switching to a different route through Skopje, Evzonoi, and Thessaloniki all the way south to Athens. Because of the diverse nationalities of the travelers, West Germans and Austrians often homogenized the E-5 into a migration route not only for Turks but also for all guest workers and "foreigners." Across nationalities, travelers often recalled similar experiences, albeit mediated by their own individual circumstances and the varying historical, social, and cultural ties they had to the countries that they passed through. Nevertheless, given that Turks became West Germany's largest ethnic minority in the late 1970s – and hence numerically the largest group of vacationing migrants – the E-5 gradually became associated primarily with them. While each migrant had a distinct narrative of their journey, their accounts converged into a collective experience that fundamentally shaped their identities and broader Cold War tensions.

The E-5 earned numerous monikers and substantially shaped the way that all Turks, not just guest workers, imagined migration. Guest workers typically referred to it fondly as "the road home" (*sıla yolu*), emphasizing its importance to their national identities. West German names ranged from "the guest worker street" (*Gastarbeiterstraße*), which emphasized that not only Turks but also guest workers from Greece and Yugoslavia traveled along it, to "the road of death" (*Todesstrecke*), which sensationalized its dangerous conditions and the high prevalence of fatal accidents. The highway was also ubiquitous in Turkish popular culture. *E-5* is the title of Turkish author Güney Dal's 1979 novel in

---

[36] Aşık Ali Kabadayı, "Zwischen Köln und Ankara," in Aytaç Yılmaz and Mathilde Jamin, eds., *Fremde Heimat. Yaban, Sılan olur. Eine Geschichte der Einwanderung aus der Türkei. Ausstellungskatalog des Essener Ruhrmuseums und des DOMiT* (Essen: Klartext, 1998), 278–79.

which a man transports his deceased father along the highway for burial in his home country; this theme also appears in Turkish-German director Yasemin Şamdereli's acclaimed 2011 film *Almanya – Willkommen in Deutschland* (Almanya – Welcome to Germany).[37] In 1992, Tünç Okan's internationally released film *Sarı Mercedes* (Mercedes Mon Amour), based on Adalet Ağaoğlu's 1976 novel, told the story of a guest worker's journey along the E-5 to marry a woman in Turkey and show off his luxurious car.[38] The sixty-minute documentary *E5 – Die Gastarbeiterstraße*, directed by Turkish filmmaker Tuncel Kurtiz, was broadcast on Swedish television in 1978, and in 1988, the Turkish television series *Korkmazlar* aired an episode titled "Tatil" (The Vacation) in which guest workers travel along the E-5 to visit relatives in Turkey, giving rise to comedic cultural conflict along the way.[39] The road also appeared in music. "E-5" was the name of a Turkish-German music group formed in the 1980s, whose style – a mixture of rock n' roll, jazz, and Turkish folk music – paid homage to the road connecting the "Occident" and the "Orient." In 1997, the Turkish-German rap group Karakan recalled their childhood road trips in a song titled "Kapıkule'ye Kadar" (To Kapıkule) named after the Turkish-Bulgarian border.[40]

The most extensive media portrayal of the E-5 was an alarmist, ten-page article in the leading West German newsmagazine *Der Spiegel*, published in 1975 (Figure 2.2). The article sensationalized the treacherous conditions along the E-5 – which, it elaborated, ensured "near-murder" and "certain suicide" – and noted forebodingly that annual fatalities on E-5-registered roads exceeded those on the entire Autobahn network, as well as the number of casualties in the previous decade's Cyprus War.[41] A 330-kilometer stretch through the curvy roads of the Austrian Alps – precarious during the summer but even worse during the icy winter – was allegedly the site of over 5,000 accidents annually, and on the highway's Yugoslav portion, one person supposedly died every two hours. As the article explained, travelers who did not succumb fatally to this "rally of no return" faced psychological torment due to tedious stop-and-go

---

[37] Güney Dal, *E-5* (Istanbul: Milliyet, 1979); Yasemin Şamdereli, dir., *Almanya – Willkommen in Deutschland*, Roxy Film, 2011, DVD.

[38] Tunç Okan, dir., *Sarı Mercedes*, Gala Film, 1992, VHS; Adalet Ağaoğlu, *Fikrimin İnce Gülü* (Istanbul: Remzi Kitabevi, 1976).

[39] Tuncel Kurtiz, dir., *E5 – Die Gastarbeiterstraße*, 1978, VHS; "Tatil," *Korkmazlar*, 1988, DOMiD-Archiv, BT 0185.

[40] Karakan, "Kapıkule'ye kadar," Al Sana Karakan, Neşe Müzik, 1997.

[41] "E 5: Terror von Blech und Blut," *Der Spiegel*, August 25, 1975, 92–101.

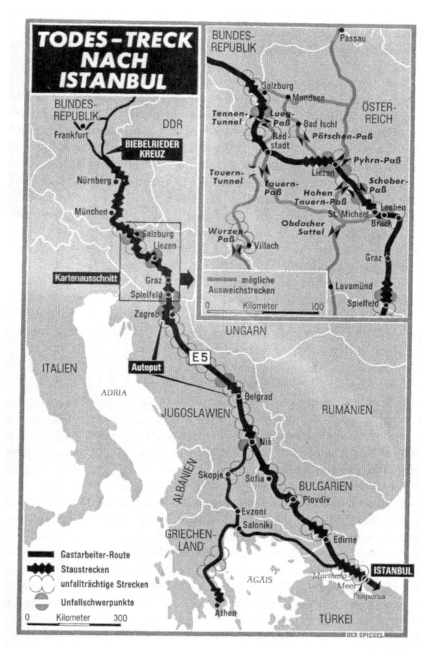

FIGURE 2.2 Map of the Europastraße 5 (E-5), titled "Death Trek to Istanbul," published in a sensationalist 1975 article. © Der Spiegel, used with permission.

traffic, with bottlenecks caused by accidents in poorly lit tunnels. Particularly notorious were two unventilated 2,400- and 1,600-meter tunnels in Austria, which plagued travelers with anxiety and shortness of breath.[42]

Reflecting anti-guest worker biases prevalent in *Der Spiegel* at the time, the same article blamed these harsh conditions not only on environmental and infrastructural problems but also on the guest workers themselves. Invoking rhetoric common in criticism of migrants, the article described the caravan of cars filled with Turkish travelers as an "irresistible and uncontrollable force" and a "mass invasion," which posed serious problems for local Austrian communities and border officials. In 1969, local officials near Graz had called upon the Austrian military for assistance in policing guest workers' traffic violations, resulting in the deployment of six tanks and 120 steel-helmeted riflemen – an incident that the newspaper jokingly called "the first military campaign against guest workers." As the years passed, officials increasingly felt their hands tied. One Senior Lieutenant of the Styrian state police expressed frustration at the number of cars needing standard ten-minute inspections at the Austrian-Yugoslav border: "If we were to catch eight Turks in a five-person car, what would we do with the surplus? Should we leave behind the grandma and the brothers, or the children? Who would take them in? The nearest hotel, the community? Or should we establish a camp for [them]? Here I am already hearing the word 'concentration camp!'"[43] While it is unclear who was beginning to invoke the term "concentration camp," the lieutenant's remark demonstrated his self-conscious concern that, in the aftermath of the Holocaust, the detention of foreign travelers – particularly elderly women and children – could devolve into public accusations of human rights violations.

Centuries-old tensions between the Ottoman and Habsburg Empires were also a reference point. Dramatically, the article quipped: "'The Turks are coming!' has become a cry of distress for Alp-dwellers and Serbs – almost as once for their forefathers when the Janissaries approached on the very same age-old path." By condemning Turkish travelers as a terrifying invasion of Janissaries, the elite corps of the Ottoman Empire's standing army, *Der Spiegel* alluded to the bloody 1683 Battle of Vienna, which occurred after the Ottoman military had occupied the Habsburg capital

---

[42] Vacationing Turkish guest workers often took photographs of these accidents. See, for example: DOMiD-Archiv, BT 0127,2.
[43] "E 5: Terror von Blech und Blut."

for two months. And by explicitly using the phrase "ancient migration route," the article characterized the region not as strictly demarcated by national borders, but rather as a space of deeply rooted travel, mobility, and exchange. However facetious, the interpretation reflected the importance of the Ottoman past in shaping twentieth-century attitudes toward Turkish guest workers. Nearly three hundred years later, ancient hatreds of "bloodthirsty Turks" and the Ottoman "other" remained a racializing anti-Turkish trope.[44]

Far from a military threat, the article continued, local Austrians' terror manifested in a constant onslaught of revving motors, piles of garbage, and human excrement. Making matters worse, the locals received little to no economic benefit from what might otherwise have constituted a touristic boon. To save money, Turkish travelers generally did not patronize Austrian restaurants, hotels, and souvenir shops. Instead, they preferred to sleep in their cars, eat pre-prepared meals, and cook using an electric stovetop. They also avoided Austrian gas stations because they considered refueling in Yugoslavia much more economical.[45] Despite these tensions, some local Austrians were willing to assist the travelers by placing cautionary Turkish-language signs on dangerous stretches of road and building a "Muslim Rest Stop" with a makeshift prayer room, meals free of pork and alcohol, and an Austrian transportation official on site.[46]

The West German government, too, expressed concern about the E-5's treacherous conditions. Around the same time as the sensationalist *Der Spiegel* article, the Federal Labor Ministry launched a public campaign to educate guest workers about proper driving habits. The forum was *Arbeitsplatz Deutschland* (Workplace Germany), a newsletter for guest workers published in multiple languages that sought to provide advice – sometimes useful, sometimes not – on aspects of life in West Germany. Many of the newsletter's articles took a didactic, paternalistic tone. Presuming that many guest workers, especially the Turks, came from rural areas stereotyped as "backward," the articles portrayed them as in need of enlightenment – or at least of a rudimentary orientation to the norms of life in "industrialized," "urbanized," and "modern" societies. In a series titled "The ABCs of the Car Driver," which ran from

---

[44] Jezernik, ed., *Imagining "The Turk"*.
[45] Dal, *E-5*, 147.
[46] Manfred Pfaffenthaler, "Die Gastarbeiterroute. Zur Geschichte eines transeuropäischen Migrationsweges," in Karin Maria Schmiedlechner et al., *Wanderarbeit, Jobnomadismus und Migration* (Graz: Karl-Franzens-Universität, 2012), 9.

the mid-1970s through the mid-1990s, the Labor Ministry instructed guest workers on traffic rules and safety, such as not driving without a license, following traffic signs and signals, paying more attention to children crossing the street, and eating a full breakfast to avoid hunger on the road.[47]

Responding to the shocking media reports on the E-5, the newsletter published a six-page, multi-article feature sponsored by the German Council on Traffic Safety, titled "Vacation Safely in Summer 1977."[48] The Turkish edition's cover featured a dark-haired husband, wife, and three children loading suitcases into a car, about to embark on the journey to the "hot countries in the South." Among the articles was a cautionary tale, in which a stereotypically named guest worker ("Mustafa" in the Turkish edition, "José Pérez" in the Spanish) had saved 4,000 DM to purchase a used van from his friend, only to find out halfway through his 3,000-kilometer journey that the brakes were defective. "Had Mustafa inspected the car beforehand? Far from it!" the article decried. "His friend had given him a 'guarantee,' saying the car was like new!" Mustafa had also failed to check alternative routes, insisting that his was the shortest, and refused to obey speed limits and to avoid forbidden entry roads. Guest workers like Mustafa, the newsletter insisted, justified their flagrant disregard for traffic safety with pride: "If you're not brave, then don't get on the road!"[49] While readership statistics are unavailable, the newsletter's continued references to inept drivers on the E-5 in the 1980s suggest that the warnings had little impact.

Amid broader Cold War geopolitics, government and media reports also perpetuated self-aggrandizing critiques of socialism and communism by blaming the Balkan countries for the E-5's dangerous conditions. While these reports typically attributed the dangers in Austria to snow, ice, and other inclement weather, *Arbeitsplatz Deutschland* echoed tropes of "Eastern" backwardness. Yugoslav roadways, the newsletter noted, were "not up to the standards of modern traffic." In contrast to Germany's esteemed Autobahn, only one-third of the E-5's Yugoslav portion was paved, and traffic officers failed to enforce safety regulations. Travelers were thus forced to endure "curves and obstacles without warning, swerving trucks, cars without lights, tractors that disregard

---

47 "Rahat ve emin yolculuk için bilgiler," *İş Yeri Almanya*, no. 2 (1977): 12–13; "La seguridad comienza al desayunar," *Arbeitsplatz Deutschland*, no. 4 (1977): 12.
48 "İzine emniyetle gidiniz," *İş Yeri Almanya*, no. 2 (1977).
49 "Mustafa emniyetli bir yolculuk için gerekenleri yapmış mıydı?" *İş Yeri Almanya*, no. 2 (1977).

the right of way, and agricultural vehicles or even animals crossing the road." Accompanying photographs depicted a large herd of sheep alongside a smashed car.[50]

Guest workers, too, perceived an immediate change as soon as they crossed the Austrian-Yugoslav border into the Balkans. On the one hand, they took comfort in knowing that every kilometer they drove eastward brought them closer to their homeland. Some even felt a "comfortable ease and relaxation" in Yugoslavia and Bulgaria.[51] Murad recalled that one of the highlights of the trip was eating at a roadside restaurant in Yugoslavia that served *ćevapi*, a minced-meat kebab similar to the Turkish *köfte*, which reminded him of home.[52] Others recalled that Bulgarians were able to communicate using Turkish words, many of which had long entered the Bulgarian language.[53] This sense of shared culture, like *Der Spiegel*'s remark about Janissaries, further reflects the legacy of centuries-long Ottoman rule in the region.

Yet, overwhelmingly, Turkish travelers perceived extreme animosity from local Yugoslavs and Bulgarians, making the drive east of the Iron Curtain especially fearsome. This animosity, as *Der Spiegel*'s comment about Janissaries evidenced, owed in part to the especially bitter memory of Ottoman conquest in the Balkans.[54] Whereas Austrians' fears of Ottoman invasion reached a height at the 1683 Battle of Vienna, Balkan populations endured both indirect and direct Ottoman rule that lasted in some areas from the fourteenth through the early twentieth centuries. Although Western European disdain for Turks subsided somewhat during Ottoman "westernization" campaigns of the Tanzimat Era (1839–1876), resistance to the oppressive "Ottoman yoke" spurred the Balkan nationalist movements and bloodshed of the nineteenth century.[55] In Bulgaria in particular, tensions persisted long after the downfall of Ottoman rule, and guest workers traveling on the E-5 in the 1980s did so in a climate in which Bulgaria's communist government was engaged in a campaign of forced assimilation, expulsion, and ethnic cleansing against the country's Muslim Turkish ethnic minority population.[56]

[50] "Yugoslavya'da yılda iki defa yapılan ölüm yarışı," *İş Yeri Almanya*, no. 1 (1985): 15.
[51] Mandel, *Cosmopolitan Anxieties*, 239.
[52] Murad B., interview.
[53] Cavit Ş., interview by author, Şarköy, 2016.
[54] Kahn, "Rethinking Central Europe as a Migration Space."
[55] Todorova, *Imagining the Balkans*, 180.
[56] Ayşe Parla, *Precarious Hope: Migration and the Limits of Belonging in Turkey* (Stanford: Stanford University Press, 2019).

These animosities assumed another layer during the Cold War. Socialism and communism in the Balkans contrasted with Turkey's democracy and NATO membership, and the reality that guest workers were traveling from West Germany tied them further to the "West." While they neither looked stereotypically German nor conversed primarily in the German language, the association reflected Cold War economic inequalities. The cars they drove were highly reputed Western brands (commonly BMW, Mercedes-Benz, Volkswagen, Audi, Opel, and Ford), and, when they exchanged money with local populations, they were identified not only by the materiality of their West German bills and coins, but also by their purchasing power. By contrast, access to Western consumer goods was rarer in Yugoslavia and Bulgaria. Although some Yugoslavs were able to acquire such products – either through international trade, shopping trips to neighboring Italy, or gifts from vacationing Yugoslav guest workers – scarcities and their less valuable currency imbued Western products with a cachet of luxury.[57] Such products were even harder to obtain in Bulgaria, even though, as Theodora Dragostinova has shown, Bulgaria was a crucial actor on the global cultural scene.[58]

Although both Yugoslavia and Bulgaria were far more entangled with the "West" than Cold War rhetoric has historically maintained, Turkish travelers envisioned the Balkans in terms of "Eastern" backwardness and underdevelopment. These lasting prejudices solidified due to their everyday encounters with local populations, which were marred by violence, bribery, and corruption. Yugoslavia, exclaimed the Turkish rap group Karakan in their song about the E-5, was "full of crooks."[59] One guest worker, Cavit, complained that rowdy Yugoslav teenagers would scatter rocks along the highway to cause flat tires and then rob and vandalize the cars when the weary drivers pulled over for assistance.[60] Tensions also occurred with Yugoslav police officers and border guards, who had a sweet spot for bribes. When Zehrin's husband made a dangerous turn into a gas station, the police arrested him, confiscated the family's passports, demanded a fine of 520 DM, and refused to release him until he gave them his watch as a bribe.[61] Another

---

[57] On Yugoslav guest workers, see: Molnar, *Memory, Politics, and Yugoslav Migrations to Postwar Germany*; Le Normand, *Citizens Without Borders*.
[58] Theodora K. Dragostinova, *The Cold War from the Margins: A Small Socialist State on the Global Cultural Scene* (Ithaca: Cornell University Press, 2021).
[59] Karakan, "Kapıkule'ye kadar."
[60] Cavit S., interview.
[61] Zehrin Ö., interview by author, Şarköy, 2016.

traveler recalled "sadistic" border guards who, in search of contra-
band, forced her family to completely empty their car. Fortunately, she
remembered poetically, "Sweets and cigarettes appeased the gods of the
border, and my cheap red Walkman worked to make one-sided friendships."[62] Avoiding conflict was easier for Erdoğan, whose mother had
grown up in Sarajevo and could communicate with the border guards,
but his family still stocked up on extra Marlboro cigarettes, Coca-Cola,
and chocolate bars just in case.[63]

For many travelers, driving through Bulgaria was even worse than
Yugoslavia. One child admitted to not knowing much about politics,
but he recalled vividly that his first impression of communism was the
absence of color: everything was gray. The only color was on the building
façades, which were adorned with ideological murals touting the benefits
of communism by depicting happy young workers – a stark contrast to
the depressing faces he saw on the streets.[64] An additional stressor for
him were visa laws that permitted Turkish citizens a mere twelve hours
to pass through the entire width of the country. If a policeman caught a
car idling, he would not hesitate to tap on the driver's window, grunting
"*komşu, komşu*" (neighbor, neighbor), a Turkish word that had become
part of the Bulgarian lexicon.[65] Bulgarian children, too, apparently had a
taste for bribes and would tap on travelers' windows demanding chocolate and cigarettes. When Cavit refused, the children cursed him: "I hope
your mother and father die!"[66]

The anxiety-provoking time in Yugoslavia and Bulgaria, which confirmed guest workers' preconceived distinctions between Western and
Eastern Europe, did not entirely disappear when they crossed into Turkey.
Far from a peaceful relief, the Bulgarian-Turkish border at Kapıkule was
just as chaotic as the others they had crossed (Figure 2.3). The Turkish
novelist Güney Dal described the scene in his 1979 book *E-5*: "German
marks, Turkish lira; papers that have to be filled out and signed … exhaust
fumes, dirt, loud yelling, police officers' whistling, chaos, motor noises …
pushing and shoving."[67] Just like their Yugoslav and Bulgarian counterparts, Turkish border guards enriched themselves through bribery and

---

[62] "Karambolage," DOMiD-Archiv, DV 0089.
[63] Erdoğan Ü., interview by author.
[64] "Ayhan (1971), Karlsruhe-Istanbul, 2.250 km, Ford Taunus, Ford Granada,"
www.yolculuk.de/deutsch/mein-reisebericht/.
[65] Zehrin Ö., interview.
[66] Cavit Ş., interview.
[67] Dal, *E-5*, 248.

FIGURE 2.3 Border guards inspect guest workers' cars at the Bulgarian-Turkish border at Kapıkule, mid-1970s. The woman's trunk is stuffed full of consumer goods, including a bag from the West German department store Hertie. © DOMiD-Archiv, Cologne, used with permission.

extortion, and guest workers reported having to wait in hours-long lines of cars just to cross the border.[68] Murad rejoiced that his family was able to skip the lines because his uncle was the wealthy mayor of a local community.[69]

Despite the massive corruption, the Turkish media romanticized the treatment that guest workers received from Turkish border guards, compared to officials in the Balkans. In 1978, the Turkish newspaper *Cumhuriyet* published an overly rosy portrayal of the Kapıkule border crossing. Guest workers are warmly welcomed by "cleanly dressed and smiling customs officials" and "friendly but cautious police officers," who are "very courteous and take care of you." The passport check and customs inspection proceed "quickly." Upon crossing the border, guest workers encounter local villagers who "smile, say hello, and wave to one another." The experience is so pleasant that the guest workers "are

[68] Photographs in DOMiD-Archiv, BT 0484,128b; BT 0484,108; BT 0341; and E 1086,12.
[69] Murad B., interview.

filled with pride": "With an expansive joy in your heart, you say, 'This is my home.'"[70] While this report certainly contradicted reality, its stark contrast to the long lines and corruption in Yugoslavia and Bulgaria supported a nationalist narrative that touted the supposed superiority of Turkish hospitality and efficiency.

The *Cumhuriyet* report was more accurate, however, in its portrayal of the "pride" and "expansive joy" after the physically and emotionally exhausting three-day journey. In the travelers' recollections of the Kapıkule border crossing, complaints about corruption are overshadowed by happiness and relief. One child recalled the joyous cries of "Geldik!" (We've arrived!) as her family's car crossed the border, which seemed "like a gate of paradise."[71] Another woman explained: "When we drive over the border in Edirne, I feel very relieved. I don't know why. Maybe because it's my own country, or maybe it comes from the dirt or the water. It doesn't matter which one. There is a saying: a bird locked in a golden cage is still in its homeland ... No matter how bad it is."[72] As a symbol of this feeling of relief and renewal, many guest workers kissed the ground, washed their cars, and enjoyed fresh watermelon.[73]

Not all travelers, however, felt a sense of familiarity. For many children who had been born and raised in Germany, Turkey seemed just as strange as Yugoslavia and Bulgaria – at least the first time they encountered it – and they described it not as their "homeland" but rather as a "vacation country" (*Urlaubsland*). Though long regaled with their parents' happy tales of Turkey, some children felt a sense of culture shock. "I thought everything was very ugly," Fatma recalled, criticizing Turkey's infrastructure as "wild" compared to Germany's "standardized" and "orderly" urban planning. "The bridges were sometimes not high enough to drive under. The buildings were partially crumbling. As a child, I thought: 'What is this place?'"[74] In Gülten Dayıoğlu's 1986 book of short stories, a teenage boy expresses a similar sentiment: he derides his parents' village as little more than "mud, dirt, and crumbling houses," and he mocks the villagers for living "primitively" and

---

[70] Selim Yalçıner, "Kapıkule gümrük tesisleri sekiz yıldır bir türlü bitirilemiyor," *Cumhuriyet*, August 10, 1978, 4.

[71] "Karambolage."

[72] Merlyn Solakhan, dir., *Hier und Dort. Erzählungen Eingewanderter*, 1992, VHS, DOMiD-Archiv, VI 0098.

[73] Murad B., interview.

[74] Fatma U., interview.

being "stupid, backward, conservative, strange people."[75] Even the guest worker generation, who had grown up in the villages, sometimes came to view their former neighbors with disdain. People who remained in the villages, they noted, were "dumb," "ignorant," "uneducated," "uncultured," "old-fashioned," "rigid," and even "crazy."[76]

This derision of Turkey's shoddy infrastructure and villagers' cultural "backwardness" reflects the power that the journey along the E-5 had in shaping the migrants' identities. Their unsavory experiences driving through Yugoslavia and Bulgaria made them disdain life in the communist and socialist East and solidified their identification with the perceived freedom, democracy, modernity, and wealth of the West. By bribing Yugoslav and Bulgarian police officers and border guards with Marlboro cigarettes, Coca-Cola, and Deutschmarks, vacationing guest workers not only testified to the porosity of the Iron Curtain but also assumed small roles as purveyors of Western consumer goods in the Cold War's underground economy. And some migrants, particularly children, transmuted their disdain for Yugoslavia and Bulgaria's perceived economic underdevelopment onto their parents' home villages, employing the same tropes of Turkish "backwardness" that West Germans used to condemn Turks as unable to integrate. The E-5 was not only paved with potholes, ice, and accidents, but also with paradoxes: while it transported the migrants to Turkey, it also solidified the West German part of their identity.

FANCY CARS AND SUITCASES FULL OF DEUTSCHMARKS

Like the journey itself, the happy reunions upon the guest workers' arrival were also marked by new tensions of identity, national belonging, and cultural estrangement. Every year, as guest workers returned to their home villages, the friends and relatives they had left behind gradually detected that something about them had changed. These local-level perceptions of the migrants' newfound difference soon crystallized into Turkish public discourse and became crucial to the development of discourses about the *Almancı*, or "Germanized Turks." Visual depictions of the *Almancı* evolved with the changing demographics of migration. Whereas the depictions of the 1980s emphasized the forlorn faces of the second-generation children who had grown up abroad and could barely

---

[75] Gülten Dayıoğlu, "Ertürk mit dem Ohrring," in *Rückkehr zwischen zwei Grenzen. Gespräche und Erzählungen*, trans. Feridun Altuna (Berlin: ikoo, 1986), 136–47.

[76] Schiffauer, *Die Migranten aus Subay*, 372.

speak Turkish, those of the 1960s and early 1970s focused on the first generation, the guest workers themselves, usually portraying the average *Almancı* in similar fashion: as a mustachioed man in button-down shirt, vest, and work boots, donning a feathered fedora, and – more often than any other accessory – carrying a transistor radio.[77]

The prevalence of the transistor radio in the images of the first-generation *Almancı* points to the important role that Western consumer goods played in delineating the shifting contours of Turkish and German identities in a globalizing world. First hitting American and Western European markets in 1954, transistor radios were among the most purchased electronic communication devices of the 1960s and 1970s and were widely popular among guest workers. In fact, up to 80 percent of guest workers chose transistor radios as their first purchase in West Germany. Promising access to Turkish-language broadcasts, transistor radios became the crucial means for staying apprised of news from home.[78] In Turkey, however, transistor radios came to symbolize not the migrants' connection to their homeland but rather their estrangement from it. Here, vacations on the E-5 were critical, for they were the channel by which guest workers transported radios, along with cars and myriad other German-made consumer goods, to Turkey. The cars and consumer goods brought on the E-5 were a major factor influencing Turkish perceptions of guest workers' Germanization: the *Almancı*, according to the stereotype, had transformed into *nouveau-riche* superfluous spenders who performed their wealth and status in the face of impoverished villagers.

The association of guest workers with Western consumer goods was rooted in broader economic trends. In the 1960s and 1970s, Turkish state planners' import substitution industrialization policy, which aimed for industrialization with minimal outside influence, resulted in a largely closed economy in which foreign-made goods were rare.[79] Like Yugoslavs and Bulgarians, Turks often romanticized the variety and quality of Western European and American consumer goods compared to the allegedly inferior Turkish brands.[80] The divide was starker in villages, where the importance of local production and the absence of running

---

[77] "Almancı'da para yok," *Milliyet*, November 9, 1996, 9.
[78] Abadan-Unat, *Turks in Europe*, 62.
[79] A. Aydın Çeçen, Suut Doğruel, and Fatma Doğruel, "Economic Growth and Structural Change in Turkey, 1960–1988," *International Journal of Middle East Studies* 26, no. 1 (1994): 37–56.
[80] Emine Z., interview by author, Ankara, 2014.

water and electricity ensured that residents had virtually no exposure to emerging products like washing machines and refrigerators.[81] While villagers' previous exposure to industrial products had come through internal seasonal labor migration to Turkish cities, vacationing guest workers brought a far more astounding array of products, and the label "Made in Germany" held more cachet than "Made in Istanbul."[82]

Since the start of the guest worker program in 1961, the Turkish government encouraged guest workers to import West German goods to Turkey as part of a larger policy of using remittances to stimulate the country's economy.[83] Advertised lists of duty-free items reflected the variety of objects that guest workers brought back. In the 1960s, the category of "home furnishings" (*ev eşyası*) included pianos, dishwashers, radios, refrigerators, and washing machines, and "personal items" (*zat eşyası*) included fur coats, typewriters, handheld video recorders, cassette tapes, binoculars, gramophones, skis, tennis rackets, golf clubs, children's toys, hunting rifles, and one liter of hard alcohol.[84] Reflecting the new sorts of goods popular in Germany, the 1982 list included handheld and stationary blenders, fruit juice pressers, grills, toasters, chicken fryers, coffee machines, yogurt-making machines, and electric massagers.[85] The number of duty-free items also diminished. Previously duty-free items, such as video cameras and washing machines, now cost up to 700 DM to import, and the minuscule half-Deutschmark tax on a single child's sock or slipper reflected the government's growing desperation for revenue amid economic crisis.

No consumer goods, however, were as significant as the cars that guest workers drove along the Europastraße 5. Amid Western Europe's postwar industrialization, cars held great social meaning. As a 1960s travel guide for Germans traveling to Turkey put it, "The man of our days wants to be independent. For him, the car is not only a demonstration of his social position, but it is also the most comfortable form of transportation."[86] Guest workers' desire to purchase their own cars ran deeper,

[81] Walt Patterson, *Transforming Electricity: The Coming Generation of Change* (New York: Earthscan, 1999), 82.

[82] Karpat, *The Gecekondu*, 166, 233.

[83] B. Miller, "Reshaping the Turkish Nation-State," 149.

[84] "Yurda gümrüksüz neler götürülür?" *Anadolu Gazetesi*, December 1963, 2.

[85] T. C. Çalışma Bakanlığı Yurtdışı İşçi Sorunları Genel Müdürlüğü, *Yurtdışındaki Türk İşçiler için Rehber (F. Almanya)* (Ankara: T. C. Çalışma Bakanlığı, 1982), 68–74.

[86] Jahn, *Türkei. Mit Stadtführer Istanbul, Ankara und Reiserouten*, 155.

however. Psychologically, *Der Spiegel* insisted, cars were a "fetish" for all guest workers: "When Slavo in Sarajevo, Ali in Edirne, and Kostas in Corinth roll up with their own Ford, BMW, or even Mercedes, then the frustration of months on the assembly line in a foreign country turns into a pleasant experience of success in the homeland."[87] Through their cars' "modern" symbolism, the "scorned, mocked, and exploited pariahs of industrial society" could transcend their socioeconomic status, making their backbreaking labor worthwhile.

The cachet of guest workers' cars was especially palpable in Turkey in the 1960s and 1970s, when car ownership was rare. The first Turkish sedan, the Devrim, was produced in 1961, the same year as the start of the guest worker program, and the first mass-produced Turkish car, the Anadol, did not begin production until 1966.[88] Whether purchasing an Anadol in Turkey or paying expensive taxes to import a car from abroad, the high cost of car ownership ensured that they were a luxury available only to wealthy urbanites. Even among the wealthy, however, the number of cars remained minuscule: for every 1,000 people in Turkey, there were only four cars in 1971 and, despite increasing, the number remained relatively low in 1977, at just ten per thousand.[89] The symbolic value of a car was especially pronounced in villages and smaller towns: while Turkish urbanites were familiar with cars by the late 1960s, most villagers had never seen a car with their own eyes until vacationing guest workers returned with them. In both cities and villages, Turks in the home country began to associate guest workers nearly synonymously with West German car brands: Mercedes-Benz, BMW, Volkswagen, Audi, and Opel. Incidentally, these were the same automotive firms where many guest workers were employed, and many took special pride in showing off a car that they had helped produce. Even if their cars were rickety, used beaters that had been sold multiple times and had broken brake lights, they became symbols of the guest workers' upward mobility.

Family members, friends, and neighbors in Turkey reacted to guest workers' cars with a mixture of awe, bewilderment, and envy. In the 1960s, twenty-year-old Necla even based her decision to marry her husband, Ünsal, on his car (Figure 2.4). Before their marriage, Necla

---

[87] "E 5: Terror von Blech und Blut."
[88] Burçe Çelik, *Technology and National Identity in Turkey: Mobile Communications and the Evolution of a Post-Ottoman Nation* (London: I. B. Tauris, 2011), 70–71.
[89] Carter Vaughn Findley, *Turkey, Islam, Nationalism, and Modernity: A History, 1789–2007* (New Haven: Yale University Press, 2010), 328.

FIGURE 2.4 Ünsal Ö., Necla's husband, with his blue Opel – one of the
eighteen cars that he bought and sold during his two decades living in
West Germany before remigrating. Family photograph, given to author
with permission.

knew nothing about Ünsal – only that he was from a small village five
kilometers east of Şarköy, where she had grown up, and that he had
become captivated with her when he caught a glimpse of her during his
vacation from Germany. Although Necla's father scrutinized potential
suitors, he entertained Ünsal's request for marriage simply because he
was a guest worker. When Ünsal asked Necla's father for her hand, her
mother forced her to stay in her room, insisting that she should not see
her suitor before the formal arrangement. Nervously awaiting Ünsal's
arrival, Necla peeked out the window and was delighted at what she
saw. Although she could barely see Ünsal's appearance from far away,
one thing was certain: he had a car, a gray Mercedes-Benz. "That car had
come to me like a fairy tale," Necla gleefully recalled fifty years later.
"All I knew was that he was a wealthy man and that he was working in
Germany. I just had to marry him."[90]

Guest workers also coveted cars as an additional income source. In
1963, *Anadolu Gazetesi* reported that 500 workers at the Ford factory

[90] Necla and Ünsal Ö., interview by author.

in Cologne had purchased used cars to drive to Turkey to sell.[91] Selling West German cars in Turkey was so prevalent that the Turkish government instituted strict customs regulations to prevent competition with the emerging Turkish automotive market. In 1973, Turkish citizens who had worked in West Germany for at least two years could import one small- or medium-sized passenger vehicle – but only upon their permanent remigration. Within six months of their arrival, the returning workers had to register their cars to ensure they had a valid Turkish driver's license. Although they could import a tractor for farming, they were restricted to a list of twenty-one "permitted tractor brands," including Massey Ferguson, Ford, Caterpillar, and John Deere, and the duty-free import of trucks, vans, buses, and minibuses was "strictly forbidden."[92] Circumventing these restrictions, guest workers regularly sold cars on the black market.[93] During their thirty years in Germany, Necla and Ünsal purchased eighteen used cars, most of which they sold for cash in Turkey.

Cars were not only modes of transportation, status symbols, and income generators, but also vessels for transporting other consumer goods. Personal vehicles' capacity for mass quantities of luggage was a major factor motivating the decision to drive rather than fly to Turkey, compared to airlines' harsh baggage restrictions. One guest worker had even offered a 100 DM bribe to a baggage handler at the Düsseldorf airport to load his massively overweight suitcase onto the plane. To his dismay, however, bribes were far less successful at German airports than they were at Yugoslav, Bulgarian, and Turkish border checkpoints: an airport official wrote a formal letter of complaint to his employer, which was forwarded to the state and federal government transportation ministries.[94] The importance of cars' capacity for luggage is captured in vacationing guest workers' family photographs, which depict lines and lines of cars on the Europastraße 5 filled to the brim, complete with carefully tied-down rooftop luggage racks.[95] Güney Dal's 1979 novel *E-5* even features a curious subplot involving a blue porcelain bathtub tied to the roof of a car.[96] After the rise in family migration in the 1970s, guest

[91] "Otomobille seyahat," *Anadolu Gazetesi*, August 1963, 4.
[92] Oya Araslı and Doğan Araslı, *Almanya'daki Türk İşçilerin Hakk ve Görevleri* (Ankara: Ayyıldız, 1973), 171.
[93] Necla and Ünsal Ö., interview.
[94] Flughafen Düsseldorf to Reisebüro Varan, "Betr.: Versuch einer Gepäckunterschiebung," January 20, 1972, BArch, B 108/63800.
[95] Photographs in DOMiD-Archiv, E 0685,3 and BT 0355.
[96] Dal, *E-5*, 204.

FIGURE 2.5 Turkish vacationers at a rest stop on the E-5 in Austria, ca. 1970. Their car, an iconic Ford Transit, is loaded to the brim with consumer goods, including a rooftop luggage rack. © DiasporaTürk, used with permission.

workers deliberately opted for cars that could hold not only large quantities of luggage but also large families. The Ford Transit, a sturdy and spacious minibus first produced in 1965, became such an iconic symbol of the guest worker program that the German city of Bremen erected a statue of it in 2017 (Figure 2.5).[97]

Well aware that vacationing guest workers were loading up their cars with consumer goods, West German firms sought to take advantage of the phenomenon. In the 1960s, supermarkets and textile stores in West German cities began hiring translators to accommodate the large number of Turkish customers.[98] Local stores also advertised in newspapers oriented toward guest workers. The Frankfurt-based retailer Radio City, the self-identified "oldest and best-known Turkish firm in Germany," boasted that its inventory included well-regarded companies, such as Grundig,

---

[97] Anne Gerling, "Ein Kleinbus voller Kulturgut," *Weser Kurier*, November 16, 2017, www.weser-kurier.de/bremen/stadtteile/stadtteile-bremen-west_artikel,-ein-kleinbus-voller-kulturgut-_arid,1669550.html.
[98] "Per Moneta," *Der Spiegel*, October 7, 1964.

Telefunken, Philips, and Siemens, that employed guest workers.[99] In the most blatant example of ethno-marketing toward Turks, the home improvement and construction store OBI, located in Berlin's heavily Turkish district of Neukölln, distributed a Turkish-language flyer advertising special deals on auto equipment necessary for the drive along the E-5, including hydraulic car jacks, water pumps, and rooftop luggage racks (Figure 2.6). The ad featured a Turkish woman wearing a headscarf, shouting: "Run, run! Don't miss the deals at OBI!"[100]

While the OBI advertisement certainly exaggerated the haste of running to catch deals, it did capture the importance that guest workers placed on shopping before their vacations. Given stereotypes about guest workers' riches, friends and relatives in Turkey expected to receive not only hugs and kisses but also gifts and souvenirs. The sheer pressure of pleasing relatives – and of not being perceived as poor, unsuccessful, or stingy – turned shopping into an annual ritual, and guest workers put extensive planning, effort, and expense into purchasing gifts. Birgül explained that her mother would take several days off work before the vacation to complete the shopping. "Everyone wants something from Germany because they think that the things here are much nicer," she explained. At department stores, Turkish women would shop for dresses, skirts, blouses, shoes, and bed linens, while men generally assumed responsibility for larger items, such as radios, vacuums, and appliances. To introduce her friends to the latest fashions, Birgül brought lipstick, mascara, and nail polish, as well as copies of the magazines *Burda*, *Brigitte*, and *Petra*. Polaroid cameras, too, were hot items. Birgül recalled excitedly that when her father photographed villagers in Çorum and the prints came out, "They thought it was a miracle!"[101]

Guest workers who were interviewed for this book confirmed this broad and oddly specific range of items. "Oh, we brought everything!" exclaimed Necla, the same woman who had married her husband because of his car.[102] Necla's list contained small items, such as beauty products and cosmetics, as well as furniture, such as chairs, cabinets, and a television, even though her village did not yet have a broadcasting connection. Above all, however, Necla coveted cookware. She brought plates, pots,

---

[99] Advertisement for Radio City, *Anadolu Gazetesi*, December 1963, 3.
[100] Advertisement for OBI-Baumarkt, 1975, DOMiD-Archiv, OS 0191.
[101] Karin König, Hanne Straube, and Kamil Taylan, *Merhaba ... Guten Tag. Ein Bericht über eine türkische Familie* (Bornheim: Lamuv, 1981), 49–51.
[102] Necla Ö., interview.

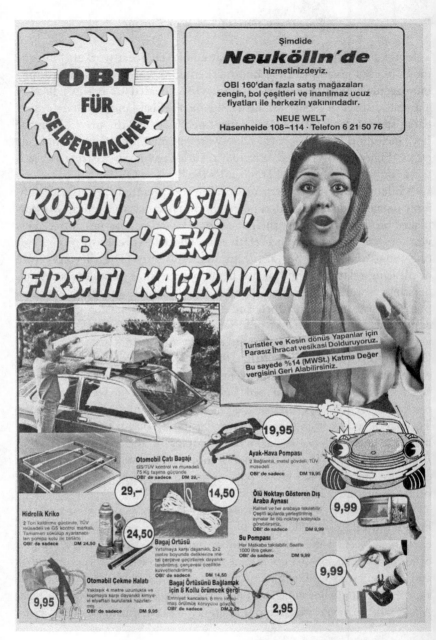

FIGURE 2.6 Turkish-language ethno-marketing flyer from the West German home improvement store OBI, advertising auto parts and rooftop luggage racks to vacationing guest workers, mid-1970s. The woman, wearing a headscarf, shouts: "Run, run, don't miss the deals at OBI!" © OBI GmbH & Co. Deutschland KG, used with permission.

and pans, including a multi-piece American set of pots and pans with a 100-year warranty that she was still using as of 2016. Burcu, who was a child while Necla and Ünsal were traveling back and forth between the two countries, remembered Necla's beautiful silver knife set even thirty years later, reminiscing, "I always loved those knives." Burcu would also get excited when "Necla Teyze" (Auntie Necla) would bring her special presents, such as balloons – since Necla worked at a balloon factory in Dortmund – and even her first Barbie doll.[103]

"Suitcase children," who lived with relatives in Turkey and traveled to West Germany to visit their parents, also transported goods between the two countries. Bengü's grandparents packed her suitcase with Turkish culinary staples like chili paste, garlic, olive oil, and dried okra, which were hard to find in Germany before the rise in Turkish markets and export stores established by former guest workers.[104] The only downside, she laughed, was that her clothes frequently smelled like garlic. Murad spoke fondly of transporting products on the other leg of the journey – from Germany to Turkey – which elevated his social status. "Turkey was like a socialist country back then," he joked, elaborating that Turkey's relatively closed trade policies made foreign products rare.[105] While his uncles asked for cigarettes and alcohol from the German airport's duty-free store, his classmates demanded sweets: "Bringing chocolates was like gold!" With its Italian origins, the chocolate hazelnut spread Nutella made Murad especially "popular," while Bengü's classmates delighted in Switzerland's Nesquik chocolate powder.

The West German media was curiously fixated on the shopping and "show-and-tell" at these reunions, emphasizing how guest workers – often arrogantly – performed their wealth and status. While newspapers mentioned vacationing guest workers, they focused on individuals who had remigrated permanently because it was then, when a guest worker had all his German-made possessions centralized in his village, that he could fully flaunt his wealth. In 1976, *Zeit-Magazin* reported on Ahmet Üstünel, a thirty-year-old farmer who had returned to Gülünce after mining coal for five years in Oberhausen. He brought not only

---

[103] Burcu K., interview by author, Şarköy, 2014.
[104] For the most part, former guest workers did not begin establishing their own businesses until the mid-1970s, and Turkish grocery stores did not begin proliferating on a mass scale until the 1990s. On Turkish migrants' entrepreneurship, see: Zeppenfeld, *Vom Gast zum Gastwirt?*
[105] Murad B., interview.

his wife and three children but also 30,000 DM (actually 28,509 DM and 33 *pfennigs*, per his meticulous calculations) saved through thrifty budgeting. Üstünel also owned not one, but two, vehicles: a brand-new McCormick 624 diesel tractor and the fully packed Volkswagen Variant. The shiny car, washed clean after the arduous three-day journey on the E-5 and boasting a West German license plate, attracted villagers' awe and envy. As he drove past a local coffee shop, a group of children chased him down the street, hoping for treats. "Cigarette! Cigarette!" they yelled.[106]

In a more comprehensive five-page article and photo series, titled "What Turks Do With Their Marks," the West German magazine *Quick* profiled ten guest workers who had returned "from the golden West" and were now viewed enviously as "capitalists" and "little kings."[107] Rather than praising the guest workers for achieving their dreams, the article belittled their frivolousness and naiveté in contrast to Germans' allegedly wise and prudent financial decisions. Jusuf Demir, who had spent three years as a garbage truck driver in Langenfeld, smiled widely for a photograph to show off his shiny new gold teeth – "a good investment," the article joked. The article further mocked Hursit Altınday, a former construction worker, for having built a "Swabian paradise on the Anatolian highlands," complete with "German" features, like a bathroom, balcony, garden, and wrought-iron railing. The article also marveled at guest workers who leveraged their wealth to secure positions in local government, implicitly criticizing Turkish politics as nepotistic. One striking example was İbrahim Öksüz, who upon returning from Wuppertal with 100,000 DM, had been elected to the Şereflikoçhisar town council and was planning to run for a seat in the parliament. But "nobody was as generous as Bünyamin Çelebi," the article continued, who used his savings to build a 125-foot minaret and was "promptly" elected mayor.

Disparaging media reports also often highlighted the negative consequences of the displays of wealth. In 1971, a fourteen-page *Der Spiegel* article on guest workers' vacations reported the emergence of Turkish discourses lambasting guest workers as extravagant spenders who squandered their hard-earned savings on items that were often entirely useless in the hinterlands of Anatolia, where electricity first arrived in the 1980s.

---

[106] Michael Holzach and Tim Rautert, "Ahmets Heimkehr," *Zeit-Magazin* 41, no. 10 (October 1976): 28–45.

[107] Oswald von Nagy, "Was Türken aus ihrer Mark machen," *Quick*, September 20, 1979.

"No one knows what to do with a camera and typewriter, so they are sold," the newspaper wrote. "The electric razor is buried at the bottom of a cabinet – until one distant day, when [the guest worker] returns or his four-year-old son sprouts his beard."[108] Even *The Sunday Times*, a British newspaper with no direct connection to the issue, condemned the "waste of the skilled men who return home": "Other than a smattering of German and perhaps the money to buy or build a house, possibly a German car or even a German wife, the vast majority have little to show for five to ten years spent in one of the world's most affluent countries."[109] In short, guest workers had filled their homes with fancy stuff that had little other purpose than to collect dust.

Although laden with stereotypes and exaggerations, these media accounts were rooted in reality. In 1971, the same year as the *Der Spiegel* feature, a governor of the Anatolian province of Cappadocia told a visiting West German official that migration had destroyed local economic life. Not only had it drained the villages of able-bodied workers, male protectors, and individuals able to participate in government, but it had also wrought no economic benefits. "Most of the workers come back without money," the governor complained. "They just spend it on frivolous things, such as cars, television sets, etc., or even items that do not correspond to their current standard of living and cannot at all be financed by them." In such cases, the items were sold or abandoned because they could not build or purchase replacement parts. The governor implored the West German official to "advise the workers in Germany to bring such items that can be used for the building of new and income-generating activity," such as tools and equipment.[110]

Such pleas proved fruitless, however. Nermin Abadan-Unat's 1975 survey of 500 returning workers in two small Turkish villages confirmed the governor's complaint that they were not bringing back "useful" items.[111] Nearly two-thirds brought clothing, tape recorders, and radios, while only 1 percent – a mere seven of the 500 surveyed workers – brought professional tools. One man built himself a five-bedroom house, by far the biggest in the village, which could fit his wife and five children, his son's wife, and his two grandchildren. While most villagers had

---

[108] "Gastarbeiter: Entwicklungshilfe für die Reiche?" *Der Spiegel*, November 21, 1971, 138–51.
[109] "Waste of the Skilled Men Who Return Home," *The Sunday Times*, July 22, 1973.
[110] Staatssekretär von Braun, "Türkische Arbeiter in Deutschland," April 5, 1971, PAAA, B 85/1046.
[111] Abadan-Unat et al., *Göç ve Gelişme*, 387.

austere decor, he adorned his guest room with "modern urban business furniture" and filled the home with accessories: two electric blankets, two lamps, a blender, an electric knife sharpener, five or six clocks, a vacuum, cups and mugs displayed in a grand showcase, a large kitchen table, a washing machine, a food compressor, a tanning bed to provide relief from rheumatism, and – most curiously – a single plastic Christmas ornament hanging from the ceiling. Despite having no electricity, he placed a refrigerator in his bedroom and stored clothing on its shelves.

This conspicuous consumption, which the survey's researchers called "gaudy" and "superfluous," was especially offensive not only because its overt ostentation highlighted villages' wealth disparities, but also because it testified to the migrants' abandonment of the rural values of hospitality and austerity amid poverty.[112] At a time when even the poorest families "were suffering for the sake of hospitality" – offering guests refreshments like sugar, perfume, food, tea, and coffee – guest workers spent their money recklessly and ostentatiously. Yet it was not entirely the workers' fault, the researchers explained: "Workers in foreign countries are accustomed to societies with excessive spending habits. As they walk along the street in the evenings, they are confronted with all kinds of advertisements and shop windows. In these countries, luxury furniture and necessities are exhibited and promoted. On the other hand, to sell to the foreign workers, the owners of stores and shops in these countries also have a tendency to exploit them, even to appeal to their chauvinistic thoughts." Tantalized by the array of products available at lower prices and buoyed by their higher wages, guest workers "fall into the trap."[113]

Although the researchers associated these excessive spending habits with the capitalist values of "foreign countries," both the guest workers and their neighbors described it as a peculiarly German problem. "I've been injected with a German sickness. I always want more," admitted one guest worker, who despite already owning multiple lavish properties in his village planned to open a huge shopping center modeled after the German department store Hertie.[114] Defensively, another guest worker attributed his spending habits to a broader sense of adopting German culture. "The workers here are slowly beginning to live like Germans," he contended. "They do not want to live in old houses. Everyone wants

---

[112] Ibid.
[113] Ibid., 389–90.
[114] Von Nagy, "Was Türken aus ihrer Mark machen."

to live in a civilized manner, not to work like a machine. Like people. As a result, our spending has increased. Isn't that our right?"[115]
This praise for "civilized" life in Germany and denigration of "old
houses" in Turkish villages, alongside the bold assertation that guest
workers were "slowly beginning to live like Germans," struck precisely
at the heart of the issue: after years abroad, guest workers, too, were
well aware of their gradual estrangement from Turkish villages and, by
proxy, from the Turkish nation. Even if they rejected the derogatory
label *Almancı*, they – to a certain extent – were willing to acknowledge,
and even embrace, the notion that they had Germanized.

* * * * *

At age eighty, reflecting on his many years of road trips along the E-5,
Cengiz was emphatic: never again would he endure the "crazy" journey, "even if someone offered me 10,000 Euros!"[116] Fortunately, as
for the vast majority of guest workers, Cengiz's last drive on the E-5
was in the mid-1980s, a time when the significance of the E-5 declined
markedly due to the increased expansion, affordability, and conve-
nience of air travel. As Turkey opened its economy to foreign influences
in the 1980s, investment in the Turkish tourism industry skyrocketed,
and the number of foreign tourists visiting from Germany rose by 12.5
percent annually between 1980 and 1987. By 1994, one-quarter of all
tourists visiting Turkey were German.[117] Competition among firms in
the expanding West German and Turkish tourism markets lowered
prices and democratized air travel, transforming it from a privilege of
the wealthy elite into one that could be enjoyed even by guest worker
families. With nonstop flights from Frankfurt to Istanbul taking just
four hours compared to three exhausting and dangerous days on the
E-5, the preference was clear for many. The long road home had
become much shorter, and the Cold War buffer zone had turned into
a flyover zone.

Guest workers' reasons for traveling to Turkey also changed in the
1980s. They increasingly vacationed to Turkey not only to visit relatives but also, as Germans did, to sightsee and take cruises. As one guest
worker remarked, "If you want to take a vacation in another country,

---

[115] Örsan Öymen, "İşçi Dövizleri. Okurlardan Kazan'a," *Milliyet*, March 20, 1979, 9.
[116] Cengiz İ., interview by author, Cologne, 2015.
[117] Faruk Şen, "Motor der Entwicklung? Die Rolle des Tourismus in der türkischen
Volkswirtschaft" (Essen: Zentrum für Türkeistudien, 1994).

you would have to pay three to five times as much." His "pockets full of Deutschmarks," he added, allowed his family to enjoy much nicer vacations than most Turks could ever imagine.[118] The number of Turkish tourism firms in Germany also grew markedly, many of them founded by entrepreneurial former guest workers. By 1987, one of the largest was AS-Sonnenreisen, which was founded by Sümer Akat, a former Volkswagen and Ford factory employee, who had begun organizing flights for Turkish mineworkers and later expanded to include German tourists. Just two decades after his menial labor as a guest worker, Akat's initiative in anticipating the lucrative new market had allowed him to manage 300 employees, several Turkish hotels, and his own airline with regular flights from Düsseldorf, Frankfurt, Hamburg, and Munich to Istanbul, Izmir, Dalaman, and Antalya.[119]

By the late 1980s, the fixation on guest workers' cars and consumer goods declined in importance as the Turkish government overhauled the country's macroeconomic system. Not only had guest workers' friends and families become accustomed to the consumer goods they had brought back over the past two decades, but Turkey's neoliberal external economic reorientation of the 1980s, which vastly reduced import duties, made foreign products available to a broader stratum of Turkish society.[120] The migrants recalled that the products they brought with them no longer had the same social cachet. The highly coveted Coca-Cola bottles and Nutella chocolate spread that Murad brought to Istanbul were now available in Turkish stores and no longer made him as "popular" as they had before. And as the economic reforms bridged the rural–urban divide by bringing running water and electricity to even the most remote parts of Anatolia, items like refrigerators, dishwashers, and electric chicken fryers no longer inspired the same awe.

If the rise of the airline and tourism industries marked the first death knells of the road trip, the post–Cold War upheaval cemented it in its grave. Travel across the E-5 was abruptly cut off upon the 1991 outbreak of the Yugoslav Wars, which made the stretch from Zagreb to Belgrade impassable. In the words of one British newspaper, the ironically named "Road of Fraternity and Unity" had transformed into little more than "a deserted concrete strip between the two capitals used only by United

---

[118] Güner Yüreklik, "Türkiye'de tatil," *Bizim Almanca*, July 1986, 47–49.
[119] "Turizm işinde iş var," *Bizim Almanca*, June 1987, 43–45.
[120] Ziya Öniş and Steven B. Webb, *Political Economy of Policy Reform in Turkey in the 1980s* (The World Bank, 1992).

Nation peacekeeping convoys."[121] Guest workers corroborated this claim, explaining that the chaos in Yugoslavia forced them to fly rather than drive.[122] Following the cessation of the fighting, the portion of the E-5 spanning from Salzburg to Thessaloniki through Ljubliana, Zagreb, Belgrade, and Skopje was reconstructed and incorporated into the Pan-European Corridor system, which the European Union devised in the mid-1990s as part of its efforts to draw southern and eastern European countries into the growing supranational transport network, as "Corridor X."[123] A highway named "E-5" continues to exist, though related to the original one in name only. As part of the United Nations international E-road network, it spans north–south from Scotland to Algeciras through England and western France.[124]

Despite these developments, the notion that guest workers had transformed into a *nouveau-riche* class of spenders out of touch with village needs remained permanently ingrained in discourses surrounding the culturally estranged *Almancı*, or Germanized Turks – so much so that condemnation of guest workers replaced sympathy for them. As one West German news report put it, "Anyone who counts the number of minivans with German license plates on Turkish streets will no longer want to hear that the passengers were 'sacrificed' for the German economic miracle."[125] Although performances of wealth and status often belied the reality that guest workers were struggling financially in West Germany, the consequences of these discourses were both concrete and lasting. One man who returned to Turkey in the 1980s explained that villagers still charged him higher prices because "they think our pockets are full."[126] When he went to a mechanic to repair his car, he was

[121] "The Bosnia Crisis: Belgrade and Zagreb Agree to Swap PoWs," *The Independent*, August 8, 1992, www.independent.co.uk/news/world/europe/the-bosnia-crisis-belgrade-and-zagreb-agree-to-swap-pows-1539120.html.

[122] Cengiz İ. and Murad B., interviews.

[123] Marios Miltiadou et al., "Pan-European Corridor X Development: Case of Literal Implementation of the European Transport Strategy Itself or of Change of the General Environment in the Region?" *Procedia – Social and Behavioral Sciences* 48 (2012): 2361–73.

[124] United Nations Economic and Social Council – Economic Commission for Europe – Inland Transport Committee, "European Agreement on Main International Traffic Arteries," 111th Session of the Working Party on Road Transport, Geneva, October 25–26, 2016, www.unece.org/fileadmin/DAM/trans/doc/2016/sc1/ECE-TRANS-SC1-2016-03-Rev1e.pdf.

[125] Heinz Barth, "Enttäuschte Freundschaft," *Die Welt*, July 7, 1983.

[126] Barbara Trottnow and Alfred Engler, "Aber die Türkei ist doch meine Heimat ... Türkische Rückwanderer berichten," undated (most likely mid-1980s), DOMiD-Archiv, CC 0041.

charged 4,000 lira – twice the usual price – simply because it was a German car. The overcharging was so rampant that one woman tried to hide the fact that she had worked in Germany even decades later.[127] Yet the secret was out: her *Almancı* identity was inescapable, and neighbors continued to gossip behind her back. Vacations across Cold War Europe – with all their twists, turns, and bottlenecks – not only physically brought the guest workers closer to Turkey, but also widened the emotional distance from "home."

---

[127] Zehrin Ö., interview.

3

Remittance Machines

Even more so than annual vacations, the "final return" to Turkey was expensive. Not only did returning migrants have to finance the moving costs themselves, but they also had to secure housing and find a new job. After years of toiling in West German factories and mines, and wary of Turkey's high unemployment rate, they generally wished to become their own bosses. But, despite performing their wealth and status, they often struggled to afford the high start-up costs of entrepreneurship. Alongside pooling money from friends and relatives, some sought governmental assistance. In 1976, Hüseyin Şen asked the West German government for a "small loan" of 100,000 DM, explaining that he had purchased a fifteen-acre plot of land that could fit forty cows, and he had already transported five cows and a bull from Germany to Turkey. "If you would give me this opportunity," Şen promised, "I am ready to leave Germany and return to Turkey forever."[1] Levent Mercan, who had spent one of his vacations purchasing an acre for cattle rearing, had a similar request – albeit for far less money.[2] Nesip Aslan tried his luck in the industrial sector, seeking a loan to build an electrical power plant in rural Hatay.[3] None of these men, however, received a response. Abandoned in the bureaucratic black hole, they were left to fend for themselves.

Failing to respond, however, did not mean that the Turkish and West German governments were not interested in guest workers' return

[1] Hüseyin Şen to BMZ, March 10, 1976, BArch, B 213/5636.
[2] Levent Mercan to Büro für die Förderung türkischer Arbeitnehmer-Investitionen, August 23, 1980, BArch, B 213/13896.
[3] Nesip Aslan to Internationaler Bund für Sozialarbeit, November 29, 1973, BArch, B 213/5621.

migration, nor did it signal a lack of interest in how guest workers spent their money. On the contrary, the connection between return migration and financial investments dominated bilateral discussions at the time. In the early 1970s, as part of a broader effort to determine how to send the Turks home, West German officials attempted to implement a bilateral program that would pay Turkey millions of Deutschmarks in development aid in exchange for assistance in reintegrating returning migrants who were interested in starting their own small businesses in Turkey. At first, the West German government had every reason to believe that Turkey would be amenable to such a program. After all, as Brian J. K. Miller has extensively documented, Turkey initially claimed to welcome the guest workers' return on the basis that they would bring new knowledge and skills to spark their home country's internal economic development and modernization.[4] By the 1970s, however, the Turkish government switched its stance and began *opposing* guest workers' return. As West German officials decried in 1984, "The Turkish government wants to avoid everything that could intensify the reverse flow of Turkish citizens."[5]

The reason for Turkey's newfound opposition to return migration, as this chapter shows, was primarily financial. Just as the exigencies of global labor markets sparked guest workers' recruitment to Germany, so too was the tense question of their return enmeshed in economic forces beyond their control. The 1970s, the decade when West Germany first devised policies to promote guest workers' return migration, marked the highpoint of neoliberalism and the globalization of international financial institutions such as the World Bank and the International Monetary Fund.[6] Turkey's relationship to the global economy was volatile, however. Throughout the 1960s and early 1970s, Turkey's official policy of import substitution industrialization had yielded steady economic growth, particularly in the nascent manufacturing and industrial sectors that the government prioritized.[7] But the OPEC oil crisis of 1973 spiraled Turkey

---

[4] B. Miller, "Reshaping the Turkish Nation-State."

[5] "Betr.: 10. Sitzung der deutsch-türkischen Arbeitsgruppe Reintegration am 21.-23.05.1984; hier: Ressortbesprechung am 03.05.1984," May 8, 1984, 2, PAAA, B 58/182487.

[6] The concept of neoliberalism has deeper historical origins. Quinn Slobodian, *Globalists: The End of Empire and the Birth of Neoliberalism* (Cambridge, MA: Harvard University Press, 2018).

[7] Despite a decline in exports and agriculture and the 1970 currency devaluation, Turkey achieved a 6–7 percent annual rise in gross national product from 1963 through 1977. Aydın Çeçen, A. Suut Doğruel, and Fatma Doğruel, "Economic Growth and Structural Change in Turkey 1960–88," *International Journal of Middle East Studies* 26, no. 1 (1994): 38.

into years of unemployment, hyperinflation, parliamentary instability, and political violence.[8] The government's excessive borrowing from international institutions and foreign countries exacerbated the problem, ultimately leading to the 1980 military coup. The situation remained dire until the mid-1980s, when democratically elected Prime Minister Turgut Özal, a neoliberal-minded former World Bank employee, overhauled the public sector, privatized firms, and promoted exports.[9]

As part of their broader impact on their home country, guest workers played a significant role in mitigating Turkey's economic crisis. To repay its foreign debt, Turkey became increasingly dependent on guest workers' remittance payments in high-performing Deutschmarks, which were far more valuable than the Turkish lira. Among migrants, this was no secret. The renowned Turkish novelist Bekir Yıldız, who had returned to Turkey after a four-year stint as a guest worker in Heidelberg, satirized the home country's views in his 1974 novel *Alman Ekmeği* (German Bread):

Give up eating, Ahmets. Give up eating, Jales. Load your stuff on trains, Osmans and Ayşes ... Fly home with your marks ... Buy land in our big cities ... Buy stocks and shares in new factories. When you return, you could become industrialists. What's wrong with that?[10]

Turkey's need for investment was so severe, Yıldız insisted, that the Turkish government expected them to put all their Deutschmarks toward farming, industrial production, and the stock market – even if that forced them to "give up eating" in the process. But Yıldız's satire went further: despite rhetoric promising guest workers the chance of future economic success in Turkey, the Turkish government did not, in fact, want them to return.

To be sure, this dependence on remittances was a pattern that prevailed in many other cases of labor migration across the globe.[11] But the Turkish-German case stands out because of the timing: the late 1970s, the time when remittance payments became especially crucial, was the very same moment that they starkly declined, since guest workers who

---

[8] Victor Lavy and Hillel Rapoport, "External Debt and Structural Adjustment: Recent Experience in Turkey," *Middle Eastern Studies* 28, no. 2 (April 1992): 313–32.

[9] Ziya Öniş, "Turgut Özal and His Economic Legacy: Turkish Neo-Liberalism in Critical Perspective," *Middle Eastern Studies* 40, no. 4 (2004): 113–34.

[10] Bekir Yıldız, *Alman Ekmeği* (Istanbul: Everest Yayınları, 2011 [1974]), 52. Translation adapted from Abadan-Unat, *Turkish Workers in Europe*, 135.

[11] The case of Mexican migration to the United States is particularly instructive here. Alfredo Cuecuecha and Carla Pederzini, eds., *Migration and Remittances from Mexico: Trends, Impacts, and New Challenges* (Lanham: Lexington Books, 2012); Lopez, *The Remittance Landscape*.

had brought their families to Germany had less need to send money home. On the flip side, the Turkish government knew that if guest workers returned to Turkey, the stream of Deutschmarks would dry up even more. This realization, alongside fears of returning guest workers inundating the labor market, made their return a nightmarish prospect. Even when it contradicted guest workers' best interests, and even when it created bilateral tensions with the West German government, officials in Ankara strove to prevent a mass return migration at all costs.

Although both countries' governments treated them like pawns on the chessboard of global finance, the migrants strategically navigated the dual pressures from above. They sent remittances home, invested in Turkish industry, and placed their savings in Turkish banks – but they did so on their own terms, when it suited their own wallets rather than Turkey's federal coffers. And they vocally pushed back against Turkey's blatant efforts to expropriate their Deutschmarks, with guest workers' children even initiating an activist movement throughout West Germany to protest the exorbitant cost of paying their way out of Turkey's mandatory military service in the 1980s. Overall, the knowledge that they were not only unwanted in Germany, but also in Turkey, whose government wanted to *prevent* them from returning at all costs, widened the rift between the migrants and their home country. Increasingly mistrustful of the Turkish government, the migrants lamented that their home country viewed them not only as "Germanized" *Almancı* but also as "remittance machines" (*döviz makinesi*), who posed the least risk and greatest reward to the nation if they kept their physical bodies far away but their Deutschmarks close.[12] Although they remained tied to the nation, their own government valued them not for their physical *presence* in their homeland, but rather for the economic benefits reaped on account of their *absence*.

DEVELOPMENT AID FOR RETURN MIGRATION

In the early 1970s, just one decade after initially welcoming Turks as guest workers, the West German government began strategizing about how to send them home. Multiple factors underlay this shift. The economy had vastly improved throughout the 1960s, and, despite guest workers' significant contributions to Germany's postwar "economic

---

[12] Eva Østergaard-Nielsen has likewise applied the idea of "remittance machines" to the case of Turkish-German migration, particularly in her study of Kurdish migrants. Østergaard-Nielsen, *Transnational Politics*.

miracle," many West Germans praised their own initiative and failed to acknowledge the guest workers' role. The German population had also restabilized, as rising birthrates helped make up for wartime deaths and alleviated the shortage of able-bodied men. As this new generation of Germans reached adulthood and began entering the labor market in the late 1960s, and as German women increasingly began working outside the home, guest workers were no longer perceived as necessary. Growing condemnation of guest workers "taking the jobs" of Germans – though far less egregious than in the 1980s – both reflected and fueled rising anti-Turkish racism. For West Germany, as for the Turkish government, guest workers represented a financial threat, albeit of a different kind.

West Germany's evolving solutions to the so-called "Turkish problem," both in the 1970s and 1980s, rested on one core premise: financial incentives for return migration. Whereas in the 1980s the West German government would *directly* – and controversially – pay individual guest workers to leave, in the 1970s they initially attempted to work bilaterally with the Turkish government to *indirectly* incentivize guest workers' return. Throughout the 1970s, officials at the West German Foreign Office and the Federal Ministry for Economic Development and Cooperation (BMZ) worked tirelessly to convince the Turkish government to cooperate on programs that would promote guest workers' return under the umbrella of "development aid" (*Entwicklungshilfe*) to Turkey. West Germany's basic idea was simple: by improving the Turkish economy through development aid, and by giving jointly administered financial assistance to individual guest workers who wanted to start their own small businesses, they could convince them to leave.[13] As Matthew Sohm has compellingly argued, tying Turkish return migration to development aid was also part of West Germany's broader strategy of managing the crises of the 1970s and 1980s by "offloading" perceived domestic problems onto countries in the southern European periphery.[14]

Offering development aid to Turkey served not only the goals of domestic policy, but also its Cold War geopolitical goals. In 1961, the same year as the start of the Turkish-German guest worker program, the West German government had institutionalized its newfound commitment to "Third World" development aid in the establishment of the

---

[13] BMA, "Rückkehrförderung ausländischer Arbeitnehmer und ihrer Familienangehörigen," March 5, 1982, PAAA, B 85/1604.
[14] Matthew Sohm, "Paying for the Post-Industrial: The Global Costs of West German and European Capitalist Crisis and Revival, 1972–1988" (PhD diss., Harvard University, 2022).

BMZ. While policymakers genuinely believed in supporting these countries' "modernization," they also aimed to jockey for global influence against their East German rival, which had already begun an extensive development aid program the previous decade.[15] Strategically positioned as a "bridge" between communist Eastern Europe and the oil-rich Middle East, Turkey was especially important to this strategy. Although its 1952 NATO membership aligned it formally with the "First World," and although Turkey's accession to the EEC was a realistic possibility, the BMZ's classification of Turkey as "Third World" reflected West Germans' core belief – bolstered by their impressions of rural guest workers' difficulties integrating into West Germany's modern industrial society – in Turkey's "backwardness."

West Germany had been giving Turkey development aid since 1958, but their attempt to tie the funds to guest workers' return migration began in late 1969, when the BMZ asked the German Confederation of Trade Unions (DGB) to help develop a training program to incentivize guest workers' return.[16] The DGB was instrumental to such a program because trade unions, which represented workers of all nationalities in West Germany, were among the key institutions with close formal ties to guest workers. Coordinated by West Germany's International Federation for Social Work, one of whose board members worked for the DGB, the program solicited guest workers who wished to become mechanics or electricians in Turkey. After completing a twelve-month course, the participants would relocate to Turkey, where they would attend a two-month training course organized by the Turkish government and then search for a job or start their own business. Most enticingly, participants would enjoy a monthly stipend of 150 DM, plus 600 DM if their family returned with them.[17] But there was a catch: they had to remain in

---

[15] William Glenn Gray, *Germany's Cold War: The Global Campaign to Isolate East Germany, 1949–1969* (Chapel Hill: The University of North Carolina Press, 2003), Chapter 5; Young-Sun Hong, *Cold War Germany, the Third World, and the Global Humanitarian Regime* (Cambridge, UK: Cambridge University Press, 2015), 239–49; Sara Lorenzini, *Global Development: A Cold War History* (Princeton: Princeton University Press, 2019). On West German development aid along the inter-German border, see: Astrid M. Eckert, "West German Borderland Aid and European State Aid Control," *Jahrbuch für Wirtschaftsgeschichte* 58, no. 1 (2017): 107–36.

[16] Jelden (BMZ) to Bundesvorstand des DGB, "Betr.: Entwicklungspolitische Förderung und Nutzung der Rückkehr ausländischer Arbeitnehmer (Gastarbeiter) aus Entwicklungsländern in ihre Heimat; hier: Einberufung einer Arbeitsgruppe I," December 18, 1969, AdsD, DGB-Archiv, 5/DGAZ000899.

[17] "Meslek eğitim anlaşması yapıldı," *Anadolu Gazetesi*, September 14, 1972.

Turkey. Violating their signed "commitment to return" agreement would result in an enormous fine of 20,000 DM.

The program was exclusively oriented toward guest workers from Turkey, not only because they were the largest guest worker nationality, but also because West Germany had strong diplomatic relations with Turkey and assumed that Turkey was still eager to embrace guest workers' return. As the organizers put it, "in negotiations in Turkey – in comparison to other countries – one can expect the fewest political hindrances."[18] This optimism, however, was severely misguided. For over a decade, the Turkish government continually frustrated the BMZ with its refusal to cooperate – even when it contradicted the guest workers' best interests. As one official noted with dismay, West Germany was apparently striving to "represent the interests of the Turkish guest workers more strongly than their own government."[19]

Ede Şevki was one of the hundreds of guest workers who applied for the pilot program in 1972. For him, like for many guest workers, the "final return" was not a far-off illusion, but rather a plan that he aimed to put into practice. Hoping to return to Istanbul to open his own auto repair shop, he boldly inquired as to the "exact" amount of money he would receive.[20] He was also enticed by the program's colorful Turkish-language advertisements, which depicted men listening to lectures while looking at mathematical equations on a chalkboard, drafting mechanical schematics with protractors, and wearing smart-looking glasses while supervising the factory floor.[21] The message of professional advancement was simple: joining the program would help them become their own bosses rather than mere peons. Although the translator of Şevki's Turkish-language application letter was impressed that his vocabulary and grammar were at an "exceptionally high level (for a guest worker)," the program had attracted such a large applicant pool that Şevki was not chosen. In fact, organizers were surprised to encounter over 600 potential applicants, whom they praised as "intelligent," "eager to learn," and "goal-oriented."[22] Many of the applicants' interest in West German

[18] "Vorläufiges Ergebnis der Tagung der Arbeitsgruppe I (Aus- und Fortbildung) am 29. Januar 1970," February 4, 1970, AdsD, DGB-Archiv, 5/DGAZ000899.
[19] Deutscher Bundestag, Stenografisches Protokoll, "20. Sitzung des Ausschusses für wirtschaftliche Zusammenarbeit," December 10, 1970, 21, BArch, B 213/5616.
[20] Ede Şevki to Jugendsozialwerk e.V., September 6, 1971, BArch, B 213/5616.
[21] Pamphlet, "Meslekî Eğitim Programı. Makinateknik ve Elektrikteknik," DGB-Archiv, 5/DGAZ000899.
[22] Internationaler Bund für Sozialwerk/Jugendsozialwerk e.V., "Sachbericht," May 1972, BArch, B 213/5617.

assistance, they further reported, stemmed from their "deep mistrust of their own government," which just months before had undergone the 1971 military coup.

Guest workers' experiences of the training program, however, actually intensified their mistrust of the Turkish government. Soon after its inception, the program began to crumble. By May 1972, fifty participants were enrolled in programs in Nuremberg, Cologne, and Frankfurt.[23] Yet, with just two weeks before the Nuremberg trainees' graduation ceremony and scheduled departure for Turkey, details surrounding Turkey's portion of the training program were still unclear. One West German organizer described the program as "still up in the air," with "all questions open." Despite extensive conversations with the Turkish Ministry of Culture and the Turkish Planning Office, he still had no idea "where, when, and how the training courses planned in Turkey would take place." Turkey, he concluded, had "no interest at all" in the program and, by extension, no interest in assisting returning workers. Rather than ensuring their smooth reintegration into Turkey's economy, Turkey was treating its own citizens like "guinea pigs."[24] As Bundestag Vice President Carlo Schmid complained, "I am very troubled by the thought that this useful program, which was initially off to a good start, could fail at the intractability of several subordinate authorities in Turkey."[25] In the words of one German bureaucrat, "These Turks feel that they have been cheated and ditched by the Turkish government."[26]

Despite these difficulties, the two countries agreed to a broader implementation of the program in the December 7, 1972, Treaty of Ankara. Based on the "friendly relations between both countries and their peoples," the treaty aimed to "promote economic and social progress in Turkey" by capitalizing on the guest workers' newly acquired "knowledge and skills."[27] Overseen by a joint committee and funded primarily

[23] Vahit Halefoğlu (Turkish Embassy in Bonn) to Ebersbach, May 15, 1972, AdsD, DGB-Archiv, 5/DGAZ000899.

[24] S. Mete Atsu to Heinz Richter, "Betr.: Positive Entwicklung bei der entwicklungspolitischen Förderung und Nutzung der Rückkehr ausländischer Arbeitnehmer in ihrer Heimat," June 5, 1972, AdsD, DGB-Archiv, 5/DGAZ000899.

[25] Carl Schmid to Erhard Eppler (BMZ), October 10, 1972, AdsD, DGB-Archiv, 5/DGAZ000899.

[26] Erich Arndt to Franz Woschech, DGB Abteilung Organisation Referat Ausländische Arbeitnehmer, "Betr.: Rückgliederungsprogramme für türkische Arbeitnehmer," October 17, 1972, AdsD, DGB-Archiv, 5/DGAZ000899.

[27] *Bundesgesetzblatt*, Teil II, Nr. 33, July 18, 1973; "Bekanntmachung der Abkommen zwischen der Bundesrepublik Deutschland und der Regierung der Republik Türkei über

by West Germany, the project operated on what BMZ officials called the "individual support model": providing funding to the Turkish government, which in turn would support individual returning workers. While this model resembled the pilot program in terms of structure and educational content, it offered increased financial incentives to participants who were interested in starting their own firms in Turkey, including start-up cash, low-interest loans, tax credits, subsidies for materials, and business advice.

The original purpose of the 1972 treaty, as predicated on the individual support model, never materialized. In a 1977 evaluation, BMZ officials complained that Turkey's failure to follow through with the "unmistakable and detailed provisions" owed not to a lack of funding but to the government's "deep-seated indifference to promoting return migration."[28] Still, this "indifference," which BMZ officials later sheepishly realized was a vehement "hostility" to return migration, did not impede Turkey from milking the West German government for millions of Deutschmarks in development aid. Through its heavy-handed negotiation skills and opposition to the individual support model, Turkish officials manipulated the flexibility of the 1972 Treaty of Ankara to convince the West German government to redirect funds earmarked for the program toward their main goal: receiving development aid without an influx of returning guest workers.

In negotiations, Turkish economic planners made it clear that supporting the small businesses of individual returning guest workers who dreamt of owning their own farms, opening local grocery stores, or working as taxi drivers was simply not a macroeconomic priority. Instead, they sought to redirect the development aid toward the financing of large infrastructure projects in the energy, transportation, and urban planning sectors.[29] Specific plans included the construction of the Istanbul subway system and the Atatürk Dam on the Euphrates River, as well as the maintenance of the Bosphorus Bridge connecting the European and Asian sides of Istanbul.[30] Reflecting the Turkish government's disconnect from the needs of its

die Förderung der beruflichen Wiedereingliederung nebst Zusatzprotokoll und über finanzielle Maßnahmen zur Einrichtung eines Kreditsonderfonds," 747–55.
[28] Projektgruppe "Rückkehrförderung" der BMZ und BMA, "Überlegungen und Vorschläge zur Förderung der Rückwanderung ausländischer Arbeitnehmer und Fachkräfte," October 31, 1977, 48, BArch, B 213/13900.
[29] Karl-Otto Henze (BMWi) to Rudolf Vogel, December 27, 1976, PAAA B 26/115913.
[30] German Embassy in Ankara to AA, "Betr.: Zusammenarbeit mit der Türkei; hier: Förderung türkischer Arbeitnehmergesellschaften," April 16, 1982, PAAA, B 58/182485; "Wir haben Deutschland fliehen müssen," *Der Spiegel*, July 8, 1984, 86–94.

citizens abroad, one guest worker complained: "The people say, why a bridge? Instead, they could be building factories so that the people have work ... This is a capitalist government that does little for the workers."[31]

While Turkish officials failed to convince West Germany that supporting major infrastructure projects would indirectly convince guest workers to return, there was one approach upon which the two countries could compromise: the financing of Turkish Workers Collectives (TANGs). Founded on the self-help initiative of groups of guest workers in West Germany, these collectives were joint-stock companies that provided individual guest workers the opportunity to purchase stock in a new firm to be established in Turkey, usually in the agrarian regions from which they came. Guest workers' primary motivation was financial. They wished to secure a job in anticipation of their eventual return to Turkey, reap income from dividends, and compensate for their inability to finance their own individual large investments by jointly purchasing stocks. But, as Turkish sociologist Faruk Şen revealed in his extensive 1980 study of the Workers Collectives, there was also an emotional motivation: investing in the development of their home communities was a means of making a contribution or giving back (Figure 3.1).[32]

The first Workers Collective, Türksan, was founded in December 1966, when a small group of Turkish guest workers living in Cologne gathered in a sports hall and pitched a promising business plan to 2,800 of their colleagues. After pooling their savings, the guest workers would become shareholders in the soon-to-be established industrial firms in Turkey and, upon their return, they would be first in line for jobs. The plan attracted widespread interest. By 1971, thousands of guest workers had invested a total of twenty million DM in Türksan. The company had purchased several plots of land to sell for profit and had opened a wallpaper factory near Istanbul (although, as one West German consular official joked in a pejorative comment on Turkey's underdevelopment, "Who there needs wallpaper?!"). Türksan also planned several schemes to address guest worker families' unique needs: a tourism business offering charter flights for vacationing workers, and grocery stores and duty-free shops for Turks abroad.[33]

---

[31] Hasan K., quoted in Kammrad, »Gast«-Arbeiter-Report, 56.
[32] Faruk Şen, *Türkische Arbeitnehmergesellschaften. Gründung, Struktur und wirtschaftliche Funktion der türkischen Arbeitnehmergesellschaften in der Bundesrepublik Deutschland für die sozioökonomische Lage der Türkei* (Frankfurt am Main: Peter D. Lang, 1980), 57.
[33] "Gastarbeiter: Entwicklungshilfe für die Reiche?" *Der Spiegel*, November 29, 1971, 118–29.

FIGURE 3.1 A vacationing guest worker in a pristine suit stands in front of straw-roofed houses in his impoverished home village, representing guest workers' desire to help Turkey's economic development and modernization, 1970. © Thorsten Scharnhorst/DOMiD-Archiv, Cologne, used with permission.

Reports on Türksan's success spurred guest workers' enthusiasm for investing in other collectives. İbrahim Karakaya, who had worked in Bremen for eight years, was intrigued when he received a letter in 1972 from Örgi-Aktiengesellschaft, a Workers Collective in the Central Anatolian province of Nevşehir. The collective planned to open a textile factory in Kalaba, seven miles from his home village, and asked him to contribute some capital. The offer proved enticing, as Karakaya's prior attempt to start a delivery business in Turkey with a used truck he had bought in Germany had embarrassingly flopped. Eager to make passive income before attempting to establish another potentially unsuccessful business, Karakaya invested 3,000 DM in the collective, paying one-quarter upfront, and he continued to invest more over the years.[34]

---

[34] Michael Weisfeld, "Unter Wölfen. Oder: In Anatolien ist alles beim Alten," *Konkret*, September 1985, 44–47, DOMiD-Archiv, P-15576.

While West Germany reluctantly accepted Workers Collectives as the only viable alternative to their prized individual support model, Turkey embraced them. The 1973 platform of Bülent Ecevit's victorious Republican People's Party (CHP) named Workers Collectives as part of its new "people's sector" (*halk sektörü*) ideology, by which the state would promote economic organization carried out by "individuals and small groups that normally have no possibility to invest."[35] In a television interview years later, Ecevit even publicly attributed the inspiration for the concept of the people's sector to his conversations with guest workers.[36] To facilitate credit acquisition, in 1975 the Turkish government founded the State Industry and Laborer Investment Bank (DESİYAB), which worked closely with Halk-İş, an organization representing Workers Collectives.[37] To evaluate and advise the Workers Collectives, the West German government contracted a private consulting firm.

The Workers Collectives proved an economic boon. By 1975, the number of collectives had doubled to fifty-six, comprising a total of nearly 54,000 shareholders abroad.[38] Within just five years, these numbers quadrupled to 208 collectives and 236,171 shareholders.[39] By 1980, Workers Collectives had invested around 1.5 million DM in Turkey, established ninety-eight new companies, and created 10,000 jobs, with an estimated additional 20,000 jobs being created indirectly.[40] In 1979 and 1980, approximately 10 percent of investments in Turkey were carried out by Turkish Workers Collectives, amounting to a total of two million DM since 1972.[41]

Despite preferring the individual support model, the West German government yielded to Turkish pressure due to a genuine belief in the potential for Workers Collectives to fulfill the dual goals of improving the Turkish economy and promoting remigration. A German bureaucrat who traveled to Turkey's Black Sea region to evaluate eight local Workers Collectives marveled at the "positive effect" on the local economy. Funding the Workers Collectives, he wrote, "currently appears to be the best form of assistance

---

[35] Şen, *Türkische Arbeitnehmergesellschaften*, 65; Ayşe Buğra and Osman Savaşkan, *New Capitalism in Turkey: The Relationship Between Politics, Religion and Business* (Cheltenham: Edward Elgar, 2014), 44.

[36] Murat Ergin Günçe, "Turkey: Turkish Workers' Companies" (Bonn: Friedrich-Ebert Stiftung, 1978), 8, BArch 213/5650.

[37] Şen, *Türkische Arbeitnehmergesellschaften*, 68.

[38] Ibid.

[39] "Wir haben Deutschland fliehen müssen," *Der Spiegel*, July 8, 1984, 86–94.

[40] "Türkische Arbeitnehmer investierten 1,5 Milliarden Mark," *Informationsdienst Entwicklungspolitik*, May 20, 1980, BArch, B 213/13896.

[41] Roland Klein, "Kann finanzielle Hilfe die Türken zur Rückkehr bewegen?" *Frankfurter Allgemeine Zeitung* (*FAZ*), February 1982, 12.

for Turkey."[42] In a 1980 report, West German officials announced that creating 20,000 industrial jobs for returning workers would be a "realistic goal." Although the number of jobs that actually went to returning guest workers "wavers from case to case," the report took comfort in the observation that the bylaws of the Workers Collectives "generally give priority to members who return to Turkey in job placement."[43]

This assumption was severely misguided. After pouring a massive 60 million DM into Workers Collectives over the past decade, West Germany learned a startling truth: most guest workers who had purchased stock in the firms were not planning to return to Turkey to work at them.[44] On the contrary, an extensive 1982 program evaluation revealed that the shareholders had an "irrational" motivation: much like "planting a tree," they desired only to "symbolically support" their home regions, "precisely because of their permanent absence."[45] Even workers who genuinely wished to return were disappointed, as only three out of every hundred jobs went to returning guest workers.[46] Worse, only 10 percent of the Workers Collectives were successful.[47] The vast majority suffered from poor planning, inexperienced management, and insufficient capital.[48] Despite "good intentions," even the first collective, the celebrated Türksan, had distributed dividends only once in the decade since its founding – and a meager 6 percent at that.[49]

These problems were compounded by the realization that the BMZ's definition of a Workers Collective was so lax that it permitted private Turkish businesspeople, who had not migrated to Germany, to exploit West German development aid. Given that only a majority of shareholders needed to be guest workers living in West Germany, Turkish

---

[42] Rudolf Jung, "Bericht über meine Dienstreise in die Türkei vom 23.04-30.04.1980," May 12, 1980, BArch, B 213/13896.
[43] Isoplan, *Türkische Arbeitnehmergesellschaften. Zwischenbericht zur Entwicklung und Beratung wirtschaftlicher Selbsthilfeinitiativen in der Türkei und der Förderung der beruflichen Wiedereingliederung von in der Bundesrepublik beschäftigten Arbeitnehmern in die türkische Wirtschaft*, 3rd edition (Saarbrücken and Istanbul: Isoplan, 1980), 20–21.
[44] BMZ, "Förderung von Arbeitnehmergesellschaften in Entwicklungsländern," 1981, 3, BArch, B 213/13910.
[45] Kreditanstalt für Wiederaufbau to BMZ, AA, BMWi, and Bundesministerium für Finanzen, "Betr.: L I a / Türkei, Rahmenplanung 1982 / Förderung von Arbeitnehmergesellschaften. DM 30 Mio für Arbeitnehmergesellschaften aus Soforthilfemitteln," May 3, 1982, Anlage 2, 1–2, PAAA, B 58/182485.
[46] AA to Frau Dr. Schröder (BMA), "Betr.: Reintegration ausländischer Arbeitnehmer; hier: Deutsch-französische Konsultation, Mai 1984," May 3, 1984, PAAA, B 89/190384.
[47] "Türkisches Modell nur selten erfolgreich," *Handelsblatt*, February 2, 1982.
[48] Şen, *Türkische Arbeitnehmergesellschaften*, 133–63.
[49] Günçe, "Turkey: Turkish Workers' Companies."

businesspeople found a loophole: they could establish a private firm and retain a 49 percent ownership share and, as long as the remaining 51 percent was held by Turks abroad, they could receive the subsidies and benefits of being classified as a Workers Collective.[50] Firms sponsored by private Turkish businesspeople had no incentive to employ guest workers seeking to return. Some, like the textile firm Meric-Textilen-Aktiengesellschaft in Edirne, even expressed reluctance to hire its own shareholders. Instead, the firm believed that returning guest workers, who had become accustomed to the higher income and social services in West Germany, would not be willing to accept the minimum wage typically paid to local agricultural workers (in 1980, 3,300 TL or 236 DM).[51]

Even amid these revelations, Turkey continued to exploit West German naiveté. Desperate to maintain the flow of Deutschmarks, Prime Minister Ecevit jumped to the Workers Collectives' defense: "Whatever has been achieved is the accomplishment of the Turkish worker," and "whatever mistakes have been committed are the fault of others!"[52] When West Germany tried to return to the individual support model throughout the 1980s, Turkish officials' reactions were "not especially encouraging."[53] The final result was bleak. By 1988, sixteen years after signing the Treaty of Ankara and envisioning a large-scale training program to promote return migration through the individual support model, the West German government had distributed only four hundred loans directly to returning guest workers and a mere five hundred had participated in a training program.[54] Although West Germany had succeeded in assisting the Turkish economy, it had failed in its primary goal of convincing guest workers to leave, and was thus wasting its money.[55] As the *Frankfurter Allgemeine Zeitung* put it, this "quite excellent idea" turned out to be a "flop."[56]

---

[50] Şen, *Türkische Arbeitnehmergesellschaften*, 88–91.

[51] Ibid., 183.

[52] Günçe, "Turkey: Turkish Workers' Companies," 35.

[53] "Betr.: 10. Sitzung der deutsch-türkischen Arbeitsgruppe Reintegration am 21.–23.05.1984; hier: Ressortbesprechung am 03.05.1984," May 8, 1984, 2, PAAA, B 58/182487.

[54] "Hilfen für Türken: Schon 400 Kredite," *Ruhr-Nachrichten*, February 13, 1988, AdsD, DGB-Archiv, 5/DGAZ001214.

[55] German Embassy in Ankara to AA, "Betr.: Veranstaltung der DESIYAB-Bank über Arbeitnehmergesellschaften vom 1. –3. September 1983 in Van/Türkei," September 7, 1983, PAAA, B 58/182486.

[56] Detlef Puhl, "Die Rückkehrer haben die Rückkehr selber bezahlt," *FAZ*, September 27, 1985.

MONEY, MANIPULATION, MISTRUST

If the Turkish government sought to portray itself as the caretaker of its citizens abroad, then why did it vehemently oppose programs that would help them realize their dreams of returning to Turkey and starting their own businesses? One important reason was Turkish economic planners' conviction that funneling West German development aid into Workers Collectives would be far more lucrative than helping individual guest workers with what they regarded as frivolous ventures, such as buying a couple dozen cows, opening a bakery, or starting a taxi business. Yet supporting the Workers Collectives did not necessarily preclude entertaining the possibility of West Germany's individual support model. Pursuing both options simultaneously, moreover, would have helped far more guest workers than it did. The real reason cut much deeper: fundamentally, for financial reasons, the Turkish government did not want the guest workers to return.

Since the 1961 start of the guest worker program, the Turkish government made no secret that guest workers were crucial to its economy. Turkey's 1963–1967 development plan touted the program for mitigating unemployment by "exporting surplus labor."[57] But in 1973, the bubble burst. Fearing its own rise in unemployment amid the OPEC oil crisis, West Germany abruptly ceased all new guest worker recruitment. The recruitment stop proved devastating not only to hundreds of thousands of Turks, many of whom were literally standing in line at recruitment offices at the time of the announcement, but also to the Turkish government. In the months before the recruitment stop, a BMZ official involved in the development aid negotiations called it "urgently necessary" to warn the Turkish government of the harsh reality: West Germany "cannot permanently solve the Turkish unemployment problem."[58]

Unable to export additional labor to Germany, the Turkish government desperately hoped that the guest workers who were already there would stay put. During a 1974 visit to Bonn, Turkish Ambassador Vahit Halefoğlu expressed "fears of a mass remigration," as unemployment was expected to double by 1987, compounded by an estimated population growth from 37.5 to 55 million.[59] A decade later, following a

---

[57] T. C. Başbakanlık Devlet Planlama Teşkilatı, *Kalkınma Planı (Birinci Beş Yıl), 1963–1967* (Ankara: DPT, 1963), 455.
[58] BMZ, "Betr.: Wiedereingliederungsprogramm für türkische Arbeitnehmer," June 6, 1973, BArch, B 213/5621.
[59] "Furcht vor einer Massenrückwanderung," *FAZ*, March 16, 1974.

bilateral development aid meeting in 1983, BMZ officials reported that "there is a general fear here that the dam against remigration could break" – even "if one makes exceptions."[60] Returning guest workers, the Turkish government further insisted, "expect too high a salary" and "return to such provinces where no need for their labor exists." Such statements revealed a lack of confidence in the guest workers. Skeptical that even the best-laid and best-financed plans to start small businesses would ever materialize, Turkish officials categorically assumed that returning guest workers would reenter the labor market. Their own government viewed them as destined to fail and, in this way, helped perpetuate their failure.[61]

Even more worrisome than unemployment was the prospect that a mass remigration would lead to a decline in remittance payments, which were crucial not only to guest workers' families but also to the Turkish economy. Like exporting surplus labor, remittances had been a crucial part of Turkey's various Five-Year Development Plans. The 1968–1972 plan affirmed the need to redirect remittances toward investments in productive sectors,[62] the 1973–1977 plan praised remittances as the "most important" factor allowing the country to repay its foreign debt,[63] and the 1979–1983 plan expressed the need for greater state control over remittances and to direct them "rationally" to the National Treasury and State Economic Enterprises.[64] The growing reliance on remittances reflected that they were among the few sources of foreign currency at a time of limited exports and foreign debt.[65] In short, explained *Cumhuriyet* in 1971, Turkey viewed the guest workers as "hens that lay golden eggs," whose key duty was to "fill the vaults of the Central Bank."[66]

As early as the 1960s, the Turkish government enacted measures to facilitate the transfer of guest workers' Deutschmarks. The Turkish Postal Service prepared bilingual remittance forms, and the government

[60] German Embassy in Ankara to AA, "Betr.: Zusammenarbeit mit Türkei; hier: Einzelförderung Rückkehr interessierter türkischer Arbeitnehmer," June 28, 1983, PAAA, B 85/1605.

[61] Ibid.

[62] T. C. Başbakanlık Devlet Planlama Teşkilatı, *Kalkınma Planı (İkinci Beş Yıl)*, 1968–1972 (Ankara: DPT), 93.

[63] T. C. Başbakanlık Devlet Planlama Teşkilatı, *Kalkınma Planı (Üçüncü Beş Yıl)*, 1973–1978 (Ankara: DPT, 1973).

[64] T. C. Başbakanlık Devlet Planlama Teşkilatı, *Kalkınma Planı (Dördüncü Beş Yıl)*, 1979–1983 (Ankara: DPT, 1979), 267.

[65] Zülküf Aydın, *The Political Economy of Turkey* (London: Press, 2005), 37.

[66] "İşçilerimiz sadece altın yumurtlayan tavuk değil," *Cumhuriyet*, December 6, 1971.

detailed the step-by-step process in advice books printed for workers living abroad.[67] To ensure that guest workers' money yielded interest for the government, a 1973 advice book cautioned guest workers against sending cash home in envelopes – a crime that, if caught, could lead to federal prosecution.[68] While guest workers seeking to transfer money by mail could fill out a handwritten remittance form at a German post office, the advice book warned them about numerous problems, such as having insufficient language skills to handwrite the sum in German, and that transferring sums larger than 1,300 DM required two forms. The best option, the advice book counseled, was to use the special postal checks offered by Turkish banks, as the German employees representing the banks could help fill out the forms. Efforts to direct guest workers' remittances through formal channels thus tightened the two countries' institutional relationships.

Filling out remittance forms was a central part of guest workers' everyday lives, and Turks sent more money home on a regular basis than other guest worker nationalities (Figure 3.2).[69] Murad, whose father opened a tailor shop in Witten after spending several years as a guest worker, marveled at the number of guest workers who visited the tailor shop daily not to have their pants hemmed or suits taken in, but rather to fill out paperwork. Although Murad did not fully understand the process as a child, his father told him that the pieces of paper featuring colorful pictures of Turkish landmarks that he stored behind the counter were remittance forms (*havale deftleri*). Often with assistance from Murad's father, who could speak both Turkish and German and was thus in a relatively privileged position, the guest workers filled out the forms, indicating the number of Deutschmarks to transfer, the recipient's name, and the bank branch in Turkey where the money would be picked up. The guest workers then took the forms to a German bank or a Turkish bank with branches in Germany, basing their decisions on the lowest transaction fees.[70]

The Turkish government also developed schemes to incentivize guest workers to deposit their Deutschmarks in savings accounts at Turkish banks. With the introduction of convertible Turkish lira deposits (CTLDs) in 1967, guest workers could open special accounts in Turkish commercial banks at an interest rate that was 1.75 percent higher than

[67] "Türkiye'ye posta ile para gönderme sağlandı," *Anadolu Gazetesi*, December 1963, 4.
[68] Araslı and Araslı, *Almanya'daki Türk İşçilerin Hak ve Görevleri*, 193–95.
[69] Østergaard-Nielsen, *Transnational Politics*, 35.
[70] Murad B., interview.

FIGURE 3.2 Guest workers send remittances at Türkiye Halk Bankası, one of
the many Turkish banks with branches in West Germany, ca. 1970.
© DOMiD-Archiv, Cologne, used with permission.

the Euromarket rate. Sweetening the deal, the publicly owned Turkish
Republican Central Bank guaranteed the principal and interest against
the risk of a potential lira devaluation. The Turkish government, too,
benefitted from the CTLDs, which constituted short-term loans in
Deutschmarks. In terms of process, the commercial banks transferred
guest workers' deposited Deutschmarks directly to the Turkish Central
Bank, which returned the adjusted sum in lira and further loaned the
Deutschmarks to state-owned enterprises for the financing of imports,
long-term investment projects, and the repayment of foreign debt. In
1975, luxuriating in the massive influx of foreign currency, the Turkish
government extended the opportunity to hold CTLDs to all nonresidents,
including foreign corporations.[71]

---

[71] Merih Celâsun and Dani Rodrik, "Economic Boom and Debt Crisis, 1973–77," in
Jeffrey D. Sachs and Susan M. Collins, eds., *Developing Country Debt and Economic
Performance* (Chicago: University of Chicago Press, 1989), 640.

As part of the CTLD scheme, the Turkish government also sought out a West German partnership. In a 1976 agreement between the Turkish Central Bank and West Germany's Dresdner Bank, the Turkish government offered up to an additional 1 percent in interest for guest workers who opened convertible accounts at Dresdner Bank, which would then transfer the Deutschmarks to the Turkish Central Bank in exchange for lira.[72] The two banks, cooperating with West Berlin's Bank for Trade and Industry, advertised their joint services to guest workers in a colorful pamphlet featuring the bold Turkish text "How to Open a Foreign Savings Account" over a backdrop of alternating lira and Deutschmark bills.[73] The back cover provided examples in both languages to assist customers in voicing their requests for transfers, withdrawals, and deposits. In another pamphlet, the Turkish Central Bank boasted about its advantageous exchange rate due to its partnerships and cautioned workers to avoid trading money on the black market. Appealing to the guest workers' nostalgia and nationalism, the pamphlet suggested that investing would offer "endless possibilities, both for you and for your country."[74]

The Dresdner Bank partnership notwithstanding, West German and Turkish banks typically engaged in fierce competition for guest workers' Deutschmarks. In one ethno-marketing advertisement, the West German bank Sparkasse boasted in Turkish that "Every Sparkasse is ready to help you" (Figure 3.3).[75] Yet West German banks could hardly compete: a survey of guest workers in Duisburg revealed that 83.5 percent of their deposits were in Turkish banks, and only 13.5 percent in German ones.[76] Turkish banks' success lay partially in their savvy appeals to guest workers' nostalgia for their homeland and separation from their loved ones. Yapı ve Kredi Bankası distributed an advertisement depicting a guest worker family in their living room with a framed photo of a faraway relative hanging on the wall, captioned: "When exchanging currency or sending remittances, the savings account you have opened at Yapı Kredi guarantees high returns for the relatives you have left behind

---

[72] Lavy and Rapoport, "External Debt and Structural Adjustment," 325.
[73] Türkiye Cumhuriyet Merkez Bankası, "Döviz hesabı nasil açılır?" 1970s, DOMiD-Archiv, SD 0311,0000a.
[74] Türkiye Cumhuriyet Merkez Bankası, "Her türlü işçi dövizi için 1 DM = 726,54 kuruş," 1976, DOMiD-Archiv, BR 0622.
[75] Advertisement for Sparkasse, in Erdoğan Olcayto, ed., *Almanya İş Rehberi 1981* (Bonn: Anadolu Yayınları, 1981), DOMiD-Archiv, OS 0082.
[76] Ölçen, *Türken und Rückkehr*, 90.

FIGURE 3.3 The West German bank Sparkasse courted Turkish clients with a Turkish-language ethno-marketing advertisement stating, "Every Sparkasse is ready to help you," ca. 1980. © Deutscher Sparkassen- und Giroverband e. V., used with permission.

in the homeland."⁷⁷ Türkiye İş Bankası appealed to Turkish nationalism, insisting that its financial advisors were not only "friendly people eager to answer your questions" but also, most importantly, "your own people who speak your own language."⁷⁸

Not only banks but also consumer goods corporations courted guest workers' Deutschmarks through nationalist appeals. This trend was particularly pronounced in the cigarette market. An advertisement for the Turkish cigarette brand Topkapı, targeting guest workers, depicted a cartoon cigarette box with a speech bubble uttering Atatürk's famous assertion, "How happy I am to be a Turk." The accompanying text reported that Turks in West Germany spent 500 million DM annually on cigarettes and argued that, if they gave this to Topkapı instead of foreign companies, then they would "support the development of our homeland."⁷⁹ Even non-Turkish companies pursued this strategy. A competing advertisement for the American cigarette company Camel touted the tobacco's Turkish origin. Because Camel's tobacco was cultivated in Izmir and was a "Turkish and American blend," even this US-based company could be considered "part of the homeland."⁸⁰

The push to court guest workers' Deutschmarks did not always work. Strategically navigating the competing options, guest workers made their investment and purchasing decisions based on their and their families' consumer preferences and financial interests rather than on nationalist rhetoric. To diversify their portfolios and take advantage of offers of high interest rates, many deposited their savings in multiple banks. One guest worker in Dortmund, Osman Gürlük, divided the minimal savings from his low monthly salary of 1,200 DM between three Turkish and West German banks – one in Istanbul and two in Dortmund – and boasted that he had saved 5,000 DM in three years, not including the remittances he sent to his wife and child in Turkey.⁸¹ Guest workers' financial prioritization of family over nation became especially apparent amid the rise in family migration of the 1970s. As they increasingly brought their spouses and children to West Germany and began to settle there more

---

⁷⁷ Advertisement for Yapı ve Kredi Bankası, on the back cover of Olcayto, ed., *Almanya İş Rehberi 1981*.
⁷⁸ Advertisement for the Frankfurt branch of Türkiye İş Bankası, in ibid.
⁷⁹ Advertisement for Topkapı Cigarettes, in ibid.
⁸⁰ Advertisement for Camel Turkish and American Blend Cigarettes, in ibid.
⁸¹ Von der Grün, *Leben im gelobten Land*, 12.

permanently, they had less need to send money home. Simultaneously, the economic downturn and rising unemployment after the 1973 OPEC oil crisis left many guest workers strapped for cash and unable to deposit as much into Turkish banks.

These factors, alongside West Germany's decision to stop recruiting guest workers in 1973, led to a stark decline in remittances during the 1970s. The percentage of guest workers who regularly sent money to Turkey declined from two-thirds in 1971 to just 43 percent in 1980.[82] Between 1965 and 1974, the total amount of money guest workers sent to Turkey had quadrupled to 4.6 billion USD.[83] But abruptly, the annual remittance sum plummeted by nearly one-third, from 1.4 billion USD in 1974 to just 980 million USD in 1976, and hovered there through 1978. Remittances temporarily recovered in the first half of 1979 due to the 44 percent devaluation of the lira and a brief return to confidence in investment, but they declined again later that year due to continued political and economic instability. Not until the 1980s, when the economy began to recover following the postcoup neoliberal economic overhaul, did remittances return to a steady rate.

The nosedive in remittances had serious consequences (Figure 3.4). Not only did the decline cost Turkey 1.7 percent of its Gross National Product (GNP) for 1974–1976, but it also exacerbated the country's foreign debt crisis amid the international oil shocks of the 1970s. Between 1973 and 1977, the same period as the decline in remittances, Turkey's foreign debt jumped from 3 billion USD to 11 billion USD, accounting for a rise from 8 percent to 23 percent of the country's GNP.[84] The political instability and repeated changing of governments throughout the 1970s – coupled with policymakers' refusal to reform their failing economic policies – made Turkey highly susceptible to global recessions and price fluctuations, and the Turkish Central Bank's excessive short-term borrowing through guest workers' CTLDs contributed markedly to the accumulation of debt. Of all the debtor countries, Turkey's situation was particularly dire: Turkey alone held 69 percent of the total debt among the developing countries that worked with the IMF and the World Bank to reschedule their foreign payment obligations and

---

[82] Pagenstecher, "Die 'Illusion' der Rückkehr," 154.
[83] Abadan-Unat et al., *Migration and Development*, 101. See the chart in Güzin Emel Akkuş, "The Contribution of the Remittances of Turkish Workers in Germany to the Balance of Payments of Turkey (1963–2013)," in Elif Nuroğlu et al., eds., *Turkish German Affairs from an Interdisciplinary Perspective* (Frankfurt am Main: Peter Lang, 2015), 185–212.
[84] Lavy and Rapoport, "External Debt and Structural Adjustment," 314, 316.

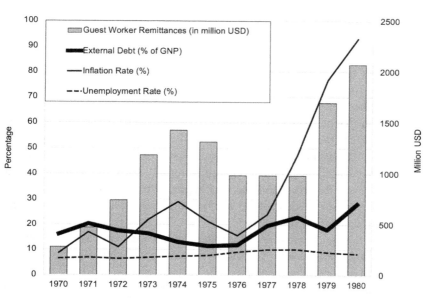

FIGURE 3.4 Significance of guest workers' remittances to the Turkish economy. Examining the 1976–1978 period in particular reveals that the stark decline in remittances exacerbated Turkey's economic crisis by coinciding with a detrimental rise in external debt, inflation, and unemployment. Graph created by author.[85]

to implement structural adjustment and austerity programs between 1978 and 1980.[86] Although Turkey's foreign debt as percentage of GNP continued to rise throughout the 1980s, the growth reflects the five Structural Adjustment Loans granted by the World Bank and the IMF from 1980 to 1984, which had an overall stabilizing effect on the Turkish economy.[87]

[85] Data were compiled from the following sources: Akkuş, "The Contribution of the Remittances of Turkish Workers in Germany to the Balance of Payments of Turkey (1963–2013)"; Levent Şahin and Kadir Yıldırım, "On Dukuzuncu Yüzyıldan Günümüze Türkiye'de İşsizlikle Mücadele Politikalarının Gelişimi," *Çalışma ve Toplum*, vol. 45 (2015), 123–25; The World Bank, "External Debt Stocks (% of GNI) - Turkey," data.worldbank .org/indicator/DT.DOD.DECT.GN.ZS?locations=TR; The World Bank, "Inflation, GDP deflator (annual %) – Turkey," data.worldbank.org/indicator/NY.GDP.DEFL .KD.ZG?end=1992&locations=TR&start=1961&view=chart.
[86] Celâsun and Rodrik, "Economic Boom and Debt Crisis, 1973–77," 631.
[87] Ziya Öniş, "The Evolution of Privatization in Turkey: The Institutional Context of Public-Enterprise Reform," *International Journal of Middle East Studies* 23, no. 3 (1991): 165.

But for ordinary individuals living in the throes of the 1977–1979 debt crisis, the economic recovery of the 1980s was difficult to imagine, and any optimism was overshadowed by the turmoil they confronted in their everyday lives. By 1980, inflation had skyrocketed to over 90 percent, leading to a 250 percent increase in the price of oil.[88] Policymakers hurriedly implemented austerity measures in January through a 30 percent devaluation of the lira and a prioritization of exports over internal consumption. Still, the winter months proved especially harsh. Individuals and families who were unable to afford oil and coal endured freezing, unheated homes.[89] They likewise struggled to afford everyday commodities like sugar, coffee, cigarettes, and alcohol.[90] This misery exacerbated the ongoing political unrest that motivated the 1980 military coup.

Aware that guest workers' declining remittances were aggravating the debt crisis, observers who had not migrated, particularly in the Turkish media and government, began openly criticizing guest workers' spending habits. Among the most vocal was *Milliyet* columnist Örsan Öymen, who had lived in West Germany while working as an editor at Westdeutscher Rundfunk. In a provocative column, Öymen blamed Turkey's woes on the guest workers' selfish refusal to send remittances. Remittances, he argued, were guest workers' civic duty – their means of giving back to their homeland in exchange for their special privileges, such as the ability to import certain goods duty-free. To boost remittances, and to help Turkey escape the "yoke of foreign financial capital institutions," Öymen proposed a law that would force guest workers to remit a mandatory sum set by the Turkish government. By his calculation, if each guest worker transferred 20 DM daily in remittances to their families or bank accounts in Turkey, that would amount to 7.2 billion DM or 4 billion USD annually. "Is it not the state's right to demand a sacrifice from these workers, such as sending remittances to their country?" he inquired. "Why would that be unfair?"[91]

Incensed by Öymen's column, guest workers flooded his mailbox with a storm of angry letters and derided him as an "intellectual" who was out

---

[88] Findley, *Turkey, Islam, Nationalism, and Modernity: A History*, 329.
[89] Öniş and Webb, *Political Economy of Policy Reform in Turkey in the 1980s*, 4.
[90] Feroz Ahmad, *Turkey: The Quest for Identity*, revised ed. (London: OneWorld, 2014), 147.
[91] Örsan Öymen, "Yurt dışına ayrıcalık," *Milliyet*, February 24, 1979, 9; Örsan Öymen, "İşçi dövizleri," *Milliyet*, March 20, 1979, 9.

of touch with their problems.[92] At fault were not the guest workers themselves, one insisted, but rather the corrupt and profiteering Turkish banks, which "think of nothing other than snatching the marks from the workers' hands." The most outrage, however, was directed at the Turkish government, which had spent the remittances "irresponsibly" through failed import–export policies and had not offered an exchange rate that was competitive with the black market, where it was possible to get a 50 percent return on the sale of Deutschmarks. Without referencing the bilateral development aid negotiations directly, another man questioned why the Turkish government had refused to provide loans to individual guest workers who wanted to invest in Turkey or had encountered financial problems. The government's seeming apathy or hostility toward its citizens' needs was all the worse, one man wrote, because "we are masses of patriotic workers," who have "contributed to the country's development" by "pouring out sweat" and "scavenging European countries' waste and trash off the streets."

Amid this outcry, the Turkish government made no secret of its economically based opposition to return migration. In April 1982, *Der Tagesspiegel* reported that after four days of intensive talks with Turkish Foreign Minister İlter Türkmen and Prime Minister Bülent Ulusu, West Berlin Mayor Richard von Weizsäcker "now understands better than before that Turkey, amid its economic situation and high native unemployment, cannot be interested in a large wave of remigration."[93] Several months later, the Turkish tabloid *Güneş* ran a front-page article reporting the guest workers' concerns that their countrymen would be hostile to their return. The migrants had learned of the Turkish population's fears that they would overburden the labor market and "evaporate any hopes that those currently unemployed would ever find a job."[94] A *Der Spiegel* article exposed the central tension clearly: while the Turkish government "appears" to harbor a "humane concern for the fate of their countrymen," they are primarily concerned with "tangible economic interests" and a mass remigration would "plague" the country.[95]

The association between the guest workers' remittances and the Turkish government's disinterest in their return was clearest during a tense January

[92] Örsan Öymen, "İşçi Dövizleri. Okurlardan Kazan'a," *Milliyet*, March 20, 1979, 9.
[93] Axel Göritz, "Kein deutscher Druck zum Heimkehr von Türken aus Berlin," *Der Tagesspiegel*, April 1, 1982.
[94] *Güneş*, October 7, 1982, quoted in German Embassy in Ankara to AA, "Betr.: Ausländerpolitik; hier: türkische Presse," October 7, 1982, PAAA, B 85/1614.
[95] "Deutsche abgestempelt," *Der Spiegel*, July 29, 1983, 20.

1983 meeting in the northwestern Turkish city of Bolu, where representatives of several local Turkish Workers Collectives, Turkey's DESİYAB Bank, and West German and Turkish government officials met to discuss how guest workers' savings could be used to finance the development of the Turkish economy.[96] The Turkish newspaper *Hürriyet* reported that these tensions came to a head in a contentious "duel of words" between West German State Secretary Siegfried Lengl of the BMZ and Turkish Finance Minister Adnan Başer Kafaoğlu. When Lengl began to plea for Turkish understanding of West Germany's labor market concerns and the urgent need for workers to return to their home country, Kafaoğlu abandoned his prepared speech and firmly underscored the significance of guest worker remittance payments to the Turkish national economy. "Turkey needs the workers' remittances for many years to come," the newspaper paraphrased, "and she will not pull back her workers."[97]

The realization that the Turkish government prioritized guest workers' Deutschmarks over their own well-being soured the migrants' impression of their homeland. Saim Çetinbaş, a former guest worker who had opened a Turkish grocery store in West Berlin, explained how he had repeatedly sought to heed the call for investment but had received no official assistance and only trouble from the Turkish government. The most devastating of his many failed business ventures involved a pickle factory that he opened from West Germany on a 22,000 square-meter plot of land in Çerkezköy. After he closed the factory at a loss of 2 million DM, the municipal government apparently seized the rest of the land with no notice and no recompense. Rather than "thanking" him for investing his Deutschmarks, the government "always makes things more difficult," he complained. His scorn, however, extended to the Turkish population as a whole: "In the eyes of Turkey, we are all viewed as marks. No one thinks about us as having flesh and blood." Outraged, Çetinbaş swore never to permanently return to Turkey. For him, it was only a "beautiful vacation country," where his children happily sunbathed along the Mediterranean Sea each summer. As for any deeper connection to Turkey, "I don't think about those who don't think about me."[98]

---

[96] German Embassy in Ankara to AA, "Betr.: Seminar über das Thema 'Die Finanzierung unseres wirtschaftlichen Wachstums' vom 20. bis 23.01.1983 in der Türkei," January 25, 1983, PAAA, B 58/182486.

[97] German Embassy in Ankara to AA, "Betr.: Veranstaltung türkischer Arbeitnehmergesellschaften vom 21. –23.01.1983 in Bolu," January 26, 1983, PAAA, B 58(ZA)/182486.

[98] "Türkiye, benim için artık güzel bir tatil ülkesi," *Cumhuriyet*, May 15, 1984.

This mistrust and sense of betrayal went much further, however, and became a core component of the way that guest workers viewed their changing relationship to Turkey. A 1983 study conducted by the University of Ankara and the University of Duisburg–Essen revealed that a startling 90 percent of Turkish guest workers in West Germany believed that the Turkish government viewed them only as sources of remittances.[99] İsmail Akar, who had worked in Germany from 1963 to 1980, encapsulated this sentiment in a scathing interview with *Milliyet*: "If you ask me, the first priority of past politicians was to abandon our workers in Germany like a burdensome, barren herd. They view us as remittance machines."[100] By viewing the guest workers so starkly in economic terms – not just as laborers, but as machines churning out Deutschmarks – Turkey stripped guest workers of their humanity and relegated their wishes to the back-burner. Although West Germany also viewed guest workers in economic terms, the pain stung worse when it came from a faraway homeland to which many guest workers yearned to return.

SERVE IN THE MILITARY – OR PAY

The Turkish government also exploited the Deutschmarks of guest work-ers' children by providing the option for military-age youths living in West Germany to serve only two rather than twenty months of mandatory mil-itary service. This "military service by payment" (*bedelli askerlik*), as it was called, came with a catch: a price of 20,000 DM. This hefty sum, over six months of wages for the average Turkish migrant, was an impos-sibility for the up to 400,000 young men between the ages of eighteen and thirty-two affected by the policy. Facing the prospect of losing their jobs after long absences, they resorted to desperate measures to come up with the money. By the mid-1980s, the notion that the Turkish govern-ment was maliciously exploiting its young countrymen's Deutschmarks prompted a wave of grassroots activism, attracting the support of sympa-thetic West German observers eager to criticize the Turkish government.

Mandatory military service in Turkey had a long history. The 1927 Military Law, passed just four years after the fall of the Ottoman Empire and the establishment of the Turkish Republic, applied not only to

---

[99] "Fast die Hälfte der Türken möchte nicht mehr zurück," *Westdeutsche Allgemeine Zeitung* (*WAZ*), September 18, 1984. This statistic is also cited in: Ölçen, *Türken und Rückkehr*, 127.

[100] "Bunalım ikinci ve üçüncü kuşakta," *Milliyet*, January 22, 1983, 9.

able-bodied men born in Turkey but also, explicitly, to "immigrants" and "foreigners" who had Turkish citizenship, even if they lived abroad. Because those between twenty and forty-one years of age were subject to an eighteen-month basic training and draft lottery, the law posed a particular conundrum for guest workers, many of whom had migrated to Germany at precisely that age and who, due to unscrupulous employers eager to fire Turks, encountered difficulties returning to Turkey without losing their jobs. The law also affected guest workers' children born in Turkey but brought to Germany, who reached adulthood abroad. To remedy the situation, the Turkish government amended the law in 1976. Whereas citizens living in Turkey could postpone their military service for only two years, those living abroad could petition the consulate for postponement every two years until age thirty-eight.[101]

In 1979, at the height of Turkey's foreign currency crisis, the Turkish government revised the Military Law to permit citizens abroad to pay their way into a shortened two-month military service. As so often with Turkish policies toward the migrants abroad, the goal was primarily financial. Prime Minister Bülent Ecevit's major announcement of the draft amendment came in a speech on plans to strengthen the economy and to "make use of" guest workers' remittances, while Defense Minister Neşet Akmandor publicly explained that the policy would be the "most efficient and effective use of a large and important resource."[102] Reflecting the policy's orientation particularly toward Turks in West Germany, the revised Military Law explicitly cast the sum not in lira but in "Deutschmarks or the equivalent in other currencies." While Ecevit set the price at 5,000 DM, the amendment, as passed the next year under the new prime minister, Süleyman Demirel, reduced the period of service to one month and doubled the price to 10,000 DM.

The price abruptly doubled again to 20,000 DM following Turkey's 1980 military coup, when the authoritarian government ushered in an era of increased societal militarization and attacked the economic crisis by decree. By January 1982, Turkey had pocketed an impressive 2.4 billion lira in military exemption fees, the vast majority of which went to the Defense Ministry budget.[103] A few years later, this number climbed

---

[101] *Turkey: Law No. 111 of 1927, Military Law*, trans. UN Refugee Agency (UNHCR), www.refworld.org/docid/3ae6b4do2o.html.

[102] Bülent Ecevit, Speech to CHP Concerning the Program to Strengthen the Economy, trans. George T. Park, March 21, 1979, BArch, B 213/5650; "Dövizle askerlik tasarısı yeniden düzenleniyor," *Cumhuriyet*, April 9, 1979.

[103] "MSB, dövizli askerlikten 2 milyarlık gelir elde etti," *Cumhuriyet*, January 15, 1982, 10.

to 500 million DM – a "welcome injection of cash," marveled one West German newspaper, considering that Turkey had over 30 billion USD in foreign debt.[104]

Always eager to report on guest workers' relationships to their home countries, and to portray the Turkish government negatively, the West German media expressed a curious fascination with the topic of "guest workers in uniform." Repeatedly, journalists emphasized that the exorbitant 20,000 DM price tag reflected not only the postcoup authoritarianism and militarization of Turkish society but also the government's desire to exploit the workers' Deutschmarks. Compared to other guest worker nationalities, this assessment rang true. By the 1980s, military-age Greek citizens living abroad could pay between 500 and 1,000 DM for an exemption, Portuguese men could pay a meager 90 DM, and Italians and Spaniards enjoyed exemptions free of charge. Only Yugoslavs faced harsher restrictions than Turks, as the outright lack of exemptions meant that they had to return to Yugoslavia for a fifteen-month period of service.[105]

Still, even paying the 20,000 DM did not free guest workers from conflicts with their employers, which became matters of dispute in West German courts. Amid unemployment and rising anti-Turkish racism, even a two-month absence for a shortened military service could cost a Turkish worker his job, or at least several months of wages. While West Germany's 1957 Law for Job Protection in Case of Conscription guaranteed that workers would not be terminated from their jobs during their military service, the law did not apply to guest workers.[106] In 1981, a thirty-two-year-old Turkish guest worker successfully sued the Krupp steel factory for refusing to grant him unpaid vacation for his military service (thereby firing him) and won 4,000 DM in wages.[107] Others lost their cases. Several months later, a Regional Labor Court in Hamm ruled against a guest worker in a similar situation, determining that the employer had not violated his "duty of care."[108]

---

[104] "Türkische Wehrpflichtige vor Wahl: Freikaufen oder Arbeitsplatzverlust," *Neue Westfälische Zeitung*, July 25, 1986.
[105] Roland Kirbach, "Wenn die Heimat ruft," *Die Zeit*, October 26, 1984.
[106] *Gesetz über den Schutz des Arbeitsplatzes bei Einberufung zum Wehrdienst* (*ArbPlSchG*), April 1, 1957, www.gesetze-im-internet.de/arbplschg/.
[107] Arbeitsgericht Bochum, Geschäfts-Nr.: 3 Ca 1/81, May 13, 1981, AdsD, DGB-Archiv, 5/DGAZ000988.
[108] "Landesarbeitsrichter entschieden: Türke ohne Anspruch auf Sonderurlaub für den Kurz-Wehrdienst," *WAZ*, June 3, 1982.

The judicial ambivalence was finally settled in September 1983, when the Federal Labor Court in Kassel ruled that "German employers must grant leave to and later reemploy Turkish citizens for the length of the shortened mandatory military service in Turkey."[109] This victory, however, was limited. Privileging wealthier guest workers, the protection applied only to those who had enough money to finance the 20,000 DM for a shortened military service, meaning that employers could still legally fire guest workers whose inability to pay the sum required them to complete the full eighteen months. As Mete Atsu, a Turkish board member of the German Confederation of Trade Unions, complained, "What employer is voluntarily willing to keep a job open for a Turk for eighteen months?"[110] This discrepancy was especially troubling to guest workers' children, who, upon reaching adulthood and entering the job market, were not only lower-paid but also dispensable. "Normally, twenty- to thirty-year-olds would be establishing their livelihoods," noted a Turkish social worker. "Now they have to give the money to the state."[111]

Horror stories of the harsh conditions in the postcoup Turkish military, widely reported in the West German media, intensified the need to scramble together the 20,000 DM. An exposé in *Vorwärts*, the Social Democratic Party's official newspaper, publicized the miserable experience of Ramazan Türkoğlu, a telecommunications worker in Cologne who had returned from his two-month basic training in Burdur: he and the other eighty recruits were forced to sleep in a small and poorly ventilated room, he had observed a corporal brutally beating a recruit, and rumor had it that the food was laced with medications to suppress their libidos.[112] For regime opponents, the sheer prospect of returning to Turkey posed a threat. Hamza Sinanoğlu, who had lobbied on behalf of Kurdish asylum seekers in West Germany, was detained for a week immediately upon arriving in Turkey for his military service. Sahabedin Buz was tortured for five months after the military courts accused him of reading the IG Metall trade union newspaper and collaborating with communists.[113]

---

[109] Karl-Heinz Bernhard, "BAG-Urteil schützt Türken. Recht auf Weiterbeschäftigung nach verkürztem Wehrdienst," *FR*, October 23, 1982. The article refers to the case number as 7 AZR 433/82.

[110] Kirbach, "Wenn die Heimat ruft."

[111] Dieter Wonka, "Da kannst du dir nur den Finger abschneiden," *Neue Presse*, April 24, 1985.

[112] Dirk Kurbjuweit, "Mit Schlagen und Fußtritten auf Linie getrimmt," *Vorwärts*, July 26, 1984.

[113] Ulrich Schauen, "In Haft, weil unbequem. Türken: Vom Wehrdienst ins Gefängnis," *WAZ*, July 26, 1984.

With these dual anxieties of losing their jobs and subjecting themselves to the harsh conditions in Turkey, many military-age youths scrambled to pay their way out of military service by any means necessary – even if they could not afford the 20,000 DM. For those who had become self-sufficient, one option was to sell their businesses. One man living in Bockenheim placed a personal advertisement in the Turkish newspaper *Hürriyet*, announcing his intent to sell his specialty Balkan grocery store in West Germany to make "the money necessary for my military service," while another sought to sell his tailor shop "urgently" for the same reason.[114] Given that most military-age youths were wage laborers, however, a more common option was to turn to their parents for financial assistance. But even if their parents had worked in Germany for two decades, they could often not afford the 20,000 DM price tag and, even if they could, they planned to use it toward their dream of returning to Turkey. The burden on parents' wallets was especially difficult for families with multiple children. A family with four sons, for example, would be required to come up with 80,000 DM – an impossibility for the vast majority of parents. Parents were thus forced to choose which of their children they would assist, if any.

Absent financial assistance from their parents, many young men attempted to finance the 20,000 DM by taking out loans. Going through formal channels, however, proved difficult. Wary of taking risks on Turkish youths they deemed likely to lose their jobs and thus default on their loans, West German banks generally granted a maximum of 6,000 DM.[115] The banks also required loan-seeking Turkish customers to provide financial guarantees (*Bürgschaften*) from two other individuals, one of whom had to be German.[116] To circumvent these hindrances, many men resorted to taking loans from wealthy private individuals, "dubious money-lenders," and "loan sharks," all of whom charged exorbitant interest rates.[117] West German journalists emphasized that the pressure to repay the loans forced the young men into money-making criminal activities such as the illicit drug trade – an assessment reflecting long-standing tropes about Turkish men's criminality.[118] In one sensationalist article, *Hürriyet* reported the case of a twenty-eight-year-old migrant in

---

[114] Personal advertisements in *Hürriyet*, February 11, 1984, and June 2, 1984.
[115] Kirbach, "Wenn die Heimat ruft."
[116] Andreas Fritzenkötter, "Junge Türken sind verzweifelt," *Rheinische Post* (*RP*), November 3, 1984.
[117] Wonka, "Da kannst du dir nur den Finger abschneiden."
[118] Kirbach, "Wenn die Heimat ruft."

Bielefeld who was allegedly murdered by a family member for demanding that his father-in-law repay a 20,000 DM loan so that he could use it to pay his way out of military service.[119]

Those who simply ignored their military conscription faced harsh long-term consequences. Under Turkey's 1930 Law on Absentee Conscripts and Draft Evaders, even a one-day delay in arrival to military service during peacetime could result in imprisonment of up to one month.[120] And given that Turkey, unlike West Germany, did not recognize conscientious objection, saving face by claiming to oppose military service on moral or religious grounds was not an option. One young man who decided not to report to basic training told the *Rheinische Post* that he had come to deeply regret the decision. The Turkish consulate had refused to renew his passport and was threatening to revoke his Turkish citizenship altogether. As a "stateless person" without a passport, he would face deportation to Turkey, where he would surely be imprisoned for draft evasion.[121]

Feeling exploited not only by the loan sharks but also by the Turkish government, young Turkish men living in West Germany spoke out against the 20,000 DM and banded together in activism. In March 1984, discussions in schools, coffee houses, and workplaces consolidated into a formal protest movement with the establishment of the Federal Initiative of Military-Age Youth from Turkey (FEBAG). The grassroots organization, run by military-age youths themselves, initiated a letter-writing campaign to the Turkish government demanding a reduction of the price to a more manageable 5,000 DM.[122] With initial branches in the Ruhr cities of Bochum, Gelsenkirchen, and Herne, FEBAG quickly spread to nearly one hundred West German cities, where its members staged well-attended demonstrations featuring Turkish food and recreational activities like soccer tournaments and breakdancing. The organization also distributed a Turkish-language newsletter called *Bedel*, which alongside well-argued articles about the cause also contained effective cartoons, such as a drawing of a man being crushed by the weight of a 20,000 DM money bag. In another particularly striking cartoon, a man

---

[119] "Mehmet'i kim öldürdü?" *Hürriyet*, June 24, 1984.
[120] *Turkey: Law of 1930 on Absentee Conscripts, Draft Evaders, Persons Unregistered [For Military Service], and Deserters*, www.refworld.org/docid/3ae6b4d01c.html.
[121] Fritzenkötter, "Junge Türken sind verzweifelt."
[122] "Bedel 5 Bine indirilsin iş güvencesi sağlansın!" *Bedel*, April 1984. All issues of *Bedel* are available at Türkiye Sosyal Tarih Araştırma Vakfı (TÜSTAV), www.tustav.org/sureli-yayinlar-arsivi/bedel/.

dressed in women's clothing begs a German doctor for help: "By God, Herr Doctor, I don't have 20,000 marks, but I do have 200 bucks for you if you'll do an operation to make me a woman and save me from military service" (Figure 3.5). This strategy paid off: the FEBAG activists collected the signatures of 20,000 young men and their fathers, who in many cases would be the ones shelling out the money.

While the struggle surrounding military service affected Turkish men living in West Germany, FEBAG connected its activism fundamentally to the question of return migration. Not only did the activists argue that paying the 20,000 DM would be a waste of money that they might have otherwise spent toward the costs of remigrating to Turkey, but they also condemned the government's overall failure to create jobs and training opportunities for individuals who wished to return. "What has been done with the 500 million marks we have sent?" the activists questioned, chastising the Turkish government for using their remittances for the defense budget rather than the "development of the homeland."[123] Although Defense Minister Zeki Yavuztürk attempted to stifle these concerns by insisting that military-age youths who paid the 20,000 DM were "performing a national service," the activists saw through the rhetoric and continued to emphasize the Turkish government's failure to address the difficulties faced by return migrants.[124] As one young man who had grown up in West Germany and now faced unemployment explained, "I need the money to return to Turkey" but "I have no chance of finding a job in Turkey either."[125]

Soon, FEBAG's platform not only spread to Turkish migrants in the Netherlands but also attracted the support of important stakeholders throughout West Germany and Turkey. FEBAG's allies tended to be left or center-left organizations that generally supported Turkish migrants: the German Confederation of Trade Unions (DGB), the metalworkers' trade union IG Metall, and the Protestant churches. Individuals with similar political inclinations also supported FEBAG, including select Social Democratic and Green Party parliamentarians and Liselotte Funcke, the Federal Commissioner for the Integration of Foreigners. FEBAG's cause also resonated with Turkey's Confederation of Turkish Trade Unions (Türk-İş), as well as organizations founded by Turkish migrants in West

---

[123] "Bugüne kadar gönderdiğimiz 500 milyon mark ile ne yapıldı?" *Bedel*, November 1985, TÜSTAV.
[124] "Türkiye'de iş, öğrenim ve eğitim yerleri için!" *Bedel*, November 1985, TÜSTAV.
[125] "15 Bin dile kolay! Kim ödeyecek?" *Bedel*, July 1984, TÜSTAV.

FIGURE 3.5 FEBAG activists published a humorous cartoon in their newsletter, conveying the desperation that young migrants felt when trying to pay their way out of military service, 1984. The caption reads: "By God, Herr Doctor, I don't have 20,000 marks, but I do have 200 bucks for you if you'll do an operation to make me a woman and save me from military service." © TÜSTAV, used with permission.

Germany, such as the Federation of Workers Associations (FİDEF), the Federation of Progressive People's Associations in Europe (HDF), and the Turkish Youth Association in West Berlin.

For these allies, FEBAG's platform fit into a broader political message: condemning Turkey for abuses that continued after the military coup, despite the country's professed transition to democracy with the 1983 elections. Expressing their support for FEBAG, West German DGB representatives disparaged the "immoral" 20,000 DM sum as a "shameless exploitation of your emergency situation in the service of financing a military dictatorship, which is painstakingly trying to hide behind a guise of democracy."[126] The West Berlin Turkish Youth Association, which like many left-wing organizations criticized Cold War militarism, connected FEBAG's platform to a broader critique of Turkey's geopolitical ties to NATO and the United States. Given that the military exemption fees were going to the defense budget, the association insisted that supporting FEBAG would help "liberate Turkey from the yoke of the NATO aggressor," "ensure the security of Turkey against imperialism," and "protect the democratic rights of working people."[127]

West German newspapers, which were likewise eager to criticize the abuses of Turkey's military government, expressed sympathy for FEBAG. The *Westfälische Rundschau* argued that the 20,000 DM sum was "immoral," described it as "plundering," and suggested that the Turkish government was using "robber baron methods" to steal the migrants' money.[128] As Hanover's *Neue Presse* put it, "Ankara apparently values the foreign currency more than the young soldiers."[129] Another publication drew a parallel to the Ottoman Empire – frequently used as a negative foil to highlight the glory of West German democracy against Turkish authoritarianism – during which young men sold into slavery and military service were forced to "passively acquiesce to their fates."[130] Forceful quotations from FEBAG's supporters hammered the

---

[126] "Ratenzahlung: 20000 DM in zehn Jahren. Unterschriften gegen Freikauf-Methoden," *Westfälische Rundschau*, April 24, 1984.
[127] Batı Berlin Türkiye Gençlik Birliği, "Yurtdışındaki gençler ve askerlik sorunu," mid-1980s, TÜSTAV.
[128] "Türken klagen: Wer Vaterland nicht dienen will, ist ruiniert," *Westfälische Rundschau*, April 24, 1984.
[129] Wonka, "Da kannst du dir nur den Finger abschneiden."
[130] "Junge Türken wehren sich gegen zu hohe Summe zum Freikauf vom Militärdienst," *Aktuelles aus dem Wurmgebiet*, July 5, 1984.

message home. "We work and work and save a bit, and then we send the money to our government," one supporter complained.[131] "The government does not want us at all. They just want the money," another complained. In the most memorable quote, which allegedly "shocked" reporters, one man hyperbolized: "The easiest thing you can do is cut off your index finger because when you're missing a body part, you don't have to go to military service."[132]

Bolstered by West German media coverage, FEBAG successfully reshaped Turkish policy. In May 1984, just two months after FEBAG's founding, Turkish Defense Minister Yavuztürk announced the existence of a proposal to reduce the price but cautioned the activists not to get their hopes up.[133] Although Yavuztürk did not mention FEBAG directly, his justification for the proposed reduction echoed the organization's main talking points. "Our citizens abroad consider this price too high and report that it is a heavy burden," he noted, adding that individuals who took out predatory loans often had to pay an additional 10,000 DM in interest, for a total of 30,000 DM.[134] The proposal was successful: a month after Yavuztürk's announcement, the government submitted a bill to parliament decreasing the price from 20,000 to 15,000 DM, reducing the length of service from twenty to eighteen months, and raising the age deadline from thirty to thirty-two.[135]

Still not satisfied, FEBAG continued to demand a reduction of the sum to 5,000 DM and increased their efforts to lobby politicians. In November 1984, the SPD fraction of the Hamburg city council petitioned the state senate to mitigate the problem by guaranteeing that the young men be allowed to return to Germany without losing their jobs even after serving the full eighteen-month military service, and the state senate enacted the law the following spring.[136] West German politicians' willingness to accommodate young Turkish migrants made the Turkish government's continued refusal to lower the price to 5,000

---

[131] Hubert Wolf, "Wir arbeiten und schenken das Geld unserer Regierung," *WAZ*, May 15, 1984.

[132] Wonka, "Da kannst du dir nur den Finger abschneiden."

[133] "Ayda 96 marka bedelli askerlik," *Hürriyet*, May 19, 1984.

[134] "Askerlik kısaltılacak," *Cumhuriyet*, May 18, 1984.

[135] "Askerlik 18 aya indirildi," *Cumhuriyet*, June 16, 1984; "Geänderte Wehrpflicht für Türken," *Pro Lokalzeitung*, October 19, 1984.

[136] SPD-Fraktion, "Antrag. Betr.: Auswirkungen der Wehrpflicht auf die in der Bundesrepublik Deutschland lebenden ausländischen Mitbürger, deren Länder der NATO eingehören," Drucksache 11/2901, November 1984. Printed in "Karar tasarıları eyalet parlamentolarında," *Bedel*, 1985.

DM all the more frustrating. By 1986, FEBAG had developed more creative ways of lobbying, including protesting in front of eight Turkish consulate offices throughout West Germany while wearing nothing but their pajamas. As the organization elaborated in a flyer, "Up until now, we have worn suits and ties, and nevertheless we were ignored by the Turkish authorities. Now we are going to show up in pajamas and nightgowns."[137]

Despite such stunts, FEBAG's 5,000 DM goal never materialized. Even though Turkey reduced the price to 10,000 DM in 1988, the activists continued to portray themselves as "victims." In an elegant poem speaking to Turkish migrants' larger sense of betrayal, one activist echoed the oft-touted notion that the Turkish government viewed them as little more than "remittance machines": "Have you ever worked abroad? Do you know what it means to be a migrant? Do you understand the younger generation? You have your palms open, expecting something from our wallets. All the laws you have passed are for yourselves. You want to take advantage of the destitute migrants ... We are not remittance machines. We are Turkish youths living abroad."[138]

* * * * *

Whether redirecting West German development aid, urging guest workers to send remittance payments, or squeezing money out of young military-age men, the Turkish government's opposition to return migration throughout the 1970s and 1980s reflected a consistent trend: prioritizing national economic goals over guest workers' and their children's needs. Whereas the Turkish government in the early 1960s valued the guest workers for their ability to return and contribute to their homeland using their knowledge and skills cultivated in West Germany, by the 1970s and 1980s the government derived the migrants' value as citizens precisely from their *absence* from their home country. Turks living in West Germany remained official citizens of Turkey, but their value to the nation was no longer tied to their physical presence within the borders of the Turkish nation-state. Instead, it was based on their ability to contribute to the country's economy by remaining abroad, by not inundating the overburdened Turkish labor market with their unwanted bodies, and by investing Deutschmarks in their homeland.

---

[137] FEBAG, flyer, "Bedelzede Genç!" June 21, 1986, TÜSTAV; "Keine türkischen Armee für im Ausland lebende Türken," March 2, 1984, AdsD, DGB-Archiv, 5/DGAZ000988.
[138] Poem in *Bedel*, September 1984, TÜSTAV.

This new set of relations reflected Turkey's efforts to position itself within the broader world and to make sense of its own identity. In practical terms, the obsession with guest workers' Deutschmarks was fundamentally the product of Turkey's macroeconomic struggles as it adjusted to its outward orientation in the age of global neoliberal capitalism and attempted to alleviate the debt crisis of the late 1970s. But it also reflected a deeper crisis of Turkey's national identity as those at home grappled with redefining their relationship to the *Almancı* 3,000 kilometers away.

To conceal their obsession with coopting guest workers' Deutschmarks, both the government and corporations – from banks to cigarette companies – used nationalist rhetoric that sought to embrace the ostracized migrants as core parts of the nation, or the *vatan*. But guest workers saw through this rhetoric. Many sincerely wished to return to their home country and could have greatly benefitted from Turkey's cooperation with West Germany's bilateral development programs promoting return migration. Instead, they felt as though they were being abandoned and exploited by the government of their homeland. The novelist Bekir Yıldız's satirical interpretation – that guest workers should even "give up eating" for the sake of their home country's struggling economy – rang true. Manipulation had created mistrust.

PART II

KICKING OUT THE TURKS

4

Racism in Hitler's Shadow

From the 1960s through the 1980s, Turkish migrants had to contend not only with their growing estrangement from their home country but also with rising racism in Germany. Former guest workers themselves marked the early 1980s as a turning point in their mistreatment in Germany, which represented a stark transition from the "welcome" they recalled having received when they first arrived. "Back then, Turks did not have a bad image," one former guest worker noted. "To the contrary, every other German said, 'You were our allies in the First World War.'"[1] Several other Turkish men, who had been some of the first guest workers to arrive in Duisburg, concurred. The early 1960s "were beautiful and happy times for us all." "It was an honor," they recalled, for German firms to employ Turks. But, by 1982, everything had changed. "Now we are like squeezed-out lemons that they want to throw away."[2]

This interpretation, in some respects, represents a distortion of the past through rose-colored glasses. While the situation had certainly worsened since the 1960s, this interpretation belied the reality that, as this book has shown, Turkish guest workers and their children faced discrimination as soon as they arrived. At the factories and mines where they toiled, they had been crammed into poorly outfitted dormitories, segregated along ethnic lines, and frequently discriminated against by their

[1] Can Merey, *Der ewige Gast. Wie mein türkischer Vater versuchte, Deutscher zu werden* (Munich: Karl Blessing, 2018), 18.
[2] Nermin Ertan and Thomas Bethge, "Damals sprach niemand von 'Kümmeltürken,'" *RP*, December 3, 1982.

German coworkers and higher-ups. Amid economic downturns, they had been the first to get fired from their jobs – with managers sometimes, as in the 1973 "wildcat strike" at the Ford factory, justifying their dismissal based on their tardy return from their summer vacations to Turkey. German media outlets had spread sensationalist stories of guest workers' criminality and sexual abuse, branding Turkish men as hot-headed and impulsive and associating them with their dangerously tempting "Mediterranean," "Oriental," and "Asiatic" origins. Internalizing these narratives, German women had often refused – or were afraid – to date Turks. And, all the while, the West German government had been trying to invent strategies for convincing Turks to leave. Many of these experiences of racism remained key features in migrants' everyday lives over two decades, even as they brought their children and settled into Germany more permanently.

But, as former guest workers rightly observed, the early 1980s were a peculiar beast when it came to racism. A March 1982 poll revealed that 55 percent of Germans believed that guest workers should return to their home country, compared to just 39 percent in 1978.[3] As the call "Turks out!" (*Türken raus!*) grew louder, policymakers took harsher action. Whereas they had previously promoted return migration through development aid to Turkey, they increasingly debated whether to unilaterally pass a law that would, in critics' view, "kick out" the Turks. Importantly, as Maria Alexopoulou has emphasized, West German racism was not only a matter of individual or collective attitudes toward migrants, or of the everyday racism that migrants faced in encounters with Germans, but it was also structural and institutional, pervading all aspects of migrants' lives (Figure 4.1). It manifested in local, state, and federal legislation, in unequal professional, educational, and housing opportunities, and in migrants' higher propensity for unemployment and poverty.[4]

If racism was not a new phenomenon of the 1980s, then neither was the growing emphasis on return migration. The idea of return migration, after all, was embedded in the very logic of the 1961 Turkish-German guest worker program in the ultimately unheeded "rotation principle," whereby individual guest workers were supposed to return to Turkey after two years and be replaced by new workers. And, of course, discussions of return migration were ubiquitous throughout the 1970s, as the

---

[3] Zimmer, "Betr.: Ausländerpolitik; hier: Vorschläge für Aktivitäten des Bundeskanzlers," March 2, 1982, BArch, B 145/14409.
[4] Alexopoulou, *Deutschland und die Migration*, 7–18.

FIGURE 4.1 Emblematic of rising racism, West Germans sometimes banned Turkish clientele from their establishments. This sign in Berlin-Spandau, for example, states: "Turks are not permitted in this restaurant," 1982. © picture alliance/dpa, used with permission.

West German government tried – and overwhelmingly failed – to work bilaterally with intransigent Turkish officials on development aid programs in exchange for promoting the workers' return. But, in the early 1980s, more so than ever before, the dual swords of racism and return migration clashed with and amplified each other with an unparalleled vigor and virulence. The controversial 1983 remigration law, ultimately passed under the conservative government of Helmut Kohl, was, in reality, the culmination of what the social–liberal coalition already wanted.

Given how crucial the 1980s are to this transnational story, the book now turns toward this decade and takes it as a point of focus. Part I, "Separation Anxieties," told the "Turkish" side of the story: how the migrants became gradually estranged from their home country and perceived as "Germanized" over three decades. Part II, "Kicking out the Turks," zooms in on just one decade – the 1980s – exposing the nexus between racism and return migration. To set the stage for Part II, the following chapter provides an in-depth exploration of what can be called the "racial reckoning" of the early 1980s, during which West Germans, Turkish migrants, and observers in Turkey all grappled – sometimes self-consciously, sometimes not – with the very nature of racism itself. From editorial boards to parliamentary chambers, from conversations with friends to scathing letters to elected officials, West Germans everywhere engaged with long-suppressed questions that struck at the core of the country's postwar identity. Had racism disappeared with the Nazis, or did it still exist in West Germany's prized liberal democratic society? Was racism relegated to neo-Nazis and right-wing extremists, or did it pervade the German population as a whole? Who had a claim to calling someone racist? How could one defend oneself against allegations of racism, and how could Turkish migrants – as the targets of racism – and their home country fight back?

The sheer extent of this racial reckoning in both public and private reveals an important point: even though West Germans overwhelmingly silenced the language of "race" (*Rasse*) and "racism" (*Rassismus*) after Hitler, there was in fact an explosion of public discourse about those very words at the very same time that debates about promoting Turks' return migration surged. This chapter identifies the racial reckoning of the early 1980s as the moment when the linguistic distinction between *Rassismus* and *Ausländerfeindlichkeit* crystallized, as Germans heatedly debated whether racism still existed and what they should call it. *Ausländerfeindlichkeit* ultimately became a more palatable term than *Rassismus* because it avoided the unsavory connection to Nazi eugenics and biological racism; instead, *Ausländerfeindlichkeit* connoted discrimination based on socioeconomic problems and "cultural differences" (*kulturelle Unterschiede*), cast primarily in terms of Turks' Muslim faith and allegedly "backward" rural origins.[5] But, as Maria Alexopoulou has rightly argued, *Ausländerfeindlichkeit* was "just a variation of racism, a phase in which racist thinking won legitimacy again."[6] This chapter builds on these interpretations by showing that, despite Germans' attempts to deny, deflect, and silence their racism, the "older" form of biological racism still reared its ugly head. Not only neo-Nazis but also self-proclaimed "ordinary" Germans condemned Turks as a racial "other" rather than just a cultural enemy who, through their higher

---

[5] Chin and Fehrenbach, "Introduction: What's Race Got to Do with It?"

[6] Alexopoulou, "'Ausländer' – A Racialized Concept"; Alexopoulou, *Deutschland und die Migration*, 188. For a scholarly theorization of *Ausländerfeindlichkeit* from the early 1980s, see: Georgios Tsiakalos, *Ausländerfeindlichkeit: Tatsachen und Erklärungsversuche* (Munich: C. H. Beck, 1983).

birthrates and "race-mixing," threatened to biologically "exterminate" and commit "genocide" against the German *Volk*.

The rise in Holocaust memory culture (*Erinnerungskultur*) in the 1980s is a crucial backdrop for understanding this racial reckoning. Though long suppressed and silenced, West Germans' efforts to combat the past (*Vergangenheitsbewältigung*) became a matter of public discussion even more so than amid the "New Left" student protests of the late 1960s.[7] A crucial spark was the widespread broadcasting of the 1979 American television miniseries *Holocaust*, which one-third of West Germany's population – 20 million people – had watched by the following year.[8] Attention to the crimes of Nazism grew in the mid-1980s amid the "historians' dispute" (*Historikerstreit*), which saw leading intellectuals publicly debate the singularity of the Holocaust and the proper role of the memory of the Third Reich in Germany's present. Simultaneously, the late 1970s and early 1980s witnessed an unprecedented rise in organized neo-Nazism and right-wing extremism, primarily perpetrated by a younger generation of Germans who had not grown up during the Third Reich. The neo-Nazi bombing of Munich's Oktoberfest in 1980 was the deadliest attack in West German history, stoking fears among policymakers and the public alike that a "Hitler cult" or "Hitler renaissance" was on the rise.[9]

As the memory of the past cast a shadow over the present, antisemitism became intertwined with Islamophobia, and the Nazis' abuse of Jews became a reference point for West Germans' abuse of Turks. When viewed from the perspective of both Turkish migrants and their home country, West Germany's project of commemorating the Holocaust in the 1980s was imperfect, incomplete, and – in many respects – counterproductive to the needs of other minority groups besides Jews.[10] On the one hand, the rise in Holocaust memory led many Germans to recognize

---

[7] Timothy Scott Brown, *West Germany and the Global 1960s: The Antiauthoritarian Revolt, 1962–1978* (Cambridge, UK: Cambridge University Press, 2013), 79–115; Terence Renaud, *New Lefts: The Making of a Radical Tradition* (Princeton: Princeton University Press, 2021).

[8] Peter Novick, *The Holocaust in American Life* (Boston: Houghton Mifflin, 1999); Jeffrey Shandler, *While America Watches: Televising the Holocaust* (Oxford: Oxford University Press, 2000), ch. 6; Jacob S. Eder, *Holocaust Angst: The Federal Republic of Germany and American Holocaust Memory Since the 1970s* (Oxford: Oxford University Press, 2016), chapter 1.

[9] Barbara Manthe, "The 1980 Oktoberfest Bombing – A Case with Many Question Marks," *OpenDemocracy*, July 6, 2019, www.opendemocracy.net/en/countering-radical-right/the-1980-oktoberfest-bombing-a-case-with-many-question-marks/.

[10] On Muslim migrants' relationship to Holocaust memory, see: Michael Rothberg and Yasemin Yildiz, "Memory Citizenship: Migrant Archives of Holocaust Remembrance

and to warn against the mistreatment of Turks as an unseemly historical continuity – even if they rarely invoked the words *Rasse* and *Rassismus*. On the other hand, the emphasis on the singularity of the Holocaust inadvertently made it possible for Germans to sweep the contemporary mistreatment of Turks under the rug. Most egregiously, Holocaust memory provoked a racist backlash among many right-wing Germans, who envisioned the "Turkish problem" as a new sort of "Jewish problem" and whose critique of the growing emphasis on Germans' collective guilt for the past compounded their denial of *Ausländerfeindlichkeit* in the present. Holocaust memory, in this sense, was often compatible with racism against Turks.

Focusing only on racist public discourses, however, ignores the very human element of racism – the daily grind of feeling that one does not belong, the constant microaggressions from both strangers and acquaintances, and the fear of physical violence. But despite a tendency to emphasize migrants' victimhood, neither they nor their home country stayed passive. As historian Manuela Bojadžijev has emphasized, migrants actively resisted racism since the very beginning of the guest worker program: while they rarely rallied explicitly against "racism" throughout the 1960s and 1970s, they organized local protests against a wide range of issues rooted in racism such as exorbitant rent prices, poor living conditions, discrimination in schools, reductions in child allowance payments, and tightened immigration restrictions.[11] Amid the racial reckoning of the 1980s, Turkish migrants' rhetoric of resistance evolved even further. They began invoking the language of their oppressor – the hotly debated word *Ausländerfeindlichkeit* – as a weapon in their anti-racist arsenal. Explicitly casting their discrimination as *Ausländerfeindlichkeit* allowed them to issue a broader critique that united their multifaceted experiences of structural and everyday racism under a single term that was already prominent in the public sphere. Rising Holocaust memory, too, became a tool for psychologically processing their own mistreatment, helping many – especially children – realize that it was not they, as individuals, who were the problem but rather German society itself.

in Contemporary Germany," *Parallax* 17, no. 4 (2011): 32–48; Esra Özyürek, *Subcontractors of Guilt: Holocaust Memory and Muslim Belonging in Postwar Germany* (Stanford: Stanford University Press, 2023).

[11] Bojadžijev, *Die windige Internationale*, 95. See also: Malte Borgmann, "Zwischen Integration und Gleichberechtigung. Migrationspolitik und migrantischer Aktivismus in Westberlin, 1969–1984" (M.A. thesis, Freie Universität Berlin, 2016).

Criticism of West German racism also resonated transnationally in Turkey – particularly when it came to the drafting of the 1983 remigration law. Paradoxically committed to both preventing return migration and portraying itself as the migrants' protector, the Turkish government assailed West Germans for violating the migrants' human rights and trying to kick them out. And in the same breath as they complained about the migrants turning into *Almancı*, the Turkish media and population regularly compared the treatment of Turks to the Nazis' persecution of Jews. These accusations were particularly contentious because they emerged immediately after Turkey's 1980 military coup – the same moment that Western Europeans were assailing Turkey for its own human rights violations. The transnational battle over human rights, democracy, and Holocaust memory not only strained an otherwise friendly century of international relations between the two countries but also revealed hypocrisies, denial, and deflection on both sides.

"I'M NOT A RACIST, BUT..."

In 1981, a survey commissioned by the West German Chancellor's Office revealed a startling conclusion: 13 percent of the German electorate harbored the "potential for right-wing extremist ideology," 6 percent were "inclined to violence," and another 37 percent had a "non-extreme authoritarian potential." An astonishingly large 50 percent veered toward "cultural pessimism," "anti-pluralism," and "racism" and felt threatened by "over-foreignization" (*Überfremdung*). And, perhaps most disturbingly, 18 percent still believed that "Germany had it better under Hitler."[12] After an internal leak, the news exploded not only throughout West Germany but also among its crucial Cold War allies, including France, Denmark, Canada, and the United States with headlines like "18 Percent Hail Hitler Era" and "Echo of Germany's Nazi Past."[13]

---

[12] "'Haß auf Fremde und Demokratie,'" *Der Spiegel*, March 15, 1981, 51–60.
[13] German Embassy in Washington, DC to AA Bonn, "Betr.: Studie über rechtsextremismus in der BR Deutschland," April 3, 1981; German Embassy in Ottawa to AA Bonn, "Betr.: Pressefernschreiben; hier: Spiegelumfrage zum Rechtsextremismus in der Bundesrepublik Deutschland," March 31, 1981; "13% des électeurs ont une mentalité d'extreme-droite," *Le Monde*, March 20, 1981, 5; "Germany's Far Right Not Really Different," *The Globe and Mail*, March 30, 1981; "18% Hail Hitler Era: Happiness Was the Third Reich, German Poll Finds," *The Los Angeles Times*, March 16, 1981, A1; "Anti-Jewish Prejudices Thrive in Germany," *The Atlanta Constitution*, March 19, 1981; "Troubling Currents in Germany," *The Houston Chronicle*, March 26, 1981; "Echo of Germany's Nazi Past," *The Christian Science Monitor*, March 31, 1981, 15.

Not surprisingly, many West Germans did not take lightly to being compared to Hitler. Writing to the Chancellor's Office, one man dismissed the results as "incomprehensible" and insisted that out of all his acquaintances – some 300–400 people – "I do not know a single one with that worldview!"[14] And Uwe Barschel, the Schleswig-Holstein Interior Minister, lambasted the survey as an "insult to the German *Volk*."[15]

The next year, the notorious Heidelberg Manifesto sprung to the forefront of public discourse. First published in the right-wing *Deutsche Wochenzeitung,* the manifesto cloaked racism in the guise of academic legitimacy, as it was signed by fifteen professors at major universities.[16] "With great concern," the professors wrote, "we observe the infiltration of the German *Volk* through an influx of millions of foreigners and their families, the infiltration of our language, our culture, and our traditions by foreign influences." Describing the "spiritual identity" of the German *Volk* as based on an "occidental Christian heritage" and "common history," they cast Turks, Muslims, and other "non-German foreigners" as fundamentally incompatible. Alongside this culturally based argument, however, was blatant biological racism reminiscent of eugenics and Hitler's *Mein Kampf.* "In biological and cybernetic terms," they continued, "peoples are living systems of a higher order with distinct system qualities that are passed on genetically and through tradition. The integration of large masses of non-German foreigners is therefore not possible without threatening the preservation of our people, and it will lead to the well-known ethnic catastrophes of multicultural societies." Preempting criticism, they claimed to "oppose ideological nationalism, racism, and every form of right- and left-wing extremism" and asserted that their desire to "preserve the German *Volk*" was firmly rooted in the Basic Law. Despite this denial of racism, mainstream media condemned the manifesto for being full of "prejudices, banalities, barroom wisdom, and bombastic definitions" and stoking the fires of "nationalism" and "racism."[17]

Also widely circulating at the time was a thirty-page pseudoscientific rant titled *Ausländer-Integration ist Völkermord* (Integrating Foreigners

---

[14] Hans Roschmann to Bundeskanzleramt, "Betr.: dpa-Meldung über 'rechtsextremistisches' Weltbild," April 5, 1981, BArch, B136/13322.

[15] "Barschel nennt Bonner Studie eine 'Beleidigung des deutschen Volkes,'" *Flensburger Tageblatt,* April 3, 1981.

[16] "Heidelberger Manifest," *FR,* March 4, 1982. English translation at: "The Heidelberg Manifesto of Xenophobic Professors (March 4, 1982)," *German History in Documents and Images,* https://ghdi.ghi-dc.org/sub_document.cfm?document_id=857.

[17] Quoted in Chin, *The Guest Worker Question,* 149.

is Genocide), written by retired police chief Wolfgang Seeger in 1980. Eschewing the mainstream parties' general definition of "integration" as a reciprocal process in which cultures could be preserved, Seeger criticized the term as a proxy for "assimilation" or "Germanization": a "merging, melting, and mixing" of foreigners into the "body of the German *Volk*" that "contradicts the laws of nature." Arguing that culture was determined by both "race" and "genetics," he warned that Germany would devolve first into "racial conflict" and eventually, through sex and intermarriage, into a "Eurasian-Negroid future race." All future offspring would be "half-bloods" (*Mischlinge*), he insisted, invoking the Nazi category codified in the 1935 Nuremberg Laws to denote certain Jews, Roma, and Black Germans whom the Nazis deemed genetically part-"Aryan." The overall consequences would be a dual "genocide" (*Völkermord*) – not only of the German *Volk* but also of the foreigners. The only way to prevent this genocide was for the "simple man" and the "simple woman of our *Volk*" to protest through democratic means and write their representatives demanding that they send foreigners home.[18]

As the call "Turks out!" echoed throughout the country, policymakers began hardening their stance on how to solve the "Turkish problem." In December 1981, Chancellor Helmut Schmidt's SPD-FDP government proposed an "immigration ban" (*Zuzugssperre*) that would lower the upper age limit for foreign children whose parents resided in Germany from eighteen to sixteen.[19] Two months later, return migration became the focus of a heated federal parliamentary debate, which transformed into a microcosm of the broader public reckoning with the existence, nature, and language of racism. The CDU/CSU opposition leader, Alfred Dregger, denied the feasibility of integrating Turks and expressed his party's staunch commitment to promoting return migration. Despite the secularization of Turkish society, Turks' "Muslim culture" and "distinct national pride" allegedly prevented them from being culturally "assimilated" or "Germanized," and even socially "integrating" them into schools and jobs would be "difficult." Promoting return migration validated the "natural and justified sentiment of our fellow citizens," Dregger noted, and was "in no way immoral." CDU/CSU representatives also proved eager to deny and deflect their racism altogether. "We have no reason to be accused

---

[18] Wolfgang Seeger, *Ausländer-Integration ist Völkermord. Das Verbrechen an den ausländischen Volksgruppen und am deutschen Volk* (Verlag Hohe Warte, 1980).
[19] Stokes, *Fear of the Family*, 326–29.

of _Ausländerfeindlichkeit_ by domestic or foreign critics when we insist that the Federal Republic should not become a country of immigration," Dregger explained. The current popular outcry, added CSU representative Carl-Dieter Spranger, was not an expression of "nationalistic arrogance," "racist incorrigibility," or an "_ausländerfeindlich_ attitude," but rather a reaction to the failed policies of the SPD-FDP.

On the other hand, the SPD and FDP both tied the issue of return migration fundamentally to _Ausländerfeindlichkeit,_ the legacy of the Third Reich, and the language of human rights and morality. SPD representative Hans-Eberhard Urbaniak opened the debate by asserting firmly: "We clearly and unambiguously reject any policy of 'Foreigners out,'" and "We must all emphatically fight against _Ausländerfeindlichkeit._" Although the SPD's coalition partner did not necessarily reject the promotion of return migration in theory, FDP representative Friedrich Hölstein cautioned that convincing Turks to "voluntarily return" might result in a policy of "forced deportation." Morally, such a policy would contradict West Germans' "responsibility" to atone for their "national history" of Nazism and to uphold their Cold War commitment to "human rights and human dignity." The optics alone would be detrimental, Hölstein asserted: "Do we really want to be internationally charged for violations of human rights? We, of all people, who continue to rightly point out human rights violations in the other part of Germany and throughout the world?"

Invigorated by the debate, the SPD-FDP government began developing a state-driven "campaign against _Ausländerfeindlichkeit._"[20] Strikingly, the Federal Press Office's proposed messaging strategy made no mention of migrants, let alone of the need to express sympathy toward them. Instead, it portrayed _Ausländerfeindlichkeit_ as a threat to Germans: "_Ausländerfeindlichkeit_ is immoral; we cannot afford to fall back into nationalistic thinking. _Ausländerfeindlichkeit_ endangers inner peace and accordingly the democratic state. It damages our reputation and all of us." As one staffer wrote, if the "caricature of the 'beastly German'" resurfaced on the world stage, it would destroy the "hard-earned sympathy" that Germans had rebuilt over the past four decades.[21] Although this coordinated public relations campaign

---

[20] Zimmer, "Betr.: Ausländerpolitik; hier: Vorschläge für Aktivitäten des Bundeskanzlers," March 2, 1982, BArch, B 145/14409.

[21] Franken, "Betr.: ÖA Ausländerpolitik/ÖA gegen Ausländerfeindlichkeit," July 14, 1982, BArch, B 134/14409.

never materialized, it demonstrates that West German policymakers envisioned the task of combatting *Ausländerfeindlichkeit* not only as self-serving but also as fundamentally connected to the memory – or forgetting – of the Nazi past.

Beyond surveys, media coverage, and parliamentary debates, however, understanding how ordinary Germans justified and expressed their own racism was – and is – no easy feat: they often criticized Turks privately, in passing, and in conversations with friends and family. But the West German government did have other sources they could examine, ones that testified more to everyday attitudes: letters they received from citizens. In fact, between 1980 and 1984, President Karl Carstens received no fewer than 202 letters from individual Germans complaining about foreigners and demanding – in one way or another – "Turks out!" Whether three-sentence postcards or ten-page rants, whether scribbled in illegible handwriting or meticulously typed, 50 percent of the writers complained about Turks explicitly, whereas other migrant groups – from Yugoslav guest workers to Vietnamese asylum seekers – were mentioned in fewer than five letters each. Although the letters ranged in tone from civil and matter-of-fact to irreverent and vulgar, the president's aide tasked with reading them cataloged them under the all-encompassing label "Ausländerfeindlichkeit." The lumping together of these diverse letters reveals that, for the aide, any criticism of Turks, no matter how mild, was indicative of *Ausländerfeindlichkeit*.

Analyzed together as a dataset, these letters are a crucial source for uncovering the bottom-up history of German racism in the early 1980s because, unlike surveys, they capture the specific patterns, nuances, and raw visceral emotion with which Germans expressed and attempted to justify their concerns about Turks.[22] In fact, Christopher Molnar has examined another set of letters written to the subsequent president, Richard von Weizsäcker, in the early 1990s, coming to a similar conclusion about the persistence of biological racism and "apocalyptical fear."[23] The letter writers' names and addresses indicate that they were relatively evenly split by gender and lived all throughout the country, from cities to smaller towns. They were not politicians, journalists, intellectuals, or other elite shapers of public opinion. Nor do most of

---

[22] As a testament to these letters' importance, Maria Alexopoulou also references them in her analysis of *Ausländerfeindlichkeit*. Alexopoulou, *Deutschland und die Migration*, 201–4.

[23] Molnar, "'Greetings from the Apocalypse.'"

them come across as hardcore neo-Nazis hellbent on mass murdering foreigners and bringing about the restoration of the Third Reich, or even as voters of the right-wing National Democratic Party (NPD). Instead, to distance themselves from radical right-wing extremists, many identified themselves mundanely: a "concerned citizen," "normal German," "retired man," "average woman," "housewife," or "elementary school student," who believed in airing their grievances through formal democratic channels. Still, their alleged "ordinariness" demands scrutiny. On the one hand, the claim of being an "ordinary citizen" was a form of self-styling that helped these letter writers rhetorically distance their beliefs from those of right-wing extremists. On the other hand, many of them were likely the so-called _Wutbürger_, or angry citizens who regularly sent politicians scathing letters about various issues or public statements. In fact, many of these writers explicitly referenced a June 10, 1982, interview with Carstens, in which he stated that foreigners are our "fellow citizens" (_Mitbürger_) and called upon Germans to "thank foreigners for contributing to the welfare of our country," to "help foreigners feel at home here," and to "oppose all forms of _Ausländerfeindlichkeit_."[24] Carstens's statement had incensed them.

Collectively, the hundreds of letters to Carstens speak strongly to the silences, denial, and deflection surrounding not only the word _Rassismus_ but also the allegedly more palatable word _Ausländerfeindlichkeit_. Strikingly, one-fourth of the writers – some fifty people – explicitly denied that they harbored racist or _ausländerfeindlich_ views. A common strategy was to preface a long letter ranting about Turks and other migrants with variations on a simple phrase: "I'm not a racist, but...," "I'm not an _Ausländerfeind_, but...," "I'm not a right-winger, but...," "I'm not an extremist, but....," "I'm not a neo-Nazi, but..."[25] Many objected to the term _Ausländerfeindlichkeit_ itself. Claiming that _Ausländerfeindlichkeit_ was "overhyped" and little more than a "stupid buzzword," several insisted that their concerns were a "reasonable critique of particular problematic developments" and a "justified rage."[26] "Whenever someone stands up and expresses his concern about foreigner policy," decried Jürgen Feucht, he is "immediately vilified as a 'fascist' or 'neo-Nazi.'"[27]

---

[24] Michael H. Spreng and Richard Voelkel, "Wir müssen den Ausländern helfen, heimisch zu werden," _BILD_, June 10, 1982.

[25] Lydia Neumann to Carstens, August 16, 1982, BArch, B 122/23885.

[26] Erich Nietsch to Carstens, May 29, 1983, BArch, B 122/23885; H. Schmidt to Carstens, March 6, 1982, BArch, B 122/23886.

[27] Jürgen Feucht to Carstens, October 12, 1981, BArch, B 122/23884.

This "tactless" association, claimed Kurt Nagel, denigrated them into "unteachable, irredeemable, conservative reactionary people with narrow-minded prejudices or people who support political demagoguery."[28] By differentiating themselves from neo-Nazis and right-wing extremists, these "ordinary" Germans deflected their guilt: they contended that their concerns, articulated through words rather than violence, were rational and justified.

Far more vividly than surveys alone, the letters to Carstens also reveal the multifaceted reasons why Germans opposed foreigners. By far the most important was the perception of foreigners' culpability for Germany's socioeconomic woes: half of the letters mentioned unemployment, while one-third mentioned guest workers' perceived abuse of the social welfare system. Fred Reymund called all foreigners a "lazy *Volk*" and complained that West Germans "have to support the Third World."[29] Irmtraud Wagner, a 61-year-old woman, asserted that Turks' exploitation of the social welfare system made them wealthier than many German retirees, whose meager pensions left them "degraded into beggars."[30] Two particularly inflammatory issues were family reunification and the child allowance benefit (*Kindergeld*), both of which had been consistent points of contention for the past decade.[31] Alongside the image of the exploitative "welfare migrant," nearly 20 percent of the letters referenced the changing neighborhoods and establishment of ethnically homogenous "Turkish ghettoes," such as Berlin's heavily Turkish neighborhood of Kreuzberg, and the challenges posed to the education system by the high percentages of migrant children.

Along with unemployment and alleged abuses of the social welfare system, perceived threats to public safety were another leading concern of letter writers. One-third referenced the migrants' criminality, lamenting that West Germany had become a "paradise for criminals" and that the jails were filled with "criminal foreigners."[32] While these complaints focused primarily on drug trafficking, 10 percent centered on sexual violence – a crime that, due to longstanding Orientalist tropes, was particularly associated with Turkish and Middle Eastern men. Two elderly women, Ingeborg Hoffmann and Helma Zinkel, each noted that German women and girls could not walk down the street even in broad

---

[28] Kurt Nagel to Carstens, January 9, 1981, BArch, B 122/23885.
[29] Fred Reymund to Carstens, June 25, 1983, BArch, B 122/23883.
[30] Irmtraud Wagner to Carstens, May 20, 1983, BArch, B 122/23886.
[31] Stokes, "'An Invasion of Guest Worker Children.'"
[32] M. Meier to Carstens, December 2, 1982, BArch, B 122/23883.

daylight because Turkish men viewed them as "prey."[33] In the most troubling letter, a thirteen-year-old girl relayed her traumatic experience of
being sexually assaulted by a group of Turkish teenagers who – "like they
always do" – were loitering at a park after dark. Although she and her
friend attempted to avoid "the group of foreigners," they "came up to us
and grabbed me, in order to flagrantly touch me." The incident, the girl
suggested, was not isolated, but rather characteristic of foreign men as a
whole: "Have we reached the point in Germany that we, at thirteen years
old, can no longer be outside at 7 o'clock at night without being molested
by foreigners? ... Pity, poor Germany!"[34] Given that no other children
sent letters, it is possible that this letter was written by adults posing as
a thirteen-year-old girl to draw the president's attention to a particularly
egregious case of sexual violation.

Twenty percent of the writers expressed cultural racism through condemning Turks' Muslim faith. Far more harshly than simply pointing out
that the two cultures were "different," most of these writers took a particularly essentialist and racialized view of Islam, with Ingrid Eschkötter
denigrating Turks as a "disgusting Mohammedan *Volk*" and another
writer demanding that the government "Kick out the Turks, this Muslim
scum!"[35] Only four of the writers mentioned headscarves – a reflection
that the letters were written primarily by political centrists and conservatives rather than the leftist feminists who since the late 1970s had
begun to condemn Muslim migrants' perceived patriarchal treatment
of women.[36] Instead, they portended a "fearsome" future of Germany's
"Islamicization by infinitely primitive Turks," in which Germans would
"burn the Bible and switch it out for the Koran!" and the Muslim call
to prayer would "drown out the church bells."[37] Muslims' Halal dietary
restrictions, they further contended, not only made them unwilling to
eat Germany's pork-based national cuisine but also posed a physical
threat. As Georg Walter wrote, Turks "consider us Germans to be pork
eaters, whom they can cheat, steal from, and even murder." Recycling

---

[33] Ingeborg Hoffmann to Carstens, August 14, 1982, BArch B 122/23884; Helma Zinkel
to Carstens, January 12, 1982, BArch, B 122/23886.
[34] Melanie Riesner to Carstens, August 26, 1982, BArch, B 122/23886.
[35] Ingrid Eschkötter to Carstens, May 20, 1983, BArch, B 122/23883; Wobschall to
Carstens, June 1, 1982, BArch B 122/23886.
[36] Rita Chin, "Turkish Women, West German Feminists."
[37] Hellmuth Greiner to Carstens, June 11, 1982, BArch B 122/23884; Max Gottschalk
to Carstens, May 23, 1983, BArch B 122/23884; Weihermüller to Carstens, June 25,
1982, BArch B 122/23884.

longstanding antisemitic tropes regarding the Jewish law of Kashrut, they insisted that the process of preparing Halal meat – ritually and humanely slaughtering the animal by cutting its throat and letting it bleed out – was a violent attack on innocent life that could lead to future violence. "They slaughter humans like they do sheep," declared Ellie Schützeberg, a housewife and grandmother married to a retired police officer.[38]

In associating Islam with primitivity and violence, several writers reiterated Orientalist tropes rooted in the centuries-old Ottoman-Habsburg conflicts. They warned that Germans would soon suffer the "downfall of the Occident," succumb to the rule of "Christian slaughterers" and the "plundering *Volk* from the empire of Allah," and be inundated by "Mustafas, Mohameds, and Ali Babas" walking around in "Oriental robes."[39] The fear of the Turks exists "everywhere where Turks show up in large masses," one man stated matter-of-factly, imploring Carstens to "think of the Mohács, the entire Balkans, and Vienna."[40] The 1683 Battle of Vienna, when the Ottoman army stormed the gates of the Habsburg capital, proved a particularly powerful reference point. "Did the friendship with the Turks begin 300 years ago at the gates of Vienna?" Heinz Schambach quipped, while Berta Maier suggested that Süleyman II, the Ottoman emperor during the 1683 battle, would be "rolling in his grave because he hadn't come up with the idea of guest workers."[41] Georg Kretschmer emphasized Ottoman violence in the modern era, recalling the 1915–1916 Armenian Genocide in which "the Turks tried to exterminate the Armenians with the most brutal of methods."[42] The irony that the legal definition of genocide would not have existed without Germans' having perpetrated the Holocaust was lost on them.

These socioeconomic concerns and cultural racism were compounded by the increase in asylum seekers migrating to West Germany in the early 1980s.[43] Lambasting asylum seekers as criminals, many of the writers

---

[38] Ellie Schützeberg to Carstens, June 1983, BArch, B 122/23886.
[39] H. Schönfels to Carstens, November 10, 1980, BArch, B 122/23886; Rudolf Zeller to Carstens, December 11, 1982, BArch, B 122/23886; Helmut Grimm to Carstens, September 18, 1983, BArch, B 122/23884.
[40] Weihermüller to Carstens, June 25, 1982, BArch B 122/23884.
[41] Heinz Schambach to Carstens, June 14, 1984, BArch, B 122/23886; Berta Maier to Carstens, January 4, 1983, BArch, B 122/23885.
[42] Georg Kretschmer to Carstens, December 21, 1981, BArch, B 122/23885.
[43] On asylum in German history, see: Miltiadis Oulios, *Blackbox Abschiebung: Geschichte, Theorie und Praxis der deutschen Migrationspolitik*, 2nd ed. (Berlin: Suhrkamp, 2015); Patrice G. Poutrus, *Umkämpftes Asyl. Vom Nachkriegsdeutschland bis in die Gegenwart* (Berlin: Christoph Links Verlag, 2019).

argued that they were "fake asylum seekers" (*Scheinasylanten*) or "economic refugees" (*Wirtschaftsflüchtlinge*) who lied about their political persecution in order to seek jobs in West Germany and exploit the country's welfare system. Criticism of asylum seekers applied most harshly to the thousands of Turkish citizens, predominantly Kurds, who applied for asylum following Turkey's September 1980 military coup. Most of the writers conflated asylum seekers and guest workers from Turkey into one homogenous category of migrants who, as one writer pointed out, wanted to turn West Germany into a "hotbed for the expansion of Greater Turkey."[44]

For 10 percent of the writers, the "Turkish problem" was inextricable from the Cold War context. Several facetiously asserted that even East German dictatorship and poverty was preferable to the large proportion of foreigners in West Germany, although such statements erased the thousands of contract workers and asylum seekers living in East Germany. "It's probably nicer to live in the GDR than in our own country among Asians and Africans," scribbled Ernst Bender on a three-sentence postcard, while Ellie Schützeberg concurred: "I'd prefer to go back to the GDR, which I left 39 years ago and where I would be protected and safe from this *Türkenvolk*."[45] Volker Arendt from Iserslohn contended that reunification could only be achieved if Germans on both sides of the Berlin Wall embraced "the feeling that we are a nation with a collective past, culture, and language," noting that a high proportion of foreigners "without any connection" to the other part of Germany would impede this process.[46] Ottilie Vogel, an elderly woman, put it even more blatantly: "GDR citizens do not want reunification with an Orientalized FRG."[47]

The letters also reflect Germans' efforts to distance themselves from the Nazi past. A remarkable 20 percent of the letters referenced Hitler, Nazism, and World War II. To support their claim that they were not right-wing extremists or neo-Nazis, several of the elderly writers emphasized that they had resisted the Third Reich. Peter Bursch claimed that he had been "thrown out" of the Hitler Youth and had only fought in World War II because he was a "good soldier" and the war "was about Germany, not about Hitler."[48] Another denied that he was a "right-wing

---

44 Weihermüller to Carstens, June 25, 1982, BArch, B 122/23886.
45 Ernst Bender to Carstens, January 16, 1981, BArch, B 122/23883; Schützeberg to Carstens, June 1983, BArch, B 122/23886.
46 Volker Arendt to Carstens, January 27, 1981, BArch, B 122/23883.
47 Ottilie Vogel to Carstens, February 14, 1982, BArch, B 122/23886.
48 Peter Bursch to Carstens, January 18, 1984, BArch, B 122/23883.

pig" by claiming that he had been an "iron antifascist," that his two best friends were Jews, and that his own great-grandfather had been Jewish. In another selective interpretation of the past, some writers criticized Turks in relation to postwar narratives of German victimhood. Twenty percent rejected the argument that Germans should thank guest workers for helping rebuild the country after World War II. Alfred Gonska from Essen, who boasted that he had participated in "clearing the rubble" of cities that had been bombed into "debris and ashes," insisted that the task of Germany's rebuilding was undertaken by "*all* Germans, and *only* Germans, under unspeakably immense sacrifices and difficulties and with great idealism."[49] Several writers also compared guest workers and asylum seekers to the twelve million ethnic German expellees (*Heimatvertriebene*) who fled Eastern Europe for Germany in 1945.[50] Identifying herself as an expellee, Elisabeth Stellma complained that today's migrants were receiving too generous treatment even though they were not ethnically Germany: "Back then, no one cared if we had nothing to eat."[51]

On the other hand, the letters also demonstrated continuities of Nazi ideology and terminology. Georg Kretschmer criticized migrants for West Germany's perceived overpopulation by invoking the Nazi phrase "*Volk* without space" (*Volk ohne Raum*), while three other writers used the highly taboo term "living space" (*Lebensraum*), the Nazi ideology that justified expansion, war, and genocide in terms of an existential need to secure land, food, and natural resources for "Aryan" Germans.[52] Several others, including 70-year-old Irmgard Recke, mentioned "Rump Germany" (*Restdeutschland*) – a rhyming play on the German word for West Germany (*Westdeutschland*) – which, in the early Cold War decades, opponents of Germany's division had used to criticize West Germany as the meager leftover half of Germany following the break-off of the GDR.[53] But the term "Rump Germany" had a deeper history. After World War I, "Rump Germany" became a rallying cry against the 1919 Treaty of Versailles, which stripped the former German Empire of

---

[49] Alfred Gonska to Carstens, May 29, 1983, BArch, B 122/23884.
[50] On *Heimatvertriebene* and the memory of World War II, see: Moeller, *War Stories*; Gengler, "'New Citizens' or 'Community of Fate'?"
[51] Elisabeth Stellma to Carstens, November 16, 1982, BArch, B 122/23886.
[52] Kretschmer to Carstens, December 21, 1981, BArch, B 122/23885; Fritz Angelkort to Carstens, March 2, 1982, BArch, B 122/23883; Rotraut Binsteiner to Carstens, May 23, 1982, BArch, B 122/23883; Wilhelm Christiansen to Carstens, May 24, 1983, BArch, B 122/23883.
[53] Irmgard Recke to Carstens, September 17, 1980, BArch, B 122/23886.

13 percent of its European territories and all its overseas colonies. As the desire to restore "Rump Germany" to "Greater Germany" became central to the Nazi expansionism, invoking the term during the Cold War reflected nostalgia for the Third Reich.[54]

A striking continuity to eugenics was the persistence of biological racism, dehumanizing language, judgments based on skin color, and the term "race" (*Rasse*) itself. Overwhelmingly, the writers who invoked the language of "race" tended to be elderly retirees, who had lived through the Third Reich and had been indoctrinated into Nazi ideology. Germany did not just have a "foreigner problem," explained Dieter Baumann from Würzheim, but rather a "racial problem" (*Rassenproblem*) caused by "colored" (*farbige*) migrants.[55] Wilhelmine Richtscheid, a retired woman from Münster, cast Turkish nationality as a skin color and railed against "yellow, brown, black, and Turkish" asylum seekers.[56] A former World War II soldier, Werner Weber, complained that Turks were a "hard to discipline race" and warned against the "yellow danger" (*gelbe Gefahr*) of Vietnamese asylum seekers.[57] After fleeing East Germany's socialist dictatorship in 1949, Hedwig Kubatta bemoaned that she was now forced to live together with "Negroes, Turks, and other half-apes."[58]

The letters also included defamatory tropes surrounding "race-mixing" (*Rassenmischung*), a eugenic concept that the Nazis had taken to the extreme in the 1935 Nuremberg Laws that banned sexual relations between Jews and "Aryans" and categorized part-"Aryans" as "half-bloods" (*Mischlinge*). Although only one of the writers explicitly mentioned the Nuremberg Laws' criminal category of "racial defilement" (*Rassenschande*), several cautioned against the perils of sexual reproduction between individuals of "different *Völker* and *Rassen*," which posed the "danger that individual races would be destroyed."[59] Two of

---

54 On the Nazi connotations of *Restdeutschland*, see: Norbert Götz, "German-Speaking People and German Heritage: Nazi Germany and the Problem of *Volksgemeinschaft*," 58–82, in K. Molley O'Donnell, Nancy Reagin, and Renate Bridenthal, eds., *The Heimat Abroad: The Boundaries of Germanness* (Ann Arbor: University of Michigan Press, 2010), 60. A nostalgic song called "Restdeutschland" also circulated in right-wing circles: Rainer Fromm, *Schwarze Geister, neue Nazis: Jugendliche im Visier totalitärer Bewegungen* (Reinbek: Olzog, 2007), 263.

55 Dieter Baumann to Carstens, January 13, 1983, BArch, B 122/23883.

56 Wilhelmine Richtscheid to Carstens, October 21, 1981, BArch, B 122/23886.

57 Werner Weber to Carstens, February 16, 1981, BArch, B 122/23886.

58 Hedwig Kubatta to Carstens, November 24, 1982, BArch, B 122/23885; Herbert Kawlewski to Carstens, February 2, 1982, BArch, B 122/23885.

59 M. Kalthof to Carstens, November 11, 1982, BArch, B 122/23885.

the writers who invoked the most blatant Nazi terminologies, Hedwig Kubatta and Georg Kretschmer, contended that Germany had already become a "dirty *Mischvolk*" and asserted that integrating foreigners was "unnatural" because "God did not put any *Mischvölker* on this earth."[60] In particularly eugenic and dehumanizing language, 80-year-old Hugo Gebhard warned that if "various skin colors and face shapes" came to West Germany, the country would devolve into a "zoological garden" that, just like the "mixed society" (*Mischgesellschaft*) of the United States, would be plagued by "race riots" (*Rassenunruhen*).[61] Jürgen Feucht and Heinz Schambach both invoked the term "Eurasian-Negroid future race" (*eurasisch-negroiden Zukunftsrasse*), directly citing Seeger's pamphlet "Integrating Foreigners is Genocide."[62] In this sense, several insisted that their opposition to Turks was not a matter of racism or *Ausländerfeindlichkeit* but rather a "natural" and "very healthy" "self-preservation instinct."[63]

Further mobilizing Seeger's inflammatory rhetoric of "genocide," many writers argued that "race-mixing" threatened the "biological downfall of one's own *Volk*."[64] These fears were particularly common among the 25 percent of writers who criticized migrants' high birthrates. Berta Maier, one of the most vociferous critics, complained that Turkish women – with their "wombs always full" and their children "multiplying like mushrooms" – were committing an "embryo mass murder" or a "new style of genocide" against Germans.[65] Turning the blame on West Germans themselves, Bernhard Machemer from Osthofen said that West Germans were committing a "*Volk* suicide" (*Volkssuizid*) by allowing themselves to become the "modern slaves of the foreigners."[66] Seven letters invoked the parallel term "extermination" (*Ausrottung*), with two directly referencing the genocide of Native Americans perpetrated by Europeans conquering the Americas. Only one letter, from Alfred Kolbe of Nuremberg, alluded to Germans' "genocide" or "extermination" of Jews, but it did so in a way that

[60] Kubatta to Carstens, November 24, 1982, BArch, B 122/23885; Kretschmer to Carstens, December 21, 1981, BArch, B 122/23885.
[61] Hugo Gebhard to Carstens, May 21, 1983, BArch, B 122/23884.
[62] Feucht to Carstens, October 12, 1981; Schambach to Carstens, June 14, 1984, BArch, B 122/23886.
[63] Baumann to Carstens, January 13, 1983, BArch, B 122/23883; Hans Zeller to Carstens, July 1, 1983, BArch, B 122/23886.
[64] Hans Georg Föller to Carstens, June 10, 1982, BArch, B 122/23884.
[65] B. Maier to Carstens, January 4, 1983, BArch, B 122/23885.
[66] Bernhard Machemer to Carstens, December 21, 1980, BArch, B 122/23885.

absolved Germans of guilt: "This is the fate of the German _Volk,_ just as what happened to the Jewish _Volk._"[67]

Showing no remorse for the victims, 5 percent of the writers blamed the "Turkish problem" on Jews and Roma, the latter of whom they continued to stigmatize as "Gypsies" (_Zigeuener_). Sigismund Stucke, who expressed his strong commitment to protecting the "still existing German Reich," demanded that the government hold a popular referendum on a simple yes-or-no question: whether "Jews and other foreigners" should be allowed to stay in West Germany.[68] Rudolf Okun from Hunfeld argued that mass migration was a conspiracy concocted by an amorphous "world Jewry" (_Weltjüdentum_) that, invoking the derogatory Yiddish term for non-Jews, sought to "destroy all _goyim._"[69] Reflecting the connection between Islamophobia and anti-Zionism, one writer argued that "the current anti-Turkish _Ausländerfeindlichkeit_ is actually an act of revenge by the state of Israel" and by the entire "Jewish race." Several, moreover, demanded that Germany "kick out the Gypsy gangs," who were "murderers," "gang robbers," and "parasites."[70] Turkish children, ranted Ilse Vogel, were so unkempt that they "look like Gypsy children," while Georg Walter warned that "Germany is on its way to becoming a motley international Gypsy _Volk._"[71]

Expressing varying degrees of Holocaust denial and revisionism, Heinz Schambach and several other writers condemned the "guilt complex" (_Schuldkomplex_) or "collective guilt thesis" (_Kollektivschuldthese_), which portrayed all Germans as culpable for Nazism. Jürgen Feucht railed against the media's "endlessly prostituted" rhetoric of "previously-we-murdered-six-million-Jews-and-now-the-foreigners-are-next," while Robert Streit complained that the current media was "worse than under [Joseph] Goebbels," the Nazi propaganda minister.[72] Calling the widely broadcasted 1979 miniseries _Holocaust_ a "fictional, lying hate film" (_Hetzfilm_), Margarete Völkl complained that the fixation on the "so-called 'German past'" was denigrating Germans as "immoral,

[67] Alfred Kolbe to Carstens, May 22, 1982, BArch B 122/23885.
[68] Sigismund Stucke to Carstens, January 10, 1982, BArch, B 122/23886.
[69] Rudolf Okun to Carstens, June 20, 1983, BArch, B 122/23885.
[70] Matlinger to Carstens, undated, BArch B 122/23883; Gerhard Finkbeiner to Carstens, November 29, 1981, BArch, B 122/23884.
[71] Ilse Vogel to Carstens, May 26, 1983, BArch B 122/23886; Georg Walter to Carstens, May 27, 1983, BArch B 122/23886.
[72] Feucht to Carstens, October 12, 1981, BArch, B 122/23884; Robert Streit to Carstens, January 3, 1983, BArch B 122/23886.

criminal, horrible, and *ausländerfeindlich.*" She further espoused a frequent neo-Nazi rallying cry: demanding the release of Nazi Deputy Führer Rudolf Hess, now eighty-eight years old, who had been serving life in prison since 1945. Hess, Völkl cried, was "innocent," his family was "suffering greatly," and his imprisonment was "inhumane!"[73] Yet, in one of the most unconvincing denials of racism, she questioned: "Why do they have to call us Nazis?"

From complaints about unemployment, to racialized and Orientalist criticism of Islam, to blatant Holocaust denial, the wide range of opinions in these letters reveals the nuances and patterns of West German racism in the early 1980s. Despite attempting to justify their criticism as "rational" and "legitimate," these self-proclaimed "ordinary Germans" inadvertently exposed themselves as harboring the same racial prejudices that they tried to suppress. Emphasizing cultural racism alone belies that 10 percent of them displayed biological racism: they invoked Nazi terminology, ranted about inferior "races," decried "race-mixing," and bemoaned the "biological downfall," "genocide," or "extermination" of the German *Volk*. They denied or downplayed the Holocaust and denigrated Jews and Roma as connected to – and even responsible for – the "Turkish problem." While not a single writer praised Hitler, drew a swastika, or tied themselves directly to organized neo-Nazism, they had clearly absorbed the messages of sensationalist mainstream media and right-wing extremist tracts. And the knowledge that policymakers were drafting a law to promote guest workers' return migration normalized their racism as politically legitimate.

EVERYDAY RACISM AND ANTI-RACIST ACTIVISM

Racism, however, was also an everyday phenomenon and a collective experience, with real material and physical consequences for Turkish migrants. But crucially, the migrants fought back. If the early 1980s saw a rise in racism, then they also witnessed an attendant rise in anti-racist activism. Although Turks' anti-racist activism has generally been underacknowledged in the memory of the guest worker program, it is important to emphasize that Turkish migrants played an active role in the racial reckoning of the 1980s, challenging West German society to confront uncomfortable and silenced truths. Both individually and collectively, they worked to defend themselves against both structural and everyday

[73] Margarete Völkl to Carstens, July 29, 1982, BArch, B 122/23886.

racism. Forms of racism ranged from anti-Turkish jokes and slurs to discriminatory treatment in workplaces, schools, and neighborhoods and – importantly for this book – the drafting of the 1983 remigration law. Anti-racism, like racism itself, took many shapes.[74] It was usually peaceful but sometimes violent. It was public and private, loud and quiet, political and personal. It was a matter of looking outward and searching inward. Ultimately, everyone had their own relationship to anti-racist activism, guided by common but sometimes unspoken goals: improving their status, securing better treatment in their everyday lives, and staking a claim to membership in West German society while still maintaining ties to home.

In the overall memory of the racial reckoning of the early 1980s, one of the most striking and powerful anti-racist protests is the case of the young Turkish-German poet Semra Ertan (Figure 4.2). Born and raised in the port city of Mersin on Turkey's Mediterranean coast, Ertan had migrated to Kiel in 1971 at the age of fifteen to reunite with her parents, both of whom were guest workers of Alevi background. As she entered adulthood, leveraging her language skills to write poetry and work as a German-Turkish interpreter, she felt growing estrangement from both countries. While poetry provided a creative outlet to privately express her concerns, she turned to public anti-racist activism. Her many hunger strikes, however, had gone unnoticed. In a final attempt to bring attention to racism, she resorted to committing suicide publicly. On May 24, 1982, just one week before her twenty-sixth birthday, she doused herself with five liters of gasoline and set herself on fire in the middle of a busy street corner in Hamburg. Although a police officer rushed to smother the flames with blanket, she died in the hospital two days later.

The suicide of Semra Ertan is a powerful reminder that Turkish migrants' experiences of racism were – all at once – personal, public, and politicized, with effects that crossed national borders. Calculated and deliberate, Ertan intended for both Germans and Turks to understand her suicide as an act of anti-racism. To ensure that her message spread, she had notified two of West Germany's largest news outlets ahead of time. One reporter rushed to speak with her. In their interview, later printed verbatim in newspapers in both West Germany and Turkey, she made her protest clear. "The Germans should be ashamed of themselves," she insisted. "In 1961, they said, 'Welcome, guest workers.' If we all went back, who would do the dirty work? ... And even if they did, who would work for such a low wage? They would certainly say: No, I would not

---

[74] For an important study of the plurality of anti-racist discourses in Western Europe, see: Alana Lentin, *Racism and Anti-Racism in Europe* (London: Pluto Press, 2004).

FIGURE 4.2 Semra Ertan, Turkish-German poet and anti-
racism activist, ca. 1980. Ertan brought transnational attention
to West Germans' mistreatment of Turks when she committed
suicide publicly in protest in Hamburg. © Bilir-Meier
Family Archive, used with permission.

work for such a low wage." She concluded powerfully: "I want foreigners not only to have the right to live like human beings, but rather to also have the right to be treated like human beings. That is all. I want people to love and accept themselves. And I want them to think about my death."[75]

Ertan's call to action, however, was hotly contested both within and across borders. Reflecting the broader debates over racism, Ertan's suicide elicited mixed responses from West German politicians. While local SPD and Green Party representatives admitted that Turks were facing a "concrete threat" that could "move in the direction of pogroms," a CDU representative cautioned against "generalizing" Ertan's case, since the "overwhelming majority of Germans do not hate foreigners."[76] Ignoring her anti-racist motivation entirely, Foreign Minister Hans-Dietrich Genscher dismissed her suicide as "an act of desperation," while the State Interior Minister of Schleswig-Holstein called her a "victim of her own problems."[77] To be sure, Ertan had struggled greatly with her mental health, and she had previously attempted suicide. For politicians, however, emphasizing her mental health problems served the political purpose of deflecting attention away from racism. Such victim-blaming not only repeated gendered tropes of female psychiatric problems, but also reflected a pervasive tendency to attribute the "Turkish problem" to Turks' alleged unwillingness to integrate rather than to West Germany's lack of any comprehensive policy to integrate them.

In Turkey, observers were far more eager to emphasize Ertan's suicide as an anti-racism protest. Whereas West German reports of the suicide faded after several days, Turkish newspaper coverage persisted for weeks on end, condemning West German politicians' dismissive responses. In a *Milliyet* interview, her father attributed her suicide to West German policy, rightly pointing out that just two weeks before her suicide, Chancellor Helmut Schmidt had announced that foreigners should either integrate into Germany or go home.[78] *Hürriyet* published a multi-page feature on how her suicide had affected her friends, neighbors, and family in her Turkish home city of Mersin, juxtaposing

---

[75] Quoted in Zühal Bilir-Meier and Cana Bilir-Meier, Foreword to Semra Ertan, *Mein Name ist Ausländer: Gedichte*, eds. Zühal Bilir-Meier and Cana Bilir Meier (Münster: Edition Assemblage, 2020), 10–12.

[76] DPA, "Bestürzung über 'Verzweiflungstat,'" May 1982.

[77] DPA, "Ausländer. Zurückhaltendere Reaktionen in Ankara auf Selbstmord junger Türkin," June 1982, in BArch B 136/15048.

[78] *Milliyet*, quoted in "Im Feuer," *Die Tageszeitung*, May 26, 2021, www.taz.de/Todestag-von-Semra-Ertan/!5774155/.

photographs of her repatriated casket with those of her happy childhood before she followed her parents to Germany, where "the true tragedy began."[79]

The week after her suicide, *Hürriyet* published a short blurb urging Turks in Germany to write directly to the West German president. *Hürriyet*'s sample letter, printed in both languages, read: "We as members of the Turkish minority who have been working in Germany for many years deplore the recent events. We are suffering the most under unemployment, and *Ausländerfeindlichkeit* threatens our very existence. The aggressors are known, but no action is taken against them. On the other hand, we also pay taxes and contribute to Germany's welfare. Is 'peace' not our right? Our request to you is to urgently pass a law against *Ausländerfeindlichkeit*."[80] The call resonated broadly. The president's office received fifty-six letters with the verbatim text, one of which had twenty-six signatories, while a dozen others wrote their own messages. Reflecting the importance of Ertan's suicide, one attached the *Hürriyet* newspaper article about the funeral in Mersin, while others noted that "a woman in Hamburg set herself on fire" and that "there are others like Semra."[81] Most extremely, one woman threatened: "If this situation does not change immediately, then I too will set myself on fire in the middle of the street like Semra Ertan, because we are sick and tired of this horrible treatment and we want to be free of it."[82]

As these letters reflect, Ertan's suicide resonated so deeply and personally not only because of sympathy toward her as a young woman, but also because her protest spoke to a collective everyday experience of anti-Turkish racism. Even when simply walking down the streets, the migrants had metaphorical targets on their backs. Speaking Turkish, or speaking German with a Turkish accent, was an audible marker of difference. And West Germans' racialization of Turks as predominantly dark-skinned with so-called "Mediterranean," "Oriental," or "Asiatic" features made many migrants – especially women and girls who wore headscarves – visually identifiable even before they spoke. Some migrants, however, recalled that they experienced less overt discrimination because they were able to racially "pass" as German due to their blonde hair and

---

[79] "İşte Semra..." *Hürriyet*, June 1982.
[80] "Mektup örneği" *Hürriyet*, June 2, 1982.
[81] Başak B. to Carstens, June 30, 1982, BArch, B 122/23883; Aynal Süleyman to Carstens, September 5, 1982, BArch, B 122/23886.
[82] Hassan Hüseyin Aydemir to Carstens, June 22, 1982, BArch, B 122/23883; Yeter Gök to Carstens, June 6, 1982, BArch, B 122/23884.

blue eyes.[83] One girl also explained that because her parents came from Istanbul, were educated, and were "western-minded," she was better able to fit in socially and culturally with Germans.[84] Nevertheless, because Germans tended to homogenize Turks as coming from predominantly rural areas, Turks' ability "pass" on the basis of urban origins was limited.

Germans verbally assaulted them with racist slurs, whether screaming at them across the street or mumbling quietly on streetcars. Besides more generic hateful names like "shit Turks" (*Scheiß-Türken*) and "Turkish pigs" (*Türken-Schweine*), these slurs also reflected age-old Orientalist stereotypes. Especially common were insults like "camel driver" (*Kameltreiber*), "garlic eaters" (*Knoblauchfresser*), and "cumin Turk" (*Kümmeltürken*), which associated Turks not only with the seemingly "exotic" foods that they brought to West Germany's otherwise bland culinary scene, but also with backwardness and underdevelopment. Increasingly throughout the 1980s, the racial slur *Kanaken* – which Germans had applied since the early twentieth century to an evolving variety of primarily working-class migrant populations from Southern and Eastern Europe, North Africa, and the Middle East – became nearly exclusively associated with Turks.[85]

Alongside foreboding signs banning them from entering German businesses, migrants also confronted racist graffiti spray-painted by organized neo-Nazis or just rowdy teenagers looking for a laugh. In one iconic photograph taken in Berlin-Kreuzberg, a Turkish man named Ali Topaloğlu and his two young nieces walk somberly past graffiti that states "Turks out!" (Türken raus!).[86] Given the strong emotions that this image evoked, it was reprinted in media outlets throughout West Germany, including on the front page of *Metall,* the publication of the metalworkers' trade union. The proliferation of such images in the mass media and through migrant networks ensured that guest workers and their children knew about this graffiti even if they had not directly confronted it. Especially disturbing was that anti-Turkish graffiti was often accompanied by swastikas, which visually implied that Turks and other "foreigners" were destined to a similar fate as Jews. Amid the public

[83] Gülmisâl E., interview.
[84] Sebnem, in Meyer, *Rückkehrkinder Berichten*, 97.
[85] The term *Kanaken* has since been reappropriated by some second- and third-generation Turkish migrants, who use it as a point of pride and self-identification. See: Feridun Zaimoğlu, *Kanak Sprak: 24 Mißtöne vom Rande der Gesellschaft* (Berlin: Rotbuch, 2013).
[86] See cover image of this book. Another photograph that captured the same scene a few seconds later has also circulated prominently; only one girl is visible in the frame, often mistakenly assumed to be the man's daughter.

reckoning with how the resurgence of neo-Nazism threatened both public order and the very project of liberal democracy itself, the Turkish-Jewish comparison threatened not only migrants but also West German society.

The so-called Turkish jokes (*Türkenwitze*) put migrants at further unease.[87] Reflecting the stereotype that Turks often worked in "dirty" jobs like garbage collectors, street cleaners, and construction workers, one joke questioned: "Why are some garbage cans made of glass? So that even Turks have a window to look out of." In dehumanizing and misogynistic language, another joke went: "What is the difference between a Turkish woman and a pig? One wears a headscarf." The most common jokes, however, made light of death and even murder. Many directly alluded to the Holocaust, particularly the murder of Jews in the gas chambers:

What is the difference between a Turk and the median on the Autobahn? You can't drive over the median.

What is a misfortune? When a ship full of Turks sinks. What is a catastrophe? When a Turk survives.

Have you heard that Turks carry a knife all the time? Between their shoulder blades and ten centimeters deep.

Have you seen the latest microwave oven? There's room in it for a whole family of Turks.

How many Turks fit in a Volkswagen? A hundred! Four on the seats, and the rest in the ashtray!

A trainload of Turks leaves Istanbul but arrives in Hamburg empty. How come? It came by way of Auschwitz.

The German scholar Richard Albrecht, writing at the time, interpreted these jokes as revealing the latent racism among the mainstream German population.[88] Equally important to understand, however, is the sheer impact that these hateful words had on the migrants themselves.

Jokes, slurs, and bullying were especially common – and traumatic – for children. Everyday contact with German classmates, teachers, and school administrators was a double-edged sword. On the one hand, many Turkish

---

[87] The "jokes" listed here come from these sources: Abadan-Unat, *Turks in Europe*, 188; Jess Nierenberg, "'Ich möchte das Geschwür loswerden.' Türkenhaß in Witzen in der Bundesrepublik Deutschland," *Fabula* 25, no. 3 (1984): 232; Tuba Tarcan and Dilek Zaptcıoğlu, "'Unser Schweigen muss sich in Widerstand verwandeln!.' 'Ausländerfeindlichkeit' und die Türken in der Bundesrepublik," *Bizim Almanca*, March 1986, 10–13.

[88] Richard Albrecht, "'Was ist der Unterschied zwischen Türken und Juden?': (Anti) Türkenwitze in der Bundesrepublik Deutschland," *Zeitschrift für Volkskunde* 78 (1982): 220.

children achieved academic success, built strong relationships with their teachers and classmates, and viewed school fondly. On the other hand, schools were also sites of racist encounters that left children wavering between belonging and rejection. In one particularly blatant example of West Germans using the language of "race" and "race-mixing," a German mother attempted to enroll her half-Turkish son in a German international school during a stay abroad, but the principal immediately rejected them, noting abruptly: "Sorry, but in our kindergarten, we only accept pure-blooded (*reinrassige*) children."[89] Especially hurtful was when racism came from the mouths of their peers, who often reiterated their parents' condemnation of Turks. When an eleven-year-old girl named Nirgül walked into her fourth-grade classroom for the first time, she was greeted with jeers. "Eww, we have another Turk," her classmates complained, refusing to sit next to her, while one boy insisted, "I have to be a meter away from a Turk."[90] Of course, there were instances in which German classmates attempted to intervene on behalf of their Turkish friends – but the bullies typically pressed on. "Even if you scream at them," one German high schooler complained, "they still are not convinced ... I don't think they know that it hurts his feelings."[91]

Given the rising attention to Holocaust education in the 1980s, schools also provided a space for Turkish children to contextualize their personal experiences of racism within the longer-term continuities of Germany's Nazi past.[92] Although they did not have personal or family connections to the Third Reich, they were able to draw parallels to their own experiences. One Turkish girl named Çiğdem, who later returned to Turkey with her parents, recalled how sitting in the classroom with German students and learning about their grandparents' crimes proved crucial to her journey of self-discovery. While learning about the Nazis' persecution of Jews, Çiğdem "realized that we Turks are affected exactly the same way and are next in line." Comparing her experience to the Holocaust also provided her with a new weapon in her arsenal to fight back. When one of her elderly neighbors screamed that she was a "stinking Turk," she became so angry that she called him a "Jew eater" (*Judenfresser*).[93]

Turkish migrants had legitimate reason to fear that hateful words might turn into physical – or fatal – violence. The media regularly

[89] Merey, *Der ewige Gast*, 73.
[90] "Wir können nicht mal sagen, was wir fühlen," *Der Spiegel*, November 14, 1982, 85–97.
[91] "Das sind doch nicht alles Kanaken," *PZ*, May 1982, AfsB, IGBE-Archiv, 14997.
[92] On Holocaust education and Muslim migrants, see: Özyürek, *Subcontractors of Guilt*.
[93] Quoted in Meyer, *Rückkehrkinder Berichten*, 27.

covered the concurrent rise in organized neo-Nazism and neo-Nazi violence. Their fears were heightened by the well-publicized shooting at the Twenty Five discotheque in Nuremberg, an establishment that was often frequented by foreigners and people of color. On June 24, 1982, the twenty-six-year-old West German neo-Nazi Helmut Oxner pulled out a high-caliber Smith & Wesson revolver and started shooting at people on the dancefloor. He murdered two African-American men – one a civilian, and one a military sergeant – and near fatally injured a Korean woman and a Turkish waiter. After fleeing the discotheque, he pulled out another gun and proceeded to shoot with two guns at foreigners passing by on the sidewalk. There, he murdered an Egyptian exchange student and crushed the jaw of a man from Libya. Before turning the gun on himself, Oxner shouted, "I only shoot at Turks!"[94] Oxner had been known by police: just two days before, he and another neo-Nazi had anonymously telephoned the police station, lambasting Turks and Jews as "camel drivers," "foreigner pigs," and "Jew pigs."

In the weeks immediately following the shooting, leading West German newspapers emphasized the pervasiveness of anti-Turkish physical violence throughout the country, tying together smaller incidents into a narrative of rising danger. This "everyday violence," as *Die Zeit* put it, was no longer exceptional: "Not a day goes by without news of bloody attacks against a minority that was once enthusiastically invited."[95] In Hamburg, *Der Spiegel* reported, Turkish teachers were "terrorized" with death threats. In Berlin, two men accosted a Turkish man in the subway, remarking that "previously something like that would have been gassed." In Munich, two other men stabbed a Turkish teenager in the throat with a broken beer bottle, shouting that he was a "foreigner pig that belongs in Dachau." In Witten, a wall was defaced with graffiti warning: "The Jews have it behind them, the Turks still in front of them."[96] In Frankfurt, a German man horrifically threw a three-year-old Turkish girl into a trashcan because, in his words, "the filthy people (*Dreckvolk*) must go." At the core of these discussions was a central question, which struck at the heart of West Germany's broader racial reckoning: were the culprits all neo-Nazis and skinheads, or were they also ordinary people unaffiliated with extremist groups? For *Der Spiegel*, the answer was clear: this violence was "in no way" perpetrated only by "organized neo-Nazis."

---

[94] "Rechtsradikale: Lebende Zeitbomben," *Der Spiegel*, July 4, 1982.
[95] *Zeit-Magazin*, 1982, quoted in Tsiakalos, *Ausländerfeindlichkeit*, 12.
[96] "'Nutten und Bastarde erschlagen wir,'" *Der Spiegel*, July 4, 1982.

Rather than acquiesce to racist rhetoric and violence, Turks engaged in varying forms of anti-racist activism, which operated on a spectrum from peaceful protest to the formation of violent gangs. As early as the 1970s, Turks living in the slums – or what Germans denigrated as "Turkish ghettos" – banded together into gangs to defend themselves.[97] As the West German Embassy in Ankara put it in 1982, these gangs functioned as "self-protection organizations": "I wouldn't be surprised if the Turks began to fight back," wrote one embassy official forebodingly, which he feared could lead to "blood vengeance" (*Blutrache*).[98] One of the most prominent of these gangs was the 36 Boys, founded in 1987 in West Berlin's heavily Turkish district of Kreuzberg, often called "Little Istanbul" (Figure 4.3). In a 2005 interview, a former member of the 36 Boys named Ali explained that he joined at age twelve because he knew many of the members and craved a sense of community. Embracing African-American culture, Ali and his friends went to rap and hip-hop parties, learned how to breakdance, and sprayed graffiti art on walls.[99] But, on the darker side, Ali also recalled many nights out on the streets with his fellow gang members fighting neo-Nazis and watching his friends die from stab wounds.[100] Turkish gang violence rose in the early 1990s, as a means of defense against the onslaught of neo-Nazi attacks after reunification.[101] Although West German media coverage acknowledged the justification of self-defense, they tended to place the blame primarily on Turkish gangs themselves, even though German neo-Nazis and right-wing extremists were responsible for instigating the violence and posed a greater threat.[102]

---

[97] On gangs, see: Klaus Farin and Eberhard Seidel, *Krieg in den Städten: Jugendgangs in Deutschland* (Berlin: Archiv der Jugendkulturen e. V., 2012).

[98] German Embassy in Ankara to AA Bonn, "Situation der Türken in Deutschland," July 7, 1982.

[99] On rap and hip-hop in Kreuzberg, see: Levent Sosyal, "Rap, HipHop, Kreuzberg: Scripts of/for Migrant Youth Culture in the WorldCity Berlin," *New German Critique* 92 (2004): 62–81. Regarding Afro-German activists, see: Fatima El-Tayeb, "'If You Can't Pronounce My Name, You Can Just Call Me Pride': Afro-German Activism, Gender, and Hip Hop," *Gender & History* 15, no. 3 (2004): 460–86.

[100] Ali Atmaca, interview by DOMiD, March 2005, DOMiD-Archiv, R0015.MS 04 R.

[101] On the case of a prominent gang in the 1990s, the Frankfurt-based Turkish Power Boys, see: Hermann Tertilt, *Turkish Power Boys: Ethnographie einer Jugendbande* (Frankfurt am Main: Suhrkamp, 1996).

[102] See, among many examples: "'Es muß nur einer von uns sterben...'" *Die Tageszeitung*, January 26, 1990; "'So ein Gefühl der Befreiung,'" *Der Spiegel*, November 11, 1990; "'Jeder Deutsche rein Nazi,'" *Der Spiegel*, November 18, 1990; "Zeitbomben in den Vorstädten," *Der Spiegel*, April 13, 1997.

FIGURE 4.3 Members of the prominent Turkish gang 36 Boys in Berlin-Kreuzberg proudly stand in front of "36" graffiti, 1990.
© Ergun Çagatay/Fotoarchiv Ruhr Museum/Stadtmuseum Berlin/Stiftung Historische Museen Hamburg, used with permission.

Far more often, however, the fight against racism was peaceful. Turkish workers overwhelmingly chose the pen over the sword, lobbying their political representatives and labor union leaders. In March 1982, for example, Turkish mineworkers in Gelsenkirchen wrote a scathing letter to the president of the Industrial Union of Mining and Energy (IGBE). When reading an article in the Turkish newspaper *Hürriyet,* the workers were shocked that the newspaper had quoted the mine's director as being "very satisfied with the performance of the Turks." Appalled at the director's seeming disingenuousness, the workers complained: "How is something like that even possible at our mine? Here we are despised and suppressed, and we suffer under *Ausländerfeindlichkeit.*"[103] Within the past year, four of their Turkish colleagues, including one with a disability, had been brutally beaten by Germans on the job. That year, the IGBE president also received a letter from a Turkish union member who, without using the word "race," invoked the legacy of Nazism and

---

[103] Letter from Turkish Mineworkers to Adolf Schmidt, March 10, 1982, AfsB, IGBE-Archiv, 14997.

worried that the past might repeat itself. Germans, he explained, viewed foreigners as a "threat to the pure German culture" and as a "problem that was waiting for its final solution (*Endlösung*)." Both politicians and academics, he wrote after the Heidelberg Manifesto's publication, were striving to create "a clean world of 'blue-eyed and blonde-haired people.'"[104]

Neighborhoods and apartments were also sites of protests against discriminatory local ordinances.[105] One particularly well-publicized incident took place in the district of Merkenich in the outskirts of Cologne, where during the 1960s, Turkish migrants had built their own houses on the largely abandoned Causemannstraße. By 1981, twenty-eight families were living there, frequently receiving threatening letters from the district government commanding them to leave as part of a broader effort to gentrify the district and rid it of Turks. Overnight in August 1982, while many of these families were on vacation in Turkey, the Cologne city government sent construction workers to tear down five houses. In a flyer that circulated throughout Cologne, the migrants maintained that all they had done was attempt to make "their own homes, simple wood and stone houses, almost a small village with vegetable gardens, courtyards, and pergolas," with places for children to play and where "men and women can maintain the sociability and hospitality they are accustomed to at home undisturbed by German landlords." Tearing down the five houses, they asserted, was an act of *Ausländerfeindlichkeit* on the part of the municipal government.[106]

Turks also took to the streets to peacefully protest, often joined by sympathetic Germans. In November 1982, the local Protestant pastor in Gelsenkirchen worked alongside Turkish residents to organize a large "protest against *Ausländerfeindlichkeit*," which attracted 500 demonstrators. This protest came in response to a spate of neo-Nazi violence that occurred in early November, the same week as the 44th anniversary of Kristallnacht. The Gelsenkirchen attack saw neo-Nazis ignite a fire at the office of the local Turkish workers association, spraypaint racist graffiti and swastikas on some two dozen storefronts owned by migrants, and send death threats to Turkish workers."[107] The pastor defended the

[104] R. Kartal, Letter, 1982, AfsB, IGBE-Archiv, folder unnamed.
[105] On housing activism among Italian guest workers, see: Sarah Jacobsen, "Squatting to Make Ends Meet: Southern Italian Migrants and the Right to a Home in 1970s Italy and West Germany" (PhD diss., Michigan State University, 2021).
[106] Flyer, "Türkei in Köln, Türkei in Merkenich," 1982, DOMiD-Archiv, E 0536,9.
[107] "Demonstration gegen Ausländerfeindlichkeit," *Ruhr Nachrichten*, November 29, 1982.

FIGURE 4.4 Young Turkish protesters march with a banner that states: "We do not want to be the Jews of tomorrow," 1981. © picture alliance/dpa, used with permission.

migrants: "They are not 'Kanaken,' they are not 'pigs'... They are not 'overrunning us ... They are not 'infiltrating' us."[108] He insisted that combatting *Ausländerfeindlichkeit* began first and foremost with Germans themselves. Germans, he cautioned, should not "bite our tongues when harmful, false words want to come out of our lips," nor should they continue to "laugh at jokes about foreigners." Importantly, amid the rise of Holocaust memory in the 1980s, these protests sometimes directly referenced the Holocaust, with Turks overtly comparing their situation to that of Jews during the Third Reich (Figures 4.4 and 4.5).

Protests of this sort, however, also revealed the fissures between Turks and Germans – or what Jennifer A. Miller has called "imperfect solidarities."[109] Like in the Gelsenkirchen case above, protests were frequently organized by Germans, with relatively minimal input and participation from Turkish migrants. So, too, were protests often performative, with even the most well-meaning of German demonstrators taking to the streets without working to dismantle the elements of structural racism.

---

[108] Richard Walter, "Aussprache auf der Abschlußkundgebung der Demonstration gegen Ausländerfeindlichkeit," November 27, 1982, AfsB, IGBE-Archiv, folder unnamed.
[109] J. Miller, *Turkish Guest Workers in Germany*, 135–61.

FIGURE 4.5 Protesters somberly hold yellow Stars of David, which the
Nazis forced Jews to wear, to draw a powerful visual connection between
past and present persecution, 1982. Written in the stars are "asylum seeker,"
"foreigner," and "Jew," although it is unclear whether the individuals holding
the signs belong to those respective groups. © Deutsche Fotothek/Martin
Langer, used with permission.

One particularly striking example occurred in 1991 amid the wave
of neo-Nazi violence after reunification in the heavily Turkish city of
Duisburg. There, some two hundred people demonstrated in a silent
march in the middle of a hailstorm, carrying signs with catchy slogans,
such as "People eat gyros and döner kebab, so why do they try to get
rid of the cook?" and "Do we only need foreigners for German garbage disposal?"[110] However, this protest was organized on the initiative of German doctors, nurses, and social workers at a local hospital
without consulting any migrants, and both German and Turkish passersby appeared disinterested. In fact, one Turkish representative on the

---

[110] On the politicization of migrants' cuisine including döner kebab, see: Ayşe Çağlar,
"McDöner. Dönerkebab und der Kampf der Deutsch-Türken um soziale Stellung,"
Sociologus 48, no. 1 (1998): 17–41; Maren Möhring, *Fremdes Essen. Die Geschichte
der ausländischen Gastronomie in der Bundesrepublik Deutschland* (Munich: De
Gruyter, 2012).

Duisburg's Foreigner Council (Ausländerbeirat) even questioned why so few Turks were willing to participate alongside Germans.[111]

Ultimately, examining Turks' anti-racist activism reveals that – just like in matters of determining who counted as "German" – West Germans did not have a singular claim to reckoning with racism. And, just like racism itself, anti-racist activism existed on a spectrum. The case of Semra Ertan, who publicly set herself on fire in protest, is a powerful reminder not only of just how deeply racism was embedded in migrants' psyches but also of the sheer frustration and desperation that many migrants felt. To be sure, not all migrants who engaged in forms of protest considered themselves political activists. Rather, fighting back against both structural and everyday racism – whether in workplaces, schools, or neighborhoods – was often simply a matter of everyday necessity to improve their living conditions and prevent further discriminatory acts. That some Germans leapt to Turks' defense provides an encouraging counterpart to others' blatant racism. Still, moments of solidarity proved fraught. When Germans defended Turks, they did so not necessarily out of sympathy for migrants, but mostly to mount a show of strength against the rising tide of right-wing extremism and neo-Nazism. Germans' allyship thus slipped into what feminist scholar Linda Alcoff has called "the problem of speaking for others," whereby "the practice of privileged persons speaking for or on behalf of less privileged persons has actually resulted (in many cases) in increasing and reinforcing the oppression of the group spoken for."[112] Enjoying comfort in public space, and safe from the threat of retribution, Germans – despite their best intentions – drowned out the voices of the migrants themselves.

TURKEY'S 1980 COUP, HUMAN RIGHTS, AND HOLOCAUST MEMORY

As performativity eclipsed real change, it became up to those in the home country to defend the migrants against the forces of hate. As news of a possible remigration law spread in the early 1980s, the racial reckoning echoed abroad, enflaming bilateral tensions with Turkey. The Turkish government staunchly opposed the proposed remigration law not only

---

[111] Martin Ziecke, "Demonstranten hielt auch der Hagel nicht auf," *Neue Ruhr Zeitung*, October 18, 1991.
[112] Linda Alcoff, "The Problem of Speaking for Others," *Cultural Critique* 20 (1991–92): 7.

for policy reasons, as it blatantly contradicted Turkey's financially based opposition to the guest workers' return, but also as a matter of political strategy and principle. While Turkish officials did not always act in the migrants' best interests, they envisioned themselves – at least outwardly – as the protectors of their mistreated citizens abroad. Turkish media outlets and ordinary citizens also rushed to the migrants' defense, even though they simultaneously ostracized the migrants as "Germanized." Generalizing all Germans as inherently racist, Turkish critics accused them of violating the migrants' human rights and drew direct comparisons to the Nazi past: Turks were the new Jews, Schmidt was the new Hitler, and the 1980s had become the 1930s. The Holocaust thus became a usable past for Turks, one that could be deployed in debates about return migration or used, alternatively, to whitewash Turkey's own past and present abuses against minority groups.

But this rhetoric was accompanied by a great irony: it occurred in the immediate aftermath of the September 12, 1980, military coup, when Turkey's authoritarian government became the target of international scorn for committing egregious human rights violations against political dissidents, Kurds, and other minority populations. The coup was a major turning point in Turkey's relationship with Europe, as it brought Turkey's status as a "European" country into question and strained its relations with the EEC. Just three weeks after the coup, both West Germany and France introduced obligatory visas for Turkish citizens, and other EEC countries followed suit.[113] The West German government under Chancellor Helmut Schmidt found itself in a particularly tricky situation and had to tread lightly. For West Germany, many issues were at stake: Turkey was a crucial NATO ally against the Soviet Union, West Germany was the second largest provider of military and economic aid to Turkey, and Turkey's cooperation on the question of guest workers' return migration was paramount.[114] Moreover, the coup government's heightened emphasis on Turkish nationalism and militarism contradicted West Germans' growing wariness of nationalism and their turn toward a "postnational" identity rooted in broader ties to Europe. But Schmidt's government also had to balance its diplomatic support for Turkey with domestic criticism. SPD parliamentarians expressed concerns that Turkey might "abuse" West German military aid to "suppress" the Kurdish

---

[113] Comte, *The History of the European Migration Regime*, 115.
[114] İhsan Dağı, "Democratic Transition in Turkey, 1980–83: The Impact of European Diplomacy," *Middle Eastern Studies* 32, no. 2 (1996): 126.

minority and Turkish dissidents. In solidarity with Turkish and Kurdish activists, West German students, journalists, churches, trade unions, and migrant advocacy organizations complained that the West German government was "dismissing" or "watering down" Turkey's abuses.[115] Still, even the mild reproach of Turkey by Foreign Minister Hans-Dietrich Genscher "clearly offended the Turkish leaders."[116]

The 1980 military coup alarmed West German policymakers not only because of the authoritarian government and blatant human rights violations, but also because the resulting rise in asylum seekers posed a further impediment to solving the domestic "Turkish problem." They argued that granting asylum to Turkish citizens would not only result in far greater numbers of "Islamic," "Asiatic," and "Oriental" people coming to West German, but would also create a "Kurdish minority problem" by transferring Turkey's "ethnic tensions" to West Germany.[117] As a result, West Germany continued to label Turkey a "safe country," excluded Kurds and Yazidis from its narrow definition of "political persecution," and accepted only 2 percent of asylum seekers from Turkey between January 1979 and August 1983.[118] Policymakers also feared that granting asylum to dissidents would heighten political violence among migrants. Particularly worrisome were the Grey Wolves (*Bozkurtlar*), a militant, right-wing extremist, pan-Turkist organization tied to Turkey's Nationalist Movement Party (MHP) founded in 1969. In the words of *Der Spiegel,* the MHP was "racist" and "fascist," and its founder Alparslan Türkeş was a "Hitler admirer" who "dreams of a new Greater Turkish Empire."[119] The West German Interior Ministry did not hesitate to describe Türkeş's "true goals" in terms of Nazism: seizing power "exactly as the Nazis," implementing "National Socialist doctrine" in Turkey through "oppressive measures," "liquidating" all ethnic minorities, and uniting all Turks on the Earth under the principle of 'One People, One Empire' (*ein Volk, ein Reich*)."[120] Although Turkey's post-coup government outlawed the MHP and imprisoned Türkeş, many West

---

[115] Pamphlet, Münchner Komitee Solidarität mit den verfolgten Gewerkschaften in der Türkei, March 1982, TÜSTAV, www.tustav.org/kutuphane/yurtdisi-kutuphanesi/solidaritat-mit-den-verfolgten-gewerkschaften-in-der-turkei/.

[116] AA Bonn to Bundespresseamt, "Betr.: Britische Presse zum Türkei-Besuch von BM Genscher," November 6, 1981, BArch, B 136/23601.

[117] German Embassy in Ankara to AA, "Betr.: EG-Vollmitgliedschaft der Türkei; hier: politische Aspekte," July 14, 1981, PAAA, B 26/1610.

[118] Stokes, "The Permanent Refugee Crisis," 36.

[119] "Rache für Hamido," *Der Spiegel,* May 7, 1978.

[120] "Mit Bozkurt zum Licht," *Der Spiegel,* September 7, 1980.

Germans continued to associate the Grey Wolves with Turkish authoritarianism and worried that extremism lurked among guest workers.

The situation was further compounded by Turkey's looming full membership in the EEC, which was planned for 1986 but never materialized. Just three days after the coup, the EEC declared that discussions about Turkey's full membership could only continue if the military government "quickly reinstated democratic institutions and respected human rights."[121] Yet it soon became clear that Turkey was failing to "announce a precise timeline" for returning to democracy and that discussions about full membership would therefore be "frozen."[122] With the highest proportion of Turkish immigrants, West Germany had the largest stake in Turkey's membership – particularly regarding the provision that citizens of member states be granted freedom of mobility. Already grappling with how to limit the number of Turks allowed to enter the country, West German officials desperately sought to twist the terms of the EEC's discussions such that Turkey could become a member without receiving freedom of mobility. As one internal memorandum on the issue stated emphatically, underlined for emphasis, "We must permanently exclude Turks from having unlimited access to our labor market!"[123] Behind closed doors, the Belgian and Danish governments, which also had sizable Turkish populations, agreed. West Germans thus weaponized Turkey's authoritarianism and human rights violations to express their concerns about freedom of mobility for unwanted Turkish citizens.

West Germans' general reproach of Turkey's military coup, alongside their rising racism against migrants, incensed Turks in the home country. To expose West Germans' hypocrisy, Turkish critics often used the language of human rights against them. In an especially frustrating blow, some of the most vocal criticism of the nexus between racism and return migration came from the post-coup dictator, General Kenan Evren. Unequivocally guilty of perpetrating human rights violations himself, Evren invoked the language of human rights not only to portray himself as the custodian of the migrants abroad but also to deflect Europeans' criticism of him. Reflecting the Turkish government's financially based opposition to guest workers' return migration, Evren centered his criticism on the ongoing discussions of a remigration law. In his

---

[121] AA Bonn, "Betr.: EU-Türkei; hier: Türkischer Antrag auf Einberufung des Assoziationsrates auf Botschafterebene," April 29, 1981, BArch, B 136/23601.

[122] European Economic Community in Brussels to AA Bonn, December 3, 1981, BArch, B 126/23601.

[123] "Freizügigkeit Türkei," November 18, 1981, BArch, B 136/23601.

New Year's speech in 1982, Evren proclaimed: "We are following with horror and dismay how the very same countries that previously called for cheap laborers in order to drive their own economic progress are now attempting to expel the country's same workers in defiance of their human rights. Our government opposes this injustice with full force."[124] Four months later, Evren pledged to do everything in his power to prevent West Germany from sending guest worker families back but noted that he would try to make life pleasant for families who returned.[125]

The battle over human rights played out primarily in the Turkish press. Although Turkey's 1961 constitution had enshrined freedom of the press as a fundamental right, the leaders of the 1980 military coup banned several communist newspapers and arrested hundreds of journalists and editors. The country's oldest and most reputable newspaper, *Cumhuriyet*, was even closed for ten days after a critical editorial.[126] To avoid problems, mainstream newspapers generally exercised self-censorship and avoided harsh criticism of the government, whereas those on the right side of the political spectrum often functioned as government mouthpieces. Despite their persuasions, journalists eagerly criticized West German racism and leapt to the migrants' defense. Some were attuned to the nuances of the West German debate over terminology. In an article about the December 1981 survey that classified 49 percent of West Germans as "ausländer-feindlich," *Cumhuriyet* explained that West Germans deliberately used the word *Ausländerfeindlichkeit* (*yabancı düşmanlığı*) to distinguish it from biological racism or "blood-based hatred" (*kan düşmanlığı*).[127] The most inflammatory editorials often invoked the Turkish term for "racism" (*ırkçılık*), especially when comparing the migrants' situation to the Nazis' persecution of Jews.

The rhetoric in Turkish articles, particularly in editorials and columns, was often virulent. Several portrayed West Germany as a new enemy who was destroying the otherwise "friendly" history of Prussian-Ottoman and German-Turkish international affairs. The notion of "friendliness" recalled their close economic and diplomatic ties since the nineteenth century, the German-Ottoman military alliance during World War I, Turkey's neutrality in World War II despite the atrocities

---

[124] Bernd Geiss, "Zusammenfassung. Türkische Standpunkte zur deutschen Ausländerpolitik," February 1982, PAAA, B 85/1611.
[125] German Embassy in Ankara to AA, "Betr.: Türkische Innenpolitik; hier: Rede General Evrens in Bursa am 03.04.1982," April 5, 1982, PAAA, B 85/1604.
[126] Zürcher, *Turkey: A Modern History*, 284.
[127] "İki Almandan biri yabancı düşmanı," *Cumhuriyet*, May 3, 1982, 11.

of Nazism, their ongoing NATO alliance during the Cold War, and the signing of the guest worker recruitment treaty itself. Emblematic of this rhetoric of broken friendship, in January 1981, *Milliyet* insisted that it made no sense to continue "wearing the guise of friendship and brotherhood" given that West Germans wanted the migrants to leave.[128] While an official at the West German Consulate in Istanbul dismissed this article as a "rarity" with limited public resonance, Chancellor Helmut Schmidt made a point of mentioning that Turkey remained a "good friend" in a *Milliyet* interview several months later.[129] Tropes of destroyed friendship continued to increase, however, as all three major West German parties hardened their stance on migration policy. "It is sad," wrote *Hürriyet* several months later, "that the old friendship between our countries, which outlasted the defeat of the First World War, the troubled Weimar period, and even the Hitler dictatorship, is now being destroyed by a Germany that calls itself democratic."[130] The concluding phrase, "a Germany that calls itself democratic," burns with sarcasm. Its implication, reiterated in numerous other Turkish newspaper articles of the time, was that West Germany had no claim to moral superiority in matters of democracy, human rights, and freedom.

In scathing editorials, Turkish journalists insinuated that the West German government's various restrictions on Turkish migrants constituted an act of ethnic discrimination that was more discordant with democracy and human rights than their own country's military coup. The Turkish newspaper *Son Havadis* denounced Schmidt's proposal to restrict the age of family reunification as a "violation of all humanitarian principles," and *Milliyet* called the proposed new visa requirement for Turkish tourists a matter of "international solidarity and human rights" that "built a Berlin Wall against the Turkish workers."[131] *Günaydın* denounced a controversial Baden-Württemberg law that forbade the marriage of any workers who resided in an apartment smaller than thirty square meters as a restriction on the Turks' "human rights" and, in another article, decried the treatment of Turks in general: "The Germans

---

[128] Feyyaz Tokar, *Milliyet,* June 19, 2021, quoted in West German Consulate in Istanbul to AA, "Betr.: Das Bild des türkischen Gastarbeiters in der hiesigen Presse," January 20, 1981, PAAA, B 85/1610.

[129] Bundespresseagentur to AA, "Betr.: Bundeskanzler-Interview mit der türkischen Tageszeitung 'Milliyet,'" July 7, 1981, PAAA, B 85/1610.

[130] *Hürriyet,* November 8, 1981, quoted in "Betr.: BM-Besuch in Ankara 05.–06.11.1981; hier: Türkische Presse," November 9, 1981, PAAA, B 85/1610.

[131] *Son Havadis,* November 8, 1981, and *Milliyet,* November 9, 1981, quoted in ibid.

themselves constitute the first class, Christian guest workers the second class, and Turkish guest workers are the third class."[132]

Turkish commentators also supported their claims with generalizations and stereotypes about Germans' personalities and worldviews in the aftermath of Nazism. In 1981, the humorist Aziz Nesin penned a series of scathing articles attributing West Germans' "oppression" of Turkish migrants to their national degradation after their defeat in World War II – a means of re-exerting their power by targeting an internal minority population.[133] Nesin further argued that Germans' hatred of foreigners was the consequence of their post-fascist malaise. Psychologically combatting the excesses of Nazism, both East and West Germans were staid, bland, and humorless, preferring "food without taste, flowers without fragrance, streets without children." German train stations were overrun with prostitutes, and Germans were so obsessed with money that they opted to remain in unhappy marriages rather than get divorced and relinquish their tax breaks. Although Germans appeared to derive joy from their pet dogs, Nesin reminded his readers that the Nazis, too, had loved dogs – not because they loved animals, but because they hated humans.

Defying West Germans' efforts to combat their Nazi past, Turkish journalists repeatedly framed anti-Turkish racism as a continuity of Nazism and drew overt parallels to the persecution of Jews during the Third Reich. *Günaydın* printed photographs of graffiti that stated "Turks out!" and "We don't sell to Turks!" alongside the iconic 1933 photograph of Nazi stormtroopers holding the antisemitic sign, "Germans! Protect yourselves! Do not buy from Jews!"[134] Demanding that the Turkish government protect its citizens abroad, the newspaper threatened: "Those who want to relive the spirit of Nazism should know that we live in another time. We won't remain passive. We are in the position to cause great difficulties."[135] *Tercüman* expressed a similar sentiment: "Even though the 1920s and 1930s are not repeating themselves," Turkish

[132] *Günaydın,* October 12, 1981, quoted in German Embassy in Ankara to AA, October 13, 1981, PAAA, B 85/1610; *Günaydın,* January 4, 1982, quoted in "Betr.: Ausländerpolitik; hier: General Evren und türkische Presse," January 5, 1982, PAAA, B 85/1611.
[133] Aziz Nesin, "Almanya? Almanya?" quoted in German Embassy in Ankara to AA, October 13, 1981, PAAA, B 85/1610.
[134] *Günaydın,* December 9, 1981, quoted in German Embassy in Ankara to AA, "Betr.: Beschluss der Bundesregierung zur Ausländerpolitik; hier: Türkische Reaktion," December 10, 1981, in PAAA B 85/1610.
[135] *Günaydın,* March 15, 1982, quoted in German Embassy in Ankara to AA, "Betr.: Deutschlandbild in türkischer Presse," March 15, 1982, PAAA B 85/1611.

migrants in Europe needed to establish lobbies and pressure groups to prevent the situation from escalating.[136]

For the West German Foreign Office, the Turkish press's most frustrating comparisons were between Chancellor Helmut Schmidt and Adolf Hitler. A 1981 front-page article in *Milliyet,* headlined "From Hitler to Schmidt," contended that the Social Democrats' discussions of restricting the family reunification policy "do not surprise us."[137] In their "desire that all non-German races be crushed," the Nazis, too, had "separated women from their children, husbands from their wives." The article concluded: "Perhaps one thinks that Nazism is dead in Germany because there is no more Adolf Hitler in the beer halls of Munich. But the situation has not changed. Hitler is dead, but now we have Helmut Schmidt." The comparison remained a sore spot between the two countries. In 1983, when Turkish officials demanded that West Germany deport regime opponents, one West German official retorted that they had not even deported Turkish citizens who had written news articles defaming the former chancellor as "Adolf Schmidt."[138]

The Turkish media's comparisons to Hitler and Nazism made their way back to German citizens in mainstream media reports. The *Rheinische Post* reported that the "Turkish public follows anti-foreigner activities in the Federal Republic with great attention.... Every right-radical graffiti in German cities is sensationalized as an attack. The Turks in the Federal Republic are compared more and more with the Jews in the time of National Socialism. Chancellor Schmidt was placed in the same political tradition as Adolf Hitler."[139] West German newspapers even referenced specific Turkish news articles, such as *Yankı*'s recounting the story of a German woman who faced condemnation simply for having married a Turk. While acquiring a visa for her husband at the consulate in Istanbul, an immigration officer had berated her choice of spouse. "All Turks are pigs," he reportedly said. "Is it your responsibility to help them? Shame on you as a German."[140]

---

[136] *Tercüman*, March 15, 1982, quoted in ibid.

[137] "Hitler'den Schmidt'e," *Milliyet*, April 12, 1981, 1.

[138] German Embassy in Ankara to AA, "Betr.: Besuch BM Graf Lambsdorff in Ankara 22. –24.5.1983; hier: Gespräche mit Industrieminister Turgut und Leiter Planungsamt Aktürk," May 25, 1983, PAAA B 85/182486.

[139] Laszlo Trankovits, "Als die Deutschen uns noch brauchten..." *RP*, March 13, 1982.

[140] "'Schweine-Türken.' Die Sünde der deutschen Diplomatie," *Yankı*, March 15, 1982, trans. into German, PAAA, B 85/1611.

For the West German Ambassador to Turkey, Dirk Oncken, who served during the tumultuous period of 1979 to 1984, the Turkish press's allegations of West German racism were both a daily annoyance and a matter of great diplomatic concern.[141] Oncken dismissed the most inflammatory articles as propagandistic "smear campaigns" (*Hetzkampagne*) grounded in "emotion" rather than "rationality" and reflective of Turks' innate "lust for conflict" and "mania for creating foreign scapegoats."[142] Still, he rushed to the defense of West Germany's reputation in a series of interviews with Turkish journalists. In a March 1982 interview with *Anadolu Ajansı*, he insisted that "signs of *Ausländerfeindlichkeit*" were "isolated cases" and that the notorious Heidelberg Manifesto was "a private opinion that reflects the opinions of neither the federal government nor the majority of the German population."[143] In September, he toughened his stance, denying the existence of *Ausländerfeindlichkeit* altogether. All forms of intolerance were "repugnant," Oncken maintained. "But in which countries do such sentiments not exist?"[144] Yet Oncken's efforts to downplay West German *Ausländerfeindlichkeit* by portraying it as a universal phenomenon proved a poor diplomatic strategy. In a combative article, which explicitly cited Semra Ertan's suicide as an example of the pervasiveness of West German racism, *Yankı* questioned: "Is the German ambassador telling the truth?"[145]

The media's skepticism toward Oncken's optimistic portrayal trickled down to their target readership, the Turkish population within Turkey, who sent hate mail to the embassy. One man, İlhan Düzgit, accused Oncken of pretending to be friendly to the Turks: "If you think that the Turks are so dumb that they believe you, then you are crazy."[146] The writers of the hate mail echoed the media's criticisms by arguing that West Germans' mistreatment of the migrants had destroyed the historical friendship between the two countries. It was "a shame," Düzgit further lamented, "that our longstanding friendship has come to an end, and that you have lost a real friend ... The Germans today are only foreign and

---

[141] The most extensive discussion of Oncken is in: Szatkowski, *Die Bundesrepublik Deutschland und die Türkei.*

[142] German Embassy in Ankara to AA, "Betr.: Ausländerpolitik; hier: General Evren und türkische Presse," January 5, 1982, PAAA, B 85/1611.

[143] Interview with Dirk Oncken, *Anadolu Ajansı*, March 26, 1982, trans. into German, PAAA, B 85/1611.

[144] *Tercüman*, July 14, 1982, 3, trans. into German, PAAA, B 85/1611.

[145] "Sagt der deutsche Botschafter die Wahrheit?" *Yankı*, June 21, 1982, trans. into German, PAAA, B 85/1611.

[146] İlhan Düzgit to Dirk Oncken, July 30, 1982, PAAA, B 85/1612.

even enemies for us."[147] As another of Oncken's critics put it, "It was the Turks' own fault" that "we trusted you" as allies in World War I and that "we had mercy for you and did not backstab you like the others." In short, "We have begun to hate you."[148]

Because they had not migrated to West Germany themselves, the writers of the hate mail based their impressions on horror stories they heard from friends and relatives living abroad and on their own experiences navigating West Germany's immigration bureaucracy from afar. Ahmet Kanun told Oncken that he had collected enough stories about racist incidents to "write a novel" and that Germans mistreated the migrants not only in the immigration office, but also in mundane settings like the butcher shop, the beach, and the movie theater.[149] Kanun also complained about West Germans' restrictions on entry visas for Turkish citizens: "Because I have no personal apartment, no car, no fat bank account, I can't visit my aunt who lives in Germany ... My request for a visa was denied, as if I were an anarchist or a suspicious person."[150] Another writer had heard nightmarish tales about West Germany's perceived religious impiety, which he used to contradict the notion that Turks were unable or unwilling to integrate: "To which of your buffoonery should we assimilate? To your Fasching? Or to the shameless way that you celebrate the birth of your prophet at the end of the year? Instead of praying!"[151]

The hate mail that observers in the home country sent both to Oncken and to West German President Karl Carstens also reflects the tendency among observers in the home country to whitewash Turkey's own human rights violations by construing West German racism as a foil against which to tout Turkish nationalist narratives. Writing to Oncken, Kanun made the comparison directly. "Because of his psychological master-race complex," he explained, "every German between seven and seventy years old is an *Ausländerfeind*."[152] Whereas racism had "invaded the blood of Germans" and was embedded in "German culture" itself, "the concept of a 'master race,'" is "unheard of" in the "character" of Turks, who had always granted minorities the utmost "tolerance" and "rights." Several guest workers writing to Carstens also pursued this strategy. Kenan Cengiz, for one, argued that West Germans

---

[147] Ibid.
[148] Anonymous to Dirk Oncken, August 2, 1982, PAAA, B 85/1612.
[149] Ahmet Kanun to Dirk Oncken, July 28, 1982, PAAA, B 85/1612.
[150] Ibid.
[151] Anonymous to Oncken.
[152] Kanun to Oncken.

had no right to criticize Turkey's military coup because their abuse of Turkish migrants was "worse" than the "pain inflicted on the Jews in 1945." Espousing a right-wing nationalist narrative, he defended the 1980 coup as an intervention to protect the "human rights" of the Turkish population, rejected the accusation that Turks had ever committed "inhumane torture," and portrayed West German sympathy for Kurds as a veiled attempt to sow division among guest workers.[153] Another man, Feyaz Aksungar, professed his love of Germany in general but told Carstens that West Germans' racism and criticism of the coup "breaks Turks' hearts." He further insisted that the coup's dictator, Evren, had improved the Turkish economy and was making progress toward restoring democracy.[154]

Taken together, the myriad political speeches, newspaper articles, and hate letters make a much deeper point about the entangled history of Turks and Germans, reshaping and expanding our understanding of their transnational relationship. On the one hand, these rich sources introduce the early 1980s as the precise moment when the two countries' historical "friendship" gradually transformed into "enmity," or at least lurched catastrophically off balance. This transformation was fueled by multiple overlapping factors, both domestic and international: Turkey's 1980 military coup and authoritarian turn, West Germany's drafting of the 1983 remigration law despite the Turkish government's opposition to return migration, the home country's concern for the rising racism against migrants, West Germany's opposition to accepting asylum seekers from Turkey, and West Germany's hesitation to grant freedom of mobility to Turks despite Turkey's planned EEC accession in 1986. In short, the issue of migration was not peripheral to the grander narrative of Turkish-German geopolitics but rather central to it. And Turkey's 1980 military coup was not relegated to Turkey's domestic history but rather reverberated across borders, reshaping both international affairs and migration policy.

Turkish observers' pervasive rhetoric of broken "friendship" further testifies to both countries' selective memory, and to their abuses and whitewashing of history. Their historical friendship was undeniably tainted by the two countries' collaboration in violence, human rights violations, and genocides throughout the early twentieth century. As allies during World War I, Prussians had defended the Ottomans'

---

[153] Kenan Cengiz to Carstens, November 22, 1982, BArch, B 122/23883.
[154] Feyaz Aksungar to Carstens, February 6, 1983, BArch, B 122/23883.

violent suppression of minority groups, even going as far as defending the 1915–1916 Armenian Genocide. As Stefan Ihrig has shown, many Prussian officials justified the extermination of the Armenians on the basis that they posed not only an internal security threat to their Ottoman ally, but also because they represented a "racial problem" as the "Jews of the Orient."[155] The two countries' "friendship" was also rooted in the exchange of transnational eugenic ideologies: many Turkish scientists admired Nazi Germany's "racial hygiene" policies and authoritarian regime as a model for achieving a state-mandated improvement of Turkey's genetic stock through promoting reproduction, preventing sexual "race-mixing," and eliminating hereditarily "inferior" people.[156] And, despite being aware of the Nazis' persecution of Jews, the Turkish government chose to maintain friendly diplomatic relations with Hitler's regime until it switched to the Allies' side in February 1945 – once it was clear that the Nazis would lose.

Even more damning is Turkey's collaboration in the Holocaust. To this day, Turkey denies its culpability in Nazi atrocities, insisting that it saved Jews and welcomed them with open arms.[157] However, as Corry Guttstadt has shown, Turkey persecuted far more Jews than it saved.[158] Many Turkish officials and diplomats were outspoken Nazi sympathizers and supported fascism as a political model. From 1933 to 1945, Turkey persecuted the 75,000 Jews within its borders, alongside other non-Muslim minorities, through high tax rates, dispossession of property, and forced labor. Turkey accepted only about 600 Jewish refugees from Nazi Germany in the 1930s, mostly elite intellectuals; instead, international Jewish organizations and Istanbul's local Jewish community bypassed restrictions to save additional Jews illegally. Although 13,000 European Jews passed through Turkey to Palestine in the early 1940s, the Turkish government generally strove to block this transit route. Turkey also withdrew citizenship from several thousand ethnically Turkish Jews living in Nazi-occupied territories, which deprived them of protections like the right to enter Turkey, and it repatriated only 114 of the 3,000

---

[155] Ihrig, *Justifying Genocide.*
[156] Ergin, "Is the Turk a White Man?", 114–16.
[157] Yağmur Karakaya and Alejandro Baer, "'Such Hatred Has Never Flourished on Our Soil': The Politics of Holocaust Memory in Turkey and Spain," *Sociological Forum* 34, no. 3 (2019): 705–28.
[158] Guttstadt, *Turkey, the Jews, and the Holocaust.* For a concise articulation of this argument, see: Corry Guttstadt, "La politique de la Turquie pendant la Shoah," trans. Olivier Mannoni, *Revue d'Histoire de la Shoah* 203, no. 2 (2015): 195–231.

Jews that the Nazis deemed eligible in early 1945. Overall, the Nazis deported approximately 3,000 Jews of Turkish origin to extermination and concentration camps – and Turkey was complicit.

Paradoxically, then, the rhetoric with which Turks assailed West Germans' racism and the proposed return migration law in the early 1980s reveals more similarities than differences between the two countries: on both sides, the denial and deflection of both past and present racism, human rights violations, and genocide reigned supreme. When West Germans criticized Turkey's 1980 military coup, Turks in the home country fought back by accusing West Germans of treating Turks like Jews and promoting a resurgence of the Third Reich. West Germans, in turn, used the language of "genocide" to express existential fears that migrants were biologically exterminating the German *Volk*. At the same time, Turkish observers failed – and refused – to recognize their own abuses, from the Armenian Genocide to the military dictatorship's human rights violations against Kurds, political leftists, and other internal minorities. Instead, by deflecting sole blame for genocide and human rights violations onto Germans, and by espousing right-wing nationalist narratives, Turks in the home country attempted to absolve themselves of guilt. While they defended the migrants against racism, they also used them as pawns in a battle over the politics of history and memory. As both countries grappled with the question of guest workers' return migration in the early 1980s, silencing the past became an urgent political goal.

* * * * *

West Germany's racial reckoning and the debates surrounding a remigration law extended far beyond its borders. From policymakers to self-proclaimed "ordinary" citizens, many of the same Germans who rejected the racist rallying cry "Turks out!" were unwilling to acknowledge their own complicity in perpetuating racism. Through denial and deflection, they changed the terms of the discussion: concerns about Turks constituted *Ausländerfeindlichkeit*, not *Rassismus*, and Turks posed a particular threat because of "cultural difference," not biology. For some, there was even no such thing as *Ausländerfeindlichkeit* – and if it did exist, then it was a phenomenon relegated to fringe radical neo-Nazis. But just like in matters of national identity, West Germans did not have a singular claim to defining whether they were racist, what counted as racism, what to call racism, and whether anti-Turkish racism marked a continuity with Nazism. And as in earlier discussions about bilateral development aid for promoting return migration, Turkey's government, media, and population all exerted power and agency by intervening into these debates from afar. Likewise, the migrants themselves fought back as well. Invoking the language of human rights, they made their views clear: West Germany had not fully reckoned with Nazism, and Hitler's shadow continued to loom.

It is worth returning here to the legacy and memory of Semra Ertan, the young Turkish-German activist whose suicide in 1982 provided a powerful emotional anchor to these debates. Six months after her death, Turkish newspapers reported that a young man replicated her protest by setting himself on fire in the very same Hamburg market-place.[159] In 1990, West German novelist Sten Nadolny honored Ertan's memory in a fictional character named Ayse, who leaps off a rooftop in protest of racism, sparking German and Turkish officials to debate the cause of her suicide.[160] And Ertan's most prominent poem, "Benim Adım Yabancı" (My Name is Foreigner), later became a mainstay in public school curricula in Turkey, introducing Turkish students to the historical struggles of the diaspora in Germany. In this sense, her death was not in vain but rather has lived on in both countries' memory for decades.

But the overall memory of anti-racist struggles in Germany, and of Ertan's suicide, is also riddled with a major problem: it has, in many respects, been coopted and overshadowed by Germans. One of the most prominent references to Ertan, for example, came in 1985, when the West German journalist Günter Wallraff dedicated his famous book *Ganz unten* (Lowest of the Low) to her, as well as to Cemal Kemal Altun, a twenty-three-year-old asylum seeker who had recently killed himself in fear of being deported back to Turkey.[161] A powerful undercover exposé of anti-Turkish racism, Wallraff's book recounted the two years he spent assuming the identity of a Turkish man named Ali Siniroğlu – disguising himself with blackface, brown contact lenses, a dark-haired wig, a mustache, and a stereotypical Turkish accent – and working in various unskilled jobs, including at the Thyssen steel factor in Duisburg. Within two years, the book sold nearly three million copies and was

---

[159] *Hürriyet*, November 10, 1982, trans. in Michel Helweg, *Türkei-Infodienst*, November 22, 1982.
[160] Sten Nadolny, *Selim oder die Gabe der Rede* (Munich: Piper, 1990); Tom Cheeseman, *Novels of Turkish-German Settlement: Cosmopolite Fictions* (Rochester: Camden House, 2007), 141.
[161] Günter Wallraff, *Ganz unten* (Cologne: Kiepenheuer & Witsch, 1985).

translated into fourteen languages, garnering international sympathy for Turkish migrants.[162] Crucially, however, Ali Siniroğlu, the man who had lent Wallraff his identity documents, called the author "two-faced" for unevenly splitting his colossal royalties and abandoning the many Turkish migrants who had helped him with his investigation.[163] Overall, it is striking that today far more Germans know the name Günter Wallraff than Semra Ertan.[164]

Even among those who have brought – and are continuing to bring – serious attention to Semra Ertan's activism, a crucial part of her message is sometimes forgotten: she sought to direct attention not only to racism in West Germany but also to the discrimination she felt when she returned to Turkey. In her poem "My Name is Foreigner," she lamented: "My country sold us to Germany, like stepchildren, like useless people. But it still needs remittances."[165] In another, she questioned: "Where do I belong? In Turkey, or am I a foreigner? … In my homeland, they look at us differently after years of living far away. Everything is foreign to us."[166] Ertan's observations force us to reexamine the Turkish rhetoric surrounding West German racism and the proposed remigration law. Despite their sympathy, the Turkish media and population engaged in their own criticism of the migrants, treating them as "Germanized" *Almancı* who were no longer fully Turkish.

Despite all these transnational concerns about racism, the passing of the remigration law came closer and closer to becoming a reality. In July 1982, after months of publicly opposing the CDU/CSU's desire to pass the remigration law, the SPD government under Helmut Schmidt introduced its own version of a "Foreigner Consolidation Law" (*Ausländerkonsolidierungsgesetz*), which for the first time expressed the

---

[162] "'Dieses Buch ist wie ein Fluch für mich,'" *Der Spiegel*, June 14, 1987.

[163] See the interview with Siniroğlu: "'Vielleicht seinen Feinden ähnlich geworden,'" *Der Spiegel*, June 14, 1987.

[164] There is reason to believe, however, that this may change in the future, as more and more Germans take note of Ertan's life and legacy. In July 2023, for instance, the city of Kiel renamed a public square in her honor: Semra-Ertan-Platz. The growing attention to Ertan's legacy has been spearheaded by her sister and niece, Zühal and Cana Bilir-Meier, who in 2018 founded the Semra Ertan Initiative: https://semraertaninitiative.wordpress.com/. On the renaming process in Kiel, see: "Von Fremdenfeindlichkeit erzählt," *Die Tageszeitung*, July 7, 2023, https://taz.de/Aktivist-ueber-die-Dichterin-Semra-Ertan/!5942118/.

[165] Semra Ertan, "Mein Name ist Ausländer," 1981, in Ertan, *Mein Name ist Ausländer: Gedichte*, 176.

[166] Semra Ertan, "Nereye aitim," 1981, in ibid., 186.

party's commitment to promoting return migration through domestic policy.[167] The proposed law included another controversial provision – further reducing the age limit for family reunification to just six years old – which Interior Minister Gerhart Baum and Foreigner Commissioner Liselotte Funcke opposed on the grounds of "humanity" and "morality."[168] But Schmidt's government never passed its consolidation law, since the SPD's thirteen-year control over the parliament ended in October 1982. After a vote of no confidence, the FDP entered a coalition with the CDU/CSU as the dominant partner, and Helmut Kohl replaced Schmidt as chancellor. Under the new Christian Democratic majority government, the stage was set for passing a morally controversial law that promoted return migration in the service of racism.

---

[167] Deutscher Bundestag, 9. Wahlperiode, "Entwurf eines Gesetzes zur Konsolidierung des Zuzugs und zur Förderung der Rückkehrbereitschaft von Ausländern," July 21, 1982, Drucksache 9/1865.

[168] DPA, "Baum gegen SPD-Pläne zur verschärften Nachzugsbeschränkung," July 13, 1982, BArch, B 106/117687; DPA, "Funcke gegen Senkung des Nachzugsalters," July 20, 1982, BArch, B 106/117687.

5

The Mass Exodus

When CDU leader Helmut Kohl was sworn in as West Germany's new chancellor on October 4, 1982, he resolved to fulfill his party's promise of turning a remigration law into reality. Even though Schmidt and the Social Democrats had begun developing their own version of a remigration law several months before, Kohl's goal was far more extreme. In a secret meeting with British Prime Minister Margaret Thatcher just three weeks after taking office, Kohl expressed his desire to "reduce the number of Turks in Germany by 50 percent." Due to the public outrage surrounding racism, however, "he could not say that publicly yet."[1]

For both guest workers and Turks in the home country, the change in government proved ominous. Continuing the tradition of likening German chancellors to Hitler, the tabloid *Bulvar* printed a cartoon depicting Kohl with swastikas on his glasses.[2] The guest workers, wrote *Güneş*, were especially "worried" about Kohl.[3] As *Milliyet* columnist Örsan Öymen explained, "Whereas the old government wanted to freeze the number of guest workers, the new government wants to send them home."[4]

---

[1] British Prime Minister's Office, "Secret: Record of a Conversation Between the Prime Minister and the Chancellor of the Federal Republic of Germany," October 28, 1982, The National Archives of the UK (TNA), Kew, PREM 19/1036.

[2] *Bulvar*, October 14, 1982, quoted in German Embassy in Ankara to AA, "Betr.: Ausländerpolitik; hier: MP Ulusu in PK 16.10 und türkische Presse," October 18, 1982, PAAA, B 85/1614.

[3] *Güneş*, October 3, 1982, quoted in German Embassy in Ankara to AA, "Betr.: Neue Bundesregierung; hier: türkische Presse zur Lage Türken in Deutschland," October 4, 1982, PAAA, B 85/1614.

[4] Örsan Öymen, *Milliyet*, October 6, 1982, quoted in German Embassy in Ankara to AA, "Betr.: Ausländerpolitik; hier: türkische Presse," October 7, 1982, PAAA, B 85/1614.

Milliyet further urged the Turkish government to "intervene to protect the rights of guest workers."[5] Columnist Rauf Tamer suggested that his fellow citizens initiate a form of "collective resistance": "If the Turkish workers are forced to leave Germany, we must boycott German goods and stop flying with Lufthansa," because "money is the only thing that interests [Germans]."[6]

Given such criticism both domestically and abroad, Kohl and his CDU/CSU-FDP coalition knew that getting rid of half of the Turkish migrant population would be no easy feat. In crafting the remigration law, they grappled with a political and ethical dilemma: How, after perpetrating the Holocaust forty years prior, could they kick out the Turks without compromising their post-fascist values of liberalism and democracy? How, amid Germany's Cold War division, could they skirt the issue of human rights violations while still upholding their international status as an ally of the Free World? How could they defend their domestic claim to being the true heir to pre-1933 German liberalism and the presumptive future leaders of a one-day reunified German nation? And how could they do so in a way that maximized their appearance of generosity and minimized criticism from the Turkish government? Surely, they knew that they could not forcibly deport half of the Turkish migrant population.

Their answer, ultimately codified in the Law for the Promotion of the Voluntary Return of Foreigners (*Rückkehrförderungsgesetz*) of November 28, 1983, was to pay Turks to leave. Under the guise of generosity, the West German government offered unemployed former guest workers a "remigration premium" (*Rückkehrprämie*) of 10,500 DM (approximately 20,000 USD today) to pack their bags, take their spouses and children, and leave the country. But there was a catch: even though taking the money was voluntary, they had to exit West German borders by a strict deadline: September 30, 1984. Tired of waiting for guest workers as they wavered on the difficult question of staying or leaving, West German policymakers wanted to force guest worker families to decide, within just ten months, whether they were willing to permanently abandon their jobs, schools, lives, and residence permits – with no option to return.

---

[5] *Milliyet*, October 3, 1982, quoted in German Embassy in Ankara to AA, "Betr.: Neue Bundesregierung; hier: türkische Presse zur Lage Türken in Deutschland."
[6] Rauf Tamer, newspaper and date not provided (likely October 6, 1982), quoted in German Embassy in Ankara to AA, "Betr.: Ausländerpolitik; hier: türkische Presse."

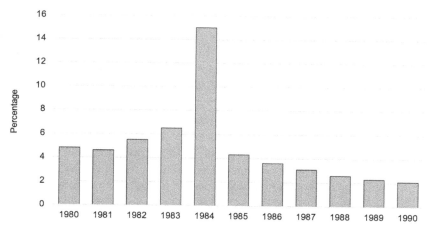

FIGURE 5.1 Annual percentage of West Germany's Turkish migrant population who returned "permanently," 1980–1990.[7] In 1984, due to the West German government's remigration law, the rate of return migration skyrocketed to 15 percent. It then declined sharply to just over 2 percent throughout the decade's latter half. Created by author.

While the remigration law did not fulfill Kohl's extreme 50 percent goal, it did spark one of the largest mass remigrations in modern European history. Between November 1983 and September 1984, within just ten months, 15 percent of the Turkish migrant population – 250,000 men, women, and children – returned to Turkey (Figure 5.1). For some, the decision to leave was easy. Having been on the fence about returning, the financial incentive was enticing. With the money, they believed they could finally return to their homeland, start their own small businesses, retire comfortably, and no longer face uncertainty. For others, the decision was difficult. Decrying the 10,500 DM as a mere pittance, they criticized the West German government's initial refusal to pay out their social security contributions in full. But they also wanted to escape the racist climate of West Germany, which had only worsened in recent years, and to prevent their children's further "Germanization" by bringing them back to Turkey. With many children having spent time in Turkey only on their vacations, parents' decision to leave sometimes tore families apart.

---

[7] Data based on *Statistische Jahrbücher*, as compiled in: Beate Jankowitsch, Thomas Klein, and Stefan Weick, "Die Rückkehr ausländischer Arbeitsmigranten seit Mitte der achtziger Jahre," 93–109, in Richard Alba, Peter Schmidt, and Martina Wasme, eds., *Deutsche und Ausländer: Freunde, Fremde oder Feinde?* (Wiesbaden: Verlag für Sozialwissenschaften, 2000), 96.

Once they returned to Turkey, their dreams often turned into nightmares. Nearly half the guest workers who returned to Turkey with the 1983 remigration law came to regret their decisions, as they encountered parallel difficulties "reintegrating" into their own homeland. For some, the happy homecoming turned sour, as years of seeing their friends, family, and neighbors only on their vacations left them ostracized as "Germanized" and culturally estranged. Others went bankrupt after failed business ventures, having underestimated Turkey's dire economic situation and hyperinflation. But failure also came at a psychological cost – forcing guest workers and their families to question whether all the years of separation had truly been worth it. The mass exodus became a cautionary tale that discouraged other guest workers from remigrating in later years, leading to a stark decline in return migration throughout the 1980s.

PAYING TURKS TO LEAVE

To solve the "Turkish problem," the West German government paid them to leave. With the 1983 Law for the Promotion of the Voluntary Return of Foreigners, the federal government offered money directly to unemployed guest workers in the form of a "return premium," more euphemistically described as "remigration assistance" (*Rückkehrhilfe*): a one-time cash transfer of 10,500 DM, plus an additional 1,500 DM per underage child. To receive the money, the worker's entire family, including his or her spouse and underage children, would need to exit West German borders. Once a guest worker had taken the money, he or she could return to the country only as a tourist. Even children who had been born in West Germany or had spent most of their lives there would require an entrance visa. Upon their departure, a border official would stamp all family members' residence permits "invalid," marking their official severance from a country where many had lived for nearly two decades.

The basic concept behind this remigration law was actually developed many years before Kohl assumed the chancellorship. In 1975, the state government of Baden-Württemberg began lobbying for the development of a federal plan to "relieve the labor market" through "a significant reduction of excessive guest worker employment." The mechanism would be the provision of "return assistance" (*Rückkehrhilfe*) financed by the Federal Labor Office (Bundesanstalt für Arbeit). Proponents within the Baden-Württemberg government lauded the success of a "spectacular" model case among workers at the Audi factory in the area surrounding Heilbronn and Neckarsulm. Within only fourteen days in May 1975, an offer of 8,000 DM severance paid by the state of Baden-Württemberg had convinced nearly 2,000 guest workers to return to their home country.[8] "In contrast to many initially skeptical voices," Baden-Württemberg Minister President Hans Filbinger declared, the program "demonstrated that a large number of guest workers are ready to take advantage of such an offer." According to the *Kölner Stadt-Anzeiger*, Filbinger's proposal found a "wide echo" in the public and piqued the interest of other state minister presidents.[9] But it also drew criticism. The metalworkers' trade union IG Metall wrote, "For the trade unions, the foreign workers are not a maneuverable mass that can be hired and gotten rid of as one pleases, even under today's increasingly difficult circumstances."[10]

There was also international precedent for paying foreign workers to leave. France was a frequent point of comparison.[11] At the time, France was experiencing an economic downturn similar to that in West Germany, complete with mass layoffs in the iron industry. French statistics in 1977 reported the presence of over 100,000 unemployed foreigners who had registered for unemployment assistance at the Labor Office.[12] While over 10 percent were citizens of countries that enjoyed freedom of movement throughout France (including 8,611 Italians), the remainder came from countries outside the EEC, including Algeria, Morocco, Portugal, Spain, Tunisia, Yugoslavia, and what French media lumped together as "Black Africa." Hoping to rid itself particularly of non-European, non-white, and non-Christian postcolonial migrants from North and Sub-Saharan Africa, the French government offered unemployed foreign laborers 10,000 Francs (approximately 4,300 DM), as well as an additional 10,000 per unemployed spouse and 5,000 per child. Informational materials distributed in local labor and immigration offices were enticing:

---

[8] "Gastarbeiter – ab nach Hause?" *Der Spiegel*, February 23, 1976. See also: "Filbinger: Abfindung soll arbeitslose Ausländer zur Rückkehr in ihre Heimat ermutigen," *FAZ*, June 5, 1985; "Filbinger regt Rückkehrhilfen für Ausländer an," *Stuttgarter Zeitung*, June 5, 1975.

[9] Heinz Murmann, "Einfach abgeschoben?" *KSA*, February 3, 1976.

[10] Metall Pressedienst, "IG Metall gegen Filbingers Vorschlag über Rückkehrprämien für ausländische Arbeitnehmer," February 12, 1976, AdsD, IG Metall-Archiv, 5/IGMA45190018.

[11] On France's remigration program, see: Comte, *The History of the European Migration Regime*, 137–40.

[12] "Les immigrés victimes de la crise," *Le Monde*, June 20, 1977.

"Because you have worked in France, you have the same rights as French workers. But would you not perhaps prefer, if you had the means, to return to your homeland and to settle there again?"[13] By 1981, however, the French law had proven a failure. Not only had it drawn criticism, but only 87,500 workers had taken the remigration premium, most from Spain and Portugal rather than North and Sub-Saharan Africa.

Likewise, inspiration came from concurrent efforts to pay asylum seekers to leave. In 1979, the West German federal and state governments established the Reintegration and Emigration Program for Asylum Seekers in Germany (REAG).[14] The program, implemented by the Intergovernmental Committee for European Migration, offered asylum seekers 930 DM to permanently leave West Germany and either return to their home country or migrate onward to a third country. By 1982, over 9,000 asylum seekers had taken this premium, costing the government an average of two million DM annually. Although billed as a "humanitarian assistance program" that would "correct" asylum seekers' "failed expectations," the REAG program had ulterior motives – namely of saving West Germany money in the long run and solving the asylum question with fewer controversial deportations.[15] Throughout the 1980s, Belgium, Switzerland, and the Netherlands followed West Germany's lead.[16]

But convincing Turkish guest workers to go home was a more complex task. Having earned Deutschmarks in West Germany for up to two decades, and well aware of the disastrous economic situation in their home country, Turks had long deferred their dream of return migration (Figure 5.2). Although government surveys revealed that 75 percent of guest workers had a "latent" desire to return home, the number of Turks who actually did so had decreased by half, from 148,000 in 1975 to 70,000 in 1980.[17] A 1982 survey of Turkish guest workers living in Nuremberg revealed a variety of conditions under which Turkish workers would

[13] "L'aide au retour: une prime au départ définitif," *Le Monde*, June 17, 1977.
[14] Bundesamt für Migration und Flüchtlinge, "Rückkehr aus Deutschland. Forschungsstudie 2006 im Rahmen des Europäischen Migrationsnetzwerks" (2006), www.bamf.de/SharedDocs/Anlagen/DE/Forschung/Forschungsberichte/fb04-rueckkehr-emn.pdf?_blob=publicationFile&v=11, 63.
[15] Deutscher Bundestag, 9. Wahlperiode, May 26, 1982, 6140.
[16] Austin Crane, "Assisted Voluntary Return: Negotiating the Politics of Humanitarianism and Security in Migration Management" (PhD diss.: University of Washington, 2021), 87.
[17] "Bericht der Arbeitsgruppe 'Rückkehrförderung,'" November 1981, BArch, B 106/117686.

FIGURE 5.2 Cartoon depicting Turkish guest workers' difficult decision regarding remigration, 1979. Should they return to their homeland, or should they remain in West Germany and continue to save Deutschmarks?[18] © Cumhuriyet, used with permission.

return to their home country. These ranged from general improvements in living conditions in Turkey ("when the living standard in Turkey is exactly as it is in Germany") to specific material concerns ("when I have a car, television, washing machine, record player, video machine, dish-washer, a large refrigerator, electrical kitchen appliances, and money"). Some less commonly listed conditions, though probably offered in jest, were "when war breaks out in the Federal Republic," "when I win the lottery," and "when the Germans kick me out."[19] Another 1982 survey of 312 workers in Saarland and Rhineland-Palatinate revealed that 50

[18] Cartoon by Memet, in "Bizler yurtsız insanlarız; ortada kalmış gurbetçiyiz, Alman ellerinde ücretli zenciler!'" *Cumhuriyet*, May 10, 1978.
[19] Safa A. Bostancı, *Zum Leben und zu den Rückkehr- bzw. Verbleibeabsichten der türkischen Gastarbeiter in Nürnberg. Eine empirische Regionaluntersuchung* (Berlin: Express Edition, 1982), 67–68.

percent feared that they would not be able to find a job in Turkey, would not be able to work independently in Turkey, and would earn less in Turkey than in Germany.[20]

Given that guest workers' reasons for staying were primarily economic, policymakers knew that the meager 930 DM they were offering to asylum seekers would not fit the bill. After much calculation, they settled on offering unemployed guest workers 10,500 DM plus 1,500 DM per underage child. This number corresponded to the government benefits that a typical guest worker received during seven months without a job, including unemployment pay, health insurance, social security contributions, and child allowances.[21] Despite the upfront cost, West German policymakers anticipated far more substantial long-term savings. For every unemployed guest worker who left, the government anticipated saving up to 10,000 DM per year in social welfare spending – even after paying out the one-time 10,500 DM premium.[22] As one Foreign Office memorandum concluded optimistically, "These measures are already cost-neutral in the mid-term (3–4 years) and then – because of the decline in entitlements – even yield saving effects."[23] Critics, however, were skeptical of the cost savings. SPD politician Rudolf Dreßler condemned the draft law as "nonsense," arguing that it constituted "nothing more than hidden state debt" and would "throw money out the window."[24]

The government also carefully deliberated which guest worker nationalities would be eligible for the remigration premium. Although the primary interest was in reducing the Turkish population, policymakers knew that they would endure both domestic and international scorn – certainly from the Turkish government – if the law singled out Turkish citizens. In an October 1982 memorandum issued two weeks after Kohl became chancellor, tellingly titled "Turkey Policy," one bureaucrat

---

[20] Manfred Werth, et al., *Rückkehr- und Verbleibabsichten türkischer Arbeitnehmer. Analyse der Rückkehrbereitschaft und des Wanderungsverhaltens sowie des Sparverhaltens und der Anlagepläne türkischer Arbeitnehmer im Raum Rheinland-Pfalz/Saarland* (Saarbrücken: Isoplan, 1983), 62.

[21] "Begründung," May 10, 1983, BArch, B 106/177694.

[22] Calculated based on statistics in: "Bericht der Arbeitsgruppe 'Rückkehrförderung,'" 1982, BArch, B 106/117686; BMA to Mitglieder der Arbeitsgruppe "Rückkehrförderung," "Betr.: Rückkehrförderung ausländischer Arbeitnehmer und ihrer Familienangehörigen," May 18, 1982, Tabelle 1, BArch, B 106/117694.

[23] Kroneck, "Betr.: Türkeipolitik; hier: Aspekt Rückkehrförderung," October 19, 1982, PAAA, B 85/1604.

[24] Information der Sozialdemokratischen Bundestagsfraktion, "Gesetzentwurf der Bundesregierung zur Rückkehrförderung für ausländische Arbeitnehmer Unsinn," September 28, 1983, BArch, B 106/117965.

warned against portraying the law as "exclusively oriented toward the Turkish workers ... although we are internally conceptualizing this policy with regard to this group."[25] But they also wanted to avoid making the category too broad since they feared that guest workers from Italy and Greece, who, as citizens of EEC member states, enjoyed freedom of mobility, might abuse the law by taking the 10,500 DM, exiting West German borders briefly, and quickly returning.[26] Ultimately, they offered the premium only to unemployed guest workers from non-EEC countries who were not married to a West German citizen. Besides Turkey, the eligible countries were Spain, Portugal, Yugoslavia, Morocco, Tunisia, and South Korea.[27]

German policymakers debated several other provisions. One was the "return option" (*Wiederkehroption*) – the question of whether guest workers who took the 10,500 DM premium would be allowed to return to West Germany. When first conceptualizing the law in the summer of 1982, the Social Democratic government proposed allowing guest workers to return to West Germany within six months of their departure. This option aimed to assuage guest workers' concerns about their home countries' unstable economic situations: "As long as a foreign worker cannot be sure that he can actually invest his capital in his homeland or that there is actually a job for him there, then he will not be willing to leave the FRG forever."[28] To avoid exploitation, the premium would only be paid out if a guest worker stayed in Turkey beyond the six months. But the version of the law passed under Kohl's government nixed the return option. To ensure that guest workers and their family members would leave the country permanently, West German border officials would stamp their residence permits "invalid." The Interior Senator of West Berlin proposed an even harsher measure, not included in the final version of the law, which

---

[25] Kroneck, "Betr.: Türkeipolitik."
[26] BMA to AA, "Betr.: Rückkehrförderung ausländischer Arbeitnehmer und ihrer Familienangehörigen," May 3, 1982, PAAA, B 85/1604.
[27] The West German government had also recruited male mineworkers and female nurses from South Korea as foreign laborers. The invitation, which was not a formal part of the guest worker program, aimed not only to address the labor shortage but also to demonstrate support for South Korea, whose citizens too had endured national division amid the Cold War. Arnd Kolb, ed., *Unbekannte Vielfalt. Einblicke in die koreanische Migrationsgeschichte in Deutschland* (Cologne: DOMiD, 2014).
[28] Bundesministerium des Innern, "Betr.: Kabinettvorlage zur Förderung der Rückkehr ausländischer Arbeitnehmer; hier: Wiederkehroption," June 28, 1982, BArch, B 106/117686.

would have prevented Turks from returning even as tourists for at least several years.[29]

Even more controversial was the question of whether – and if so, then when – returning guest workers could receive their social security contributions. This problem lay largely in the difference between the Turkish and West German retirement ages. While West Germany paid social security benefits only after age sixty-five, individuals in Turkey typically retired at forty-five or fifty.[30] This discrepancy meant that middle-aged guest workers who planned to fulfill their dream of retiring in Turkey might need to wait over a decade before receiving their West German social security payouts. Although a previous policy permitted guest workers to receive their employee social security contributions early after a two-year waiting period, the draft laws under both the SPD and CDU governments offered an immediate payout. But there was a huge catch: they would lose their employer social security contributions entirely.[31] In criticizing the law, the Citizens Initiative of Foreign Workers in Hanover tabulated the potential lost wages in the hypothetical scenario of a guest worker who had worked in West Germany for eleven years and retired at age sixty-three.[32] Assuming that the worker had contributed 23,000 DM overall to social security, he would receive 100,000 DM by age seventy-five if he stayed in Germany. But if he returned to Turkey, he would only receive his 23,000 DM employee contribution, and the extra 67,000 DM in employer contributions would remain in the government's social security fund. Though devastating to the migrants, this provision was a welcome boon to the federal budget.

After devising the remigration law, the next challenge was how to sell it. Given ongoing debates about racism and the longstanding critique of the general idea of a remigration law, proponents portrayed it in a way that sought to reconcile the morally controversial policy with their post-Holocaust commitment to upholding the rights of minority populations. To save face, CDU/CSU members repeatedly made it clear in the press, as well as in heated discussions with Turkish government officials, that the law did not constitute a forced deportation. During parliamentary

---

[29] Interior Senator of West Berlin, "Betr.: Ausländerrecht; hier: Erlöschen des Aufenthaltsrechts von Ausländern, die Rückkehrhilfe in Anspruch nehmen," July 22, 1983, BArch, B 106/117694.

[30] Presse- und Informationsamt der Bundesregierung, "Türkische Arbeitnehmer: Rückkehr und Rente," *Sozialpolitische Umschau*, May 11, 1984.

[31] *Gesetz zur Förderung der Rückkehrbereitschaft von Ausländern*, November 28, 1983, BArch, B 149/161888.

[32] "Reise ohne Wiederkehr," *Die Zeit*, May 11, 1984.

debates throughout 1983, Federal Labor Minister Norbert Blüm assured critics that the key word in the law's title was "voluntary." Invoking the politically correct term "foreign fellow citizens" (*ausländische Mitbürger*), Blüm framed the law as a voluntary collaboration between the government and guest worker families. The law, in Blüm's words, was "simply an offer." Because the law's foundation was "voluntariness," it "cannot be exercised against the will of our foreign fellow citizens, but rather only with them ... Therefore, it cannot be a law against the foreigners, but rather it is a law for our foreign fellow citizens."[33] Blüm further insisted that the law would benefit the guest workers not only financially but also psychologically. After years of "unclarity" and "sitting on packed suitcases," they could finally decide to go home.[34]

Yet, with the dual pressures of unemployment and racism, the law's voluntariness came into question. Although the Federal Senate (Bundesrat) overwhelmingly supported the law, opposition parties in the parliament saw through the guise of generosity. In an extensive debate just two weeks before the law was passed, Green Party representative Gabriele Potthast argued that the law conceded to the population's "fears" and "racist attitudes" and subjected foreigners to "moral, psychological, and political pressure." The SPD, despite having initially developed earlier versions of the law under Helmut Schmidt's chancellorship, now changed its tune. The law, argued SPD representative Rudolf Dreßler, constituted a "deportation premium" and "bargain for the government" that "incites *Ausländerfeindlichkeit*." Even when factoring in their employee social security contributions, Dreßler argued that guest workers would spend much of the payout on their journey home. In his party's estimation, moving a two-and-a-half-bedroom apartment from Stuttgart to Istanbul would cost 6,000 DM on average and up to 8,000 DM if a guest worker traveled even farther to Mersin or Sivas along the Anatolian coast. But FDP representative Carl-Junius Cronenberg, whose party supported the law as the CDU/CSU's coalition partner, pointed out the SPD's "hypocrisy" and noted that they had no ground on which to stand.[35]

Outside parliamentary chambers, efforts to frame the law as voluntary and magnanimous failed miserably.[36] DGB board member Siegfried

---

[33] Bundesrat, 526. Sitzung, September 2, 1983, 290, BArch, B 106/117965.
[34] Deutscher Bundestag, 10. Wahlperiode, November 10, 1983, 2219.
[35] Ibid., 2230.
[36] Rainer Zunder, "Keine Lösung. Rückkehr-Prämie für Ausländer geplant," *Westfälische Rundschau*, June 15, 1983.

Bleicher called the law a "false," "illusionary," and socially irresponsible "political miscarriage," and IG Metall condemned it as a "continuation of the federal government's kicking out policy" (Figure 5.3).[37] For *Die Tageszeitung*, the 10,500 DM was just "pocket money for an uncertain future."[38] A *Spiegel* article titled "Take Your Premium and Get Out" featured a photograph of a Turkish family loading their belongings into their van and was captioned "Splendid deal for the Germans."[39] One Turkish migrant called the law "singularly and solely about saving the German state the social services to which these foreigners are legally entitled."[40] Ordinary Germans expressed their concerns in letters to the editor of *Stern*, noting that they were "ashamed" that politicians were rendering migrants "powerless" and "watching the deportation of the Turks with vicious delight."[41] Although foreign workers were "oppressed" elsewhere, "only the Germans have a special ability to make these people suffer, both as a society and a state." If "parties who call themselves 'Christian'" ever opened the Bible, perhaps they would learn the scripture: "Love thy neighbor as you love yourself."

While the state of West Berlin preempted the federal government by passing its own version of a remigration law in July 1983, other local governments warned against the detrimental effects of a mass exodus of Turks.[42] In a report called "Zero Hour," referencing the abrupt transition after the fall of Nazism in 1945, the city of Düsseldorf conjured an apocalyptical vision of what would happen when the last guest worker left. The report predicted that Düsseldorf would lose much more than "the pizzeria on the corner" (a stand-in for guest workers' beloved gastronomic contributions) and the guest workers' "friendliness," "warmth," and "hospitality" (stereotypical personality traits that contrasted with Germans' cold affect). Local businesses would lose at least 50 million

---

[37] "Rückkehrprämie ist politische Fehlgeburt," *Gewerkschaftspost*, 1983 (most likely November or December); DPA, "IG Metall nennt Rückkehrhilfe ein Blendwerk,'" *Volksblatt*, December 1, 1983.

[38] Klaus Weizel, "Taschengeld für ungewisse Zukunft," *Die Tageszeitung*, February 24, 1984.

[39] "Nimm deine Prämie und hau ab," *Der Spiegel*, August 22, 1983, 26–31.

[40] Hakki Keskin, "Rückkehrförderungsmaßnahmen bieten den Ausländern nichts an," *Arkadaş*, November 1982, 6–8.

[41] *Stern*, trans. in Mehmet Yaşin, "Naklihaneciler Kapıkule'den ancak 3–4 günde çıkabılıyor," *Cumhuriyet*, May 16, 1984.

[42] Deutscher Depeschendienst, "Senat beschloß Rückkehrhilfe für Ausländer," July 12, 1983, BArch, B 106/117694.

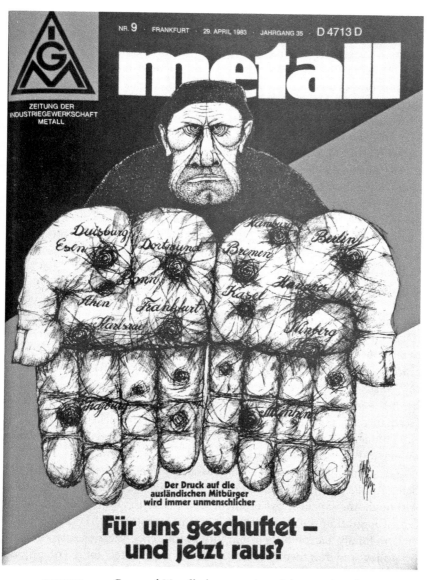

FIGURE 5.3 Cover of *Metall,* the magazine of the metalworkers trade union, opposing the remigration law, 1983. The text reads: "Toiled for us – and now out? The pressure on our foreign fellow citizens is becoming increasingly inhumane." © IG Metall, used with permission.

DM in revenue. Public transportation would literally screech to a halt, as local trains employed nearly 500 foreign workers. Amid declining German birthrates, the loss of foreign children would force kindergartens and elementary schools to close. The dilapidated buildings in the large housing blocks where guest workers lived would continue to deteriorate – surely, the report maintained, no Germans would want to live under such poor conditions, and no landlords would be interested in investing there. The message was clear. As the headline of an article on the Düsseldorf report put it: "Germany Could Not Survive Without the Foreigners."[43]

The Turkish government, too, took up the call for resistance. The two countries' labor ministers, Norbert Blüm and Turhan Esener, clashed on the remigration law in a July 1983 meeting in Ankara. The meeting made it clear, in the words of *Der Tagesspiegel,* that the Turkish government had "no understanding for Bonn's problems with the more than 4.6 million foreigners – a third of them Turks – in the Federal Republic." Calling the proposed law "inappropriate," "unacceptable," and "detrimental to our workers," Esener expressed concerns that Bonn would impose harsher measures against Turkish guest worker families if the law failed to achieve its goals.[44] Returning guest workers, Esener added ominously, "will be doomed to misery."[45] At a press conference later that month, Turkish Minister President Bülent Ulusu called the remigration law "unjust and to the disadvantage of our workers" and urged the West German government not to "resort to measures not supported by the Turkish government."[46] Ulusu demanded further that the West German government pay out the returning guest workers' social security payments, remaining unemployment premiums, and child allowance money in full.

Yet even the prospect of deteriorating bilateral relations did not deter Kohl's government from passing the law on November 28, 1983. Although the Turkish government continued to oppose all forms of return migration out of a fear of declining remittances, Turkish policymakers finally accepted their inability to influence West German domestic policy and resigned themselves to an anticipated influx of 70,000

[43] Joachim Schucht, "Deutschland könnte ohne die Ausländer nicht auskommen," *Kölnische Rundschau,* October 30, 1983.
[44] "Türkische Regierung gegen Pläne Bonns zur Rückkehrförderung," *Der Tagesspiegel,* July 5, 1983.
[45] "Ankara 'dönüş primine' zam, Alman Bakan 'anlayış' istedi," *Cumhuriyet,* July 5, 1983, 1.
[46] German Embassy in Ankara to AA, "Betr.: Rückkehrförderung: Äußerungen MP Ulusus, 08.07.1983," July 13, 1983, PAAA, B 85/1605.

return migrants – a vast underestimation of the approximately 250,000 men, women, and children who would return within the following ten months.[47] Official condemnation of the law, however, persisted. Three months after the law was passed, Turkish minister Mesut Yılmaz complained colorfully: "After an invitation sealed in gold ink, they now want to send the Turkish workers home like squeezed-out lemons."[48]

TO STAY OR TO LEAVE?

"The time has come to make a decision," wrote guest worker İlyas Suran in a poem. "The Germans have run out of marks and jobs. It makes no sense to stay here any longer. ... Helmut Kohl no longer cares about us." He continued powerfully: "Do not stay stuck between two mountains. Do not estrange yourself from your nation. Do not end your life in a foreign land. Go on your way friend, back to Turkey."[49] As a young man, Suran had migrated from Gaziantep to West Germany as a textile worker and had turned to poetry and music to quell his homesickness. While he chose not to return until the 1990s, his poem captures Turkish migrants' collective spirit as they navigated both the challenge and the opportunity that the 1983 remigration law presented. Should they stay, or should they leave?

Although the CDU publicly praised the remigration law as a "full success," Kohl failed to achieve his goal of reducing the Turkish population by 50 percent.[50] As the June 30, 1984, application deadline neared, the Turkish newspaper *Cumhuriyet* reported that Turkish guest workers "show less interest than expected."[51] The meager 10,500 DM and the loss of their employer social security contributions turned off most guest workers, who knew they would encounter difficulties in Turkey's struggling economy. Others stayed in Germany for personal or family reasons, or out of fear of losing their freedom of mobility between the two countries. Still, the remigration law prompted one of the largest mass remigrations in modern European history. In 1984 alone, 15 percent of the

---

[47] *Volksblatt*, December 10, 1983, DOMiD-Archiv, P-15528.
[48] "Ankara fordert von Bonn 'vernünftigere Lösung,'" *Der Tagesspiegel*, January 5, 1984.
[49] İlyas Suran, "Almancıya," May 28, 1986, in Magistrat der Stadt Frankfurt am Main, »*Mit Koffern voller Träume...*«, 56.
[50] For one of many examples of the CDU praising the "full success" of the remigration premium, see the party's 1986 publication: *CDU-Dokumentation* 32/1986, 29, www .kas.de/wf/doc/kas_26763-544-1-30.pdf?110826092553.
[51] "Turk işçileri geri primine yüz vermedi," *Cumhuriyet*, June 27, 1984.

Turkish immigrant population – approximately 250,000 men, women, and children – made the difficult decision to leave a country where they had lived for over a decade.

The law's implementation had a rough start. Beginning on December 1, 1983, the day the law went into effect, the six employees of the Rhineland-Palatinate State Insurance Agency in Düsseldorf were bombarded with an average of 240 guest workers per day, primarily Turks, demanding the immediate cash payout of their social security.[52] This rush continued through January 1984. The *Neue-Ruhr-Zeitung* reported that the workers who "stormed" the office reacted with "resignation, disappointment, and outbursts of anger" when they learned that they would lose their employer contributions and that they would receive the money only after they could provide proof of having exited West German borders. Others were dismayed that individuals who had become unemployed before the October 30, 1983, cutoff or had not worked reduced hours (*Kurzarbeit*) for the past six months were ineligible. One man shouted at a social security advisor, "Even upon our departure, we are financing your pension!" "I always had the impression that my countrymen were being scammed," another concurred.[53] Overall, this experience was consistent with accusations that the law did not have guest workers' best interests in mind.

Although statistics varied, the 10,500 DM premium proved far less attractive than the social security payouts. By mid-January 1984, two months into the program's eight-month application period, only 3,200 people had applied for the 10,500 DM.[54] While policymakers were delighted that 80 percent of the applicants were Turks, they lamented that this number amounted to only one out of every ten who were eligible.[55] In late February, the DGB reported that only 4,200 out of 300,000 eligible workers of all nationalities had applied for the 10,500 DM premium – "less than a drop on the hot stone."[56] To sweeten the deal, the government permitted returning workers to receive up to 75 percent of the premium and the employee social security refund before they returned to Turkey if they paid a small upfront fee.[57] Applications for social

---

[52] Klaus-Dieter Oehler, "Sie lassen sich die Rente jetzt auszahlen," *RP*, December 13, 1983.

[53] "Die Kredithaie lauern schon im Kellerbüro," *Neue Ruhr Zeitung*, January 25, 1984.

[54] "3200 Ausländer stellten Anträge auf Rückkehrhilfe," *Der Tagesspiegel*, January 27, 1984.

[55] "Zehn Prozent der Türken machen von dem neuen Gesetz Gebrauch," *Volksblatt*, January 18, 1984.

[56] "Kaum Wirkung der Rückkehrhilfen," *Einigkeit*, April 1984.

[57] "Nur wenige Anträge auf Rückkehrhilfe," *Die Welt*, April 25, 1984.

security payouts immediately skyrocketed, outpacing applications for the 10,500 DM premium eightfold. All in all, the Labor Ministry reported that 16,833 applicants of all nationalities – 14,459, or 86 percent, of whom were Turks – were accepted for the 10,500 DM premium, and 2,500 were rejected as not fulfilling all the law's conditions. Whereas the government initially estimated that 55,000 people would apply for their social security contributions, a massive 140,000 applicants – 120,000 of whom were Turks – chose to do so.[58] Of those, 70 percent took the new option to receive the money while still in Germany so they could finance the expensive homeward journey without succumbing to shady loan sharks.[59] Hasan Karabiber, an advisor at the Workers' Welfare Organization in Ingolstadt, confirmed that the social security payout – not the 10,500 DM – was the crucial factor motivating the workers he had advised.[60]

Eager to rid themselves of unwanted Turkish workers and avoid mass layoffs, private companies also seized the opportunity to downsize by offering severance packages to any foreign worker willing to voluntarily quit. The timing was enticing: while they could not receive the full governmental payout until they returned to Turkey, they could cash in on the firm's severance package immediately. Ruhrkohle AG, a large mining company in Essen and the largest West German employer of Turkish citizens, was among the first to pursue this strategy. By June 1984, 2,700 Turkish workers – or every eighth foreign worker at the company – had taken a severance package of approximately 11,200 DM.[61] An internal study boasted that 26.5 percent of all the men who had taken the government's remigration premium had been employed at Ruhrkohle AG.[62] The Gelsenkirchen mining company Bergbau AG Lippe followed suit. Employees who quit before the remigration law's June 30, 1984, application deadline would receive two-and-a-half months of wages, the remainder of their paid vacation days for the whole year, and a 2,600 DM Christmas bonus – all tax-free.[63] Combining all the incentives, Bergbau

[58] "300.000 Ausländer planen Heimkehr," *KSA*, August 2, 1984.
[59] "300.000 nahmen Rückkehrhilfen," *RP*, August 2, 1984.
[60] "Wirtschaftskrise fraß die Rückkehrhilfe," *Donau Kurier*, May 1985, AdsD, DGB-Archiv, 5/DGAZ001214.
[61] Leonhard Spielhofer, "Türken sagen der Ruhrkohle ade," *KSA*, August 22, 1984.
[62] Heinz Esken, *Bericht über die in die Türkei zurückgekehrten Mitarbeiter der Ruhrkohle AG* (Essen: Ruhrkohle AG, 1985).
[63] Bergbau AG Lippe, "Aufhebungsvertrag zwischen der Bergbau ASG Lippe / Werksdirektion," AdsD, DGB-Archiv, 5/DGAZ000902.

AG Lippe estimated that a Turkish worker with two children could return to his or her homeland with a hefty amount of cash: 58,481 DM if the worker had been with the company for over twelve years, and 64,929 DM for a period of employment in excess of eighteen years.[64]

Guest workers' reasons for leaving were not only financial. The Turkish Central Bank reported that over 80 percent of the applicants were men between thirty-eight and fifty-five years of age who had lived in West Germany between ten and twenty years.[65] Nearly all were married with at least one child, and 70 percent had children who lived in Turkey. The vast majority earned 1,000–3,000 DM per month, meaning that the 10,500 DM premium barely amounted to a year of their salary. Eighteen percent were motivated by the 10,500 DM premium initially, while 93 percent attributed their final decision to the social security payouts and 8 percent to the employer severance packages. The Center for Turkish Studies offered a more complex portrait. Only one-third of the surveyed return migrants attributed their decision primarily to financial reasons – split between having already reached their financial goals (16 percent), being unemployed (8 percent), wanting to retire (4 percent), and planning to start their own small businesses in Turkey (6 percent).[66] For 10 percent of the migrants, either homesickness, personal/family reasons, their children's education, or old age/illness was the primary motivator. Approximately 5 percent each were leaving on account of integration problems, because they no longer wanted to live in Germany, or because they missed their family and friends in Turkey. Despite the varying statistics, the pattern is clear: individual decisions were motivated by a complex constellation of financial, personal, and familial reasons in which the remigration law played a supporting role.[67]

Even though racism was just one of many reasons, the Turkish media emphasized it in numerous reports on returning guest workers – even before the remigration law came into effect (Figure 5.4). One man told *Milliyet* that he was returning because Germans treated Turks "like dogs" or "as though we had leprosy," similar to how he

---

[64] Bergbau AG Lippe, "Rückkehrhilfegesetz – Beispiele über zu erwartende Leistungen," February 10, 1984, AdsD, DGB-Archiv, 5/DGAZ000902.

[65] Türkiye Cumhuriyet Merkez Bankası, "Yurt Dışındaki Vatandaşlarımızın Tasarruf Eğilimleri Araştırması: Yurda Kesin Dönenler" (December 1986).

[66] Zentrum für Türkeistudien, "Türkische Remigranten" (Essen: Zentrum für Türkeistudien, 1992).

[67] See also the statistics in Elmar Hönekopp, "Rückkehrförderung und Rückkehr ausländischer Arbeitnehmer," 323–25.

FIGURE 5.4 Cartoon in *Hürriyet* emphasizing West German racism as a main reason for return migration, ca. 1984. The text states: "In my opinion, the most effective remigration incentives are some people's facial expressions." © Oğuz Peker, used with permission.

had seen African-Americans treated in an American film.[68] Other men told *Cumhuriyet* that they feared the "Turks, get out!" graffiti and the "aggressive German youths with motorcycles ... Enough already!"[69] The most extensive account came from Turkish novelist Bekir Yıldız, who wrote a series of *Cumhuriyet* articles based on his interactions with return migrants even before the remigration law was passed. "Perhaps if Turks had blonde hair, blue eyes, and could speak proper German, Germans would not consider them foreigners," one man quipped. "Christians and Muslims are incompatible," another asserted, and now "we are in the situation of the old Jews." Just like "how Hitler did it," the Germans "will slaughter people on the streets."[70] In short, Yıldız implied, guest workers who went back to Turkey did not return feeling wealthy and triumphant but rather like "prisoners" who had been locked up in Germany for fifteen years.[71]

Yet, because Turkish guest workers were not a homogenous population, the decision to stay or leave was far more complicated. Ethnic, religious, and political affiliations circumscribed their mobility, especially because the 1983 remigration law came three years after 1980 Turkey's military coup. Understandably, guest workers who were political leftists

[68] Erhan Akyıldız, "Kapıkule'de her gün 20 işçi ailesi kesin dönüş yapıyor," *Milliyet*, April 17, 1982, 8.
[69] Fatih Güllapoğlu, "Kapıkule'de 'büyük göç' zilleri çalıyor," *Cumhuriyet*, August 10, 1983, 1.
[70] Bekir Yıldız, "Alacağım son kuruşuna kadar almadan dönmem," *Cumhuriyet*, September 9, 1983.
[71] Bekir Yıldız, "Odediğimiz işsizlik parasını istiyoruz," *Cumhuriyet*, September 10, 1983.

or who were members of Turkey's internal ethnic minority groups like
Kurds and Yazidis feared that upon their return they would be arrested,
tortured, or executed. They also knew that if they wished to reenter West
Germany yet again to escape persecution, they would face a dual set of
barriers: they would not only be subject to West Germany's harsh visa
restrictions against Turkish citizens, in general, but they would also likely
be denied asylum.[72] For them, staying in West Germany – even if they
wished to return with the remigration premium – was far preferable to
precarity in Turkey.

Sometimes, guest workers' fates depended on circumstances beyond
their control, such as old age or illness. Guest workers' parents who
remained in Turkey, now in their twilight years, sometimes begged their
middle-aged children to take care of them or to spend time together
before they died. Forty-eight-year-old Osman İşleyen wanted to stay in
Germany after living there for fifteen years but resigned himself to returning to his hometown of Burdur. His eighty-year-old mother had fallen ill
and could no longer tend to their farm, nor raise his three children who
lived with her.[73] Burcu İkçilli's family was deterred from returning by
her father's health condition. Although her father had planned to quit his
job just two weeks before the remigration law's application deadline, he
had suffered a severe work accident and had broken three vertebrae. His
seven-month hospital stay prevented his family from returning to Turkey,
even though he had already purchased a home there and furnished it with
German furniture brought back on their summer vacations. Fifteen years
later, they still had not returned and had resorted to renting their Turkish
house to a family with three children. The story turned tragic: an earth-
quake destroyed the house and killed all three children.[74]

Many guest workers decided to stay because they viewed the remigration law with "skepticism," "insecurity," and "mistrust," and they
knew that returning to Turkey would mean losing their freedom of
mobility between the two countries.[75] Although Necla and Ünsal Ö. had
strongly considered taking the premium, a German colleague convinced

[72] Stokes, "The Permanent Refugee Crisis," 35–36.
[73] Mehmet Yaşin, "80 yaşındaki anam yüzünden kesin dönüşe karar verdim," *Cumhuriyet*,
May 16, 1984.
[74] Burcu İkçilli, "Deutschland mein Zuhause?!" in Bernardino Di Croce, Manfred
Budzinski, and Verein Migration & Integration in der Bundesrepublik Deutschland,
eds., *Nicht auf Augenhöhe? Erfahrungen und Lebensgeschichten zum Thema Migration
und Zweiter Generation in Deutschland* (Karlsruhe: Loeper, 2009), 70–74.
[75] Ölçen, *Türken und Rückkehr*, 9–10.

Ünsal otherwise. Anyone taking the money was "an idiot," the colleague insisted, because they would only be receiving their employee social security contributions and foregoing their employer contributions.[76] The couple also did not want to detach themselves from West Germany, where they had lived for two decades, and they knew that taking the premium would mean relinquishing their residence permits at a time of heightened visa restrictions on Turkish citizens. Ultimately, Necla and Ünsal decided to return to Turkey in the 1990s, retiring in the quaint beach town of Şarköy rather than their bustling home city of Istanbul. In an interview thirty years later, the couple expressed no regrets, because their decision to wait allowed them to maintain their lives in both countries, and they could still travel back and forth on their annual vacations.

For many families, the decision to stay or leave was unclear. Murad B., a self-identified "suitcase child" who was born in Germany but sent to Istanbul to live with his grandparents, recalled that his parents had repeatedly promised to return. They had even stored unopened boxes of German consumer goods in their attic, in anticipation of one day bringing them to Turkey. Although the 10,500 DM remigration premium was "clearly attractive" to Murad's parents, and although they feared the rising racism, his parents lived well and had become accustomed to life in Germany. "They traveled, they had a car, they were driving to places they probably never could have gone to otherwise," Murad explained, and "they didn't want to let go of these possibilities." Crucial to his parents' decision was that his father, like thousands of former guest workers, had opened his own business.[77] Returning to Turkey – with or without the 10,500 DM premium – would require him to close his relatively lucrative tailor shop and try his luck in Turkey's volatile economy. The tailor shop had also given his parents "very good contact" with German customers, whom they considered close friends. Murad's parents were thus left wavering back and forth – "Are we going, are we not? Are we going, are we not?" – and eventually decided to stay.[78] Thousands of miles away, Murad continued to see his parents and younger sister only during their vacations.

The Uğur family, profiled in a West German television report, was also split along a generational divide. The father, Ali, had become

76 Necla and Ünsal Ö., interview.
77 On former guest workers who started their own businesses in Germany, see: Zeppenfeld, *Vom Gast zum Gastwirt?*, chapter 6.
78 Murad B., interview.

unemployed, and the meager unemployment money was insufficient to feed his wife and three children. His thirty-six-year-old wife, Nezat, also wished to return to Turkey, since she felt isolated and missed her large family, especially her female relatives. For both parents, the rising racism of recent years was cause for concern. The tea house that Ali frequently visited had recently been vandalized: rowdy German youths had thrown a rock through the window, sprayed graffiti reading "Foreigners out!" on the walls, and attacked a Turkish customer. But Ali and Nezat also had to act in the best interest of their children, who loved living in Germany. The youngest two spoke German fluently and had many friends at their kindergarten. The older daughter, Şerife, was earning all "A"s in her middle school and was worried about switching to a Turkish school. The Uğur family was thus relegated to a liminal position between staying and leaving, perched on a generational divide.[79]

Whereas the Uğurs wanted to keep their children in Germany, other parents returned precisely because they wanted to prevent the "Germanization" of their children, who had long been derided as Almancı. In a survey of eighteen returning families, 62 percent of parents cited "problems of the children" as a main motivation for their return, while another study attributed many decisions to the "fear that children could too strongly Germanize."[80] "We came here to escape Germanization and to become real Turks," one teenage boy explained.[81] Echoing longstanding discourses about the cultural estrangement of "Almancı children," parents feared the dual loss of their children's Turkish language skills and Muslim faith. For Yaşar Fuad, who identified as a pious Muslim, returning to Turkey was a means of "saving one's child," since integration necessarily entailed "forgetting God's commandments" and "acting like Christians." Children exposed to Germany for too long would become gâvur, a derogatory term for non-Muslims, and would engage in "sinful" (günah) and "forbidden" (haram) behaviors like abandoning prayer and study of the Koran, eating pork, drinking alcohol, disrespecting elders, and having premarital sex.[82]

---

[79] Engler and Trottnow, "Fremde Heimat."

[80] Topraklar, Zur Situation türkischer Rückkehrfamilien, 20; Klara Osiander and Johannes Zerger, Rückkehr in die Fremde. Die Problematik der Remigration junger Türken/-innen und deren Familien in ihr Heimatland. Oder: 'Keine Ahnung und zurück' (Augsburg: MaroVerlag, 1988), 61.

[81] Dilek Zaptıcıoğlu, "Wir kamen hierher, um Türken zu werden," Bizim Almanca, April 1987, 13–16.

[82] Schiffauer, Die Migranten aus Subay, 149, 243, 303, 350.

Since most Turks who applied for the remigration premium were married men who returned with their wives and children, the story of Fatma Koçyiğit stands out. Born in Gaziantep, the forty-eight-year-old woman had followed her husband to Germany in 1970 and begun working as a maid in hotels and restaurants. Although she sorely wished to return to Turkey, her husband had underestimated Turkey's high inflation rate and could not afford to purchase a farm there. Soon, Fatma discovered that her husband was cheating on her with their neighbor's daughter and that he wanted a divorce. When she asked for money for their children, her now ex-husband beat her – but, not knowing German, she did not go to the police. After sending her children back to Turkey to stay with relatives, Fatma became so "depressed" and "anxious" that she needed to be hospitalized and was fired from her job. But since she did not have a work permit, she could not receive unemployment benefits. In the meantime, her ex-husband was imprisoned for possessing marijuana, leaving him unable to provide any financial support. Fearing that she would "die alone," Fatma decided that her only option was to "bow my head," wait to receive the remigration premium, and finally "return from this hell."[83] Yet given that the government rejected thousands of applications for the premium, Fatma's future was likely insecure.

After they made their difficult decisions, the 250,000 men, women, and children who left Turkey with the remigration premium now embarked upon a mass exodus – packing their bags and hustling back to Turkey before the September 30, 1984, deadline for exiting West German borders (Figures 5.5 and 5.6). At the local level, the effects of this mass exodus were especially visible in cities with high Turkish populations. One of the most extreme cases was the Ruhr city of Duisburg, home to numerous coal and steel factories like Ruhrkohle, Thyssen, Krupp, and Mannesmann. "If the Turks go," warned the *Bonner Rundschau*, Duisburg will turn into a "ghost town."[84] That prophecy came true: by mid-February 1984, nearly 4,000 Turks, had left the city.[85]

Over half the Turks who left Duisburg lived in Hüttenheim, a neighborhood pejoratively nicknamed "Türkenheim" because every eleventh resident was Turkish.[86] Nearly all of them had received severance

[83] Mehmet Yaşin, "14 yılın sonunda: Bilet param bile yok," *Cumhuriyet*, May 13, 1984.
[84] Hans Wüllenweber, "Tausende von Türken packen schon die Koffer," *Bonner Rundschau*, February 7, 1984.
[85] Hannelore Schulte, "Der Abzug der Türken. Wie Duisburg viertausend Menschen verliert," *Die Zeit*, February 10, 1984, 13.
[86] "Ausländer. Dramatische Szenen," *Der Spiegel*, February 27, 1984.

FIGURE 5.5 A Turkish family packs their van with all their possessions, preparing to return to Turkey permanently after taking the remigration premium, 1984. © akg-images/Guenay Ulutuncok, used with permission.

FIGURE 5.6 Turkish women in Kreuzberg pack their cars and say goodbye as they await their families' departure, 1985. © Bayerische Staatsbibliothek/stern-Fotoarchiv/Jürgen Müller-Schneck, used with permission.

packages from the local steel plant Mannesmann AG. Although company spokespeople would not admit it, Mannesmann's climate was decidedly racist. Hasan Özen, who began working at Mannesmann in 1966 and was elected to the employee council of the metalworkers' trade union IG Metall in 1975, recalled that his German colleagues repeatedly exclaimed phrases like "Dead Turk!" and "Turks out!" – which implied that "I should leave Germany, otherwise they'd kill me." While Özen dismissed these coworkers as "just a couple of idiots," many of his Turkish colleagues took the rising racism as a cue to leave.[87] Turkish employees at Mannesmann also cited the rising racism in a new discriminatory company policy. The board had recently mandated that all employees take an allegedly "subject-oriented" mathematics and language test to determine which workers' language skills made them suitable for higher-level tasks. The exam had the indirect, although intentional, effect of motivating workers' decisions to leave. As a local Turkish social worker who had counseled many Mannesmann employees explained, the language test created a "competitive atmosphere" in which "everyone believed that they would lose their job tomorrow."[88] Derviş Zabo, who had worked at Mannesmann for fourteen years and had become a foreman, expressed his anxieties about his lack of job security in a 1984 interview: "If I do not pass the test, Mannesmann will probably send me to a temp job firm, and the temp firm will want to give us other random jobs, like road maintenance or digging trenches."[89]

As Mannesmann employees and their families abruptly left their homes, West German journalists descended on Duisburg-Hüttenheim. A ten-page photo essay in the West German magazine *Stern*, which also circulated to Turkish readers, told the story from the migrants' perspective.[90] Titled "The Expellees" (*Die Heimatvertriebenen*), in reference to the mass migration of ethnic Germans from Eastern Europe after the Second World War, the article aimed to attract sympathy. The photographs depict men on a train platform staring wistfully into the distance, old women in headscarves hugging one another, and children watching somberly as a group of men lug a washing machine into a moving van. The captions

---

[87] Hasan Özen, interview, VHS (1992), DOMiD-Archiv, VI 0310.
[88] "Aus Duisburg reisten 4000 Türken ab," *Der Tagesspiegel*, March 1, 1984, DOMiD-Archiv, P-15539.
[89] Horst Röper, "Der Türke kann gehen," *Politik Aktuell*, Westdeutscher Rundfunk (1984), DOMiD-Archiv, VI 0233(15).
[90] Gerhard Krömschröder and Mihaly Moldavy, "Die Heimatvertriebenen. Exodus der Türken," *Stern*, March 1, 1984, 20–29, DOMiD-Archiv, P-15540.

were mournful and foreboding: "Goodbye in Duisburg-Hüttenheim…
Hugs, kisses, tears. Compassion for the old and young who are leaving
Germany forever – and for those who are staying in the Turk-Ghetto
(*Türken-Ghetto*). Will they also have to go soon?" The article went
beyond most German portrayals, however, as the journalist drove with
a former Mannesmann employee and his family back to their hometown
of Kahramanmaraş, reporting on both their excitement and misgivings.

In a *Die Zeit* article also republished in the Turkish newspaper
Cumhuriyet, a German teacher in Hüttenheim shared her perspective on
the mass departure. She described the scene as both somber and chaotic –
a mad dash to leave with as many West German consumer goods as
possible. "Already many windows are missing their flower boxes, and
cardboard boxes piled high are awaiting their transport," she marveled.
"Almost daily the Duisburg department stores are delivering goods that
will be taken to the homeland: washing machines, television sets, video
recorders, and entire living room furniture sets."[91] As predicted in the City
of Düsseldorf's foreboding "Zero Hour" report, she emphasized that the
mass exodus bore serious consequences for the local economy. Duisburg's
business owners complained about a loss in profits of up to 50 percent.
Shops had closed, and many feared layoffs of German employees.[92] The
demographic changes also affected schools, where 80 percent of students
were Turkish. By the end of 1984, one of the second-grade classes in
Hüttenheim was predicted to have only six or seven children left.

Although she attempted to empathize with her students, the
Hüttenheim teacher problematically exoticized Turkish culture and
reinforced tropes of Turkish backwardness. "We are not letting go of
'our' Turks with light hearts," she lamented. She would miss the exciting
street festivals featuring kebab and Turkish pizza, honey-soaked cakes,
and girls wearing colorful "traditional" clothing. Likewise, she would
miss seeing the trash containers spill over the lawn, the elderly women in
ruffled skirts crouching down on the ground knitting to pass the time, the
loud calls of "Öğretmen, öğretmen!" (Teacher, teacher!), and the need to
develop new modes of communication based on hand and foot gestures.
All of these gave her the feeling of "being far away – somewhere on
vacation." By contrast, she noted that German parts of the city were far
less exciting, with their pristine white houses, perfectly trimmed hedges,
and orderly flowers. The only sign of children was a lone German girl

---

[91] Schulte, "Der Abzug der Türken," 13.
[92] Ibid.

wheeling back and forth on her tricycle, warned by her parents not to venture beyond the front lawn.[93] Most troubling to her, the fate of the Turkish children whom she had worked so tirelessly to educate and integrate was bleak – particularly for the girls. Not only would they be perceived as "Germanized" in Turkey, but, echoing derogatory critiques of Turkey's allegedly patriarchal culture, she feared that they would quickly be forced into marriage and motherhood. "What awaits them? … In a few years, will these outgoing girls, who are so eager to learn, turn into fat, worn-out women like most of their mothers?"

However problematic, the article revealed the underacknowledged reality that the decision to leave had consequences not only for Turkish migrants but also for Germans. After up to two decades of living and working in West Germany, Turkish guest workers and their children had undoubtedly become part of German society. But when border officials stamped their residence permits "invalid," they also stamped out their lives, friendships, and connections in West Germany – leaving only memories. As Germans watched them leave, emotions were mixed. While those who embraced the racist cry "Turks out!" cheered with delight, others truly mourned their absence. The situation had flipped. When guest workers first stepped onto the trains to West Germany in the 1960s and early 1970s, they waved goodbye to the loved ones they left behind. Over a decade later, upon the mass exodus of 1984, they stood outside their homes in German cities and waved goodbye not only to their Turkish neighbors and friends, but also – especially for children – to their German ones. School classes held goodbye parties for Turkish students who were leaving, neighbors exchanged parting gifts, and sobbing friends savored last hugs at the airport. In both moments, the rupture was both exhilarating and heartbreaking.

UNREALIZED DREAMS

"We killed our passports," return migrants regularly noted, expressing the seeming irreversibility and permanence of their "final" return.[94] For the 250,000 men, women, and children who took the 1983 remigration premium and left Germany, the homeward journey came full circle. For their final return, they either stepped onto airplanes or loaded up their cars with all their belongings and drove on the same familiar

---

[93] Ibid.
[94] Wolbert, *Der getötete Paß*, 7.

route that they took on their annual vacations: the Europastraße 5, the treacherous international highway or "road of death" through Austria, Yugoslavia, and Bulgaria. But this time, their baggage felt even heavier. While their vacations had always been temporary, a new sense of permanence and anxiety loomed: How would they fare upon their permanent return? Would they come to regret their decision? Would they finally realize their dreams of financial success? While many achieved their dreams, others missed their lives in Germany and encountered harsh difficulties *re*-integrating into Turkish society. Although they remained derided as "Germanized," the stereotype of the wealthy *Almancı* did not always materialize and many found themselves not only socially ostracized but also financially bankrupt. As *Der Tagesspiegel* put it bluntly, "This homeland may be more foreign to them than Berlin-Kreuzberg, Cologne-Ehrenfeld, or the Ruhr region."[95] *Cumhuriyet* concurred, turning the concept of "integration" on its head: "Life abroad is over. Now they must get used to Turkey."[96]

Even before the 1983 remigration law was passed, customs officials at the Bulgarian-Turkish border at Kapıkule were already estimating a problematically large increase in border traffic. In 1982, the border authorities had reported that approximately twenty or twenty-five families passed through the border for permanent remigration each day, but they expected to be overrun in 1984.[97] Officials were aware that this situation would be "different" than the traffic and chaos even during peak vacation season, and they were already building new inspection sites along the border to accommodate what they anticipated to be kilometer-long queues of guest workers transporting all their possessions and furniture, all of which needed to be inspected and accounted for on customs forms. The officials estimated that they could only accommodate 300 cars of returnees per day, and already the border guards and returning workers were "drowning" in the paperwork, with lost passports and incomplete customs forms.[98]

As anticipated, the scene at Kapıkule in the months before the September 30, 1984, deadline was far more chaotic than it had ever been on their vacations. A *Cumhuriyet* reporter accompanied guest workers on

95 "Hunderte von Türken warteten vor den deutschen Konsulaten," *Der Tagesspiegel,* October 7, 1984.
96 Yalçin Pekşen, "Gurbet bitti, sıra Türkiye'ye alışmakta..." *Cumhuriyet,* October 15, 1984.
97 Akyıldız, "Kapıkule'de her gün 20 işçi ailesi kesin dönüş yapıyor."
98 Güllapoğlu, "Kapıkule'de 'büyük göç' zilleri çalıyor"; "Kesin dönüşler arttıkça Kapıkule'de kargaşa büyüyor," *Cumhuriyet,* June 12, 1983.

the long drive back from Germany to Turkey along the Europastraße 5 – through the border check points at Austria, Yugoslavia, and Bulgaria – the same drive they had made so many times before. He drove along with one guest worker, who was heading back from West Berlin to his home village of Bakırköy. At Kapıkule, the border guards were so swamped that they resorted to dividing the cars into two lines – one for the returning workers and one for vacationers. "It takes half a day to complete the paperwork," the reporter noted. "In the remaining half day, the car is searched." A border guard quoted in the article further explained the delay: "Even if all the officers are mobilized in July and August, it will still take three or four days for all the cars to enter." Finally, the guest worker and the accompanying reporter passed through the border in one and a half days and unpacked his bags in Bakırköy – everything he had to show for thirteen years of his labor.[99]

But not all returning guest workers could breathe a sigh of relief as they unpacked their bags and settled into their homes in Turkey. Due to problems implementing the 1983 remigration law, many encountered immediate financial hardship. In the first four months after the September 30, 1984, deadline, the Braunschweig Labor Office received over one hundred handwritten letters from returning guest workers who had not yet received their money. Hursit U., who provided the most detail, described the convoluted process. In May 1984, after being advised by the Turkish language interpreter at the Braunschweig Labor Office, Hursit had filled out an application for the remigration premium. He was assigned a "remigration assistance number" and received a letter confirming that he had fulfilled all the requirements. The next step was crucial: upon exiting West German borders at either the airport or along the highway, Hursit needed to present two copies of a red and green "Confirmation of Border Crossing Form" for the border guards to sign and stamp. While Hursit was supposed to keep the green copy for his own record, the red copy went through a complex paper trail. The border guard had to forward the red copy to the Federal Labor Office, which would then forward it to the local Braunschweig Labor Office. Only upon the red copy's arrival in Braunschweig could the money transfer begin. The money would be transferred to the bank account and address that Hursit had provided.

[99] Mehmet Yaşin, "Naklihaneciler Kapıkule'den ancak 3–4 günde çıkabılıyor," *Cumhuriyet*, May 16, 1984.

Certainly, there were several places where this complex chain could break down. Many returning guest workers who wrote to the Braunschweig Labor Office were unaware that they were supposed to have the form officially signed and stamped by a border official. Nor were some border officials aware of their responsibility to mail the red copy to the Federal Labor Office. Instead, they simply handed both signed and stamped copies back to the guest workers. Mustafa K. admitted that he had "clumsily" given the form to a friend in Hanover, and Mestan P. had handed the form to a friend who was waving goodbye to them at the airport.[100] Two men had given the form to the travel agent from whom they had bought the plane tickets.[101] Others, who had chosen to drive home, opted to send the form via post at various stops along the international highway Europastraße 5. One man mailed it from an Austrian post office in Salzburg, and Hayrettin Ö. put it in a mailbox as soon as he crossed the Bulgarian-Turkish border.[102]

Problems arose even when guest workers properly submitted their forms at the West German border. One German man wrote to the Federal Labor Ministry complaining that his colleagues had witnessed the lackadaisical attitudes of the border guards at the Cologne Airport. "The personnel employed at this border protection station were apparently so overloaded," he wrote, "that it was no longer possible to issue the required border confirmation to the departing Turks."[103] Shockingly, "many of the officials were on a coffee break!" Overwhelmingly, however, border officials deflected blame onto the guest workers. Pejoratively, the Border Police Directorate complained that only half of the "partially illiterate foreigners" exiting through the Hanover Airport had accurately filled out their forms. The resulting quarrels and confusion led to "unacceptable impairments on border police control" and a "break-down of flight operations."[104] No matter who was to blame, confusion about

100 Mustafa K. to Yelkenkaya, November 14, 1984, DOMiD-Archiv, E 0987,36; Mestan P. to Yelkenkaya, November 29, 1984, DOMiD-Archiv, E 0987,36.
101 Hinditti to Yelkenkaya, October 31, 1984, DOMiD-Archiv, E 0987,36; Cemal T. to Yelkenkaya, November 29, 1984, DOMiD-Archiv, E 0987,36.
102 Anonymous to Yelkenkaya, October 7, 1984, DOMiD-Archiv, E 0987,36; Hayrettin Ö. to Yelkenkaya, September 25, 1984, DOMiD-Archiv, E 0987,36.
103 Hans Merz (Finanzagentur International) to BMA, "Betr.: Vollzug des Gesetzes zur Förderung der Rückkehrbereitschaft von Ausländern; hier: Grenzübertrittsbescheinigung," March 20, 1984, BArch, B 106/117696.
104 Grenzschutzdirektion (Eisel) to Bundesminister des Innern, "Betr.: Gesetz zur Förderung der Rückkehrbereitschaft von Ausländern (RückHG); hier: Grenzübertrittsbescheinigungen," April 19, 1984, BArch, B 106/117696.

what to do with a double-sided piece of red paper curiously led to a deterioration of West German state control.

Aware of the possibility for confusion at the border, the West German Foreign Office had authorized a backup procedure: anyone who neglected to have their forms signed, stamped, and submitted by the border officials could physically go to a West German embassy or consulate in Turkey to deliver it in person by the September 30 deadline.[105] But even this option led to chaos. *Der Tagesspiegel* described the "hectic and even tumultuous scene" at the West German Consulate Office in Istanbul in the days before the deadline. Four hundred returning guest workers were "crowding the steps" of the building, and many had slept there overnight, leaving the consular officials "totally overextended," "close to a nervous breakdown," and "on the verge of tirades."[106] Submitting the form to diplomatic offices also posed a problem for returning guest workers. Since the embassy and consulates were located only in major cities, those returning to smaller towns and villages had to make an additional costly and time-consuming trek. This provision proved especially problematic for one man, whose village was located 700 kilometers east of the nearest diplomatic office. Frustrated to find the embassy closed when he passed through Ankara during his drive home, he refused to make another trip. Instead, he put the form in the mail and hired a Düsseldorf-based financial agent to ask about the status of his premium.[107]

Transferring the money into Turkish bank accounts presented another source of confusion. Despite submitting his form properly, Şevki K. checked all his bank accounts but found no money in his name: "I went to Fakat Bank and even telephoned the bank in Ankara and the Merkez Bank in Istanbul. I called them one by one ... Which bank was it sent to?"[108] The comments in the margins of the letters to the Braunschweig Labor Office provide some insight into what might have happened. Repeatedly, labor office officials insisted that they had already transferred the money months before. On Bekir M.'s letter, one official expressed his frustration with an exclamation point: "Sent to the

[105] AA to German Embassy in Tunis, "Betr.: Gesetz zur Förderung der Rückkehrbereitschaft von Ausländern (RückHG); hier: Vordrucke 'Grenzübertrittsbescheinigung,'" January 25, 1984, PAAA, B 89(ZA)/190385.
[106] "Hunderte von Türken warteten vor den deutschen Konsulaten."
[107] Merz (Finanzagentur International) to BMA.
[108] Şevki K. to Yelkenkaya, December 2, 1984, DOMiD-Archiv, E 0987,36.

above-named account on July 10!"[109] The case of Halil A. is particularly revealing. In his letter, Halil requested that the Labor Office transfer his social security contributions to Ziraat Bank in Torbalı. The marginalia, however, indicates that the Labor Office had already sent the money three months prior in the name of a certain "Mehmet A.," likely a friend or relative of Halil, to the Sparkasse Regional Bank in Horb am Necker.[110]

Having failed to receive their money, the letter writers expressed financial difficulties. Halil S. put it bluntly: "I regret coming back."[111] "I really need the money," wrote Ahmet Y., who claimed to have only 20,000 lira left in his wallet.[112] Ramazan B. described his situation in more dire terms: "There are five of us here (my children and I), and we have run out of money."[113] Şevki K., who had hoped to retire from manual labor after over a decade of working in the Peine Steel Work in Salzgitter, found himself once again seeking factory employment.[114] Others needed the remigration premium and social security payout as start-up capital for their own small businesses. Necati T., who also wanted to start his own business, described his and his family's situation more positively: "We got to Turkey safe and sound ... Turkey really is beautiful. Everyone is happy here. Now my only concern is whether or not I will be able to start my own business here. God willing, I will be the boss of my own workplace."[115]

The delay in the payment was especially troubling because many guest workers had spent large quantities of money preparing for the homeward journey itself. Like during their annual vacations, family and friends at home expected gifts, and coming home empty-handed signaled both selfishness and economic failure. But now even more crucial was the need to load up their cars with German consumer goods, likely for the last time, to furnish their homes in Turkey. In the months and days before leaving, they rushed to buy furniture, refrigerators, washing machines, televisions, video recorders, and other household appliances.[116] As *Cumhuriyet* reported, "The remigration premium and social

[109] Bekir M. to Yelkenkaya, September 27, 1984, DOMiD-Archiv, E 0987,36.
[110] Halil A. to Yelkenkaya, December 1, 1984, DOMiD-Archiv, E 0987,36.
[111] Halil S. to Yelkenkaya, November 1, 1984, DOMiD-Archiv, E 0987,36.
[112] Ahmet Y. to Yelkenkaya, November 31, 1984, DOMiD-Archiv, E 0987,36.
[113] Ramazan B. to Yelkenkaya, October 1984, DOMiD-Archiv, E 0987,36.
[114] Şevki K. to Yelkenkaya, July 29, 1984, DOMiD-Archiv, E 0987,36.
[115] Necati T. to Yelkenkaya, undated (likely late 1984), DOMiD-Archiv, E 0987,36.
[116] Türkiye Cumhuriyet Merkez Bankası, "Yurt Dışındaki Vatandaşlarımızın."

security money enter Turkey not as marks but as goods." The West German government successfully "hit several birds with one stone," as guest workers spent the money to "stimulate the German shopping market."[117] But, because they could only receive the entire payout once they had exited German borders, many financed these purchases with loans from shady creditors who charged exorbitant interest rates of up to 50 percent.[118]

Once they had their finances in order, they settled into their new lives in Turkey. Guest workers overwhelmingly returned to the places where they had been born or had lived prior to migrating to West Germany. But for many, new locales were appealing. One survey reported that 46 percent moved to Turkish cities, 39 percent to towns or large villages, and 15 percent to small villages.[119] While statistics about their new employment varied, studies reflected a disconnect between their dreams and the reality. Dispelling the stereotype that returning guest workers dreamt of becoming taxi drivers, a survey the year before the remigration law revealed that guest workers' most desired sector was overwhelmingly manufacturing (39 percent), followed by trade (23 percent), agriculture (16 percent), service (13 percent), construction (6 percent), and transportation (3 percent).[120] By the end of 1986, however, another survey reported that only 10 percent actually owned manufacturing firms.[121] This discrepancy owed in large part to the high start-up cost of factory equipment, which – even with their 10,500 DM and employee social security contributions in hand – most guest workers simply could not afford.

For many guest workers, the dream of owning a small business turned into a nightmare. Having underestimated Turkey's economic crisis and hyperinflation, they set up businesses that flopped, and many went bankrupt. Surely, guest workers who returned with the 1983 remigration law could have anticipated these failures. In the months before the mass exodus, horror stories and news articles on the subject were rampant in both countries. The editor of *Blickpunkt* reported on numerous businesses that had failed in the coastal city of Alanya. A former Ford factory employee named Taner was struggling to keep his ice cream shop afloat. "Children never come by," he bemoaned. "They don't have money for an

[117] Yaşin, "Naklihaneciler Kapıkule'den ancak 3–4 günde çıkabılıyor."
[118] "Die Kredithaie lauern schon im Kellerbüro."
[119] Türkiye Cumhuriyet Merkez Bankası, "Yurt Dışındaki Vatandaşlarımızın."
[120] Werth, et al., *Rückkehr- und Verbleibabsichten türkischer Arbeitnehmer*, 357.
[121] Türkiye Cumhuriyet Merkez Bankası, "Yurt Dışındaki Vatandaşlarımızın."

ice cream cone ... They would rather jump into the harbor off a slanted piece of wood. It's cheaper." Taner's neighbor, Mehmet, had opened a German artisanal craft shop that sold luxury items like fancy lamps and bronze sculptures. Mehmet was clearly out of touch with the needs of Alanya's population, who were "busy scrambling together enough money for their basic subsistence." After losing all their savings, the editor wrote, Taner and Mehmet ironically reverted to the same poverty as before their migration to Germany.[122]

The most notorious and well-publicized case was that of İsmail Bahadır from Konya, the celebrated "Millionth Guest Worker from Southeastern Europe." In 1969, at age twenty-four, Bahadır was gifted a brand-new television upon his arrival at the Munich Central Train Station – a symbol of the riches to come. Upon returning to Konya in 1982, however, Bahadır lost 20,000 DM in his twice-bankrupt metalworking firm and had "nothing left" of his 27,000 DM in German social security. After resorting to selling his house, his large family moved into a tiny two-bedroom apartment in a dilapidated building. Bahadır also experienced difficulties "reorienting" himself in the now bustling city, which "was suddenly more than three times as big as before." Rather than close-knit communities, he encountered only "strangers" who had migrated to the city from the villages. "If you ask me," Bahadır explained, "when we were in Germany, we did not have as many problems." If the family had stayed in Germany, they could have saved more money, "and things probably would not have gone as badly as they did here."[123]

Reports of unfulfilled dreams and social ostracization increased markedly following the mass exodus. One West German article, tellingly titled "The Almancıs," reported on forty-two-year-old Muzaffer Kılıç, who had returned to Istanbul in 1984 with his wife and daughter after eleven years working at a manufacturing company in Bremen. Although he was making good money in Turkey in his small store selling natural gas for cooking and heating, he went broke because his liras were "worthless." Due to Turkey's exorbitant inflation, his earnings were mere *pfennigs* compared to the Deutschmarks he made in Germany. "It would have been better if I had not given up my well-paid job in Germany," he said.

---

[122] Ulrich Horb, "Nix versteh'n. Deutschtürken in der Türkei," *Blickpunkt*, September 1983, 36–39. DOMiD-Archiv, P-15515.

[123] "Rückkehrer in Konya," *Teestube*, VHS (undated, likely 1990), DOMiD-Archiv, VI 0217.

"Here I am a foreigner and on top of that still a poor man. I had not expected that."[124] Süleyman Taş, whose family returned to Mersin after fifteen years in West Berlin, also felt ostracized. "We are strangers in our own country, too. The adjective 'foreign' has stuck with us ... They have changed our name to *Almancı.*"[125]

Just like the initial migration to Germany, the return to Turkey destabilized family life and gender roles. For women who had worked grueling hours in West German factories, returning to Turkey typically meant returning to the domestic sphere – this time, however, as housewives. Although they enjoyed their new middle-class status, they encountered new marital challenges. For many, the gendered division of household labor changed dramatically. Whereas spouses who were both working typically shared housework in West Germany, many new housewives complained that their husbands – whether retirees, wage laborers, or small business owners – now expected them to handle all the cooking, cleaning, and childrearing. "My husband sits at the coffee house all day," one woman explained. "He expects his food on time and does not help at home. If I am running a bit late, he leaves and goes to a restaurant."[126]

When they were not doing housework, many women found themselves socially isolated and unsure how to spend their newfound free time. Some did not return to their homes, but rather to big cities where they knew no one. Given that Turkey was still experiencing high levels of internal rural–urban migration, women who returned to villages were dismayed that many of their closest friends and relatives had left for Turkish cities. Even in cases of reunions, years of estrangement had changed social dynamics: it was one thing to chat during a temporary vacation, and another to maintain deep friendships upon a permanent return. One woman reported that village women gossiped about her "because I am an *Almancı.*" Not only did they mistakenly envy her perceived wealth, but they also perpetuated longstanding tropes about female sexuality abroad. Believing that Germany turned women "corrupt," they viewed her more "harshly" and "suspiciously" than returning men: "One sideways glance, and they immediately think I have a boyfriend in Germany."[127] Over time, however, women began rekindling relationships or forging new ones. Curious for a glimpse inside the

---

[124] Uwe Gerig, "Die Almancis," *Frankfurter Neue Presse,* June 28, 1986.
[125] Mehmet Yaşin, "Türkçe yazamadığı için, kızımla komşular aracılığıyla mektuplaştık," *Cumhuriyet,* May 14, 1984.
[126] Topraklar, *Zur Situation türkischer Rückkehrfamilien,* 24–27.
[127] Pagenstecher, "Die 'Illusion' der Rückkehr," 159.

"*Almancı* family's" house, neighbors came over for tea to chat about the prices and quality of German-made appliances. Though superficial and boring, these conversations often evolved into close friendships that sustained them while their husbands were working or socializing with other men outside the home.

Women's experiences, however, were not homogenous. Some returned from West Germany alone, either divorced or still mourning their husbands' deaths. For them, the struggle to reintegrate required finding a new husband or, sometimes with great delight, navigating life in Turkey as a single woman. Many returning mothers assumed new roles as primary caregivers after years of leaving their children behind with grandparents or other relatives in Turkey. Yet given the years of separation, in some cases as long as a decade, they sometimes struggled to establish parental authority and to bond with their children, who in many cases resented being ripped from their grandparents' home and placed under the care of their "foreign" mother. The situation was different for women whose children had reached adulthood in West Germany and were not required to return with their parents in accordance with the 1983 law. One woman was especially upset that she had returned without her son, an in-debt alcoholic who was having an extramarital affair with an older German woman with three children. For her, reintegrating meant coming to terms not only with the separation of her family, but also with the reality that she would likely be unable to find a Turkish woman for her son to marry.[128]

Amid all these financial and social struggles, the Turkish government was nowhere to be seen. Due to their financially based opposition to the guest workers' return, officials in Ankara had taken no substantial measures to prepare for their economic or social reintegration. After a decade of Turkey blocking the West German government's proposal to direct its development aid toward helping guest workers start their own small businesses, the returning guest workers were reaping the bitter consequences. "I didn't get a single *pfennig* from the state. I just did it myself," complained Hüseyin Uysal, who built an automated carpentry factory in Ankara after fourteen years in West Germany.[129] Süleyman Taş, whose business also failed, expressed a much harsher sense of betrayal. "The state has always expected foreign currency from us, but never offered a helping hand and never spoke out against our

---

[128] Wolbert, *Der getötete Paß*, 69–70.
[129] Ümit Kivanç, "Almanya'dan gücü olan dönsün," *Cumhuriyet*, March 31, 1983, 7.

oppressors," he said. "Now the government is not taking care of us when we return."[130]

To save face, the Turkish government tried but failed to change its tune. In June 1984, in the thick of the mass exodus, Mesut Yılmaz announced that the Turkish government would take measures to integrate returning migrants into the economy. "There is a great need in the industry for workers who are young, experienced, and returning," he explained, in a vast overstatement of the truth. "Therefore they will be immediately employed."[131] But that promise was dead on arrival. In reality, the vast majority of returning guest workers were not "young" but rather middle-aged or reaching retirement, and the Turkish government did nothing to ensure their employment – let alone their immediate placement. This neglect persisted throughout the 1980s. In 1988, a Turkish Labor Ministry official told reporters that returning guest workers would receive no special treatment in the allocation of jobs.[132] The same year, in a press conference with West German journalists organized by the Association of Turkish Chambers of Commerce, Prime Minister Turgut Özal proclaimed: "The Turks who receive unemployment money in the Federal Republic of Germany should stay there and not come back."[133]

The complaints of economically struggling returning guest workers did, however, compel the Turkish government to soften its stance on the question of how to spend West German development aid. In November 1984, the two governments revised their previous cooperation on development aid programs as codified in the 1972 Treaty of Ankara. Although they continued to fund Turkish Workers Collectives, the Turkish government now conceded to implementing West Germany's originally proposed "individual support model," by which development aid would be directly placed into the hands of returning guest workers. But this time they were more cautious. Rather than the initial idea of offering aid to any guest worker who planned to return, they now restricted the criteria to individuals who had already returned and who already possessed the technical and managerial skills, as well the capital, needed to start their own businesses in industrial sectors. By August 1989, this program had distributed loans

[130] Yaşin, "Türkçe yazamadığı için, kızımla komşular aracılığıyla mektuplaştık."
[131] "Kesin dönüş yapana iş kredisi verilecek," *Cumhuriyet*, June 12, 1984.
[132] Trottnow and Engler, "Aber die Türkei ist doch meine Heimat..."
[133] Mehmet Aktan, "İşsiz Türkler Almanya'da kalsın," *Bizim Almanca*, February 1988, 8–9.

of between 50,000 and 70,000 DM to more than 600 returning workers at an advantageous interest rate of 26 percent – nearly half the typical interest rate in Turkey.[134] But, out of thousands of returning workers, assisting only 600 proved insufficient. The sense of betrayal remained as strong as ever.

* * * * *

For both the West German government and the guest workers themselves, the disputedly "voluntary" 1983 remigration law was not a success story but a cautionary tale. Not only did it concede to the passions of popular racism, but it also failed to achieve the intended outcome. Rather than fulfilling Kohl's desire to "reduce the Turkish population by 50 percent," the law prompted only 15 percent to take the money and leave. And, although celebrated as a potential boon to the West German economy, the mass exodus proved a financial disaster. At 180 million DM, the total amount spent on the payout of the 10,500 DM premium plus the additional 1,500 DM per underage child was manageable.[135] But, at 1.7 billion DM, the need to swiftly refund 140,000 employee social security contributions in 1984 alone proved devastating. By comparison, during the previous three years, the government had only paid out 250,000 DM annually in early employee social security contributions, distributed among 30,000 returning guest workers.[136] And due to a failure of administrative oversight, some guest workers had received their payout without the two-year waiting period, even though they had not actually left the country.[137] Although in 1985 these costs dropped substantially, the federal government found itself strapped for liquid cash and forced to dip into its emergency reserve. As policymakers internally lamented this failure, they attempted to publicly save face. The 1983 law, announced the Labor Ministry misleadingly, was a "full success."[138]

For the migrants themselves, returning to Turkey intensified their sense of estrangement. Turkish scorn for returnees was best captured in a 1984

---

[134] Birgit Jesske-Müller, Albert Over, and Christoph Reichert, *Existenzgründungen in Entwicklungsländern* (Kassel: Wissenschaftliches Zentrum für Berufs- und Hochschulforschung, 1991), 89–93.

[135] "300.000 Ausländer planen Heimkehr."

[136] "Beitragserstattungen von 1981 bis 1984 nach Postmeldungen," January 1985, BArch, B 149/93369.

[137] "Auswirkungen des Rückkehrförderungsgesetzes auf die Beitragserstattungen in der gesetzlichen Rentensversicherung," June 28, 1985, BArch, B 122/93369.

[138] Rolf-Dietrich Schwartz, "Rückkehrhilfe 'voller Erfolg,'" *FR*, August 2, 1984.

Hürriyet article, reprinted twice in *Der Spiegel*, which sensationalized the mass exodus as a belligerent invasion by foreign foes.

It needs not be said who the *Almancı* are. They are now coming home one after another. And they are bringing Germany with them. If they only brought cars, refrigerators, washing machines, dishwashers, or videos in their moving boxes, it would not be so alarming. But they bring something else very different from Germany, namely everything to which they got accustomed there, and that is the bad thing. Turned entirely inside-out internally, the renegades stroll in arrogantly. What they saw in Germany, they are now looking for here. Every sentence begins with, 'In Germany.' We will still have a lot more to endure with these *Almancı*. And they with us. In the end, one of us will have to give in. We'll see who.[139]

With this spirited and foreboding call to arms, the existential struggle for Turkey's national survival was there for all to see. Whether or not they chose to return, by the 1980s all migrants were homogenized into *Almancı*, feeling estranged even from their own home country.

Citing both social ostracization and economic failure, up to 50 percent of Turks – both the guest workers and their children – regretted the decision to return.[140] Despite their residence permits having been stamped "invalid," many attempted to return to West Germany. By November 1984, just two months after the end of the mass exodus, the West German Consulate in Izmir reported that dozens of Turks who had taken the money and returned were increasingly applying for West German tourist visas because they regretted their decision.[141] "I'd pay back the remigration premium with interest plus interest on the interest," one man wrote, while another promised he would be willing to work sixteen hours a day if he were allowed to return.[142] But they had no recourse. With the 250,000 men, women, and children finally out of sight and out of mind, the West German government turned its attention to the dealing with the 1.2 million Turks – and over 4 million "foreigners" of all nationalities – who remained. For the Turkish government, which had spent over a decade trying to prevent a mass remigration, assisting with the guest workers' economic reintegration was simply not a priority.

[139] *Hürriyet*, quoted in Mareike Spiess-Hohnholz, "Meine deutsche Lehrer haben mich geliebt."
[140] Zentrum für Türkeistudien, "Türkische Remigranten."
[141] West German Consulate in Izmir to AA Bonn, "Betr.: Gesetz zur Förderung der Rückkehrbereitschaft von Ausländern," November 19, 1984.
[142] Baha Güngör, "Heimweh nach dem fernen 'Almanya,'" *Der Tagesspiegel*, August 11, 1985.

Feeling abandoned by both countries, the return migrants were left to fend for themselves.

Spreading transnationally through both rumors and media accounts, horror stories of guest workers' unrealized dreams not only supported criticism of the 1983 law's sinister intentions but also contributed to a stark decline in return migration. After the rate of remigration peaked at 15 percent in 1984, it plummeted to 3–4 percent the following two years – well below its 5.5 percent average in the first three years of the decade – and hovered at just over 2 percent well through the late 1980s and into the 1990s.[143] Whereas in 1983 the West German government reported that 75 percent of guest workers wanted to return, a 1986 survey revealed that only 19 percent had concrete plans to do so.[144] This decline occurred even in the aftermath of the West German government's attempt to provide other financial incentives throughout the 1980s, such as the ability to transfer their West German real estate savings accounts to Turkey for building or purchasing houses there.[145] The decline owed not only to the reality that most of the migrants who seriously planned to return had done so in 1984, but also to horror stories of the "economically desolate situation in Turkey," as the management of the mining firm Ruhrkohle AG put it.[146] It was not uncommon, reported one Turkish journalist, for return migrants to write letters to their friends in Germany warning them, "God willing, stay where you are. We have made a huge mistake."[147]

For the 1.2 million Turkish migrants who remained in West Germany, the decision not to return provided further evidence of their "Germanization." Friends and relatives in Turkey, who hoped for the return of their loved ones, were often surprised – and even offended – to learn that they were not planning to return anytime soon, even when

---

[143] Statistische Bundesamt, cited in chart in Beate Jankowitsch, Thomas Klein, and Stefan Weick, "Die Rückkehr ausländischer Arbeitsmigranten seit der Mitte der achtziger Jahre," in Richard Goldstein, Peter Schmidt, and Martina Wasmerin, eds., *Deutsche und Ausländer. Freunde, Fremde oder Feinde?* (Berlin: Springer, 2000), 93–109.

[144] "Immer weniger ausländische Arbeitnehmer wollen in ihre Heimat zurück," *Druck und Papier* 19 (1986), DOMiD-Archiv, P-15590.

[145] Deutscher Bundestag, 10. Wahlperiode, "Entwurf eines Gesetzes über eine Wiedereingliederungshilfe im Wohnungsbau für rückkehrende Ausländer," August 28, 1985.

[146] "Türkische Bergleute der Ruhrkohle verunsichert: Wirtschaftliche Lage im Heimatland 'desolat,'" *Westfälische Rundschau*, December 6, 1988, AdsD, DGB-Archiv, 5/DGAZ001214.

[147] Güngör, "Heimweh nach dem fernen 'Almanya.'"

given the "generous" financial offer of the 1983 remigration law. In the view of the home country, it was not only the migrants' selfish spending habits, diminishing language skills, and religious abandonment that had transformed them into *Almancı* but also their fundamental decision to remain abroad. Becoming *Almancı*, in this sense, was a choice. Not only had the migrants become passively estranged through their exposure to Germany, but they had also actively chosen to estrange themselves.

6

Unhappy in the Homeland

A few months after his parents decided to take the remigration premium and move their family back to Turkey, seventeen-year-old Metin Yümüşak took a sixteen-hour bus ride from Istanbul to the West German Embassy in Ankara and begged for permission to return. But this time, "returning" meant the opposite: leaving Turkey and going back to West Germany. Born and raised in Germany, Metin was barely familiar with Turkey. He struggled to speak Turkish, and he knew the country only from his summer vacations. Though he had hoped to attend one of Turkey's several elite German schools, he had been rejected amid the surge in applications during the mass exodus of Turkish families in the summer of 1984. After waiting two hours at the embassy with all his documents, however, Metin's "world collapsed" when his request for a residence permit was categorically denied. "A permanent return to Turkey is permanent," snarked the consular official. Perhaps, she insisted, Metin should have thought about that before he made his remigration decision. "It was never my decision!" Metin cried.[1]

Outside the embassy, Metin had many supporters on his side. Not only did his German principal and teachers write him glowing recommendations, but the donors of his school in Bochum agreed to pay all his living expenses.[2] With his teachers' lobbying via letters and phone calls, Metin's case made it all the way up the governmental hierarchy. Karl Liedtke, a member of the federal parliament from Bochum, implored

---

[1] Metin Yümüşak to Peter Paraknowitsch, August 31, 1984, PAAA, B 89/190384.

[2] Oberstudiendirektor Hellweg-Schule to Metin Yümüşak, August 14, 1984, PAAA, B 89/190384.

Foreign Minister Hans-Dietrich Genscher to grant an exception.[3] Upon glancing at Metin's file, one of Genscher's staffers marveled that the boy spoke "excellent German" and had a "good report card" with especially high grades in German, mathematics, physics, politics, and sports.[4] A higher-ranking official agreed, praising Metin as "overwhelmingly integrated into the German environment," but admitted that his hands were tied: the law was the law.[5] The only way to make an exception might be to classify Metin as a professional trainee rather than a student, but even so, both the municipal Foreigner Office of Bochum and the Interior Ministry of the State of North Rhine-Westphalia would need to grant permission. The paper trail ended there, leaving Metin caught in "the eternal back and forth" and worried that he would "screw up" his life in Turkey.

For Metin and the thousands of children and teenagers who returned to Turkey with their parents during the mass exodus of summer 1984, the very concept of "return" was fraught. Though labeled "return children" (*Rückkehrkinder; kesin dönüş çocuğu*) in both countries, many viewed this category as frustratingly inaccurate. At stake in the notion of "return" was not only the physical direction in which they were traveling but also the very meaning of "home" and the fundamental question of identity (Figure 6.1). Whereas children who had spent most of their childhood in Turkey typically viewed the journey as a homecoming, those born and raised abroad like Metin often considered West Germany their home. Turkey, by contrast, was the faraway homeland of their parents, which they knew only from family stories and their limited experiences on their summer vacations. With this variety of experiences, the rigid categories used to describe migration fall apart: for many children of guest workers, leaving West Germany in the 1980s was not a return or a remigration, but rather an *immigration to* a new country as *emigrants from* West Germany.

The struggle of these archetypical "return children" was especially pronounced because they also bore the burden of another label: "*Almancı* children," or "Germanized children." As over 100,000 children set foot in Turkey in 1984, abstract anxieties about their cultural estrangement and Germanization became concrete. The Turkish media regurgitated exclusionary tropes with new vigor, reporting with both indignation and sympathy on the rowdy, undisciplined, and sexually promiscuous "lost

---

[3] Karl Liedtke to Hans-Dietrich Genscher, October 30, 1984, PAAA, B 89/190384.
[4] Ziegler, marginalia on Liedtke to Genscher, October 30, 1984, PAAA, B 89/190384.
[5] Jürgen W. Möllemann to Karl Liedtke, November 12, 1984, PAAA, B 89/190384.

FIGURE 6.1 A young Turkish child in West Germany waves the Turkish flag – a symbol of his identity and connection to his home country, 1979. © Süddeutsche Zeitung Photo/Alamy Stock Foto, used with permission.

generation" who barely spoke Turkish and had abandoned Islam. The Turkish government, having spent a decade opposing guest workers' return migration and doing next to nothing to promote "reintegration," was utterly unprepared to deal with the influx of Germanized children. To "re-Turkify" them, the Turkish Education Ministry scrambled to haphazardly implement "integration courses" (*uyum kursları*) to prepare them both linguistically and culturally for the coming school year. By bombarding students with nationalist narratives, on the one hand, and failing to address the students' actual needs, on the other, these courses inadvertently reinforced the very "problem" they attempted to solve.

Although West German policymakers initially delighted in exporting the burden of integrating these children and teenagers to Turkey, they soon developed sympathy. Sensationalist reports of Turkish teachers' psychological and physical abuse villainized Turkish parents for uprooting their children from comfortable lives in Germany and forcing them against their will into a dangerous unknown. Amplified amid criticism of Turkey's authoritarianism following the 1980 military coup, these reports became new ammunition with which to condemn Turkish migrants, as they reinforced the binary assumption that West Germany was "free," "liberal," and "democratic," while Turkish culture was "authoritarian," "backward," and "incompatible" with Europe. Though often twisted in the service of racism, expressions of sympathy for the children's plight compelled a rare relaxation of West German immigration policy. In 1989, just five years after kicking them out, Kohl's government permitted the children to return once again – this time, not to their parents' homeland but to the one that many considered their own: Germany (Figure 6.2). Unfortunately for Metin, his petition to the embassy came five years too early.

"RE-TURKIFYING" GERMANIZED CHILDREN IN THE 1970S AND 1980S

"Turkey is foreign to me," wrote the Turkish poet Bahattin Gemici, reflecting on the collective sorrow of archetypal return children. "I couldn't even get used to the toilets there. And haven't you heard what they say about me? Some said that I have become irreligious in Germany. Others have laughed about the way I speak. In reality, I am a German Turk. Papa, please let me stay here. I do not want to go to Turkey."[6]

---

[6] Bahattin Gemici, "Papa, laß mich bitte hier bleiben," in Arbeitsgruppe Ausländerfreundliche Maßnahmen, *Almancilar – Deutschländer. Bericht der "Arbeitsgruppe Ausländerfreundliche Maßnahmen" über ihre Reise in die Türkei (20.06 bis 17.07.1985)* (Schwerte: Amt für Jugendarbeit der Evangelischen Kirche von Westfalen, 1985), 3.

FIGURE 6.2 Cartoon depicting a distressed "return child" (*Rückkehrkind*) forced to remigrate to Turkey with his parents, 1989. The division of the child's body into black and white represents his identity conflict as both Turkish and German – or for many children, as neither Turkish nor German. © Erdoğan Karayel, used with permission.

Filled with sorrow and desperation, this poem is a reminder of how deeply the everyday lives of young migrants were impacted by top-down return migration policies. Beholden to their parents' decisions, children generally had minimal say in the difficult question of whether to stay or to leave. Yet they were often the ones hit hardest by the challenges of reintegrating.

From the 1973 recruitment stop through the mass exodus of 1984, 43 percent of the migrants who left West Germany and returned to Turkey were children and teenagers under eighteen years of age.[7] Numbering at over half a million, they either returned with their parents or, like many "suitcase children" (*Kofferkinder*), were sent to live with grandparents or relatives. Just like the number of returning guest workers, the annual number of children returning to Turkey peaked in 1984, since guest workers who accepted the West German government's 10,500 DM remigration premium had to take their spouses and dependents with them, receiving an extra 1,500 DM per underage child. Although guest workers

---

[7] Hönekopp, "Ausländische Jugendliche nach der 'Rückkehr,'" 480.

who took the early social security contributions were not beholden to this regulation, they typically returned with their entire families.

Just as there was no singular "second generation," so too was there no singular experience for children who returned as part of the mass exodus of 1984. Their experiences differed based on their age and gender, the country in which they were born or spent most of their lives, and whether they returned to cities or villages (Figure 6.1). While these differences shaped the children's attitudes toward and experiences of return migration, both countries' governments and media tended to homogenize them and to perpetuate the stereotype that the children were both threats and victims in need of assistance. The Turkish government, having opposed return migration and done nothing to assist children who had returned in the previous decade, now scrambled to deal with this "threat" head-on. For the Education Ministry, the challenge was clear: reintegrating this unwanted mass of Germanized children would require re-Turkifying them – turning them back into Turks.

More than their parents' struggles with unemployment and racism, the experiences of the children and teenagers who returned in 1984 called into question the already contested "voluntariness" of the remigration law. The vast majority of these so-called "return children" had little to no say in the decision and, in many cases, felt that their parents had forced them to return against their own will. This sense of an involuntary return was captured in a prominent 1984–1986 sociological survey of returning children and teenagers of all guest worker nationalities who had been born in West Germany or spent most of their lives there. Approximately one-quarter had wished to return to Turkey, while two-thirds reported that they had been "required" to return with their families or had "not opposed" their families' desire to return.[8] While only two percent of respondents used the term "forced" explicitly, the West German media sensationalized the idea of a forced return and portrayed the children as victims of their parents' decisions. Such rhetoric downplayed West Germans' complicity in kicking out the Turks by deflecting guilt onto migrant parents for having forcibly removed or even "uprooted" their children.

For many children and teenagers, the prospect of returning to Turkey was connected not only to everyday concerns about their families, social lives, and schools, but also rooted in fundamental questions of identity: where did they feel most comfortable, and which country did they consider "home"? Those who had grown up in Turkey and had migrated

[8] Ibid., 484.

at an older age to Germany sometimes considered Turkey their home and looked forward to returning. In a 2014 interview, Meliha K., who migrated to Germany as a teenager, recalled having been ecstatic when her parents decided to return to Turkey. "I hated it! I just hated it!" she exclaimed repeatedly about her life in Germany as her parents, also at the interview, erupted in laughter. "I don't even understand how they lived there!" she exclaimed.[9] Günnür, who grew up in Ankara with her grandparents, also expressed her "antipathy" toward Germany.[10] When her parents forced her to join them in Germany upon her grandparents' death, she even went on a hunger strike. For Günnür, the problems stemmed not only from her difficulties speaking German and getting used to a new country but also from her confrontation with "village Turks," whom she encountered for the very first time in West Germany and against whom she harbored prejudices. "I am not a village girl, I was born in Ankara!" she complained, noting that her only friends were German. After years of isolation due to her inability to interact with Turks "like her" from the cities, Günnür was delighted to return to Ankara in the 1980s.

The experience of leaving West Germany was generally more difficult for children and teenagers who had been born and raised primarily abroad. Many of them considered West Germany "home" and mourned their return to Turkey. "It was the most bitter day of my life," one girl sobbed, "as I had to separate myself from my friends and from the country in which I was born and raised and that I loved as my homeland."[11] Erci E., who migrated to Berlin at age four, explained the distinction: "Germany is my homeland (*Heimat*), but my country of origin (*Herkunftsland*) is Turkey."[12] This notion of a "country of origin" or, literally translated, "heritage land," reflected a nostalgia for her parents' past rather than her own individual rootedness within it. By contrast, many viewed Turkey as a "vacation country," which had inadvertently reinforced their sense of cultural estrangement. Subject to the watchful eye of the "gossip-addicted" villagers, who chastised her for not wearing a headscarf, another girl "noticed each year more clearly how much she had already become a 'German' in the eyes of her countrymen."[13]

---

[9] Meliha K., interview by author, Şarköy, July 18, 2016.

[10] "'Das ist eine Art von Sklaverei hier.' Besuch an einer Rückkehrschule in Ankara – Viele Schüler müssen erst Türkisch lernen," *Der Tagesspiegel*, May 15, 1988, 10.

[11] Topraklar, *Zur Situation türkischer Rückkehrfamilien*, 46.

[12] Erci E., interview by DOMiD, July 27, 2004, DOMiD-Archiv, R0015.MS. 04 R.

[13] "Familienurlaub in der Türkei," in Zahide Özkan-Rashed, *Hab keine Angst ... Erinnerungen* (Norderstedt: BoD, 2014), 27–32.

FIGURE 6.3 Turkish teenagers in denim pants, mocked as "*Almancı* children" in their home country, mid-1980s. Behind them are posters expressing their interest in American and European popular culture: Humphrey Bogart in *Casablanca* (1942), Gary Cooper in the western classic *High Noon* (1952), the American horror film *Tarantula* (1955), the Bruce Lee film *Fist of Fury* (1972), Freddie Mercury performing in Queen's 1977 world tour, Miss Piggy from *The Muppet Movie* (1979), and the German Eurodisco pop band Dschinghis Khan, which won fourth place at the 1979 Eurovision song contest. © akg-images/ Guenay Ulutuncok, used with permission.

Long derided in Turkey as "Germanized" and suffering from cultural estrangement, the returning children and teenagers struggled with experiences that were as much public as personal. Amid the mass exodus of 1984, Turkish references to "*Almancı* children" became more frequent and disdainful, often mocking their perceived Europeanization and even Americanization (Figure 6.3). That year, production began on the satirical film *Katma Değer Şaban* (Value Added Şaban), starring comedic actor Kemal Sunal as a teenager named Şaban who returns to Turkey after spending his childhood with relatives in West Germany.[14] Immediately, the audience sees Şaban as an object of ridicule. He arrives at the Istanbul airport sporting an outlandish outfit influenced by the 1980s punk music

---

[14] Kartal Tibet, dir., *Katma Değer Şaban*, Uğur Film, 1985, VHS.

scene – an uncommon sight in Turkey at the time, despite the subculture's popularity in the United States and Europe. His hair is partially shaved and dyed in splotches of green, blue, and purple. He sports a flashy red turtleneck, tight black leather pants, knee-high boots, a metal-studded vest, a gold earring, and a Mercedes-Benz logo on a gold chain around his neck. When greeting his father, he pulls out a guitar adorned with stickers of rock bands and sings an improvised rock song whose lyrics are a mixture of German, French, and Turkish. "Hallo Papa! Bonjour Papa!" he belts, before switching to poorly accented Turkish. Neighbors' disdainful glances and explicit criticism of him as an *Almancı* turn his estrangement into a joke.[15]

This sense of cultural estrangement was not only a social but also a political problem, particularly in the realm of public education. Schools, in Sarah Thomsen Vierra's words, were the primary institutional sites where Turkish children "began to learn what it meant to be German," as they interacted on a daily basis with West German teachers, classmates, and state curricula.[16] As Brittany Lehman has shown, migrants' home countries also intervened to varying degrees in their education, often leading to transnational tensions.[17] Brian Van Wyck has traced this involvement to 1972, when, in cooperation with the West German state governments, Turkey began implementing preparatory classes taught by Turkish teachers sent from Turkey.[18] Because guest workers were still understood as temporary residents at the time, these courses aimed less at integrating students into West Germany and more at preparing them to *reintegrate* into Turkey. With great leeway to develop their own lessons, teachers sent from Turkey generally highlighted the Turkish language, geography, history, and culture, and decorated their classrooms with nationalistic symbols such as Turkish flags and Atatürk portraits. Quickly, however, the teachers realized that replicating the content and pedagogy of Turkish classrooms did not work well with

---

[15] Alongside the image of the *Almancı*, the film also critiqued Turkey's transition to neoliberal economic policies during the 1980s. Ayça Tunç Cox, "Portrayal of Turkish-German Migratory Relations in Turkish Films of the 1980s: A Call for an Alternative Reading," *Turkish Studies* 20, no. 5 (2019): 794–811; Yunus Şaban Yaman and Engin Başçı, "'Katma Değer Şaban' ve 'Orta Direk Şaban' Filmlerinde 1980'ler Türkiye'sinin Ekonomi Politikalarının Eleştirisi," *İletişim Çalışmaları Dergisi* 6, no. 2 (2020): 223–43.

[16] Vierra, *Turkish Germans in the Federal Republic of Germany*, 123 and chapter 4.

[17] Lehman, *Teaching Migrant Children*; Van Wyck, "Turkish Teachers and Imams."

[18] Brian Van Wyck, "Guest Workers in the School? Turkish Teachers and the Production of Migrant Knowledge in West German Schools, 1971–1989," *Geschichte und Gesellschaft* 43 (2017): 466–91.

migrant students, who spent most of their day with German teachers. In explaining the pedagogical differences, observers noted that the disciplinary practices, rote memorization, and lecturing that prevailed in Turkish classrooms contrasted with West German teachers' interactive and student-centered pedagogy.

By the late 1970s, however, West German officials lamented that efforts to prepare guest workers' children for their return to Turkey were failing. The Foreign Office was particularly alarmed by a 1977 sociological survey conducted in Izmir that interviewed Turkish teachers about their experiences teaching middle school students who had returned from West Germany. Overwhelmingly, the teachers complained that the students "destroy classroom dynamics" by making rude remarks and forgetting to bring their books.[19] The problems were most apparent in German foreign language courses, where returning students allegedly acted like "little know-it-alls" and flaunted their near-native mastery of the language in the faces of their Turkish teachers, many of whom had never been to a German-speaking country.[20] Classroom conflicts were compounded by fundamental differences in the two countries' public education structures. The Turkish government's requirement that children graduate from a Turkish elementary school before being permitted to attend middle school (*orta okul*) meant that children returning with insufficient Turkish language skills were frequently held back for as long as three years.[21]

One way to avoid the language barrier was to attend an elite private or special public school with German as a partial language of instruction. The most prestigious was the German High School (Alman Lisesi), a private secondary school in Istanbul's wealthy district of Beyoğlu founded in 1868 to educate the children of German merchants, diplomats, missionaries, and cultural figures living in the cosmopolitan Ottoman city.[22] Located just three miles away was the public Istanbul High School (Erkek Lisesi), which received substantial financial and administrative support from the West German government and had taught mathematics and

---

[19] Helmut Birkenfeld, ed. *Gastarbeiterkinder aus der Türkei. Zwischen Eingliederung und Rückkehr* (Munich: C. H. Beck, 1988).
[20] Helmut Birkenfeld, "Rückkehrkinder Türkischer Gastarbeiter," 1977, PAAA, B 93/861/600.65/2.
[21] "Betreuung von Kindern zurückgekehrter Gastarbeiter," November 19, 1977, PAAA, B 93/861/600.65/2.
[22] "Betr.: Deutsche Sprache in der Türkei; a) Erkek Lisesi Istanbul; b) Alman Lisesi Istanbul" (undated, likely mid-1979), PAAA, B 93/861.

science courses in German since the 1910s. The latter was one option among the Turkish government's slate of elite merit-based Anatolian High Schools (Anadolu Lisesi) that, despite their name, were located in major Turkish cities. Yet West German officials knew that such schools, with a capacity of only 1,000 students each and with a notoriously rigorous nationwide admissions exam, could not accommodate a large influx of returning students.[23] The schools' location in a few select cities also meant that children who returned elsewhere – particularly, as most did, to villages and small towns – would remain unserved.

Motivated by these concerns, in November 1977 the West German Foreign Office reached out to the embassies of all guest workers' home countries to ask about any projects currently in place for facilitating the reintegration of guest worker families and offering bilateral cooperation on the matter.[24] Several countries already had projects underway. Greece had made the most progress, with a designated Reintegration Center for Migrant Workers with branches in both Athens and Thessaloniki set to open a few months later.[25] Although the Greek Reintegration Center was not government operated (it was funded primarily by the Greek Orthodox Church in cooperation with the Protestant Church of Germany), it was a solid step toward studying the problems of return migrants and offering them legal and practical advice. The West German Foreign Office also touted its financial support for the Association for Greek-German Education in Athens. The association planned to implement a pilot project in a small local private school attended primarily by returning guest worker children and children from Greek-German mixed marriages, which would supplement the regular curriculum with German lessons.[26]

The Turkish government, however, could not name a single organization, governmental or otherwise, that aided returning workers and their children. Turkish officials' disinterest in assisting returning guest worker families was consistent with their concurrent lack of cooperation with West Germany's proposals for facilitating the economic and professional reintegration of returning guest workers, owing to their financially based

---

[23] "Betr.: Kulturelle Verbindungen zu in ihre Heimatländer zurückgekehrten Gastarbeitern und ihren Kindern," September 4, 1979, PAAA, B 93/861.
[24] "Betreuung von Kindern zurückgekehrter Gastarbeiter," November 19, 1977, PAAA, B 93/861/600.65/2.
[25] See the collection "Beratungszentrum für Griechische Rückkehrer," AdsD, DGB-Archiv, 5/DGAZ000445.
[26] "Betr.: Kulturelle Verbindungen zu in ihre Heimatländer zurückgekehrten Gastarbeitern und ihren Kindern."

opposition to return migration. West German diplomats complained about a similar nonchalance in discussions of the educational reintegration of migrant children. According to one West German internal memorandum, Turkish embassy officials could provide no "reliable" information about the number of "returning children," and a follow-up conversation at the Education Ministry revealed that "they do not even see it as a problem."[27] To the West German government's dismay, Turkish education officials had also rejected a proposal by the prestigious Istanbul High School, which envisioned an admissions process that ranked returning children according to their success within the West German education system. Turkish officials balked at the suggestion and, as a result, only seventeen of the ninety-three returning children and teenagers who had applied in the previous months were accepted, even though in most cases their knowledge of the language was "more than sufficient."[28]

The West German government also encountered difficulties in its quest to send German teachers to educate return migrants in Turkey's German-language schools, a plan that both countries' education ministries had been discussing since the mid-1970s. Although both sides had agreed to the sending of two German teachers to the Anatolian High School in Izmir for the 1979/1980 school year, the Turkish government's "strict adherence" to the extensive review of visa application and work permit materials had made the process "exceedingly difficult" and even "impracticable." Even though the West German government had sent the required documents six months ahead of the start of the school year, the teachers' work and residence permits had not been granted by mid-summer. Because of the uncertainty, the West German state authorities gave up on the idea and placed the two teachers in West German schools.[29]

The Turkish government's unwillingness to develop programs for reintegrating migrant children reflected the overall shift of the late 1970s, when officials sought to prevent the guest workers' return for economic reasons. As Turkey's economic crisis worsened and as both countries realized that guest workers were deciding not to return to Turkey, the goal of preparing the students for their return and reintegration receded. As West German Foreign Office officials concluded, "The

---

[27] "Betr.: Kulturelle Verbindungen zu in ihre Heimatländer zurückgekehrten Gastarbeitern und ihren Kindern."
[28] "Betr.: Deutsche Sprache in der Türkei; a) Erkek Lisesi Istanbul" (undated, likely mid-1979), PAAA, B 93/861.
[29] "Betr.: Deutsche Sprache in der Türkei; c) Probleme deutscher Lehrer" (undated, likely mid-1979), PAAA, B 93/861.

Turkish government, which until recently had demanded that equal emphasis be placed on the integration of Turkish children into the German school system and on their simultaneous preparation for the smoothest possible reintegration [in Turkey], is now increasingly focusing on the desire for integration."[30] Just as in the case of guest workers' professional reintegration, the Turkish government came under fire again for its unwillingness to assist the children. In 1978, _Cumhuriyet_ complained that the Turkish government was only interested in the guest workers' remittances and therefore had abandoned the children, who were "heartbroken," unable to speak either language, and mistreated as the "stepchildren of Germany."[31]

With the September 12, 1980, military coup, the new Turkish government intensified its efforts to influence the education of Turkish children abroad, particularly in the realm of religion. This emphasis reflected the military government's broader strategy of achieving unity and stifling left-wing and Kurdish dissidents by reframing national identity in terms of Turkish ethnicity and Sunni Islam. Reflecting this "Turkish-Islamic Synthesis," as the government called it, religious education became part of the public school curriculum, with an exclusive emphasis on Sunni Islam and on portraying "patriotism and love of parents, the state, and army" as a "religious duty."[32] The coup also ushered in a heightened interest in influencing Turkish citizens abroad, whom – with the exception of leftists, dissidents, and ethnic minorities – the military government considered part of the national community. This commitment was codified in the 1982 constitution, which for the first time pledged the state's responsibility to "ensure family unity, the education of the children, the cultural needs, and the social security of Turkish citizens working abroad" and, crucially, to "safeguard their ties with the home country and to help them return home."[33] Although the government blatantly contradicted this pledge by continuing to oppose guest workers' return migration, its political interest in maintaining their connection to Turkey remained strong.

The Turkish government's new prerogative, besides attempting to oust leftist Turkish teachers from their jobs at guest worker children's

---

[30] "Betr.: Türkische Sprache in der Bundesrepublik Deutschland; b) Unterrichtsfragen türkischer Kinder" (undated, likely mid-1979), PAAA, B 93/861.
[31] Dursun Akçam, "'Bizler yurtsız insanlarız; ortada kalmış gurbetçiyiz, Alman ellerinde ücretli zenciler!'" _Cumhuriyet,_ May 10, 1978.
[32] Zürcher, _Turkey: A Modern History,_ quoted in B. Miller, 183.
[33] "Constitution of the Republic of Turkey," Article 62, global.tbmm.gov.tr/docs/constitution_en.pdf.

preparatory schools, was to promote religious education in West Germany through Koran schools. As Brian Van Wyck has explained, Koran schools in West Germany initially existed relatively independently with little influence from Turkey's secular-oriented government and were organized by Turkish religious groups such as the Süleymancı and Islamist political parties such as the National Salvation Party (Millî Selâmet Partisi, MSP) and far-right MHP.[34] During the late 1970s, as Europeans increasingly viewed Islam as an impediment to guest workers' integration, West Germans began condemning Koran schools as promoting far-right Turkish nationalist ideologies, harboring ties to the MHP's paramilitary Grey Wolves, and abusing their students through corporal punishment. Yet, after the coup, the Turkish government viewed Koran schools as venues for exporting the Turkish-Islamic Synthesis and politically influencing the diaspora. Supported by the West German government, which welcomed the intervention to regulate Islam, Turkey sent state-supported Muslim religious leaders (*imams*) to West Germany to lead prayers at mosques and teach at Koran schools.[35]

But amid the mass exodus following the 1983 remigration law, as tens of thousands of "Germanized" children and teenagers were poised to return to Turkey for the 1984/1985 school year, the Turkish government was confronted with the reality that manipulating their education in West Germany was not enough. After years of doing virtually nothing to assist them, officials in Ankara now grappled with a question that struck at the core of the postcoup conception of national identity: How, after excessively integrating into Germany, could this "lost generation" of *Almancı* children – stereotyped as speaking insufficient Turkish, having little knowledge of Turkish culture, and abandoning their Muslim faith – be *re*-integrated into Turkey? Based on previous reports, the Turkish government knew that the children could not simply be dropped into regular classes. Instead, before they were ready to join regular classes, the children desperately needed an orientation to life in Turkey – better considered as a crash course in re-Turkification. During the summer of 1984, education officials scrambled to implement what they called "integration courses" (*uyum kursları*), intensive six-week summer programs for the children of returning guest workers that aimed to prepare them for Turkish schools. Though framed primarily as language classes, the courses had an ulterior motive: teaching Germanized children how to be "real Turks."

[34] Van Wyck, "Turkish Teachers and Imams," 218.
[35] Ibid.

Ideologically charged, the integration courses' government-mandated curriculum reflected the postcoup conception of a singular national identity that was tied to Turkish ethnicity and Sunni Islam and that villainized subversive outsiders. In his analysis of the special textbook used in these courses, Brian J. K. Miller has emphasized that the Education Ministry explicitly expressed its commitment to assisting the children's reintegration into the "genuine culture of the motherland."[36] Glorifying Kemalism and the foundation of the Turkish Republic, the textbook began with the lyrics of the Independence March (*İstiklal Marşı*) and featured excerpts from nationalistic poetry and the famous speeches of Atatürk. Amid the coup government's emphasis on militarism, patriotic lessons on Ottoman and Turkish history were sometimes accompanied by lectures on contemporary "national security" in which, as one student recalled, they were required to memorize "the different ranks of the army and the external and internal enemies of Turkey, who were many."[37] Departing from the secular orientation of Kemalism, students also received religious education similar to that in Turkish public schools at the time. The courses also placed great emphasis on imparting cultural norms. As Murad B., a self-proclaimed "suitcase child" recalled, "They were teaching us not only the history of Turkey and rules in Turkey but also how you have to appear in Turkey, how you have to behave in Turkey, and that that is different from how you have to act in Germany." Most vividly, he was taught to "stand up and kiss the hand of elders" when entering their presence.[38]

Given the Turkish public's longstanding curiosity about "*Almancı* children" and the fates of return migrants, the integration courses drew widespread media coverage. In August 1984, the Turkish newspaper *Cumhuriyet* published two front-page, above-the-fold articles on the subject, one week apart (Figure 6.4). With forlorn photographs and quotations from returning students, the articles aimed to attract sympathy. In one article, fourteen-year-old Nuri wondered: "Am I a Turk or a German? I can read neither there nor here ... Who will accept me?" Seventeen-year-old Erkan, who had been living in Germany since the age of four, felt self-conscious because everyone was staring at his blue jeans, long hair, and Converse shoes. Sixteen-year-old Oya complained

---

[36] Milli Eğitim Gençlik ve Spor Bakanlığı, *Türk İşçi Çocukları İçin Türk Kültüründen Derlemeler* (Ankara: Milli Eğitim Gençlik ve Spor Bakanlığı, 1985), quoted in B. Miller, "Reshaping the Turkish Nation-State," 189.
[37] B. Miller, "Reshaping the Turkish Nation-State," 181–204.
[38] Murad B., interview.

Başka bir toplumda büyüdüler, "kesin" döndüler, şimdi...

Bize uyacaklar

Yurt dışından kesin dönüş yapan işçilerin çocukları için "uyum" kursları başladı. "Uyum dersi"nde ilk konu İstiklâl Marşı oldu.

Öğrencilere anons: Herkes velileri ile vedalaşsın. Küpelerini takılarını onlara teslim etsin. Kılık, kıyafetler düzeltilsin. Kız ve erkek öğrenciler ayrılsın.

14 yaşındaki Nuri: Ben Türk müyüm, Alman mı? Ne orada okuyabiliyorum, ne burada. Kimse birbirinin okulunu kabul etmiyor. Peki beni kim kabul edecek?

Çocuğuyla Flamanca konuşan bir anne

ALMANYA'DAN GELDİLER, UYUM KURSUNA GİRDİLER

FIGURE 6.4 Front-page *Cumhuriyet* article on the struggles of "return children" in the Turkish government's integration courses, August 14, 1984. The headline states: "They Grew up in Another Country and Made their 'Final' Return, Now … They Will Adapt to Us." © *Cumhuriyet*, used with permission.

that she and others had been held back for several years. "We are adults, but we are in the same class as small children," she said. "Everyone makes fun of me."[39] The second article attributed these difficulties to their general confusion about life in Turkey, with children rattling off lists of what they sensed as cultural differences: why people honked their car horns so frequently, why the toys broke so easily, why civil servants treated people so unkindly, why the television was so awful, why the Bay of Izmir was so polluted, why no one did their job properly and honestly, and why everyone gave commands without saying "please." After each student's quotation, the newspaper editorialized by printing the phrase "I am confused" (*şaşırdım*). The message was clear: "Germany did not adapt to their parents. Or their parents did not adapt to the Germans. Now they are to be adapted to us … For now, 'They're Not Adapting at All.'"[40]

[39] "Bize uyacaklar," *Cumhuriyet*, August 14, 1984, 1.
[40] "Gurbetçi Çocuklar Zor 'Uyacaklar' Çünkü … Şaşırdılar," *Cumhuriyet*, August 21, 1984, 1.

Discussions of the integration courses also reinforced virulent stereotypes that villainized returning students. In an interview with *Milliyet*, a Turkish teacher who taught one of the integration courses berated them as "rude children without morals and without nationalities." The problem, he insisted, was not insufficient integration into Germany but rather excessive integration. "They learned the German language like parrots in German schools. They learned their way of life like apes. And now they show up in front of us, scrunch their noses at everything, and look down on us and the 'native' peers of their age."[41] He placed the blame on the structural discrimination the students faced in West Germany, their internal identity conflict, and their parents' decisions to return against their will. But he did not end there – he also placed the blame, fundamentally, on the children themselves. Statements blaming the children for the problems of reintegration were even more powerful because they came from respected civil servants, including teachers and principals, who had firsthand insight into the children's classroom behavior. Moving beyond the echo chamber of rumors into the hallowed halls of the schoolgrounds, negative stereotypes about returning students assumed an air of legitimacy, making the children's sense of cultural estrangement more potent than ever before.

Overwhelmingly, however, the integration courses failed to accomplish their goals. Conceived and implemented at the last minute, despite ample warning about the imminent mass remigration, the courses were marred by organizational problems. During the first summer that the courses were offered, there were not enough spaces to accommodate the number of interested students. Located primarily in cities, the courses reinforced urban elitism at the expense of serving children who returned to the countryside. Although the programs continued the following summers, attendance dropped. In 1986, only 417 students participated in the courses, which were held in thirteen of the country's fifty-four provinces. The decrease was attributable not only to the declining number of returning children but also to a lack of interest.[42] Even after attending the

---

[41] Haldun Taner, "Devekuşundan mektuplar," *Milliyet*, September 26, 1984, quoted in Topraklar, *Zur Situation türkischer Rückkehrfamilien*, 52. Also quoted in Horst Widmann, "Zum schulischen Aspekt der Reintegration" in Horst Widmann and Unal Abadi, eds., *Probleme der Reintegration Migrantenkinder. Ergebnisbericht einer deutsch-türkischen Kooperationstagung der Hacettepe Üniversitesi Ankara und der Justus-Liebig-Universität Giessen vom 1.-4. September 1988 in Rauischholzhausen bei Giessen* (Giessen: Verlag Polytechnik, 1987), 28, n. 5.

[42] "Anpassungskurse wenig gefragt," *Bizim Almanca*, November 1986, 2.

courses, only 43 percent of surveyed students described them as "useful," and Murad B. had completely forgotten about his integration course until asked about it in a 2016 interview.[43] Resolving the challenge of "reintegrating" "Germanized" children into Turkish schools and society required much more than a top-down, government-sponsored, six-week crash course in what it meant to be Turkish. As *Cumhuriyet* put it, "It looks like the battle to 'reintegrate' children from other countries and other cultures, where we expect them to fit in with us, will take much longer than we thought."[44]

LIBERAL CHILDREN IN AUTHORITARIAN SCHOOLS

The failure of the integration courses set up returning children and teenagers for a difficult transition to the 1984/1985 school year and beyond. In the ubiquitous news reports from both West Germany and Turkey, one theme remains constant throughout the 1980s: the contrast between the "authoritarian" school system of Turkey and the "free" and "democratic" school system of West Germany. This binary became the focal point of West German media coverage of the struggles of remigrant children because it reinforced West German beliefs about a seemingly "backward" and "authoritarian" Turkish way of life, ideas that had already intensified following Turkey's 1980 military coup. When applied to the education of returning children, the liberal-authoritarian binary revealed a paradox in Germans' attitudes toward Turkish migrants. On the one hand, the general emphasis on Turkish authoritarianism underscored the core belief that the migrants were incapable of integrating into West Germany and therefore should continue to return to their home country. On the other hand, by portraying the children's reintegration difficulties as the result of their education in a "liberal" German milieu, it exposed the possibility that Turkish children, more so than their parents, might be considered German.

In the context of return children's education, the liberal-authoritarian binary was fundamentally rooted in an essentialist interpretation of the two countries' different approaches to pedagogy that was amplified following the 1980 military coup. Since the implementation of preparatory courses for Turkish students in West Germany in the 1970s, West German pedagogues had presented the two school systems as incompatible: West

---

[43] B. Miller, "Reshaping the Turkish Nation-State," 197; Murad B., interview.
[44] "'Uyumcular'ın savaşı daha epey sürecek," *Cumhuriyet*, August 22, 1984.

Germany's preference for student-centered and discussion-based learning allegedly clashed with Turkish teachers' lecturing and emphasis on rote memorization. Criticism of the Koran schools, though mostly detached from the state and taught by religious educators, reinforced the notion that even secular public education in Turkey emphasized discipline and rigidity to the students' detriment. The role of education in delineating the sense of cultural difference increased following the 1980 military coup and Europe-wide criticism of Turkey's slow return to democracy. For West German critics of Turkey, the authoritarian classroom went hand in hand with the authoritarian government. While these binaries were largely media discourses in both countries, they were also prominent in the recollections of the return migrant students themselves, of Turkish teachers and principals, and of those West German teachers who were sent to Turkey to assist in educating returning migrant students.

Following Turkey's military coup and crackdown on leftists, West German observers harped on the idea that those returning to Turkey, especially migrant youths, were feared by both civil servants and the military as "potential agitators" or "revolutionaries."[45] Their education in a "liberal" and "freer" education system would make them prone to ask questions critical of the government, behave improperly, and ultimately rub off on other Turkish students. This discourse was not invented by West German observers but was rather grounded in quotations from Turkish teachers and principals who complained about the students' lax behavior, lack of discipline, and irreverence. One school director paraphrased in a news report expressed concerns that remigrant children would "shake up schools' sacred framework of drilling and subordination" because West Germany's "freer" education system had socialized them to express "criticism and dissent."[46] The principal of the İnönü High School in Izmir expressed his difficulties remaining patient when dealing with returning children, who had a lax attitude toward authority figures. "I was walking through the hall, and a girl from Germany came up to talk to me. She linked arms with me and started chatting as if it were nothing. Most of them never say 'my teacher' (*hocam*). We must teach them how one speaks to a teacher. They call the teachers 'uncle' (*amca*)."[47]

---

[45] Gerig, "Die Almancis."
[46] Reiner Scholz, "Rückkehrkinder fehl am Plätze," *Die Tageszeitung*, April 3, 1985.
[47] *Cumhuriyet*, September 2, 1985, quoted in "Anpassungsklassen für die zweite Generation," *Die Tageszeitung*, September 18, 1985.

In both West German and Turkish news outlets, the figure of the school principal embodied these power dynamics. Equating having been raised abroad with a disease that only a proper Turkish education could cure, one school principal reportedly told the students on the first day of school: "You are from a foreign land. I will make you healthy again."[48] In another article, *Cumhuriyet* reported on the students' first encounter with the principal of a residential school near Ankara. As the students fooled around during his speech, the principal rattled off a list of restrictions: "There is nothing forbidden here, but there are rules. You are not to exit the dormitories. I am not saying that you may not stroll along the roads and parks, but there will be surveillance and supervision." The principal emphasized clothing restrictions along gendered lines. "I do not want students wearing blue jeans and going without neckties ... Female students will also wear clothing appropriate for students and will be dressed modestly ... Say goodbye to your parents. Hand over your earrings and jewelry to them. Straighten up your uniforms. Separate the male and female students." The students' immediate reaction reveals their negative impressions of their new schools. "This much discipline is not necessary at all," a teenage boy named Murat scoffed.[49]

The restrictions on clothing and accessories were among the most controversial, with students complaining that the uniforms stifled their identities. At the time, Turkish public schools required uniforms: girls wore skirts or dresses with done-up hair and no makeup or jewelry, and boys wore suit jackets, neckties, and had very short haircuts. But, as reflected in the cinematic caricature of the *Almancı* named Şaban as a punk rocker, many teenage boys had grown their hair out long past their chins or shoulders or had pierced one of their earlobes. That was true of Hüseyin, who returned to Turkey from Würzburg in 1984. Despite expressing his punk rock personality aesthetically with long hair, jeans, a military-style jacket, and an earring, Hüseyin was forced to take out his earring to conform to his Turkish school's dress code. As *Die Tageszeitung* put it mournfully, "Today, the small hole in his ear remains a reminder of his past."[50]

While clothing restrictions were the most visible manifestation of control, much of the controversy surrounding the liberal-authoritarian

---

[48] Sibylle Thelen, "Zurück in den alten Zwängen. Türkische Jugendliche, die lange bei uns lebten, haben Probleme in ihrer Heimat," *Die Zeit,* September 25, 1987.

[49] "Başka Bir Toplumda Büyüdüler, 'Kesin' Döndüler, Şimdi ... Bize Uyacaklar," *Cumhuriyet,* August 14, 1984, 1.

[50] Dillmann, "Dort Türkin – Hier Deutsche."

binary centered on classroom dynamics, particularly the student–teacher relationship. West German teachers sent to Turkey to teach returning children articulated the binary most explicitly. In Turkey, complained one German teacher in Istanbul, students' role required "passively listening to the teaching authority and diligently writing down everything said, learning the content more or less unreflectively by heart, repeating it back as close to verbatim as possible in the exams, neither scrutinizing nor analyzing nor criticizing it, copying down pages from books – whether understood or not – nonetheless presenting it all proudly as accessible facts." It was clear, she concluded, that "many years of attending a German school can disrupt the usual attitude towards learning in Turkey."[51] After spending the 1985/1986 school year at Istanbul's Üsküdar Anatolian High School, another teacher explained that he had needed to adapt his otherwise "liberal" teaching style. "Even I became authoritarian at this school," he admitted, calling the school "fundamentally a ghetto": "It would have been impossible to accomplish anything without disciplinary measures. This school system would never function if all were authoritarian and only one was liberal."[52] Another German teacher, about to depart for a year in Turkey, worried whether he would be compatible with Turkish schools and feared aggravating his Turkish colleagues. "I do not want to change my teaching style," he said, "but I also do not want to cause conflicts. I want to do everything to avoid provoking the Turkish side."[53]

The notion that Turkish teachers were harsh disciplinarians whereas German teachers were friendly and "liberal" was also common in West German media accounts of the time. A *Der Spiegel* article published at the beginning of the 1984/1985 school year, which recounted young return migrants' nostalgia for their German schools and their regrets about returning to Turkey, was tellingly titled "My German Teachers Loved Me."[54] Yet the West German media's emphasis on the idea that German teachers "loved" their students was an overly rosy portrayal that failed to address far more rampant accounts of tensions and abuse experienced by Turkish students in German classrooms. In a short 1980 poem, a fourteen-year-old Turkish boy named Mehmet, who had only spent four years in Germany, complained that his German classmates called him

51 Meyer, *Rückkehrkinder berichten*, 6.
52 Dilek Zaptıcıoğlu, "Bir getto'dan diğerine..." *Bizim Almanca*, April 1987, 6–12.
53 "Gut vorbereitet auf die türkische Schule?" *Nürnberger Anzeiger*, October 8, 1987, 9.
54 Spiess-Hohnholz, "Meine deutsche Lehrer haben mich geliebt," 90–94.

cruel names, such as "camel jockey," "garlic eater," and "stinker."[55] A sixteen-year-old girl named Nalan complained that her peers even tried to insult her by calling her "Atatürk" and were only nice to her – "for a very short time!" – when she would bring chips and candy to share with them.[56] In many cases, teachers did not stand up on the Turkish students' behalf. Yet, by focusing on the positive rather than the negative, West German news outlets could strengthen their arguments condemning Turkish schools to reinforce exclusionary tropes about Turks in general.

Those sympathetic to returning students also assailed the public-school curriculum for reinforcing Turkish nationalism. *Die Tageszeitung* remarked that, compared with the cautiously muted nationalist spirit of post-fascist West Germany, the requirement to sing the Turkish national anthem at the beginning of lessons was "incomprehensible" to many students and quoted one student who dismissed Turkish schools as "total shit."[57] The greatest disconnects occurred in history and geography courses, which touted the accomplishments of Atatürk alongside the centuries-old tales of Turkish military triumph. One student complained, "In history class, we are told only about Turkey. They portray Turkey as a country without negative aspects, as a country that lives in prosperity and affluence. I have had history classes for three years and we have only talked about Atatürk and his reforms. But we also have to know about the rest of the world!"[58] The Turkish journalist Baha Güngör, who regularly contributed to West German newspapers, concurred: "These young people do not want to know how the Turks won the Battle of Malazgırt in 1071 and why this battle should be so meaningful for Turkey today. They want to know why there is inflation, why Turkish democracy lags so far behind that in Western European states, and why Turkey is so harshly criticized by Europe in questions of human rights."[59]

Returning students themselves complained that attempts to deconstruct nationalistic narratives, ask critical questions, and discuss or debate the lecture material were shut down. Alongside the liberal-authoritarian binary, they also invoked the language of democracy and modernity. A teenage boy interviewed for a Turkish newspaper praised the more "democratic" environment that he had experienced in West Germany,

---

[55] Förderzentrum Jugend Schreibt, *Täglich eine Reise*, 43.
[56] Ibid., 58.
[57] Dillmann, "Dort Türkin – Hier Deutsche," 14–15.
[58] "Amsterdam-Istanbul-Route," *Bizim Almanca*, June 1987, 61–66.
[59] Baha Güngör, "Späte Liebe zu Deutschland," *Der Tagesspiegel* (undated, likely 1985).

FIGURE 6.5 Reflecting return migrants' praise of West Germany's
"democratic" teaching style versus the "authoritarian" education in Turkey,
Turkish children in a West German preparatory school eagerly raise their
hands, 1980. © picture alliance/dpa, used with permission.

where he was allowed to raise his hand, participate, and "contradict"
the teachers (Figure 6.5). "Discussion is the foundation of democracy,"
he insisted. "One cannot educate through orders. One must persuade."[60]
Another boy from Nuremberg called his experience at Turkish schools "a
type of slavery" and complained that the Turkish education system was
"not modern." "If I want to have a modern education," he quipped, "I
have to go to Germany." An eighteen-year-old at the private Ortadoğu
Lisesi described his school days as psychological torment that was
"brainwash[ing]" him into obedience: "All nerves are under pressure ...
To be able to survive here, one must not speak, not see anything, and
of course not hear anything."[61] A German teacher who worked with
returning children connected this stifling of discussion to the question of
Turkey's status as a democracy following the military coup: "The Turks

---

[60] Haldun Taner, quoted in Widmann, "Zum schulischen Aspekt der Reintegration."
[61] "Ausländer in Deutschland, Ausländer in der Heimat" *Bizim Almanca*, April 1987, 33.

must learn to handle criticism if they want to be a democratic state."[62] Most egregiously, several students flipped the script on Nazi analogies by comparing Turkish teachers to Hitler.

The strongest critiques, however, targeted Turkish teachers' verbal and physical abuse of their students. Halit, a ten-year-old boy whose family came from Fetiya on the Aegean coast, explained the disciplinary differences in Turkey. "The teachers don't know how to treat people," he complained. "If you don't pay attention to something, if you just fool around during the lesson, you'll just get slapped a couple times." In Germany, on the other hand, "the teachers would just glare at us and then we were all silent as fish."[63] Ayşe, who attended Maltepe Lisesi, revealed that she was "still very afraid of the teachers," who had often hit her.[64] Her schoolmate, Ayhan, corroborated her claim: "In Germany, we were always warned: 'Be careful, when you're in Turkey, they will make real Turks out of you.'" His fears materialized one day during a geography class. When he could not identify the name of a Turkish city, his teacher slapped him in the face as part of an apparent pedagogical technique: the name of the city, Tokat, means "slap."[65] In another article, a Turkish teacher exposed the abuse committed by her own colleagues.[66] A fellow teacher had publicly shamed a remigrant student as a "beast" for chewing gum during class. When the student responded by calling him a "pig" in German, which required translation by another remigrant, the teacher slapped him and kicked him out of the classroom. Although the teacher had escalated the incident, the disciplinary committee blamed the student.

Often it was not only teachers but also classmates who viewed the returning children disparagingly, reiterating tropes about the migrant children's excessive freedom and lack of discipline. Directly labeling his peers as *Almancı*, a student at Istanbul's Üsküdar Anatolian High School explained matter-of-factly: "They are freer than we are, and their language is ill-mannered and rude. They just have not experienced sufficient care from their parents."[67] Many remigrant children found themselves once again subject to their peers' cruel name-calling – this time,

[62] Zaptıcıoğlu, "Bir getto'dan diğerine..."
[63] Trottnow and Engler, "Aber die Türkei ist doch meine Heimat..."
[64] Zaptıcıoğlu, "Wir kamen hierher, um Türken zu werden."
[65] Ibid.
[66] Topraklar, *Zur Situation türkischer Rückkehrfamilien*, 55, 62; Pakize Türkoğlu, "Unsere Probleme..." *Bizim Almanca*, April 1987, 34–37.
[67] "Amsterdam-Istanbul-Route."

however, from their Turkish classmates. A girl named Yeşim recalled times at which her Turkish classmates had called her a "Nazi."[68] Halil, a middle-school-aged boy who had grown up in Hamburg, was taunted as a non-Muslim infidel (*gâvur*) for having eaten pork in Germany, even though he promised that he never had.[69] The ostracization from classmates meant that returning children often tended to congregate together and speak German among one another.

Outside school, the children faced similar difficulties that further reinforced preexisting stereotypes about Turkish culture as authoritarian and patriarchal. Reflecting ongoing West German narratives of Turkish women's victimization at the hands of their patriarchal husbands and fathers, reports on remigrant children drew distinctions based on gender and highlighted the struggles of teenage girls. A 1985 *Die Tageszeitung* article reported that Turkish newspapers' frequent criticism of the girls' allegedly loose morals and sexual promiscuity had affected their daily interactions with men in their home country.[70] Men of all ages, the article stated, "hit on the remigrant girls in order to go to bed with them."[71] Migrant girls' styles of dress and their refusal to wear headscarves also raised eyebrows within local communities. In one of Gülten Dayıoğlu's short stories about returnees, a middle-school girl named Yahya becomes the target of local gossip. "Why are her pants so short and tight around her bottom? People would even be embarrassed to wear that as underwear!" the neighbors complain. The gossip takes an emotional toll on Yahya. "I am like a prisoner in the village," she explains. "When I go outside, everyone looks at me. There is nowhere to go, no friends. I am going crazy trapped at home."[72]

Many girls encountered harsher restrictions in Turkey since their parents wished to respect local gender norms and fit in among their neighbors. When speaking to journalists about life in their parents' homeland, they often invoked the language of "freedom." Derya Emgin, whose family remigrated from Heidelberg, recalled feeling very "aggressive" toward her parents. "I did not want the boys on the street to think of me as an 'easy girl,'" she explained, and "I complained to my parents that I could

---

[68] Yeşim, "Als Rückkehrkind zwischen 2 Kulturen (Freier Aufsatz)," in Meyer, *Rückkehrkinder Berichten,* 37–49.
[69] Quoted in Trottnow and Engler, "Aber die Türkei ist doch meine Heimat…"
[70] Dillmann, "Dort Türkin – Hier Deutsche."
[71] Ibid.
[72] Gülten Dayıoğlu, "Sünnetli mi, Sünnetsiz mi?" in *Geriye Dönenler. "Adın Almancıya Çıkmışsa"* (Istanbul: Altın Kitaplar, 1986), 48.

have had a freer life in Germany."[73] Zemre B. reported a similar experience: "In Germany, I played volleyball very often, and we would go to the disco at night. Here I can't be seen with a boy at all and, if I were, all hell would break loose."[74] Though less commonly reported, some girls experienced new freedom of mobility. Hülya, who grew up in Siegen and accompanied her parents to Gelibolu at age fifteen, quickly realized what was not permissible, such as "smoking inside a store or smoking outside in front of my parents or kissing a guy." But Hülya's parents did permit her to go to Turkish discos, a privilege denied to her in West Germany. She attributed the shift to her parents' belief that their home country's gender relations, specifically the pressures placed on Turkish men, would prevent them from making a move on her. "Here everyone knows that the girls have to be virgins. If they were to sleep with a girl, they would have to marry her immediately. So, they're sort of afraid."[75]

Alarmed by the rise in media attention to the problems of remigrant children, some Germans traveled to Turkey to observe the situation firsthand. In 1986, a group of social workers based in North Rhine-Westphalia went on an expedition to Turkey to report on the experiences of remigrant children and compiled their diary entries and findings in a report aptly titled *Almancılar – Deutschländer*. The social workers expressed great sympathy. A woman named Anja described an encounter in Zonguldak with a teenager named Hasan, an only child who had lived in Germany from 1976 to 1984 and had returned, in his words, because he "did not wish to destroy his good relationship with his parents by marrying a German." Although he soon regretted the decision, he could not return to Germany even as a visitor due to harsh visa restrictions. "His life is destroyed," Anja wrote. "It was another one those depressing experiences that made me feel powerless and sad."[76] The impression of the students' treatment in Turkey was even worse for Monika Joseph, a German teacher who likewise traveled there that year as part of a three-week study trip with a group of her colleagues.[77] While she was initially excited to learn about the home country of her Turkish students, her observations

---

[73] Heinz Delvendahl, "Rückkehr in ein fremdes Land. Türkische Rückwanderer müssen die alten Sitten wieder lernen/250.000 betroffen," *Volksblatt*, October 11, 1986, DOMiD-Archiv, P-15589.

[74] Güngör, "Heimweh nach dem fernen 'Almanya.'"

[75] Trottnow and Engler, "Aber die Türkei ist doch meine Heimat…"

[76] Anja, "Tagebuchauszug Seite 49," June 27, 1985, in Arbeitsgruppe Ausländerfreundliche Maßnahmen, *Almancılar – Deutschländer*, 18.

[77] Monika Joseph, interview by DOMiD, June 17, 2004, DOMiD-Archiv, R0015.MS.04, R,200.

made her "less tolerant than before," since they reinforced her disdain for the poverty and religious conservatism of the countryside. A village near Hatusha, she complained, did not even have a chalkboard, and she had a "not so nice" conversation with a local religious teacher (*hoca*). Most appalling to her were the regulations of a school in the Central Anatolian province of Kayseri, where female students allegedly received a fine or even a short prison sentence for removing their headscarves.

Following widespread reports of the children's difficulties, local-level initiatives began cropping up to ameliorate their plight. In 1987, Canan Kahraman, who had spent fifteen years in West Germany, founded the Istanbul-based Culture and Assistance Association for the Children of Remigrants (Kultur- und Hilfsverein für die Kinder von Remigranten). Her motivation to found the organization stemmed from the "depressive phase" that she had endured when returning to Turkey in 1975. "It was a difficult time for me," she admitted. "No one was there to show me the way, which would have helped me very much. I at least needed someone to whom I could have told my problems." Kahraman envisioned the organization as a space for the children, teenagers, and young adults to candidly discuss their challenging experiences and to attend film screenings, museum exhibitions, concerts, seminars, and language courses.[78] Psychologists and therapists also developed programs for the children. The first was founded in 1989 as a cooperation between the German Culture Institute (Deutsche Kultur-Institut) in Istanbul and Ali Nahit Babaoğlu, director of the Bakırköy Psychiatric Hospital, who had spent fifteen years living and researching in West Germany. The goal was to create a space where local psychiatrists could meet individually with the children and, in rare cases, prescribe medication. The *Westdeutsche Allgemeine Zeitung* praised the initiative for assisting children "who have found themselves psychologically in severe distress" and who "have until now surrendered to their mostly tragic fate and therefore have ended up at emotional dead ends."[79]

THE RIGHT TO RETURN – AGAIN – TO GERMANY

With all the attention to the children's problems, it came as no surprise that the Westdeutscher Rundfunk (WDR) chose to produce the low-budget

---

[78] Hikmet Kayahan, "Die 'Deutschländer' gründeten ihren ersten Verein," *Bizim Almanca*, March 1988.

[79] Baha Güngör, "Die Füße müssen sich den Schuhen anpassen," *WAZ*, June 1, 1989.

1990 feature film *Sehnsucht* (Yearning). A joint production by Turkish writer Kadir Sözen and German director Hanno Brühl, the fictional film follows the teenage Hüseyin and his younger brother Memo as they accompany their parents to a small town near Izmir after growing up in Cologne. Upon the brothers' arrival, the townspeople treat them like outsiders. Hüseyin, who works at a small grocery store, endures the constant berating of his boss, and Memo has trouble at school. The teacher yells at him in front of the other students, complaining that he is "undisciplined" and "needs to learn respect." Walking home from school and on the soccer field, the other students tease Memo, using the word *Almancı*. Relations within their nuclear and extended family are also strained. As a punishment for Memo's poor grades and his inability to speak proper Turkish, their father sends the boys to pick cotton. Their uncle, who owns the cotton fields, screams at them for their apparently poor work ethic. "Did you learn that in Germany? Lazy twerps!" Ultimately, the brothers decide to run away, illegally cross the West German border, and reestablish their lives in Cologne.[80] Yet their plans are foiled by their lack of entry visas. Although the brothers had grown up in West Germany, the local Foreigner Office declares them illegal and orders them to return to Turkey.

Premiering at the First European Youth Film Festival in Antwerp and airing in the primetime Friday night slot on West German television, the film garnered further West German sympathy for the plight of remigrant children.[81] In the words of one reviewer, it offered an "authentic" portrayal of the children's "inner turmoil" as remigrant youths. "For many," she wrote, "the country that most know only from stories and the annual vacation, becomes a nightmare."[82] The reviewer also noted that the film had a "pedagogical" function that stood to influence policy. The timing of the film's production, the late 1980s, coincided with political debates about whether children who endured hardships after unwillingly returning to their parents' homeland might one day be granted a "return option" (*Wiederkehroption*). This time, however, the return would mean going *back* to West Germany, the place *they* considered home.

The number of returning children who, like the fictional Hüseyin and Memo, yearned to return – again – to Germany was overwhelming. In a sociological survey of returning children between ages twelve and eighteen, nearly half the children said that they were "not satisfied at all" or

---

[80] Hanno Brühl, dir., *Sehnsucht*, Westdeutscher Rundfunk, 1990.
[81] See the television schedule in "Freitag," *Der Spiegel*, October 1, 1990.
[82] Irene Schoor, "Sehnsucht," *Kinder-Jugend-Film Korrespondenz*, January 1993.

"partly unsatisfied" with their return, that their lives in Germany had been "much better" or "somewhat better," and that they would "definitely" or "very much like" to go back to Germany.[83] Evenly split by gender, these sentiments were especially strong among children who reported having been "forced" to return. Two-thirds cited "major school problems" due to both the language barrier and the school system itself. While this survey did not ask the students about their experiences outside school, their concerns about life in Turkey were multifaceted, involving their social lives, family conflicts, gender roles, and the overall feeling of being ostracized as *Almancı*. Missing their friends in Germany, with whom they now communicated only by letters or rare international telephone calls, played a major role.

For West German policymakers, a new question emerged: should these children be allowed to return to West Germany? Was there a moral or ethical imperative to alleviate the suffering of these children, whom the government had "kicked out" only a few years earlier and who considered Germany their homeland? These debates largely unfolded along party lines. Kohl's CDU/CSU-FDP coalition, having expressly excluded a "return option" from the 1983 remigration law, ardently opposed allowing them to return. The SPD and Green Party, long more willing to express sympathy for the migrants, pushed for a return option in the late 1980s.

Discussions surrounding the return option emerged at the same time as some even more controversial debates about whether to grant migrants German citizenship. Germans' longstanding and archaic racialized notion of citizenship, initially codified in 1913, perpetuated racism and social exclusion by legally classifying migrants as "foreigners." Permitting them to become citizens, as the SPD and Green Party increasingly argued throughout the 1980s, would serve as an acknowledgment – at least on paper – that they had become part of German society. In 1981, however, the attempt by Chancellor Helmut Schmidt and his SPD-FDP coalition to pass a law that would provide a path to citizenship for individuals born in Germany was silenced by the increasingly vocal call "Turks out!"[84] Reports on the plight of "Germanized" children who returned to Turkey reinvigorated the debate throughout the 1980s since they opened many Germans' eyes to the reality that many children identified – and were externally identified in Turkey – as more "German" than "Turkish."

---

[83] Hönekopp, "Ausländische Jugendliche nach der 'Rückkehr.'"
[84] Deutscher Bundestag, 9. Wahlperiode, "Antwort der Bundesregierung auf die Große Anfrage der Fraktionen der SPD und FDP," Drucksache 9/1306, May 5, 1982, 2.

If the children were not able to reintegrate into their own home country, and if their own countrymen treated them so poorly, then where did they belong? Perhaps these children – and maybe even migrants as a whole – not only deserved to live in Germany but also to become German citizens.

These questions were on the Green Party's mind in the spring of 1986, when the party's parliamentary faction pressed Kohl's government to articulate its opinion on permitting returned guest workers – and particularly their children – to move back to West Germany after difficulties "reintegrating." Did Kohl's government agree, the Green Party inquired, that West Germany had a "moral responsibility" toward children and teenagers who were either born in or "experienced most of their socialization" in West Germany? What "concrete measures" would the government take to "ease" their situation? Even more controversially, the Green Party asked whether the government would be willing to grant new residence permits for reentry in exceptional cases, such as when parents realized that their decision to return to Turkey was "significantly adversely affecting their children's future development," and if the parents were willing to repay the 10,500 DM premium and early social security reimbursement. The Green Party also proposed another exceptional situation that cast reentry into West Germany in a way that detached the children from their parents: could new residence permits be granted to children and teenagers who had spent most of their lives in West Germany, and who before age eighteen had been "forced to leave because of their parents' decision," but who wished to return to West Germany after reaching adulthood?[85]

On all counts, Kohl's government responded negatively and defensively, rejecting the notion that West Germany had a "moral responsibility" toward the children. At fault for their difficulties was not the 1983 remigration law, the government insisted, but rather their home countries' dire economic problems. Though unwilling to admit that the returning children had integrated into West Germany, the government did acknowledge that they had been passively "affected by our cultural and social environment." The overall impression was that the government had little interest in assisting the children. As for the controversial question of permitting returnees to reenter the country, the government refused. Even doing so on a case-by-case basis would "effectively result

---

[85] Deutscher Bundestag, 10. Wahlperiode, "Kleine Anfrage der Abgeordneten Fischer (Bad Hersfeld), Ströble und der Fraktion Die Grünen: Probleme ausländischer Arbeitsemigranten und ihrer Kinder, die nach dem Gesetz zur Förderung der Rückkehrbereitschaft von Ausländern in ihre Herkunftsländer zurückgekehrt sind," Drucksache 10/5293, April 8, 1986.

in an unlimited possibility for return." Flippantly, the government reminded the parliamentarians that the 1983 law had established the infrastructure for advising guest workers before they decided to take the 10,500 DM premium. Parents, in this view, were to blame since they should have been forewarned about their children's potential struggles.[86]

The push for a return option did not subside, however, and became a hot-button issue in 1988. In March 1988, the SPD parliamentary faction introduced a Law for the Permission to Return for Foreigners Who Grew up in the Federal Republic. The draft law proposed the provision of unlimited residence permits for young foreigners who had completed their education in West Germany or had spent most of their lives there between the ages of ten and eighteen, as long as they applied for the residence permit within three years of their eighteenth birthday. To justify the law, the SPD contended that one-quarter of all returned foreigners were children and teenagers under age eighteen, who were dependent upon their parents' decisions and had encountered "great difficulties reintegrating into the societal environment of their homeland."[87] According to SPD member Gerd Wartenberg, the law fit squarely into West Germany's integration policy and aimed to "help solve human difficulties and individual fates."[88] Yet given the Social Democrats' status as the opposition party, the proposed law found little traction.

Reforms quickly began at the state level, however. In May and June 1988, the State Interior Ministers of West Berlin and North Rhine-Westphalia (NRW) began granting exceptions to young foreigners wishing to return to West Germany, and Hamburg and Rhineland-Palatinate followed suit.[89] Each state imposed its own guidelines. In West Berlin, for example, foreign children could only return if they wished to complete an educational or professional training program in the state and had submitted their application within three years of their departure from West Germany.[90]

---

[86] Deutscher Bundestag, 10. Wahlperiode, "Antwort der Bundesregierung auf die Kleine Anfrage der Abgeordneten Fischer (Bad Hersfeld), Ströble und der Fraktion Die Grünen: Probleme ausländischer Arbeitsemigranten und ihrer Kinder, die nach dem Gesetz zur Förderung der Rückkehrbereitschaft von Ausländern in ihre Herkunftsländer zurückgekehrt sind," Drucksache 10/5432, May 5, 1986.

[87] Deutscher Bundestag, 10. Wahlperiode, "Gesetzentwurf der Fraktion der SPD. Entwurf eines Gesetzes über die Wiederkehrerlaubnis für in der Bundesrepublik aufgewachsene Ausländer," Drucksache 11/1931, March 3, 1988.

[88] "Wiederkehrerlaubnis – ein Weg zur Humanorientierung," *Handelsblatt*, March 4, 1988.

[89] "Funcke fordert Rückkehrrecht," *FR*, October 20, 1988.

[90] "Ausländerkinder dürfen zurückkehren," *FR*, May 3, 1988; "Recht auf Rückkehr für Gastarbeiterkinder," *FAZ*, May 3, 1988.

In justifying the reform, NRW Interior Minister Helmut Schnoor (SPD) cited "progressive" and "humane" concerns grounded in "a Christian conception of humanity."[91] Many of the children had suffered "tragic fates" and should be allowed to return if "Germany had become their actual homeland."[92] The *Kölner Stadt-Anzeiger* praised Schnoor's move: "Whoever knows about the tragedies that are occurring in Turkish families who are willing to return or have already returned can only welcome that Interior Minister Schnoor has implemented a liberal rule for the young foreigners."[93] The *Kölnische Rundschau* concurred, noting that "the Federal Republic has a human responsibility toward these young people."[94]

The tensions between the states' reforms and the federal government's obstinacy resulted in a surge in media coverage in the summer of 1988, with reports highlighting individual cases of Turkish teenagers and young adults who had been denied reentry into West Germany. The *Westdeutsche Allgemeine Zeitung* reported on twenty-one-year-old Tahsin Baki, who had accompanied his parents to Turkey in 1984 following their acceptance of the 10,500 DM remigration premium.[95] The newspaper explained that his strong Ruhr accent and poor knowledge of Turkish made him an "outsider" in Turkey. Two years later, Baki had returned to his hometown of Gelsenkirchen with a tourist visa and attempted to apply for a residence permit. Despite written confirmation that he had secured an apprenticeship at a pet shop, the local Foreigner Office denied his request. An appeal to the NRW state government proved fruitless, confirming the assessment that Tahsin was in West Germany illegally and faced deportation if he did not return to Turkey voluntarily. After a yearlong battle, the state of NRW finally granted him a limited residence permit in the fall of 1987.[96] Another well-publicized case was that of Hakan Doğan, who was born in a small town near Bergisch-Gladbach, and who lived there until his family returned to Turkey when he was fifteen years old. Only after public protests and the powerful

[91] "Rückkehr in die 'Heimat': Auch dort sind sie oft Fremde," *Neue Ruhr-Zeitung,* September 20, 1988.
[92] "Junge Ausländer dürfen bleiben," *Süddeutsche Zeitung,* July 22, 1988.
[93] "Heimat," *KSA,* July 22, 1988.
[94] Peter Weigert, "Alleingang in Düsseldorf," *Kölnische Rundschau,* July 22, 1988.
[95] Joachim Rogge, "Funcke: Rückkehr einheitlich regeln," *WAZ,* October 20, 1988.
[96] Lauren Stokes has also cited Baki's case as a prominent example that connects the "right to return" to West Germans' broader attempts to police family migration. Stokes, *Fear of the Family,* 192.

endorsement of a local government official in Cologne was he permitted to return to his West German hometown. As one headline put it, Doğan was just one of many "young Germans with Turkish names."[97]

Public opinion further shifted in 1988 with the revelation that several politicians in the governing coalition had changed their stance.[98] The most prominent was Liselotte Funcke (FDP), the Federal Commissioner for the Integration of Foreign Workers and their Families. Despite having earned the nicknames "Mother Liselotte" and "Angel of the Turks" for the "tolerance and understanding" that she showed toward guest worker families, Funcke had long toed the coalition line on the issue of a return option.[99] When she visited Istanbul's Üsküdar Anatolian High School in the spring of 1986, several children had complained to her about their inability to return to West Germany. One boy questioned: "We lived in Germany for fourteen or fifteen years. We have friends and family there. But we cannot travel to Germany. Why?" Another lamented that he required a visa to spend his vacation in the country in which he had grown up and argued that Turkish citizens who had lived in West Germany should receive preferential treatment in immigration policy: "We're not like the other normal Turks in Turkey. There have to be exceptions for us, right?" Funcke evaded the questions and defended the restrictive policy. Instead, she urged them to use their bilingualism as an "opportunity" and to come to terms with their situation as "migrants" in a globalizing world. "Living abroad is the fate of our time," she asserted.[100]

But with all the media coverage and studies of the children's struggles, Funcke changed her position. In October 1988, she made headlines throughout the country when she implored Federal Interior Minister Friedrich Zimmermann (CSU) to include the return option in the ongoing revisions to the Foreigner Law (*Ausländergesetz*), which would go into effect in 1990. Strategically, Funcke appealed not only to sympathy for the children's plight but also to the need to standardize state and federal immigration policy. State reforms should apply to the entire country, she maintained, so that the opportunity to return would no longer depend on

---

97 "Junge Deutsche mit türkischen Namen," *Aachener Nachrichten*, July 22, 1988.
98 Willy Zirngibl, "CDU fordert Recht auf Rückkehr für junge Ausländer," *WAZ*, July 22, 1988.
99 Altan Öymen, "Deutschlandbild in der türkischen Presse," *Bizim Almanca*, May 1986, 7–10.
100 Tuba Tarcan, "'Frau Funcke, wie ist das Wetter in Deutschland?' Mit Lieselotte Funcke in der 'Rückkehrschule' Üsküdar Anadolu Lisesi," *Bizim Almanca*, June 1986, 34–35.

the state in which a young foreigner had grown up.[101] To mitigate critics' concerns, Funcke promised that a federal return option would not lead to a "flood" (*Überschwemmung*) of foreign children into West German borders. As evidence, she cited a study concluding that, of the 17,000 eligible Turkish youths, only 4,000 would want to take advantage of such an offer.[102] Despite having submitted her written pleas to Zimmermann, the Interior Minister had not responded.

After nearly a year of discussion, Kohl's conservative government finally softened its stance. In late December 1988, the Federal Interior Ministry publicized its plans to implement the return option for foreign children who had spent most of their lives in West Germany. The decision, as several news outlets interpreted it, stemmed less from Interior Minister Friedrich Zimmermann's concern for the children's plight than from his desire to reconcile state and federal policy and to extend a "signal of goodwill" to the FDP and to certain Christian Democrats who had expressed support. The Interior Ministry explained that it would accept applications from young foreigners who could provide a secondary school diploma (*Hauptschulabschluß*) or had lived in Germany for seven years, and who had remigrated to their homeland at age fifteen or older. The application for reentry had to be submitted before their twentieth birthdays or within two years after their departure from West Germany. Successful applicants would receive new permanent residence permits only if they had secured a job or a training position in West Germany and if they could support themselves without social assistance.[103]

The new policy, with some alterations, was codified in the July 1990 revision of the Foreigner Law. In a section titled "Right to Return" (*Recht auf Wiederkehr*), the Foreigner Law allowed migrants to receive new residence permits if they had legally lived in West Germany for eight years before their departure as a minor, had attended a West German school for at least six of those years, and applied for reentry between their sixteenth and twenty-second birthdays, or within five years of their departure. To assuage concerns about the migrants draining the social welfare system, applicants had to prove that they could finance their stay either through their own employment or through the official registration

[101] "Funcke fordert Rückkehrrecht"; "Rückkehrrecht für Kinder verlangt. Frau Funcke strebt sofortige gesetzliche Regelungen an," *Süddeutsche Zeitung*, October 20, 1988.
[102] Ulrich Reitz, "Funcke für Wiederkehr-Option," *Die Welt*, October 20, 1988.
[103] Peter Pauls, "Regeln für Rückkehr junger Ausländer?" *KSA*, December 20, 1988.

of a third party who would overtake responsibility for their livelihood for five years. Despite these restrictions, the codified policy was more lenient than originally conceived.[104]

The 1990 revision to the Foreigner Law went one step further, however. The inescapable realization that foreign children who grew up in West Germany were, in fact, members of the national community prompted a reevaluation of the country's citizenship law altogether. In a section entitled "Facilitated Naturalization" (*Erleichterte Einbürgerung*), the law enacted two milestone changes. First, it permitted "young foreigners" between the ages of sixteen and twenty-three to naturalize under similar conditions as in the "right to return" provision: if they had continually lived in West Germany for the past eight years and if they had attended school there for six years, four of which at a public school. Second, it granted *all* foreigners the right to naturalize, as long as they had lived in West Germany regularly for the past fifteen years, could prove that they could provide for themselves and their families without requiring social welfare, and applied for citizenship before December 31, 1995. In both cases, the applicant could not have been sentenced to a crime and had to relinquish their previous citizenship. Although the "right to return" and the "facilitated citizenship" clauses pertained to all foreigners, the target groups were guest workers and their children from countries outside the EEC: the former Yugoslavia, Morocco, Tunisia, and, of course, Turkey.[105]

* * * * *

The hard-fought battle for the "right to return" to West Germany reflected years of both countries' political, scholarly, and media attention to the plight of allegedly Germanized children who had endured great hardships after returning to a homeland that they did not consider their own. Although the experiences reported in the media were not representative of all guest worker children in Turkey, and although they were often sensationalized, these reports were collectively powerful enough to garner sympathy for the children's plight. In West Germany, the archetype of the psychologically tormented "return child" was instrumentalized to reinforce preexisting discourses condemning the imagined

---

[104] *Gesetz über die Einreise und den Aufenthalt von Ausländern im Bundesgebiet (Ausländergesetz – AuslG)*, July 9, 1990, www.gesetzesweb.de/AuslG.html.

[105] Deutscher Bundestag, 11. Wahlperiode, "Gesetzentwurf der Bundesregierung. Entwurf für ein Gesetz zur Neuregelung des Ausländerrechts," Drucksache 11/6321, January 27, 1990, 85.

differences between Turkish migrants' "authoritarian," "backward" culture and West Germans' "free," "liberal," and "democratic" society. Herein lies the paradox of West Germans' attitudes toward these children caught between two countries. Within the boundaries of the West German nation-state, Turkish migrant children seemed to be anything but German. In Turkey, however, the Education Ministry's last-minute scrambling to "re-Turkify" Germanized children through integration courses underscored that the problem was not *insufficient* integration into West Germany but rather *excessive* integration.

The controversial 1990 revisions to the Foreigner Law marked a sea change in German ideas about citizenship. For the first time, most leading West German policymakers, even Kohl's Christian Democrats, formally acknowledged that guest workers and their children – even if they were Muslim – deserved the opportunity to legally become German. The timing made all the difference. Back in 1981, when Schmidt's SPD-FDP coalition government had first proposed a citizenship law, the bill was dead on arrival – drowned out by the far more vocal demand "Turks out!" Once the 1983 remigration law passed, and once West Germans increasingly realized that only 15 percent of the Turkish population had decided to leave, they had to come to terms with the reality that Turks – even when provided financial incentives – were there to stay. And, as they observed the children's struggles to reintegrate into Turkish society from afar, Germans were forced to realize that the children really had integrated into German society, so much so that they identified – or were externally identified – as German. By eroding the rigid boundaries of national identity, *Almancı* children played a key role in bringing about this milestone revision.

The timing of the citizenship reform and the "right to return" further illuminates West Germany's efforts to position itself at the end of the Cold War as reunification with socialist East Germany loomed. The Berlin Wall had fallen on November 9, 1989, less than a year before the revised Foreigner Law went into effect, and the public sphere was abuzz with heated debates about how the two Germanies, divided for the past forty-five years, would become one. Policymakers who envisioned the reunified Federal Republic as the natural heir to West German liberal democracy could flaunt their perceived benevolence toward Turkish children. Having "rescued" the children from authoritarianism in Turkey, they could now lay claim to rescuing East Germans from the shackles of socialism. But, by deflecting the children's abuse onto Turkey and their parents rather than acknowledging Germans' responsibility for their hardships, this line of thinking obscured the harsher reality: in both the migrants' perspective and the perspective of their home country, West Germany had failed to uphold its reputation as a bastion of liberal democracy. Despite the 1990 revision to the citizenship law, Turks were still viewed as "foreigners," continued to endure racism, and fell victim to a resurgence of neo-Nazi violence.

Epilogue

The Final Return?

This epilogue moves beyond the book's primary point of chronological focus, the 1960s to the 1980s, by reflecting on the past thirty years, from the early 1990s until today. It reexamines the four core themes laid out in the introduction – return migration and transnational lives, estrangement from "home," racism and the history of 1980s West Germany, and the inclusion of Turks and Muslims in European society – with an eye toward applying the analysis put forth in the previous six chapters to contemporary developments. Temporally, the first point of departure is the fall of the Berlin Wall in 1989 and the reunification of Germany in 1990. These events have long been viewed as a point of rupture in German history – a new sort of "zero hour" (*Stunde Null*) that ushered in a fundamentally different era in which liberal democracy – encapsulated in the Federal Republic – triumphed joyously over the former East Germany. Recently, though, historians like Jennifer Allen have emphasized the continuities that persisted across the 1989/1990 divide.[1] And, as Paul Betts has argued, the confusion and upheaval throughout Europe at the end of the Cold War led many Germans to fear the rise of a newly oppressive regime, perhaps even a Fourth Reich.[2]

---

[1] Allen, "Against the 1989–1990 Ending Myth."

[2] Paul Betts, "1989 at Thirty: A Recast Legacy," *Past and Present* 244, no. 1 (2019): 279. See also: Philipp Ther, *Europe since 1989: A History*, trans. Charlotte Hughes-Kreutzmiller (Princeton: Princeton University Press, 2016 [2014]). On the anxieties of West German liberal intellectuals, including Günter Grass and Jürgen Habermas, see: Jan-Werner Müller, *Another Country: German Intellectuals, Unification, and National Identity* (New Haven: Yale University Press, 2000). For German, European, and international responses to German unification, see: Harold James and Marla Stone, eds., *When the Wall Came Down: Reactions to German Unification* (New York: Routledge, 1992).

Especially pertinent to this book's narrative is the explosion of racist violence following reunification, which many migrants experienced as both a continuation and an intensification of the racism of the 1980s.[3] While some West Germans felt closer to Turkish migrants than to the more than 150,000 East Germans who crossed the inter-German border, Turks, Black Germans, Jews, Roma, and other so-called "foreigners" felt increasingly – and violently – marginalized.[4] As the renowned Afro-German poet May Ayim wrote, "A reunited Germany / celebrates itself in 1990 / without its immigrants, refugees, Jewish, and Black people. / It celebrates in its intimate circle. / It celebrates in white."[5] Turkish migrants summed up this sense of marginalization in the phrase "the Wall fell on us" (*duvar bizim üstümüze düştü*).[6] While four major anti-foreigner attacks received widespread attention – in Hoyerswerda (1991), Rostock (1992), Mölln (1992), and Solingen (1993) – thousands of lesser-known incidents turned sidewalks, streets, train stations, restaurants, community centers, refugee homes, and private residences into spaces of danger.[7] Crucially, two of the four major attacks – Mölln and Solingen – took place in the west. This geography alone complicates the prevailing notion that the explosion of violence in the early 1990s was primarily perpetrated by East German neo-Nazis. By highlighting the prevalence of racism in 1980s West Germany, this book has shown on a deeper level that it is no longer possible to absolve West Germans of guilt by dismissing the post-reunification violence solely as an East German import. On the contrary, racism, right-wing extremism, and violence are deeply rooted in the history of the Federal Republic.

The attacks of the early 1990s also remind us of the transnational character of this history. Immediately following the Mölln attack, for example, the Turkish parliament expressed its desire to form a committee to investigate the situation of the 1.8 million Turks living in Germany, and Turkey's Human Rights Committee traveled to Germany for a week.[8] The Turkish

---

3 Molnar, "Asylum Seekers"; Adaire, "This Other Germany, the Dark One."
4 Sheffer, *Burned Bridge*, 238. On Turks' feelings of marginalization, see: Nevim Çil, *Topographie des Außenseiters. Türkische Generationen und der deutsch-deutsche Wiedervereinigungsprozess* (Berlin: Hans Schiler Verlag, 2007).
5 May Ayim, "blues in black and white" (1990), in *Blues in Black and White: A Collection of Essays, Poetry, and Conversations*, trans. by Anne V. Adams (Trenton: Africa World Press, 2003), 4.
6 Mandel, *Cosmopolitan Anxieties*, 31.
7 Rita Chin and Heide Fehrenbach, "German Democracy and the Question of Difference, 1945–1995," in Chin et al., *After the Nazi Racial State*, 102–36.
8 "Keine heiße Spur nach Möllner Morden," *KSA*, 1992.

media, like in the early 1980s, continually compared the attacks to Nazi atrocities. One *Milliyet* headline called the Mölln attack an example of "Nazi brutality" and featured a photograph of German youths performing the Hitler salute. Another, on the front page, reported that Jews living near Mölln had begun to arm themselves.[9] West German reporters were likewise fixated on the attack, with some expressing a fascination with the migrants' home country, traveling to villages to interview the victims' families. Several newspapers published the same quotation – the murderers should be punished, "otherwise our pain will never end" – from the relatives of the Aslam and Yılmaz families murdered in Mölln, who lived on the Black Sea coast.[10] In the most extensive report, broadcast on the German television station ARD, a reporter traveled to Mercimek, the home village of the Genç family, five of whose members had been murdered in Solingen. Many of the interviewed villagers had themselves been guest workers before remigrating from West Germany amid the mass exodus of 1984. All feared for the safety of family members who were still in Germany. One man noted that he called his children every day and that "they could hardly speak without crying."[11]

On the policy level, the nexus between racism and return migration also reigned supreme – this time, increasingly targeting other minority groups. In January 1990, partially beholden to the whims of the West German government in the lead-up to eventual reunification, East German Prime Minister Lothar de Maizière implemented a version of the 1983 remigration law to reduce the number of unemployed "contract workers" (*Vertragsarbeiter*) from communist, socialist, and nonaligned countries.[12] As was the case in West Germany, the East German program was called "remigration assistance" (*Rückkehrhilfe*) and operated on the principle of "voluntary" return – all the more problematic because the GDR orchestrated unemployment from above. By October 3, the official date of reunification, the East German government had terminated the jobs of 60 percent of the country's 90,000 contract workers, primarily those from

---

[9] "Almanya'da Nazi Vahşeti," *Milliyet*, November 26, 1992, 12; "Yahudiler silahlanıyor," *Milliyet*, November 24, 1992, 1.

[10] "Türken in Sorge um Angehörige in Deutschland," *WAZ*, November 25, 1992.

[11] Dieter Sauter, television report about Mercimek, *ARD*, 1993, DOMiD-Archiv, VI 0134.

[12] Christiane Mende, "Lebensrealitäten der DDR-Arbeitsmigrant_innen nach 1989 – Zwischen Hochkonjunktur des Rassismus und dem Kampf um Rechte," in *Kritische Migrationsforschung? Da kann ja jeder kommen*, eds. Franziska Brückner et al. (Berlin: Netzwerk Mira, 2012), 108.

Mozambique, Angola, and Vietnam.[13] But the stipulations for acquiring the GDR remigration premium were even harsher than those set by the Federal Republic in 1983, and its benefits were even lower. Contract workers fired by the GDR had just three months to decide whether to return home with only 70 percent of the previous year's salary, a one-time "money for integration" (*Eingliederungsgeld*) stipend of 3,000 DM, and tickets for their homeward flight.[14] Reflecting ten years later, *Der Spiegel* called the contract workers "the first victims of reunification."[15]

More broadly, within several decades, paying unwanted foreigners to "voluntarily" leave became standard practice for dealing with asylum seekers – not only in Germany but also throughout Europe. This approach assumed an increasingly transnational character upon the founding of the European Union (EU) in 1993 and the Schengen Area in 1995, whereby member states turned their attention to policing the *external* borders of what has been called "Fortress Europe."[16] West Germany's 1979 REAG/ GARP program, which laid the foundation for the 1983 remigration law, became the inspiration for the EU's 2008–2013 European Return Fund, which in 2014 was recommissioned as part of the newly named Asylum, Migration, and Integration Fund (AMIF).[17] Like in the 1980s, these programs have come under fire for violating migrants' human rights and not actually being voluntary. Since the early 2000s, Human Rights Watch has denounced the International Organization for Migration (IOM) as having "no formal mandate to monitor human rights abuses" in the migrants' home countries nor to determine whether asylum seekers' remigration decisions were in fact voluntary and not made "under duress" or "coercive circumstances."[18] In matters of return migration, therefore, Germany and the EU have remained susceptible to criticism.

[13] Steven Geyer, "Die ersten Opfer der Wende," *Der Spiegel*, May 23, 2001.
[14] "Rückkehrhilfe geplant," *KSA*, September 21, 1990.
[15] Geyer, "Die ersten Opfer der Wende."
[16] On the EU's migration policy, see among many others: Andrew Geddes, *Immigration and European Integration: Beyond Fortress Europe* (Manchester: Manchester University Press, 2008); Christof Roos, *The EU and Immigration Policies: Cracks in the Walls of Fortress Europe?* (London: Palgrave Macmillan, 2013); Katharina Eisele, *The External Dimension of the EU's Migration Policy: Different Legal Positions of Third-Country Nationals in the EU: A Comparative Perspective* (Leiden: Brill, 2014).
[17] "Decision No 575/2007/EC of the European Parliament and of the Council of 23, May 2007 establishing the European Return Fund for the period 2008 to 2013 as part of the General Programme 'Solidarity and Management of Migration Flows,'" *Official Journal of the European Union*, May 23, 2007, eur-lex.europa.eu/eli/dec/2007/575/oj.
[18] Human Rights Watch, "The International Organization for Migration and Human Rights Protection in the Field: Current Concerns," IOM Governing Council Meeting,

In the new millennium, Germany has experienced new heightened moments of racial reckoning that recall the tensions of biological versus cultural racism in the 1980s. In 2010, former chancellor Angela Merkel notoriously claimed that multiculturalism, or the toleration of "cultural difference" rather than the promotion of integration or assimilation, had "utterly failed" – a statement echoed shortly thereafter by British and French leaders in reference to their own countries.[19] These debates were amplified by the simultaneous publication of the inflammatory tome *Deutschland schafft sich ab* (Germany Abolishes Itself) by Thilo Sarrazin, an SPD member and the former head of the German Federal Bank. Eerily reminiscent of the racist letters written by "ordinary Germans" to West German President Carstens in the 1980s, Sarrazin's book attributed Germany's allegedly declining intellectual stock and inauspicious future to the high birthrates of Turks and Arabs.[20] As Michael Meng has explained, Sarrazin's book, which sold a remarkable 1.3 million copies, revealed the continued silence around racism in Germany: public critiques of the book's overt racism were overshadowed by mainstream German discourse, which portrayed it as "a generally useful, if times errant, examination of the 'problem' of failed integration."[21] Intriguingly, Sarrazin's initial manuscript repeatedly invoked the word "race" (*Rasse*), but, at his publisher's urging, he replaced it with "ethnicity" (*Ethnizität*).[22]

Several years later, Germans transposed the call "Turks out!" onto a new Muslim enemy: asylum seekers fleeing the 2011 Syrian Civil War. Leading the charge against Syrians was the Dresden-based Islamophobic organization Patriotic Europeans against the Islamicization of the Occident (Patriotische Europäer gegen die Islamisierung des Abendlands, PEGIDA), whose rallies attracted up to 20,000 Germans at its peak. The racist backlash also fueled the rise of Germany's far-right Alternative

---

86th Session, November 2003, 18–21, www.hrw.org/legacy/backgrounder/migrants/iom-submission-1103.htm.

[19] On the longer history of debates surrounding multiculturalism, particularly the more recent view that multiculturalism is a "failure," see: Chin, *The Crisis of Multiculturalism*, chapter 5.

[20] Thilo Sarrazin, *Deutschland schafft sich ab: Wie wir unser Land aufs Spiel setzen* (Munich: Deutsche Verlags-Anstalt, 2010).

[21] Meng, "Silences about Sarrazin's Racism," 105. See also: Christoph Butterwege, "Sarrazynismus, Rechtspopulismus und Sprechen über Migration und Integration," in Hans-Joachim Roth, Henrike Terhart, and Charis Anastasopoulos, eds., *Sprache und Sprechen im Kontext von Migration. Worüber man sprechen kann und worüber man sprechen (nicht) soll* (Wiesbaden: Springer, 2013), 85–102.

[22] Ibid., 108.

for Germany (Alternative für Deutschland, AfD), a welcome home to neo-Nazis and Holocaust deniers, which in 2017 became the third largest party in the Bundestag.[23] In 2016, as politics shifted further to the right, Merkel stepped back from her previous "welcoming culture" (*Willkommenskultur*) by telling asylum seekers to "go back to your home country" once "there is peace in Syria again, once ISIS has been defeated in Iraq."[24] As in the past, Germany has continued to offer financial incentives for "voluntary return," although very few Syrians chose to take up the offer – just under 450 people in 2018, for example.[25]

This book's transnational narrative also provides insights for understanding Turkey's increasingly volatile relationship to Germany, Europe, and the diaspora today. During the 1980s, at the height of the debates surrounding racism and return migration, there was a distinct possibility that Turkey might join the European Economic Community, with its accession planned to take effect in 1986. Turkey signed a customs agreement with the EU in 1995 and in 1999 was recognized as a candidate for full membership. Although serious negotiations for Turkey's full membership began in 2005, these stalled due in part to Turkey's continued human rights violations and Europeans' growing concerns about Islam following the September 11, 2001, terrorist attacks. Turkey's relationship to Europe worsened considerably amid the county's turn to authoritarianism under Recep Tayyip Erdoğan, who served as prime minister from 2003 to 2014 and then, in a controversial and fraudulent election, became president.[26]

---

[23] I discuss the AfD and PEGIDA's efforts to "tiptoe around Nazism" here: Michelle Lynn Kahn, "Antisemitism, Holocaust Denial, and Germany's Far Right: How the AfD Tiptoes around Nazism," *The Journal of Holocaust Research* 36, no. 2–3 (2022): 164–85. See also: Alexander Häusler, ed., *Die Alternative für Deutschland. Programmatik, Entwicklung und politische Verortung* (Wiesbaden: Springer, 2016); Eric Langenbacher, ed., *Twilight of the Merkel Era: Power and Politics in Germany after the 2017 Bundestag Election* (New York: Berghahn, 2019); Jay Julian Rosselini, *The German New Right: AfD, PEGIDA, and the Re-Imagining of National Identity* (London: Hurst and Company, 2019); Thomas Klikauer, *The AfD: Germany's New Nazis or Another Populist Party?* (Brighton: Sussex Academic Press, 2020).

[24] Andreas Rinke and Michelle Martin, "Merkel: Refugees Must Return Home Once the War Is Over," *Reuters*, January 30, 2016, www.businessinsider.com/merkel-refugees-must-return-home-once-war-over-2016-1.

[25] Choukri Chebbi, "Syrian Refugees in Germany Contemplate Return Home," *DW*, January 27, 2017, www.dw.com/en/syrian-refugees-in-germany-contemplate-return-home/a-37305045; Benjamin Bathke, "Very Few Syrians Accept German State Support to Return Home," *InfoMigrants*, April 23, 2019, www.infomigrants.net/en/post/16462/very-few-syrians-accept-german-state-support-to-return-home.

[26] On the AKP, see: William M. Hale and Ergun Özbudun, *Islamism, Democracy, and Liberalism in Turkey: The Case of the AKP* (New York: Routledge, 2010); Kerem

Tensions were especially high after Erdoğan's attempted 2016 military coup, which prompted unsavory memories of the 1980 coup that fueled Germans' growing concerns about Turkish authoritarianism.[27] In 2018, the EU's General Affairs Council put it bluntly: "Turkey has been moving further away from the European Union."[28]

What do these vast geopolitical developments mean for the 3 million Turks who still live in Germany today, and for the hundreds of thousands who have returned? The question of citizenship, for one, has become paramount. In the first decade after the 1990 revision to the German Foreigner Law, 410,000 individuals of Turkish descent – approximately 20 percent of the population – applied for German citizenship.[29] They did so at far higher rates than other migrant groups, accounting for 44 percent of all naturalized immigrants by the year 2000.[30] Naturalizations rose upon the landmark 1999 revision to the German Nationality Law, which allowed individuals born in Germany to naturalize under certain conditions regardless of ethnic heritage.[31] Still, the debate about dual citizenship – prohibited by the 1999 German citizenship reform, though allowed in Turkey since 1981 – raged on.[32] In 2014, Germany finally abandoned its so-called "option obligation" (*Optionspflicht*) – which had controversially forced individuals born in Germany to choose only one citizenship by age twenty-three – and began offering dual citizenship

---

Öktem, *Angry Nation: Turkey since 1989* (London: Zed Books, 2011); Ümit Cizre, ed., *The Turkish AK Party and its Leader: Criticism, Opposition, and Dissent* (New York: Routledge, 2016); Bahar Başer and Ahmet Erdi Öztürk, *Authoritarian Politics in Turkey: Elections, Resistance, and the AKP* (London: I. B. Tauris, 2017); M. Hakan Yavuz and Ahmet Erdi Öztürk, *Erdoğan's Turkey: Islamism, Identity, and Memory* (New York: Routledge, 2022).

[27] Feride Çiçekoğlu and Ömer Turan, eds., *The Dubious Case of a Failed Coup: Militarism, Masculinities, and 15 July in Turkey* (Singapore: Palgrave Macmillan, 2019).

[28] Council of the European Union, "Enlargement and Stabilisation and Association Process – Council Conclusions," June 26, 2018, 13, www.consilium.europa.eu/media/35863/st10555-en18.pdf.

[29] Ayhan Kaya, "Transnational Citizenship: German-Turks and Liberalizing Citizenship Regimes," *Citizenship Studies* 16, no. 2 (2012): 153–72.

[30] Max Friedrich Steinhardt, "Does Citizenship Matter? The Economic Impact of Naturalizations in Germany," *Labour Economics* 19, no. 6 (December 2012): 813–23.

[31] Merih Anil, "No More Foreigners? The Remaking of German Naturalization and Citizenship Law, 1990–2000," *Dialectical Anthropology* 9, no. 3/4 (2005): 453–70.

[32] Simon Green, "Between Ideology and Pragmatism: The Politics of Dual Nationality in Germany," *International Migration Review* 39, no. 4 (2005): 921–52; Karen Schönwälder and Triadafilos Triadafilopoulos, "A Bridge or Barrier to Incorporation?: Germany's 1999 Citizenship Reform in Critical Perspective," *German Politics and Society* 30, no. 1 (2012): 52–70.

to those who had completed secondary school or vocational training in Germany, or who had lived there for at least eight years before reaching age twenty-two.[33] But many of those who have obtained legal citizenship continue to experience discrimination, racism, and identity conflicts. The Turkish-German rap group Karakan captured this paradox in a mid-1990s song, tellingly titled "Almancı Yabancı": "Even if there is a German flag on my passport, I cannot be German because my hair is black. ... Wherever we are, we don't fit anywhere. Turkey? Is it Germany? Where is our homeland?"[34]

Just like their decisions to travel to Germany and back, Turks' citizenship decisions have been heavily influenced not only by their enduring emotional, material, and financial ties to their home country but also by the reciprocal nature of Turkish and German policy. In 1995, Turkey introduced the "pink card" (*pembe kart*) – since 2004 called the blue card (*mavi kart*) – to provide limited rights to individuals who had relinquished their Turkish citizenship, a concept that Ayşe Çağlar has called "citizenship light."[35] These rights – which include property ownership and inheritance, but not suffrage or the right to join the civil service – reflect Turkey's desire to retain connections to one-time citizens and its hesitation to cast them out as foreigners. In 2010, the AKP systematized these connections by establishing the Presidency for Turks Abroad and Related Communities (Yurtdışı Türkler ve Akraba Topluluklar Başkanlığı) as an umbrella organization to coordinate the various official diaspora policy groups. This organization's motto reflects the ongoing – and politicized – perception that the migrants, despite their physical and cultural estrangement, are still part of the Turkish nation: "Wherever we have a citizen, kin, or relative, there we are."[36]

Whereas Turkey previously had little concrete policy toward the migrants abroad (besides courting their Deutschmarks), Erdoğan and the

---

[33] Elke Winter, Annkathrin Diehl, and Anke Patzelt, "Ethnic Nation No More? Making Sense of Germany's New Stance on Dual Citizenship by Birth," *Review of European and Russian Affairs* 9, no. 1 (2015); Susan Willis McFadden, "German Citizenship Law and the Turkish Diaspora," *German Law Journal* 20, no. 1 (2019): 72–88.

[34] Karakan, "Almancı Yabancı," *Al Sana Karakan*, Neşe Müzik, 1997.

[35] Ayşe S. Çağlar, "'Citizenship Light': Transnational Ties, Multiple Rules of Membership, and the 'Pink Card,'" in Jonathan Friedman and Shalina Randeria, eds., *Worlds on the Move: Globalization, Migration, and Cultural Security* (London: I. B. Tauris, 2004), 273–91; Zeynep Kadırbeyoğlu, "National Transnationalism: Dual Citizenship in Turkey," in Thomas Faist, ed., *Dual Citizenship in Europe: From Nationhood to Societal Integration* (Hampshire: Ashgate, 2007), 127–46.

[36] Pusch and Splitt, "Binding the Almancı to the 'Homeland,'" 144.

AKP have been much more proactive. As Ayca Arkilic has explained, since the 1990s the Turkish government has increasingly pandered to Turks abroad not because of their *financial* value – since remittances currently account for only 0.1 percent of Turkey's GDP – but rather because of their *political* value, as they are a crucial voting bloc in Erdoğan's quest for power.[37] In 2008, in response to long-term lobbying among the diaspora, Turkey began allowing citizens abroad to vote in referenda and elections by post or electronically without needing to be physically present in Turkey on election day. Since then, Erdoğan's rampant campaigning in Germany has enflamed bilateral tensions, with Turkey flinging the types of rhetorical jabs that it hurled at Germany in the 1980s. In 2017, for example, after the German government canceled one of Erdoğan's rallies, the right-wing, pro-Erdoğan Turkish tabloid *Güneş* photoshopped a Hitler mustache and an SS uniform onto a photograph of Merkel and captioned the new image "Frau Hitler."[38] Amid these tensions, the relative strength of the diaspora's support for Erdoğan has added a new layer of meaning to the term *Almancı*: that they are excessively clinging to their Turkish identity and failing to integrate in Germany. This view, which inadvertently reiterates longstanding racist German tropes about migrants' perceived failure to integrate, reflects a paradox: to be a "Germanized Turk," in this sense, is also to be a Turk who has still failed to "Germanize."

Within the last twenty years, the so-called *Almancı* have been returning at much higher rates – though never to the extent of the mass exodus of 1984.[39] An estimated three-quarters of these returnees are between 25 and 50 years old, representing guest workers' children and grandchildren.[40] This new wave of return migration has captured attention in Germany. A 2014 German government report divided returnees into two categories – "*Almancı* born in Turkey" and "*Almancı* born in Germany" – testifying to the persistence of the moniker.[41] A well-publicized 2016

[37] Ayca Arkilic, *Diaspora Diplomacy: The Politics of Turkish Emigration to Europe* (Manchester: Manchester University Press, 2022). Statistic from: World Bank, "Personal Remittances, Received (% of GDP) – Turkey," data.worldbank.org/indicator/BX.TRF.PWKR.DT.GD.ZS?locations=TR.

[38] "Dişi Hitler. #Frau Hitler," *Güneş*, March 17, 2017.

[39] Yaşar Aydın, "The Germany-Turkey Migration Corridor: Refitting Policies for a Transnational Age" (Washington, DC: Migration Policy Institute, 2016), 7.

[40] Pusch and Splitt, "Binding the Almancı to the 'Homeland,'" 137.

[41] Stefan Alscher and Axel Kreienbrink, eds., *Abwanderung von Türkeistämmigen. Wer verlässt Deutschland und warum?* (Nuremberg: Bundesamt für Migration und Flüchtlinge, 2014), 7–23.

German documentary titled *Tschüss Deutschland* (Goodbye, Germany) profiled these "educated," "well integrated," and "emancipated" *Almancı* who wished to "return to the land of their forefathers" – adding dramatically, "Not for vacations. Forever."[42] As Yaşar Aydın has shown, their motivations for returning vary greatly – from family reasons, missing "home," and cultural identity, to concerns about racism and the perception of better economic opportunities in Turkey.[43]

With the proliferation of cell phones and the advent of social media, today's return migrants experience fewer difficulties than the archetypically unhappy "return children" of the 1980s. Like the train stations where guest workers regularly gathered in the 1960s and 1970s, Facebook groups provide young and middle-aged return migrants a forum for networking with one another and exchanging information.[44] The groups' thousands of members regularly post questions in both languages on a variety of logistical and mundane topics: Where can I find a three-bedroom apartment in Istanbul? What paperwork do I need to fill out to bring a cat to Turkey? Can I watch Netflix shows in German, or do I have to watch them in Turkish? How can I watch German soccer games in Turkey?[45] Also advertised in these Facebook groups are in-person happy hours and meetups with other returnees (*Rückkehrer-Stammtische*), the first and most prominent of which was founded in Istanbul in 2006. These meetups, as Susan Rottmann has shown, provide a crucial forum for returnees to forge friendships and vent their frustrations about life in Turkey, from their criticism of Turkish politics to their ostracization as *Almancı* by non-migrants.[46] One can imagine that if these communities had existed in the 1980s, the guest workers and their children who returned to Turkey following the 1983 remigration law might not have felt so isolated.

---

[42] Ute Jurkovis and Özgür Uludağ, dirs., *Tschüss Deutschland*, Norddeutscher Rundfunk, 2006; Cirstin Listing, "Wenn Deutschtürken lieber in die Türkei zurück wollen," *Die Welt*, January 15, 2016, www.welt.de/vermischtes/article151066217/Wenn-Deutschtuerken-lieber-in-die-Tuerkei-zurueck-wollen.html.

[43] Barbara Pusch and Yaşar Aydın, "Migration of Highly Qualified German Citizens with Turkish Background from Germany to Turkey: Socio-Political Factors and Individual Motives," *International Journal of Business and Globalization* 8, no. 4 (2012): 471–90.

[44] See the Facebook groups: "Türkei-Rückkehrer / Türkiye'ye dönüş," "Deutsche und Rückkehrer in Istanbul," "Izmir Rückkehrer Stammtisch," "RückkehrerStammtisch," and "Deutsche und Rückkehrer in Antalya."

[45] On the "Rückkehrer-Stammtisch" in Istanbul, see: Rottmann, *In Pursuit of Belonging*. On return migrants in Antalya, see: Nilay Kılınç and Russell King, "The Quest for a 'Better Life': Second-Generation Turkish-Germans 'Return' to 'Paradise,'" *Demographic Research* 36, no. 49 (2017): 1491–514.

[46] Rottmann, *In Pursuit of Belonging*, 126.

The guest workers themselves, now in their twilight years, also have enduring connections to both countries. Although never to the same extent as following the 1983 remigration law, up to an average of 14,000 per year have opted to return to Turkey since 2007.[47] To be sure, some leave Germany and never look back – "I left for a reason!" shouted one of my interview partners in the beach town of Şarköy. But for many elderly returnees, vacations remain a crucial part of life. Unlike in the 1960s and 1980s, former guest workers living in Turkey travel in the opposite direction – flying to Germany to visit their children, grandchildren, nieces, and nephews who remain there. As the aging first generation finds it increasingly difficult to travel, visits from these relatives living in Germany become crucial. Another subset are the "circular migrants" who alternate, spending six months in Germany and then six months in Turkey, and who typically own or rent homes in both countries.[48] This option is especially popular among elderly migrants who rely on what they believe to be superior health care in Germany but wish to escape the cold weather.[49]

As elderly migrants contemplate their mortality, the question of where they wished to be buried is central. German cemeteries have proven unpopular options, as they have historically banned Muslim burial practices such as being buried in a loin cloth.[50] Although Turkish organizations have lobbied for reforms, most elderly migrants still wish to be buried in their home villages, where their bodies can rest alongside those of their parents and ancestors. The repatriation process is complex. The German authorities are notified of a death only after the deceased's body has been ritually washed. The deceased's documents are then submitted to the Turkish consulate, after which the casket may be driven to the airport, where it is sealed in bubble wrap, weighed, and placed into the cargo hold of a Turkish Airlines plane en route to Turkey. To facilitate the process, the Turkish-Islamic Union for Religious Affairs (Diyanet

---

47 I have estimated this figure based on the statistics in Alscher and Kreienbrink, eds., *Abwanderung von Türkeistämmigen*. The report notes that, between 2007 and 2012, an estimated 14,000 to 17,000 individuals of Turkish migration background returned annually. Around 20 percent were second or third generation.

48 Sarina Strumpen, *Ältere Pendelmigranten aus der Türkei. Alters- und Versorgungserwartungen im Kontext von Migration, Kultur und Religion* (Bielefeld: Transcript, 2018).

49 Necla and Ünsal Ö., interview.

50 Gerhard Höpp and Gerdien Jonker, eds., *In fremder Erde. Zur Geschichte und Gegenwart der islamischen Bestattung in Deutschland* (Berlin: Das Arabisches Buch, 1996).

İşleri Türk-İslam Birliği, DİTİB) has offered the opportunity to buy into a "funeral fund" (*Bestattungshilfe-Fond; Cenaze Fonu*) since 1992.[51] As of 2011, 200,000 people had purchased this funeral insurance for the affordable price of 50 Euros per year.[52]

For many Turkish migrants, only death and repatriation provide a sense of completion – a truly final return. By the early 2000s, elderly migrants expressed this sentiment with a darkly humorous saying: "We came by plane on the seats above, and we will go back in the cargo hold underneath."[53] While morbid, the notion of death as a final return to the home country marks not a break from the migrants' past but rather a comforting continuity. It is the poetic culmination of a lifelong transnational journey of moving back and forth between the two countries they considered home but from which they, to outside observers, had become gradually estranged.

Ultimately, it is worth meditating on what the word "return" actually means. As this book has shown, in the six-plus decades since the guest worker program began in 1961, the idea of return has been both politically and emotionally charged, public and private, voluntary and coercive, temporary and permanent. Among the many sorts of returns that this book has charted – from returns within the heart, to returns on vacations, to returns amid the mass exodus of the 1980s – it is the idea of permanence and finality that looms the most. But what does it really mean to make one's "final return," the *endgültige Rückkehr* or *kesin dönüs* that so dominated discussions in both countries in the 1980s? What does it mean to go back *permanently* to a place that one, at least physically, had left behind? Where does the line between temporariness and permanence lie? What does it mean to go "home," when the very notion of home is shifting and contingent? These are not questions that can be answered by policy or dictated from above. They are matters of the heart, matters of the soul, and matters of human beings who all shape their own stories.

* * * * *

By following the migrants as they moved back and forth across borders, this book has highlighted their agency and their emotional lives. From 1961 to 1990, guest workers and their children navigated the constraints

---

[51] DİTİB Sosyal Dayanışma Merkezi, "Cenaze Fonu," www.cenazefonu.eu/.
[52] Başak Özay, "Letzte Ruhestätte in Deutschland oder daheim?" *DW*, December 15, 2011, www.dw.com/de/letzte-ruhest%C3%A4tte-in-deutschland-oder-daheim/a-15473330.
[53] Mektube Taşçi, quoted in Ayhan Salar, "In Fremder Erde," Salar Film Produktion, 2000, VHS, DOMiD-Archiv, VI 0063.

of both German and Turkish domestic and international politics and economics as both countries' governments strove to police their cross-border movement – with the German government trying to *promote* their return, and the Turkish government trying to *prevent* it. But return migration was both physical and emotional. All migrants – even those who stayed in Germany – grappled with their changing relationships to their identities, their sense of "home," and the people whom they left behind. Every day was a journey back and forth between two countries, leading many to question where they belonged. Physically traveling to Turkey was not always a *return* to a static "homeland," but rather a journey to a place that had transformed in their absence and from which they had become increasingly estranged.

In the end, however, there was no such thing as a "final return." Even for those who returned to Turkey following the 1983 remigration law, whose residence permits were stamped "invalid" at the border, the attachment to Germany remained. These "permanent returnees," or *kesin dönüşçü*, remained forever connected to West Germany – in how they saw themselves, and how non-migrants in Turkey saw them. Ostracized as *Almancı*, they could never shake the association with Germany, even if they tried to hide it. It was inescapable: Germany had become part of them, and they had become part of Germany. These separation anxieties developed over time on overlapping levels, from the family and local community to the nation. And they intersected with a variety of issues: gender and sexuality, vacations across Cold War Europe, global finance and development, West German popular and state-sanctioned racism, and education. The result was that the migrants felt a parallel sense of exclusion in both countries. For them, *integrating* in Germany was just one side of the story. *Reintegrating* in Turkey posed another set of challenges.

On a larger scale, the experiences of guest workers force us to consider Turkish history as part of German history – and vice versa. Rather than a peripheral "bridge" across continents, Turkey was a crucial actor that exerted much power *vis-à-vis* Germany. By decrying the migrants as Germanized, individuals in Turkey – from policymakers and journalists to even the poorest of villagers – dictated the contours of West German national identity from afar. By comparing anti-Turkish racism to antisemitism under Nazism, Turks continually exposed the hypocrisy of West German liberalism. And Turkey's mistreatment of returning migrants, especially children following the 1980 military coup, amplified ongoing contestations over West German democracy and Turkish authoritarianism. Debates surrounding racism and return migration were fundamentally connected to larger questions about Turkey's integration into European supranational institutions and the idea of "Europe." Although migration undoubtedly tied the two countries together, it also pulled them apart – with enduring consequences today.

Bibliography

PUBLISHED PRIMARY SOURCES

Ağaoğlu, Adalet. *Fikrimin İnce Gülü*. Istanbul: Remzi Kitabevi, 1976.

Almanya'da Yabancı, Türkiye'de Almancı. *Türkiye ve Almanya'dan İlginç Yorumlar*. Ulm: Merhaba Yayınları, 1995.

Araslı, Oya, and Doğan Araslı. *Almanya'daki Türk İşçilerin Hak ve Görevleri*. Ankara: Ayyıldız, 1973.

Arbeitsgruppe Ausländerfreundliche Maßnahmen, ed. *Almancılar – Deutschländer. Bericht der "Arbeitsgruppe Ausländerfreundliche Maßnahmen" über ihre Reise in die Türkei (20.06 bis 17.07.1985)*. Schwerte: Amt für Jugendarbeit der Evangelischen Kirche von Westfalen, 1985.

Aydemir, Fatma, and Hengameh Yaghoobifarah, eds. *Eure Heimat ist unser Albtraum*. Berlin: Ullstein, 2019.

Baykurt, Fakir. *Alman Oma. Deutsche Oma*. Duisburg: no recorded publisher, 1984.

Birkenfeld, Helmut, ed. *Gastarbeiterkinder aus der Türkei. Zwischen Eingliederung und Rückkehr*. Munich: C. H. Beck, 1988.

Bostancı, Safa A. *Zum Leben und zu den Rückkehr- bzw. Verbleibeabsichten der türkischen Gastarbeiter in Nürnberg. Eine empirische Regionaluntersuchung*. Berlin: Express Edition, 1982.

Dal, Güney. *E-5*. Istanbul: Milliyet, 1979.

Dayıoğlu, Gülten. *Atıl hat Heimweh [Yurdumu Özledim]*. Translated by Feridun Altuna. Berlin: ikoo, 1985 [1980].

Dayıoğlu, Gülten. *Geride Kalanlar*. Ankara: Bilgi Yayınevi, 1975.

Dayıoğlu, Gülten. *Rückkehr zwischen zwei Grenzen. Gespräche und Erzählungen [Geriye Dönenler. "Adın Almancıya Çıkmışsa"]*. Translated by Feridun Altuna. Berlin: ikoo, 1986 [Istanbul: Altın, 1986].

Demir, Alev. *Zaman İçinde Değişim*. West Berlin: Yabanel Yayınları, 1987.

Demirci, Halim. *Almancıların Çocukları*. Berlin: Halim Demirci Yayınları, 1997.

Di Croce, Bernardino, Manfred Budzinski, and Verein Migration & Integration in der Bundesrepublik Deutschland, e.V., eds. *Nicht auf Augenhöhe? Erfahrungen und Lebensgeschichten zum Thema Migration und Zweiter Generation in Deutschland*. Karlsruhe: Loeper, 2009.

Ertan, Semra. *Mein Name ist Ausländer: Gedichte*, edited by Zühal Bilir-Meier and Cana Bilir-Meier. Münster: Edition Assemblage, 2020.

Esken, Heinz. *Bericht über die in die Türkei zurückgekehrten Mitarbeiter der Ruhrkohle AG*. Essen: Ruhrkohle AG, 1985.

Förderzentrum Jugend Schreibt. *Täglich eine Reise von der Türkei nach Deutschland. Texte der zweiten türkischen Generation in der Bundesrepublik*. Fischerhude: Verlag Atelier im Bauernhaus, 1980.

Franck, Beate, and Aytunç Kılıçsoy. *Sehnsucht nach Heimat. Hofer Gastarbeiter aus der Türkei erzählen aus ihrem Leben*. Hof: Hoermann, 2006.

Goddar, Jeannette, and Dorte Huneke. *Auf Zeit: Für immer. Zuwanderer aus der Türkei erinnern sich*. Cologne: Kiepenheuer & Witsch, 2011.

Gür, Metin. *Meine Fremde Heimat: Türkische Arbeiterfamilien in der BRD*. Cologne: Weltkreis Verlag, 1987.

Isoplan – Institut für Entwicklungsforschung und Sozialplanung GmbH. *Türkische Arbeitnehmergesellschaften. Zwischenbericht zur Entwicklung und Beratung wirtschaftlicher Selbsthilfeinitiativen in der Türkei und der Förderung der beruflichen Wiedereingliederung von in der Bundesrepublik beschäftigten Arbeitnehmern in die türkische Wirtschaft*. 3rd ed. Saarbrücken and Istanbul: Isoplan, 1980.

Jahn, Hans Edgar. *Türkei. Mit Stadtführer Istanbul, Ankara und Reiserouten*. Vol. 25 of *Mai's Auslandstaschenbücher*. Buchenhain outside Munich: Verlag 'Volks und Heimat,' 1962.

Jesske-Müller, Birgit, Albert Over, and Christoph Reichert. *Existenzgründungen in Entwicklungsländern*. Kassel: Wissenschaftliches Zentrum für Berufs- und Hochschulforschung, 1991.

Kammrad, Horst. *»Gast«-Arbeiter-Report*. Munich: Piper, 1971.

Kıroğlu, Tufan. *Die ersten Türken von Neumünster. 12 Lebensgeschichten*. Berlin: epubli, 2011.

Klee, Ernst, ed. *Gastarbeiter: Analyse und Berichte*. Frankfurt: Suhrkamp, 1972.

König, Karin, and Hanne Straube. *Kalte Heimat. Junge Ausländer in der Bundesrepublik*. Reinbek bei Hamburg: Rowohlt, 1984.

König, Karin, Hanne Straube, and Kamil Taylan. *Merhaba ... Guten Tag. Ein Bericht über eine türkische Familie*. Bornheim: Lamuv, 1981.

Magistrat der Stadt Frankfurt am Main Amt für multikulturelle Angelegenheiten. *»Mit Koffern voller Träume...«. Ältere Migrantinnen und Migranten erzählen*. Frankfurt am Main: Brandes & Apsel, 2001.

Merey, Can. *Der ewige Gast. Wie mein türkischer Vater versuchte, Deutscher zu werden*. Munich: Karl Blessing, 2018.

Meyer, Erika. *Rückkehrkinder berichten. Texte aus einem Seminar über Migrantenliteratur an der Istanbul Universität (1987/88)*. Berlin: Pädagogisches Zentrum, 1989.

Milli Eğitim Gençlik ve Spor Bakanlığı. *Türk İşçi Çocukları İçin Türk Kültüründen Derlemeler*. Ankara: Milli Eğitim Gençlik ve Spor Bakanlığı, 1985.

Müftüoğlu, Mustafa. *Yalan Söyleyen Tarih Utansın*. Istanbul: Çile, 1977.

Nadolny, Sten. *Selim oder die Gabe der Rede*. Munich: Piper, 1990.

Olcayto, Erdoğan, ed. *Almanya İş Rehberi 1981.* Bonn: Anadolu Yayınları, 1981.
Osiander, Klara, and Johannes Zerger. *Rückkehr in die Fremde. Die Problematik der Remigration junger Türken/-innen und deren Familien in ihr Heimatland. Oder: 'Keine Ahnung und zurück.'* Augsburg: MaroVerlag, 1988.
Oulios, Miltiadis. *Blackbox Abschiebung: Geschichte, Theorie und Praxis der deutschen Migrationspolitik.* 2nd ed. Berlin: Suhrkamp, 2015.
Özkan-Rashed, Zahide. *Hab keine Angst ... Erinnerungen.* Norderstedt: BoD, 2014.
Sarrazin, Thilo. *Deutschland schafft sich ab: Wie wir unser Land aufs Spiel setzen.* Munich: Deutsche Verlags-Anstalt, 2010.
Schneider, Jan, and Axel Kreienbrink. "Return Assistance in Germany: Programmes and Strategies Fostering Assisted Return to and Reintegration in Third Countries." *Working Paper 31.* Berlin: Federal Office for Migration and Refuges [BAMF], 2010.
Seeger, Wolfgang. *Ausländer-Integration ist Völkermord. Das Verbrechen an den ausländischen Volksgruppen und am deutschen Volk.* Pähl: Verlag Hohe Warte, 1980.
Sow, Noah. *Deutschland Schwarz Weiß: Der alltägliche Rassismus.* Munich: Bertelsmann, 2008.
T. C. Çalışma Bakanlığı Yurtdışı İşçi Sorunları Genel Müdürlüğü. *Yurtdışındaki Türk İşçiler için Rehber (F. Almanya).* Ankara: T. C. Çalışma Bakanlığı, 1982.
Tepecik, Ergün. *Die Situation der ersten Generation der Türken in der multikulturellen Gesellschaft.* Frankfurt am Main: Iko-Verlag, 2002.
Topraklar, Hasan. *Zur Situation türkischer Rückkehrfamilien. Ursachen, Folgen, Probleme.* Berlin: Fachhochschule für Sozialarbeit und Sozialpädagogik Berlin, 1986.
Trottnow, Barbara, and Alfred Engler. *Aber die Türkei ist doch meine Heimat ... Türkische Rückwanderer berichten. Begleitmaterial zur Tonkassette.* Marl: Deutscher Volkshochschul-Verband e.V., 1986.
Tsiakalos, Georgios. *Ausländerfeindlichkeit. Tatsachen und Erklärungsversuche.* Munich: C. H. Beck, 1983.
Üstün, Nevzat. *Almanya Beyleri ile Portekiz'in Bahçeleri.* Istanbul: Çağdaş, 1975.
Von der Grün, Max. *Leben im gelobten Land. Gastarbeiterportraits.* Darmstadt: Hermann Luchterhand, 1975.
Wallraff, Günter. *Ganz unten.* Cologne: Kiepenheuer & Witsch, 1985.
Werkkreis Literatur der Arbeitswelt, ed. *Sehnsucht im Koffer.* Frankfurt am Main: Fischer Taschenbuch, 1981.
Werth, Manfred, et al. *Rückkehr- und Verbleibabsichten türkischer Arbeitnehmer. Analyse der Rückkehrbereitschaft und des Wanderungsverhaltens sowie des Sparverhaltens und der Anlagepläne türkischer Arbeitnehmer im Raum Rheinland-Pfalz/Saarland.* Saarbrücken: Isoplan, 1983.
Widmann, Horst. *Exil und Bildungshilfe. Die deutschsprächige akademische Emigration in die Türken nach 1933.* Frankfurt am Main: Peter Lang, 1973.
Widmann, Horst, and Unal Abadi, eds. *Probleme der Reintegration Migrantenkinder. Ergebnisbericht einer deutsch-türkischen Kooperationstagung der Hacettepe Üniversitesi Ankara und der Justus-Liebig-Universität Giessen vom 1.-4. September 1988 in Rauischholzhausen bei Giessen.* Giessen: Verlag Polytechnik, 1987.

Yıldız, Bekir. *Alman Ekmeği*. Istanbul: Cem Kitabevi, 1974.
Zieris, Ernst, et al. *Betriebsunterkünfte für ausländische Mitbürger. Bericht zur Situation in Betriebsunterkünften für ausländische Arbeitnehmer in Nordrhein-Westfalen*. Düsseldorf: Minister für Arbeit, Gesundheit und Soziales des Landes Nordrhein-Westfalen, 1972.

SECONDARY SOURCES

Abadan-Unat, Nermin. *Batı Almanya'daki Türk İşçileri ve Sorunları*. Ankara: Başbakanlık DPT, 1964.
Abadan-Unat, Nermin. "Impact of External Migration on Rural Turkey." In *Culture and Economy: Changes in Turkish Villages*, edited by Paul Stirling, 201–15. Cambridgeshire: The Eothen Press, 1993.
Abadan-Unat, Nermin. "Implications of Migration on Emancipation and Pseudo-Emancipation of Turkish Women." *The International Migration Review* 11, no. 1 (1977): 31–57.
Abadan-Unat, Nermin. *Turkish Workers in Europe 1960–1975: A Socioeconomic Reappraisal*. Leiden: Brill, 1976.
Abadan-Unat, Nermin. *Turks in Europe: From Guest Worker to Transnational Citizen*. Translated by Caterine Campion. New York: Berghahn Books, 2011.
Abadan-Unat, Nermin, et al., *Göç ve Gelişme: Uluslararası İşgücü Göçünün Boğazlıyan İlçesi Üzerindeki Etkilerine İlişkin Bir Araştırma [Migration and Development: A Study of the Effects of International Labor Migration on Boğazlıyan District]*. Ankara: Ajans-Türk Matbaacılık Sanayii, 1976.
Acar, Mustafa. *Türkische Kaffeehäuser in Deutschland. Ein Integrationshindernis für die Türken in der deutschen Gesellschaft*. Saarbrücken: VDM Verlag, 2007.
Adaire, Esther. "'This Other Germany, the Dark One': Post-Wall Memory Politics Surrounding the Neo-Nazi Riots in Rostock and Hoyerswerda." *German Politics and Society* 37, no. 4 (2019): 43–57.
Ahmad, Feroz. *Turkey: The Quest for Identity*. Revised ed. London: OneWorld, 2014.
Akçam, Taner. *Killing Orders: Talat Pasha's Telegrams and the Armenian Genocide*. New York: Palgrave Macmillan, 2018.
Akgündüz, Ahmet. *Labour Migration from Turkey to Western Europe, 1960–1974: A Multidisciplinary Analysis*. Burlington: Ashgate, 2008.
Akkuş, Güzin Emel. "The Contribution of the Remittances of Turkish Workers in Germany to the Balance of Payments of Turkey (1963–2013)." In *Turkish German Affairs from an Interdisciplinary Perspective*, edited by Elif Nuroğlu et al., 185–212. Frankfurt am Main: Peter Lang, 2015.
Aktar, Ayhan. *Nationalism and Non-Muslim Minorities in Turkey, 1915–1950*. London: Transnational Press, 2021.
Albrecht, Richard. "'Was ist der Unterschied zwischen Türken und Juden?': (Anti) Türkenwitze in der Bundesrepublik Deutschland." *Zeitschrift für Volkskunde* 78 (1982): 220.
Alcoff, Linda. "The Problem of Speaking for Others." *Cultural Critique* 20 (1991–92): 5–32.

Alexopoulou, Maria. "'Ausländer' – A Racialized Concept? 'Race' as an Analytical Concept in Contemporary German Immigration History." In *Who Can Speak and Who Is Heard/Hurt? Facing Problems of Race, Racism, and Ethnic Diversity in the Humanities in Germany*, edited by Mahmoud Arghavan, et al., 45–67. Bielefeld: Transcript, 2019.

Alexopoulou, Maria. *Deutschland und die Migration. Geschichte einer Einwanderungsgesellschaft wider Willen*. Ditzingen: Reclam, 2020.

Allen, Jennifer L. "Against the 1989–1990 Ending Myth." *Central European History* 52, no. 1 (2019): 125–47.

Alscher, Stefan, and Axel Kreienbrink, eds. *Abwanderung von Türkeistämmigen. Wer verlässt Deutschland und warum?* Vol. 6 of *Beiträge zu Migration und Integration*. Nuremberg: Bundesamt für Migration und Flüchtlinge, 2014.

Andrews, Walter G., and Mehmet Kalpakli. *The Age of Beloveds: Love and the Beloved in Early Modern Ottoman and European Culture*. Durham: Duke University Press, 2005.

Anil, Merih. "No More Foreigners? The Remaking of German Naturalization and Citizenship Law, 1990–2000." *Dialectical Anthropology* 29, no. 3/4 (2005): 453–70.

Argun, Betigül Ercan. *Turkey in Germany: The Transnational Sphere of Deutschkei*. New York: Routledge, 2003.

Arkilic, Ayca. *Diaspora Diplomacy: The Politics of Turkish Emigration to Europe*. Manchester: Manchester University Press, 2022.

Aydın, Yaşar. *The Germany-Turkey Migration Corridor: Refitting Policies for a Transnational Age*. Washington, DC: Migration Policy Institute, 2016.

Aydın, Zülküf. *The Political Economy of Turkey*. London: Pluto, 2005.

Ágoston, Gábor. *The Last Muslim Conquest: The Ottoman Empire and Its Wars in Europe*. Princeton: Princeton University Press, 2021.

Bade, Klaus, ed. *Auswanderer – Wanderarbeiter – Gastarbeiter. Bevölkerung, Arbeitsmarkt und Wanderung in Deutschland seit der Mitte des 19. Jahrhunderts*. Ostfildern: Scripta Mercaturae, 1984.

Baer, Marc David. "Mistaken for Jews: Turkish PhD Students in Nazi Germany." *German Studies Review* 41, no. 1 (2018): 19–39.

Baer, Marc David. *The Ottomans: Khans, Caesars, and Caliphs*. New York: Basic Books, 2021.

Baer, Marc David. *Sultanic Saviors and Tolerant Turks: Writing Ottoman Jewish History, Denying the Armenian Genocide*. Bloomington: Indiana University Press, 2020.

Baer, Marc David. "Turk and Jew in Berlin: The First Turkish Migration to Germany and the Shoah." *Comparative Studies in Society and History* 55, no. 2 (2013): 330–55.

Bahar, İ. İzzet. *Turkey and the Rescue of European Jews*. London: Routledge, 2015.

Bailkin, Jordanna. *The Afterlife of Empire*. Berkeley: University of California Press, 2012.

Balerrama, Francisco E., and Raymond Rodríguez. *Decade of Betrayal: Mexican Repatriation in the 1930s*. Revised ed. Albuquerque: University of New Mexico Press, 2006.

Balibar, Étienne. "Is There a 'Neo-Racism'?" In *Race, Nation, Class: Ambiguous Identities*, edited by Étienne Balibar and Immanuel Maurice Wallerstein. Translated by Chris Turner, 17–28. London: Verso, 1991 [1988].

Bark, Dennis L., and David R. Gress. *A History of West Germany, Volume 1: From Shadow to Substance, 1945–1963.* 2nd ed. Cambridge, MA: Blackwell, 1993.

Barker, Martin. *The New Racism: Conservatives and the Ideology of the Tribe.* London: Junction, 1981.

Başer, Bahar, and Ahmet Erdi Öztürk. *Authoritarian Politics in Turkey: Elections, Resistance, and the AKP.* London: I. B. Tauris, 2017.

Başer, Bahar, and Paul T. Levin. *Migration from Turkey to Sweden: Integration, Belonging, and Transnational Community.* London: I. B. Tauris, 2017.

Behrends, Jan C., Thomas Lindenberger, and Patrice G. Poutrus, eds. *Fremde und Fremd-Sein in der DDR. Zu historischen Ursachen der Fremdenfeindlichkeit in Ostdeutschland.* Berlin: Metropol, 2003.

Berlinghoff, Marcel. *Das Ende der »Gastarbeit«. Europäische Anwerbestopps 1970–1974.* Paderborn: Ferdinand Schöningh Verlag, 2013.

Best, Jeremy. *Heavenly Fatherland: German Missionary Culture and Globalization in the Age of Empire.* Toronto: University of Toronto Press, 2020.

Betts, Paul. *Ruin and Renewal: Civilizing Europe after World War II.* New York: Basic Books, 2020.

Betts, Paul. "1989 at Thirty: A Recast Legacy." *Past and Present* 244, no. 1 (2019): 271–305.

Bevilacqua, Alexander. *The Republic of Arabic Letters: Islam and the European Enlightenment.* Cambridge, MA: Harvard University Press, 2018.

Biess, Frank. *German Angst: Fear and Democracy in the Federal Republic of Germany.* Oxford: Oxford University Press, 2020.

Biess, Frank. *Homecomings: Returning POWs and the Legacies of Defeat in Postwar Germany.* Princeton: Princeton University Press, 2006.

Biess, Frank, and Astrid M. Eckert. "Introduction: Why Do We Need New Narratives for the History of the Federal Republic?" *Central European History* 52, no. 1 (2019): 1–18.

Black, Monica. *A Demon-Haunted Land: Witches, Wonder Doctors, and the Ghosts of the Past in Post-WWII Germany.* New York: Metropolitan Books, 2020.

Blackler, Adam. *An Imperial Homeland: Forging German Identity in Southwest Africa.* Philadelphia: Pennsylvania State University Press, 2022.

Bojadžijev, Manuela. *Die windige Internationale. Rassismus und Kämpfe der Migration.* Münster: Dampfboot, 2008.

Borgmann, Malte. "Zwischen Integration und Gleichberechtigung. Migrationspolitik und migrantischer Aktivismus in Westberlin, 1969–1984." MA thesis, Freie Universität Berlin, 2016.

Botsch, Gideon. *Die extreme Rechte in der Bundesrepublik Deutschland: 1949 bis heute.* Bonn: wbg academic, 2012.

Brown, Timothy Scott. *West Germany and the Global Sixties: The Antiauthoritarian Revolt, 1962–1978.* Cambridge, UK: Cambridge University Press, 2013.

Brubaker, Rogers. *Citizenship and Nationhood in France and Germany.* Cambridge, MA: Harvard University Press, 1992.

Buettner, Elizabeth. *Europe after Empire: Decolonization, Society, and Culture.* Cambridge, UK: Cambridge University Press, 2016.

Buggeln, Marc. *Slave Labor in Nazi Concentration Camps.* Translated by Paul Cohen. Oxford: Oxford University Press, 2014.

Buğra, Ayşe, and Osman Savaşkan. *New Capitalism in Turkey: The Relationship between Politics, Religion and Business.* Cheltenham: Edward Elgar, 2014.

Bui, Pipo. *Envisioning Vietnamese Migrants in Germany: Ethnic Stigma, Immigrant Origin Narratives, and Partial Masking.* Münster: Lit, 2003.

Casale, Giancarlo. *The Ottoman Age of Exploration.* Oxford: Oxford University Press, 2011.

Celâsun, Merih, and Dani Rodrik. "Economic Boom and Debt Crisis, 1973–77." In *Developing Country Debt and Economic Performance*, edited by Jeffrey D. Sachs and Susan M. Collins. Chicago: University of Chicago Press, 1989.

Ceylan, Rauf. *Ethnische Kolonien. Entstehung, Funktion und Wandel am Beispiel türkischer Moscheen und Cafés.* Wiesbaden: Verlag für Sozialwissenschaften, 2006.

Chakrabarty, Dipesh. *Provincializing Europe: Postcolonial Thought and Historical Difference.* New ed. Princeton: Princeton University Press, 2007.

Chin, Rita. *The Crisis of Multiculturalism in Europe: A History.* Princeton: Princeton University Press, 2017.

Chin, Rita. "Guest Worker Migration and the Unexpected Return of Race." In *After the Nazi Racial State: Difference and Democracy in Germany and Europe*, edited by Rita Chin, Geoff Eley, Heide Fehrenbach, and Atina Grossmann, 80–102. Ann Arbor: The University of Michigan Press, 2009.

Chin, Rita. *The Guest Worker Question in Postwar Germany.* Cambridge, UK: Cambridge University Press, 2007.

Chin, Rita. "Thinking Difference in Postwar Germany: Some Epistemological Obstacles around 'Race.'" In *Migration, Memory, and Diversity: Germany from 1945 to the Present*, edited by Cornelia Wilhelm, 206–32. New York: Berghahn, 2017.

Chin, Rita. "Turkish Women, West German Feminists, and the Gendered Discourse on Muslim Cultural Difference." *Public Culture* 22, no. 3 (2010): 557–81.

Chin, Rita, Geoff Eley, Heide Fehrenbach, and Atina Grossmann. *After the Nazi Racial State: Difference and Democracy in Germany and Europe.* Ann Arbor: The University of Michigan Press, 2009.

Chin, Rita, and Heide Fehrenbach. "Introduction: What's Race Got to Do with It? Postwar German History in Context." In *After the Nazi Racial State: Difference and Democracy in Germany and Europe*, edited by Rita Chin, Geoff Eley, Heide Fehrenbach, and Atina Grossmann, 1–29. Ann Arbor: The University of Michigan Press, 2009.

Choate, Mark I. *Emigrant Nation: The Making of Italy Abroad.* Cambridge, MA: Harvard University Press, 2008.

Cizre, Ümit. "Ideology, Context and Interest: The Turkish Military." In *Turkey in the Modern World*, Vol. 4 of *The Cambridge History of Turkey*, edited by Reşat Kasaba, 301–31. Cambridge, UK: Cambridge University Press, 2008.

Clarkson, Alexander. *Fragmented Fatherland: Immigration and Cold War Conflict in the Federal Republic of Germany, 1945–1980.* Oxford: Oxford University Press, 2013.

Cohen, Deborah. *Braceros: Migrant Citizens and Transnational Subjects in the Postwar United States and Mexico.* Chapel Hill: The University of North Carolina Press, 2011.

Comte, Emmanuel. *The History of the European Migration Regime: Germany's Strategic Hegemony.* London: Routledge, 2018.

Cox, Ayça Tunç. "Portrayal of Turkish-German Migratory Relations in Turkish Films of the 1980s: A Call for an Alternative Reading." *Turkish Studies* 20, no. 5 (2019): 794–811.

Crane, Austin. "Assisted Voluntary Return: Negotiating the Politics of Humanitarianism and Security in Migration Management." PhD dissertation, University of Washington, 2021.

Cuecuecha, Alfredo, and Carla Pederzini, eds. *Migration and Remittances from Mexico: Trends, Impacts, and New Challenges*. Lanham: Lexington Books, 2012.

Çağlar, Ayşe S. "'Citizenship Light': Transnational Ties, Multiple Rules of Membership, and the 'Pink Card.'" In *Worlds on the Move: Globalization, Migration, and Cultural Security*, edited by Jonathan Friedman and Shalina Randeria, 273–91. London: I. B. Tauris, 2004.

Çağlar, Ayşe S. "McDöner. Dönerkebab und der Kampf der Deutsch-Türken um soziale Stellung." *Sociologus* 48, no. 1 (1998): 17–41.

Çalış, Şaban Halis. *Turkey's Cold War: Foreign Policy and Western Alignment in the Modern Republic*. London: I. B. Taurus, 2017.

Çeçen, Aydın, A., Suut Doğruel, and Fatma Doğruel. "Economic Growth and Structural Change in Turkey 1960–88." *International Journal of Middle East Studies* 26, no. 1 (1994): 37–56.

Çelik, Burçe. *Technology and National Identity in Turkey: Mobile Communications and the Evolution of a Post-Ottoman Nation*. London: I. B. Tauris, 2011.

Çiçekoğlu, Feride, and Ömer Turan, eds. *The Dubious Case of a Failed Coup: Militarism, Masculinities, and 15 July in Turkey*. Singapore: Palgrave Macmillan, 2019.

Crew, David F. ed. *Consuming Germany in the Cold War*. Oxford: Berg, 2003.

Dack, Mikkel. *Everyday Denazification in Postwar Germany: The Fragebogen and Political Screening During the Allied Occupation*. Cambridge, UK: Cambridge University Press, 2023.

Dağı, İhsan D. "Democratic Transition in Turkey, 1980–83: The Impact of European Diplomacy." *Middle Eastern Studies* 32, no. 2 (1996): 124–41.

De Bellaigue, Christopher. *The Islamic Enlightenment: The Modern Struggle Between Faith and Reason*. New York: Random House, 2017.

Demirović, Alex, and Manuela Bojadžijev, eds. *Konjunkturen des Rassismus*. Münster: Westfälisches Dampfboot, 2002.

Demshuk, Andrew. *The Lost German East: Forced Migration and the Politics of Memory, 1945–1970*. Cambridge, UK: Cambridge University Press, 2012.

Donnelly, Robert. Review of *Rethinking Transit Migration: Precarity, Mobility and Self-Making in Mexico*, by T. Basok, D. Bélanger, M. L. Rojas Wiesner, and G. Candiz. *Population, Space, and Place* 23 (2017).

Döşemeci, Mehmet. *Debating Turkish Modernity: Civilization, Nationalism, and the EEC*. Cambridge, UK: Cambridge University Press, 2013.

Dragostinova, Theodora K. *The Cold War from the Margins: A Small Socialist State on the Global Cultural Scene*. Ithaca: Cornell University Press, 2021.

Düvell, Franck, Irina Molodikova, and Michael Collyer, eds. *Transit Migration in Europe*. Amsterdam: University of Amsterdam Press, 2014.

Eckert, Astrid M. "West German Borderland Aid and European State Aid Control." *Jahrbuch für Wirtschaftsgeschichte* 58, no. 1 (2017): 107–36.

Eckert, Astrid M. *West Germany and the Iron Curtain: Environment, Economy, and Culture in the Borderlands.* Oxford: Oxford University Press, 2019.

Eder, Jacob S. *Holocaust Angst: The Federal Republic of Germany and American Holocaust Memory Since the 1970s.* Oxford: Oxford University Press, 2016.

Eggers, Maureen Maisha, Grada Kilomba, Peggy Piesche, and Susan Arndt, eds. *Mythen, Masken und Subjekte. Kristische Weißseinsforschung in Deutschland.* 4th ed. Münster: UNRAST, 2020 [2005].

Ehrkamp, Patricia. "'We Turks are no Germans': Assimilation Discourses and the Dialectical Construction of Identities in Germany." *Environment and Planning A* 38 (2006): 1673–92.

Eisele, Katharina. *The External Dimension of the EU's Migration Policy: Different Legal Positions of Third-Country Nationals in the EU: A Comparative Perspective.* Leiden: Brill, 2014.

El-Tayeb, Fatima. *European Others: Queering Ethnicity in Postnational Europe.* Minneapolis: University of Minnesota Press, 2011.

El-Tayeb, Fatima. "'If You Can't Pronounce My Name, You Can Just Call Me Pride: Afro-German Activism, Gender, and Hip Hop." *Gender & History* 15, no. 3 (2004): 460–86.

El-Tayeb, Fatima. *Undeutsch: Die Konstruktion des Anderen in der postmigrantischen Gesellschaft.* Bielefeld: Transcript, 2016.

Epstein, Catherine. *Model Nazi: Arthur Greiser and the Occupation of Western Poland.* Oxford: Oxford University Press, 2010.

Erdal, Marta Bivand, and Ceri Oeppen. "Forced to Leave? The Discursive and Analytical Significance of Describing Migration as Forced and Voluntary." *Journal of Ethnic and Migration Studies* 44, no. 6 (2018): 981–98.

Ergin, Murat. *"Is the Turk a White Man?": Race and Modernity in the Making of Turkish Identity.* Leiden: Brill, 2017.

Evans, Jennifer V. *Life among the Ruins: Cityscape and Sexuality in Cold War Berlin.* Basingstoke: Palgrave Macmillan, 2011.

Evans, Jennifer V. *The Queer Art of History: Queer Kinship after Fascism.* Durham: Duke University Press, 2023.

Evans, Jennifer V., and Brian J. Griffith, eds. "The Catechism Debate." *The New Fascism Syllabus.* 2021. www.newfascismsyllabus.com/category/opinions/the-catechism-debate/.

Ewing, Christopher. *The Color of Desire: The Queer Politics of Race in the Federal Republic of Germany after 1970.* Ithaca: Cornell University Press, 2023.

Ewing, Katherine Pratt. *Stolen Honor: Stigmatizing Muslim Men in Berlin.* Stanford: Stanford University Press, 2008.

Farin, Klaus, and Eberhard Seidel. *Krieg in den Städten: Jugendgangs in Deutschland.* Berlin: Archiv der Jugendkulturen e. V., 2012.

Fehrenbach, Heide. *Race after Hitler: Black Occupation Children in Postwar Germany and America.* Princeton: Princeton University Press, 2005.

Findley, Carter Vaughn. *Turkey, Islam, Nationalism, and Modernity: A History, 1789–2007.* New Haven: Yale University Press, 2010.

Florvil, Tiffany N. *Mobilizing Black Germany: Afro-German Women and the Making of a Transnational Movement.* Champaign: University of Illinois Press, 2020.

Florvil, Tiffany N., and Vanessa Plumly, eds. *Rethinking Black German Studies: Approaches, Interventions, and Histories.* Oxford: Peter Lang, 2018.

Foerster, Lena. *Hochofen, Maloche und "Gastarbeiter": Ausländerbeschäftigung in Unternehmen der Eisen- und Stahlindustrie des Ruhrgebiets in den 1950er bis 1980er Jahren.* Wiesbaden: Franz Steiner Verlag, 2021.

Foerster, Lena. "Zwischen Integration und Rückkehrförderung – türkische Arbeitnehmer bei den Kölner Ford-Werken 1961 bis 1983." *Geschichte in Köln* 62, no. 1 (2015): 237–70.

Freeland, Jane. *Feminist Transformations and Domestic Violence in Divided Berlin, 1968–2002.* Oxford: Oxford University Press, 2022.

Frei, Norbert, Christina Morina, Franka Maubach, and Maik Tändler. *Zur rechten Zeit: Wider die Rückkehr des Nationalismus.* Berlin: Ullstein Verlag, 2019.

Frevert, Ute. "Angst vor Gefühlen? Die Geschichtsmächtigkeit von Emotionen im 20. Jahrhundert." In *Perspektiven der Gesellschaftsgeschichte*, edited by Paul Nolte, Manfred Hettling, Frank-Michael Kuhlemann, and Hans-Walter Schmuhl, 95–111. Munich: C. H. Beck, 2000.

Fromm, Rainer. *Schwarze Geister, neue Nazis: Jugendliche im Visier totalitärer Bewegungen.* Reinbek: Olzog, 2007.

Gatrell, Peter. *The Unsettling of Europe: How Migration Reshaped a Continent.* New York: Basic Books, 2019.

Geddes, Andrew. *Immigration and European Integration: Beyond Fortress Europe.* Manchester: Manchester University Press, 2008.

Gengler, Peter. "'New Citizens' or 'Community of Fate'? Early Discourses and Policies on 'Flight and Expulsion' in the Two Postwar Germanies." *Central European History* 53, no. 2 (August 2020): 314–34.

Gilroy, Paul. *There Ain't No Black in the Union Jack: The Cultural Politics of Race and Nation.* Chicago: University of Chicago Press, 1987.

Gingeras, Ryan. "Last Rites for a 'Pure Bandit': Clandestine Service, Historiography, and the Origins of the Turkish 'Deep State.'" *Past & Present* 206 (February 2010): 151–74.

Gitmez, Ali. "Einwanderer aus der Türkei in Europa. Erfahrungen und Erinnerungen im Spiegel der Literatur." In *Geschichte und Gedächtnis in der Einwanderungsgesellschaft. Migration zwischen historischer Rekonstruktion und Erinnerungspolitik*, edited by Jan Motte and Rainer Ohliger, 53–72. Essen: Klartext, 2004.

Goedde, Petra. *GIs and Germans: Culture, Gender, and Foreign Relations, 1945–1949.* New Haven: Yale University Press, 2003.

Goeke, Simon. *»Wir sind alle Fremdarbeiter!«. Gewerkschaften, migrantische Kämpfe und soziale Bewegungen in Westdeutschland 1960–1980.* Paderborn: Schöningh, 2020.

Gosewinkel, Dieter. "Citizenship in Germany and France at the Turn of the Twentieth Century: Some New Observations on an Old Comparison." In *Citizenship and National Identity in Twentieth-Century Germany*, edited by Geoff Eley and Jan Palmowski, 27–39. Stanford: Stanford University Press, 2008.

Göçmen, Ararat. "Hay, Yabancı, Mensch: National Difference and Multinational Society in the Political Thought of Armenian Workers from Turkey in Postwar Germany." MA thesis. Queen Mary University of London, 2021.

Göle, Nilüfer. *The Forbidden Modern: Civilization and Veiling.* Ann Arbor: University of Michigan Press, 1996.

Götz, Norbert. "German-Speaking People and German Heritage: Nazi Germany and the Problem of *Volksgemeinschaft.*" In *The Heimat Abroad: The Boundaries of Germanness,* edited by K. Molley O'Donnell, Nancy Reagin, and Renate Bridenthal, 58–82. Ann Arbor: University of Michigan Press, 2010.

Grams, Grant W. *Coming Home to the Third Reich: Return Migration of German Nationals from the United States and Canada, 1933–1941.* Jefferson: McFarland & Company, 2021.

Gray, William Glenn. *Germany's Cold War: The Global Campaign to Isolate East Germany, 1949–1969.* Chapel Hill: University of North Carolina Press, 2003.

Greble, Emily. *Muslims and the Making of Modern Europe.* Oxford: Oxford University Press, 2021.

Green, Simon. "Between Ideology and Pragmatism: The Politics of Dual Nationality in Germany." *International Migration Review* 39, no. 4 (2005): 921–52.

Greene, Molly. *A Shared World: Christians and Muslims in the Early Modern Mediterranean.* Princeton: Princeton University Press, 2000.

Griffiths, Craig. *The Ambivalence of Gay Liberation: Homosexual Politics in 1970s West Germany.* Oxford: Oxford University Press, 2021.

Grosser, Dieter, Stephan Bierling, and Beate Neuss, eds. *Deutsche Geschichte in Quellen und Darstellungen.* Vol. 11 of *Bundesrepublik Deutschland und DDR 1969–1990.* Stuttgart: Reklam, 1996.

Grossmann, Atina. "A Question of Silence: The Rape of German Women by Occupation Soldiers." *October* 72 (1995): 43–63.

Grüßhaber, Gerhard. *The "German Spirit" in the Ottoman and Turkish Army, 1908–1938: A History of Military Knowledge Transfer.* Oldenbourg: De Gruyter, 2018.

Guttstadt, Corry. "La politique de la Turquie pendant la Shoah." Translated by Olivier Mannoni. *Revue d'Histoire de la Shoah* 203, no. 2 (2015): 195–231.

Guttstadt, Corry. *Turkey, the Jews, and the Holocaust.* Translated by Kathleen M. Dell'Orto, Sabine Bartel, and Michelle Miles. Cambridge, UK: Cambridge University Press, 2009.

Habermas, Jürgen. *Die postnationale Konstellation: Politische Essays.* Frankfurt am Main: Suhrkamp Verlag, 2001.

Hackett, Sarah E. *Foreigners, Minorities, and Integration: The Muslim Immigrant Experience in Britain and Germany.* Manchester: Manchester University Press, 2013.

Hajdarpašić, Edin. "Out of the Ruins of the Ottoman Empire: Reflections on the Ottoman Legacy in South-eastern Europe." *Middle Eastern Studies* 40, no. 5 (2008): 715–34.

Hale, William M., and Ergun Özbudun. *Islamism, Democracy, and Liberalism in Turkey: The Case of the AKP.* New York: Routledge, 2010.

Hamed-Troyansky, Vladimir. *Empire of Refugees: North Caucasian Muslims and the Late Ottoman State.* Stanford: Stanford University Press, 2024.

Hanioğlu, M. Şükrü. *Atatürk: An Intellectual Biography.* Princeton: Princeton University Press, 2011.

Hanioğlu, M. Şükrü. *A Brief History of the Late Ottoman Empire.* Princeton: Princeton University Press, 2008.

Harper, Marjory, ed. *Emigrant Homecomings: The Return Movement of Emigrants, 1600–2000.* Manchester: Manchester University Press, 2005.

Häusler, Alexander, ed. *Die Alternative für Deutschland. Programmatik, Entwicklung und politische Verortung.* Wiesbaden: Springer, 2016.

Hein, Benjamin Peter. "Emigration and the Industrial Revolution in German Europe, 1820–1900." PhD dissertation, Stanford University, 2018.

Heineman, Elizabeth. *Before Porn Was Legal: The Erotica Empire of Beate Uhse.* Chicago: University of Chicago Press, 2011.

Heineman, Elizabeth. "The Hour of the Woman: Memories of Germany's 'Crisis Years' and West German National Identity." In *The Miracle Years: A Cultural History of West Germany, 1949–1968,* edited by Hanna Schissler, 21–56. Princeton: Princeton University Press, 2001.

Herbert, Ulrich. *A History of Foreign Labor in Germany, 1880–1980: Seasonal Workers/Forced Laborers/Guest Workers.* Translated by William Templer. Ann Arbor: University of Michigan Press, 1990.

Herbert, Ulrich. *Hitler's Foreign Workers: Enforced Foreign Labor in Germany Under the Third Reich.* Translated by William Templer. Cambridge, UK: Cambridge University Press, 1997.

Herzog, Dagmar. *Sex after Fascism: Memory and Morality in Twentieth-Century Germany.* Princeton: Princeton University Press, 2005.

Hong, Young-Sun. *Cold War Germany, the Third World, and the Global Humanitarian Regime.* Cambridge, UK: Cambridge University Press, 2015.

Höpp, Gerhard, and Gerdien Jonker, eds. *In fremder Erde. Zur Geschichte und Gegenwart der islamischen Bestattung in Deutschland.* Berlin: Das Arabisches Buch, 1996.

Hubbell, Amy L. *Remembering French Algeria: Pieds-Noir, Identity, and Exile.* Lincoln: University of Nebraska Press, 2015.

Hull, Isabel V. *Absolute Destruction: Military Culture and the Practices of War in Imperial Germany.* Ithaca: Cornell University Press, 2006.

Huneke, Samuel Clowes. *States of Liberation: Gay Men Between Dictatorship and Democracy in Cold War Germany.* Toronto: University of Toronto Press, 2022.

Hunn, Karin. "'Irgendwann kam das Deutschlandfieber auch in unsere Gegend...' Türkische 'Gastarbeiter' in der Bundesrepublik Deutschland – von der Anwerbung bis zur Rückkehrförderung." In *Geschichte und Gedächtnis in der Einwanderungsgesellschaft. Migration zwischen historischer Rekonstruktion und Erinnerungspolitik,* edited by Jan Motte and Rainer Ohliger. Essen: Klartext, 2004.

Hunn, Karin. *»Nächstes Jahr kehren wir zurück...« Die Geschichte der türkischen »Gastarbeiter« in der Bundesrepublik.* Göttingen: Wallstein, 2005.

Huwer, Jörg. *"Gastarbeiter" im Streik. Die Arbeitsniederlegung bei Ford Köln im August 1973.* Cologne: Verlag edition DOMiD, 2013.

Ihrig, Stefan. *Atatürk in the Nazi Imagination.* Cambridge, MA: Harvard University Press, 2014.

Ihrig, Stefan. *Justifying Genocide: Germany and the Armenians from Bismarck to Hitler.* Cambridge, MA: Harvard University Press, 2016.

İnalcık, Halil. *The Ottoman Empire and Europe: The Ottoman Empire and Its Place in European History.* Istanbul: Kronik, 2017.

Jacobsen, Sarah. "Squatting to Make Ends Meet: Southern Italian Migrants and the Right to a Home in 1970s Italy and West Germany." PhD dissertation, Michigan State University, 2021.

James, Harold, and Marla Stone, eds. *When the Wall Came Down: Reactions to German Unification*. New York: Routledge, 1992.

Jankowitsch, Beate, Thomas Klein, and Stefan Weick. "Die Rückkehr ausländischer Arbeitsmigranten seit der Mitte der achtziger Jahre." In *Deutsche und Ausländer. Freunde, Fremde oder Feinde?*, edited by Richard Goldstein, Peter Schmidt, and Martina Wasmer, 93–109. Berlin: Springer, 2000.

Jarausch, Konrad. *After Hitler: Recivilizing Germans, 1945–1995*. Translated by Brandon Hunziker. New York: Oxford University Press, 2006.

Jezernik, Božidar, ed. *Imagining "The Turk"*. Newcastle upon Tyne: Cambridge Scholars Publishing, 2010.

Joppke, Christian. "Immigration Challenges the Nation-State." In *Challenge to the Nation-State: Immigration in Western Europe and the United States*, edited by Christian Joppke, 5–46. Oxford: Oxford University Press, 1998.

Joppke, Christian. *Immigration and the Nation-State: The United States, Germany, and Great Britain*. Oxford: Oxford University Press, 1999.

Kadırbeyoğlu, Zeynep. "National Transnationalism: Dual Citizenship in Turkey." In *Dual Citizenship in Europe: From Nationhood to Societal Integration*, edited by Thomas Faist, 127–46. Hampshire: Ashgate, 2007.

Kadıroğlu, Ayşe. "The Paradox of Turkish Nationalism and the Construction of Official Identity." *Middle Eastern Studies* 32, no. 2 (1996): 177–93.

Kahn, Michelle Lynn. "The American Influence on German Neo-Nazism: An Entangled History of Hate, 1970s–1990s." *The Journal of Holocaust Research* 35, no. 2 (2021): 91–105.

Kahn, Michelle Lynn. "Antisemitism, Holocaust Denial, and Germany's Far Right: How the AfD Tiptoes around Nazism." *The Journal of Holocaust Research* 36, no. 2–3 (2022): 164–85.

Kahn, Michelle Lynn. "The Long Road Home: Vacations and the Making of the 'Germanized Turk' across Cold War Europe." *The Journal of Modern History* 93, no. 1 (2021): 109–49.

Kahn, Michelle Lynn. "Rebels against the Homeland: Turkish Guest Workers in 1980s West German Anthropology." *Migrant Knowledge*. October 23, 2019. https://migrantknowledge.org/2019/10/23/rebels-against-the-homeland/.

Kahn, Michelle Lynn. "Rethinking Central Europe as a Migration Space: From the Ottoman Empire through the Cold War and the Refugee Crisis." *Central European History* 55, no. 1 (2022): 118–37.

Karacan, Elifcan. *Remembering the 1980 Turkish Military Coup d'État: Memory, Violence, and Trauma*. Wiesbaden: Springer, 2015.

Karakaya, Yağmur, and Alejandro Baer. "'Such Hatred Has Never Flourished on Our Soil': The Politics of Holocaust Memory in Turkey and Spain." *Sociological Forum* 34, no. 3 (2019): 705–28.

Karakayali, Serhat. *Gespenster der Migration. Zur Genealogie illegaler Einwanderung in der Bundesrepublik Deutschland*. Bielefeld: Transcript, 2015.

Karpat, Kemal. *The Gecekondu: Rural Migration and Urbanization.* Cambridge, UK: Cambridge University Press, 1976.

Kaya, Ayhan. "Transnational Citizenship: German-Turks and Liberalizing Citizenship Regimes." *Citizenship Studies* 16, no. 2 (2012): 153–72.

Kaya, Ayhan. *Turkish Origin Migrants and their Descendants: Hyphenated Identities in Transnational Space.* Wiesbaden: Springer, 2018.

Keyder, Çağlar, and Zafer Yenal. "Agrarian Change Under Globalization: Markets and Insecurity in Turkish Agriculture." *Journal of Agrarian Change* 11, no. 1 (2011): 60–86.

Kılınç, Nilay, and Russell King. "The Quest for a 'Better Life': Second-Generation Turkish-Germans 'Return' to 'Paradise.'" *Demographic Research* 36, no. 49 (May 2017): 1491–514.

Kıray, Mübeccel B. "The Family of the Immigrant Worker." In *Turkish Workers in Europe 1960–1975: A Socio-Economic Reappraisal,* edited by Nermin Abadan-Unat, 210–34. Leiden: Brill, 1976.

Klikauer, Thomas. *The AfD: Germany's New Nazis or Another Populist Party?.* Brighton: Sussex Academic Press, 2020.

Kocatürk-Schuster, Bengü, Arnd Kolb, Thanh Long, Günther Schultze, and Sascha Wölk, eds. *Unsichtbar. Vietnamesisch-Deutsche Wirklichkeiten,* Vol. 3 of *edition-DOMiD.* Cologne: DOMiD, 2017.

Kolb, Arnd, ed. *Unbekannte Vielfalt. Einblicke in die koreanische Migrationsgeschichte in Deutschland.* Cologne: DOMiD, 2014.

Kontje, Todd. *German Orientalisms.* Ann Arbor: University of Michigan Press, 2004.

Korteweg, Anna C., and Gökçe Yurdakul. *The Headscarf Debates: Conflicts of National Belonging.* Stanford: Stanford University Press, 2014.

Kostkiewicz, Janina. *Crime Without Punishment: The Extermination and Suffering of Polish Children during the German Occupation, 1939–1945.* Krakow: Jagiellonian University Press, 2021.

Köksal, Yonca. *The Ottoman Empire in the Tanzimat Era: Provincial Perspectives from Ankara to Edirne.* New York: Routledge, 2019.

Kundnani, Hans. *Eurowhiteness: Culture, Empire and Race in the European Project.* London: Hurst, 2023.

Kunuroğlu, Filiz, Kutlay Yağmur, Fons J. R. van de Vijver, and Sjaak Kroon. "Consequences of Turkish Return Migration from Western Europe." *International Journal of Intercultural Relations* 49 (2015): 198–211.

Kuschminder, Katie, and Russell King, eds. *Handbook of Return Migration.* London: Routledge, 2022.

Langenbacher, Eric. *The German Polity.* 12th ed. Lanham: Rowman & Littlefield, 2021.

Langenbacher, Eric, ed. *Twilight of the Merkel Era: Power and Politics in Germany after the 2017 Bundestag Election.* New York: Berghahn, 2019.

Lavy, Victor, and Hillel Rapoport. "External Debt and Structural Adjustment: Recent Experience in Turkey." *Middle Eastern Studies* 28, no. 2 (April 1992): 313–32.

Le Normand, Brigitte. *Citizens Without Borders: Yugoslavia and its Migrant Workers in Western Europe.* Toronto: University of Toronto Press, 2021.

Lehman, Brittany. *Teaching Migrant Children in West Germany and Europe, 1949–1992.* New York: Palgrave Macmillan, 2018.

Lentin, Alana. *Racism and Anti-Racism in Europe.* London: Pluto Press, 2004.

Lopez, Sarah Lynn. *The Remittance Landscape: Spaces of Migration in Rural Mexico and Urban USA.* Chicago: University of Chicago Press, 2015.

Lorenzini, Sara. *Global Development: A Cold War History.* Princeton: Princeton University Press, 2019.

Lucassen, Leo. *The Immigrant Threat: The Integration of Old and New Migrants in Western Europe since 1850.* Champaign: University of Illinois Press, 2005.

Lüdtke, Alf, ed. *Alltagsgeschichte. Zur Rekonstruktion historischer Erfahrungen und Lebensweisen.* Frankfurt am Main: Campus, 1989.

Lyons, Amelia H. *The Civilizing Mission in the Metropole: Algerian Families and the French Welfare State during Decolonization.* Stanford: Stanford University Press, 2013.

Mack, Mehammed Amadeus. *Sexagon: Muslims, France, and the Sexualization of National Culture.* New York: Fordham University Press, 2017.

Madianou, Mirca, and Daniel Miller. "Crafting Love: Letters and Cassette Tapes in Transnational Filipino Family Communication." *South East Asia Research* 19, no. 2 (June 2011): 249–72.

Maier, Charles. *The Unmasterable Past: History, Holocaust, and German National Identity.* Cambridge, MA: Harvard University Press, 1988.

Mandel, Ruth. *Cosmopolitan Anxieties: Turkish Challenges to Citizenship and Belonging in Germany.* Durham: Duke University Press, 2008.

Mangold-Will, Sabine. *Begrenzte Freundschaft. Deutschland und die Türkei 1918–1933.* Göttingen: Wallstein, 2013.

Manthe, Barbara. "The 1980 Oktoberfest Bombing – A Case with Many Question Marks." *OpenDemocracy.* 6 July 2019. www.opendemocracy .net/en/countering-radical-right/the-1980-oktoberfest-bombing-a-case-with-many-question-marks/.

Marchand, Suzanne L. *German Orientalism in the Age of Empire: Race, Religion, and Scholarship.* Cambridge, UK: Cambridge University Press, 2009.

Mardin, Şerif. *Religion and Social Change in Modern Turkey: The Case of Bediüzzaman Said Nursi.* Albany: State University of New York Press, 1989.

Mattes, Monika. *»Gastarbeiterinnen« in der Bundesrepublik. Anwerbepolitik, Migration und Geschlecht in den 5oer bis 7oer Jahren.* Frankfurt am Main: Campus Verlag, 2005.

Mazower, Mark. *The Balkans: A Short History.* New York: Random House, 2007.

Mazón, Patricia, and Reinhild Steingröver, eds. *Not so Plain as Black and White: Afro-German Culture and History.* Rochester: University of Rochester, 2005.

McFadden, Susan Willis. "German Citizenship Law and the Turkish Diaspora." *German Law Journal* 20, no. 1 (2019): 72–88.

McMeekin, Sean. *The Berlin-Baghdad Express: The Ottoman Empire and Germany's Bid for World Power.* Cambridge, MA: Belknap, Harvard University Press, 2010.

Meeker, Michael. *A Nation of Empire: The Ottoman Legacy of Turkish Modernity*. Berkeley: University of California Press, 2002.

Mello, Brian. "Political Process and the Development of Labor Insurgency in Turkey, 1945–1980s." *Social Movement Studies* 6, no. 3 (2007): 207–25.

Mende, Christiane. "Lebensrealitäten der DDR-Arbeitsmigrant_innen nach 1989 – Zwischen Hochkonjunktur des Rassismus und dem Kampf um Rechte." In *Kritische Migrationsforschung? Da kann ja jeder kommen*, edited by Franziska Brückner, et al., 103–22. Berlin: Netzwerk Mira, 2012.

Meng, Michael. "Silences about Sarrazin's Racism in Contemporary Germany." *The Journal of Modern History* 87, no. 1 (2015): 102–35.

Miller, Brian Joseph-Keysor. "Reshaping the Turkish Nation-State: The Turkish-German Guest Working Program and Planned Development, 1961–1985." PhD dissertation, University of Iowa, 2015.

Miller, Jennifer A. "Her Fight is Your Fight: 'Guest Worker' Labor Activism in the Early 1970s West Germany." *International Labor and Working-Class History* 84 (2013): 226–47.

Miller, Jennifer A. "On Track for West Germany: Turkish 'Guest-worker' Rail Transportation to West Germany in the Postwar Period." *German History* 30, no. 4 (November 2012): 550–73.

Miller, Jennifer A. *Turkish Guest Workers in Germany: Hidden Lives and Contested Borders, 1960s–1980s*. Toronto: University of Toronto Press, 2017.

Mills, Amy. *Streets of Memory: Landscape, Tolerance, and National Identity in Istanbul*. Athens: University of Georgia Press, 2010.

Miltiadou, Marios, et al. "Pan-European Corridor X Development: Case of Literal Implementation of the European Transport Strategy Itself or of Change of the General Environment in the Region?" *Procedia – Social and Behavioral Sciences* 48 (2012): 2361–73.

Minian, Ana Raquel. *Undocumented Lives: The Untold Story of Mexican Migration*. Cambridge, MA: Harvard University Press, 2018.

Moeller, Robert G. *Protecting Motherhood: Women and the Family in the Politics of Postwar West Germany*. Berkeley: University of California Press, 1993.

Moeller, Robert G. "The Remasculinization of Germany in the 1950s: Introduction." *Signs* 24, no. 1 (1998): 101–06.

Moeller, Robert G. *War Stories: The Search for a Usable Past in the Federal Republic of Germany*. Berkeley: University of California Press, 2001.

Molnar, Christopher A. "Asylum Seekers, Antiforeigner Violence, and Coming to Terms with the Past after German Reunification." *The Journal of Modern History* 94, no. 1 (2022): 86–126.

Molnar, Christopher A. "'Greetings from the Apocalypse': Race, Migration, and Fear after German Reunification." *Central European History* 54, no. 3 (2021): 491–515.

Molnar, Christopher A. *Memory, Politics, and Yugoslav Migrations to Postwar Germany*. Bloomington: Indiana University Press, 2019.

Morgenstern, Christine. *Rassismus – Konturen einer Ideologie. Einwanderung im politischen Diskurs der Bundesrepublik Deutschland*. Hamburg: Argument Verlag, 2002.

Moses, Dirk A. "The German Catechism." *Geschichte der Gegenwart.* May 23, 2021. www.geschichtedergegenwart.ch/the-german-catechism/.

Motte, Jan, and Rainer Ohliger, eds. *Geschichte und Gedächtnis in der Einwanderungsgesellschaft. Migration zwischen historischer Rekonstruktion und Erinnerungspolitik.* Essen: Klartext, 2004.

Motte, Jan, Rainer Ohliger, and Anne von Oswald, eds. *50 Jahre Bundesrepublik – 50 Jahre Einwanderung. Nachkriegsgeschichte als Migrationsgeschichte.* Frankfurt am Main: Campus, 1999.

Möhring, Maren. *Fremdes Essen. Die Geschichte der ausländischen Gastronomie in der Bundesrepublik Deutschland.* Munich: De Gruyter, 2012.

Mutafchieva, Vera. "The Notion of the 'Other' in Bulgaria: The Turks. A Historical Study." *Anthropological Journal of European Cultures* 4, no. 2 (1995): 53–74.

Müller, Jan-Werner. *Another Country: German Intellectuals, Unification, and National Identity.* New Haven: Yale University Press, 2000.

Müller, Jan-Werner. *Constitutional Patriotism.* Princeton: Princeton University Press, 2007.

Neiman, Susan. *Learning from the Germans: Race and the Memory of Evil.* New York: Farrar, Straus, and Giroux, 2019.

Newsome, Jake W. *Pink Triangle Legacies: Coming Out in the Shadow of the Holocaust.* Ithaca: Cornell University Press, 2022.

Nichols, Bradley Jared. "The Hunt for Lost Blood: Nazi Germanization Policy in Occupied Europe." PhD dissertation, University of Tennessee at Knoxville, 2016.

Nierenberg, Jess. "'Ich möchte das Geschwür loswerden.' Türkenhaß in Witzen in der Bundesrepublik Deutschland." *Fabula* 25, no. 3 (January 1984): 229–40.

Niven, Bill, ed. *Germans and Victims: Remembering the Past in Contemporary Germany.* New York: Palgrave Macmillan, 2006.

Nobrega, Onur Suzan, Matthias Quent, and Jonas Zipf, eds. *Rassimus. Macht. Vergessen. Von München über den NSU bis Hanau: Symbolische und materielle Kämpfe entlang rechten Terrors.* Bielefeld: transcript Verlag, 2021.

Novick, Peter. *The Holocaust in American Life.* Boston: Houghton Mifflin, 1999.

Olusoga, David, and Casper W. Erichsen. *The Kaiser's Holocaust: Germany's Forgotten Genocide and the Colonial Roots of Nazism.* London: Faber and Faber, 2011.

Orhon, Göze. *The Weight of the Past: Memory and Turkey's 12 September Coup.* Newcastle upon Tyne: Cambridge Scholars Publishing, 2015.

Öktem, Kerem. *Angry Nation: Turkey since 1989.* London: Zed Books, 2011.

Ölçen, Ali Nejat. *Türken und Rückkehr. Eine Untersuchung in Duisburg über die Rückkehrneigung türkischer Arbeitnehmer als Funktion ökonomischer und sozialer Faktoren.* Frankfurt am Main: Dağyeli, 1986.

Öniş, Ziya. "The Evolution of Privatization in Turkey: The Institutional Context of Public-Enterprise Reform." *International Journal of Middle East Studies* 21 (1991): 163–76.

Öniş, Ziya. "Turgut Özal and His Economic Legacy: Turkish Neo-Liberalism in Critical Perspective." *Middle Eastern Studies* 40, no. 4 (July 2004): 113–34.

Öniş, Ziya, and Steven B. Webb. *Political Economy of Policy Reform in Turkey in the 1980s*. Policy Research Working Papers: Transition and Macro-Adjustment. The World Bank, 1992.

Özkan, Behlül. *From the Abode of Islam to the Turkish Vatan: The Making of a National Homeland in Turkey*. New Haven: Yale University Press, 2012.

Özyüksel, Murat. *The Berlin-Baghdad Railway and the Ottoman Empire: Industrialization, Imperial Germany, and the Middle East*. London: I. B. Tauris, 2016.

Özyürek, Esra. *Being German, Becoming Muslim: Race, Religion, and Conversion in the New Europe*. Princeton: Princeton University Press, 2015.

Özyürek, Esra. *Nostalgia for the Modern: State Secularism and Everyday Politics in Turkey*. Durham: Duke University Press, 2006.

Özyürek, Esra. "Muslim Minorities as Germany's Past Future: Islam Critics, Holocaust Memory, and Immigrant Integration." *Memory Studies* 15, no. 1 (2019): 139–54.

Özyürek, Esra. "Rethinking Empathy: Emotions Triggered by the Holocaust among the Muslim-Minority in Germany." *Anthropological Theory* 18, no. 4 (2018): 456–77.

Özyürek, Esra. *Subcontractors of Guilt: Holocaust Memory and Muslim Belonging in Postwar Germany* Stanford: Stanford University Press, 2023.

Østergaard-Nielsen, Eva. *Transnational Politics: Turks and Kurds in Germany*. Vol. 8 of *Transnationalism*, edited by Steven Vertovec. London: Routledge, 2003.

Pagenstecher, Cord. "Die 'Illusion' der Rückkehr: Zur Mentalitätsgeschichte von 'Gastarbeit' und Einwanderung." *Soziale Welt* 41, no. 2 (1996): 149–79.

Palmowski, Jan. "In Search of the German Nation: Citizenship and the Challenge of Integration." *Citizenship Studies* 12, no. 6 (2008): 547–63.

Panayi, Panikos. *Ethnic Minorities in Nineteenth and Twentieth Century Germany: Jews, Gypsies, Poles, Turks and Others*. Harlow: Pearson, 2000.

Papadopoulou-Kourkoula, Aspasia. *Transit Migration: The Missing Link Between Emigration and Settlement*. London: Palgrave Macmillan, 2008.

Parla, Ayşe. *Precarious Hope: Migration and the Limits of Belonging in Turkey*. Stanford: Stanford University Press, 2019.

Partridge, Damani J. *Hypersexuality and Headscarves: Race, Sex, and Citizenship in the New Germany*. Bloomington: Indiana University Press, 2012.

Patterson, Walt. *Transforming Electricity: The Coming Generation of Change*. New York: Earthscan, 1999.

Petkova, Lilia. "The Ethnic Turks in Bulgaria: Social Integration and Impact on Bulgarian-Turkish Relations, 1947–2000." *The Global Review of Ethnopolitics* 1, no. 4 (June 2002): 42–59.

Pfaffenthaler, Manfred. "Die Gastarbeiterroute. Zur Geschichte eines transeuropäischen Migrationsweges." In *Mobilitäten. Beiträge der Vortragenden der Montagsakademie*, edited by Ulrike Bechmann and Christian Friedl, 154–64. Graz, 2012.

Plamper, Jan. *Das neue Wir: Warum Migration dazugehört: Eine andere Geschichte der Deutschen*. Frankfurt am Main: S. Fischer, 2019.

Poiger, Ute G. *Jazz, Rock, and Rebels: Cold War Politics and American Culture in a Divided Germany*. Berkeley: University of California Press, 2000.

Poutrus, Patrice G. *Umkämpftes Asyl. Vom Nachkriegsdeutschland bis in die Gegenwart.* Berlin: Christoph Links Verlag, 2019.

Press, Steven. *Blood and Diamonds: Germany's Imperial Ambitions in Africa.* Cambridge, MA: Harvard University Press, 2021.

Pugach, Sara. *African Students in East Germany, 1949–1975.* Ann Arbor: University of Michigan Press, 2022.

Pusch, Barbara, ed. *Transnationale Migration am Beispiel Deutschland und Türkei.* Wiesbaden: Springer, 2012.

Pusch, Barbara, and Julia Splitt. "Binding the *Almancı* to the 'Homeland' – Notes from Turkey." *Perceptions* 18, no. 3 (2013): 129–66.

Pusch, Barbara, and Yaşar Aydın. "Migration of Highly Qualified German Citizens with Turkish Background from Germany to Turkey: Socio-Political Factors and Individual Motives." *International Journal of Business and Globalization* 8, no. 4 (2012): 471–90.

Reddy, William M. *The Navigation of Feeling: A Framework for the History of Emotions.* New York: Columbia University Press, 2001.

Renaud, Terence. *New Lefts: The Making of a Radical Tradition.* Princeton: Princeton University Press, 2021.

Richardson-Little, Ned. *The Human Rights Dictatorship: Socialism, Global Solidarity, and Revolution in East Germany.* Cambridge, UK: Cambridge University Press, 2020.

Robins, Kevin, and David Morley. "Almancı, Yabancı." *Cultural Studies* 10, no. 2 (2006): 248–54.

Roesch, Claudia. "Of Turkish Women and Other Foreigners: Family Planning and Guest Workers in 1980s West Germany." In *Family in Crisis?: Crossing Borders, Crossing Narratives,* edited by Eva-Sabine Zehelein, Andrea Carosso, and Aida Rosende-Pérez, 193–204. Bielefeld: Transcript, 2020.

Roos, Christof. *The EU and Immigration Policies: Cracks in the Walls of Fortress Europe?* London: Palgrave Macmillan, 2013.

Roos, Julia. "The Race to Forget? Bi-Racial Descendants of the First Rhineland Occupation in 1950s West German Debates about the Children of African American GIs." *German History* 37, no. 4 (2019): 517–39.

Rosas, Ana Elizabeth. *Abrazando El Espíritu: Bracero Families Confront the U.S.-Mexico Border.* Berkeley: University of California Press, 2014.

Rosenwein, Barbara H. "Worrying about Emotions in History." *American Historical Review* 107, no. 3 (2002): 821–45.

Rosselini, Jay Julian. *The German New Right: AfD, PEGIDA, and the Re-Imagining of National Identity.* London: Hurst and Company, 2019.

Rothberg, Michael. *Multidirectional Memory: Remembering the Holocaust in the Age of Decolonization.* Stanford: Stanford University Press, 2009.

Rothberg, Michael, and Yasemin Yildiz. "Memory Citizenship: Migrant Archives of Holocaust Remembrance in Contemporary Germany." *Parallax* 17, no. 4 (2011): 32–48.

Rottmann, Susan Beth. *In Pursuit of Belonging: Forging an Ethical Life in European-Turkish Spaces.* New York: Berghahn, 2019.

Rottmann, Susan Beth. "Negotiating Modernity and Europeanness in the Germany-Turkey Transnational Social Field." *Insight Turkey* 16, no. 4 (2014): 143–58.

Rottmann, Susan Beth, and Myra Marx Ferree. "Citizenship and Intersectionality: German Feminist Debates about Headscarf and Antidiscrimination Laws." *Social Politics* 15, no. 4 (2008): 481–513.

Ruble, Alexandria. *Entangled Emancipation: Women's Rights in Cold War Germany*. Toronto: University of Toronto Press, 2023.

Said, Edward W. *Orientalism*. New York: Pantheon Books, 1978.

Samudzi, Zoe. "Capturing German South West Africa: Racial Production, Land Claims, and Belonging in the Afterlife of the Herero and Nama Genocide." PhD dissertation, University of California San Francisco, 2021.

Sayılan, Fevziye and Ahmet Yıldız. "The Historical and Political Context of Adult Literacy in Turkey." *International Journal of Lifelong Education* 28, no. 6 (2009): 735–49.

Sayyid, Salman. *A Fundamental Fear: Eurocentrism and the Emergence of Islamism*. New York: Zed Books, 1997.

Schenck, Marcia C. *Remembering African Labor Migration to the Second World: Socialist Mobilities between Angola, Mozambique, and East Germany*. New York: Palgrave Macmillan, 2023.

Schiffauer, Werner. *Die Migranten aus Subay: Türken in Deutschland: Eine Ethnographie*. Stuttgart: Ernst Klett Verlag, 1991.

Schissler, Hanna, ed. *The Miracle Years: A Cultural History of West Germany, 1949–1968*. Princeton: Princeton University Press, 2001.

Schönwälder, Karen, and Triadafilos Triadafilopoulos. "A Bridge or Barrier to Incorporation?: Germany's 1999 Citizenship Reform in Critical Perspective." *German Politics and Society* 30, no. 1 (2012): 52–70.

Schulz, Kristina. *Der lange Atem der Provokation: Die Frauenbewegung in der Bundesrepublik Deutschland und in Frankreich, 1968–1976*. Frankfurt am Main: Campus, 2002.

Scott, Joan Wallach. *The Politics of the Veil*. Princeton: Princeton University Press, 2010.

Shandler, Jeffrey. *While America Watches: Televising the Holocaust*. Oxford: Oxford University Press, 2000.

Shaw, Stanford J. *Turkey and the Holocaust: Turkey's Role in Rescuing Turkish and European Jewry from Nazi Persecution*. London: Macmillan, 1992.

Shefer-Mossensohn, Miri. *Science among the Ottomans: The Cultural Creation and Exchange of Knowledge*. Austin: University of Texas Press, 2015.

Sheffer, Edith. *Burned Bridge: How East and West Germans Made the Iron Curtain*. Oxford: Oxford University Press, 2007.

Shepard, Todd. *The Invention of Decolonization: The Algerian War and the Remaking of France*. Ithaca: Cornell University Press, 2006.

Shepard, Todd. *Sex, France, and Arab Men, 1962–1979*. Chicago: University of Chicago Press, 2021.

Silies, Eva-Maria. "Taking the Pill after the 'Sexual Revolution': Female Contraceptive Decisions in England and West Germany in the 1970s." *European Review of History* 22, no. 1 (2015): 41–59.

Silverstein, Paul A. *Algeria in France: Transpolitics, Race, and Nation*. Bloomington: Indiana University Press, 2004.

Sirkeci, İbrahim. *The Environment of Insecurity in Turkey and the Emigration of Turkish Kurds to Germany*. Lewiston: Edwin Mellen Press, 2006.

Slobodian, Quinn, ed. *Comrades of Color: East Germany in the Cold War World.* New York: Berghahn, 2015.

Slobodian, Quinn. *Globalists: The End of Empire and the Birth of Neoliberalism.* Cambridge, MA: Harvard University Press, 2018.

Smith, Andrea L. *Europe's Invisible Migrants.* Amsterdam: Amsterdam University Press, 2003.

Sohm, Matthew. "Paying for the Post-Industrial: The Global Costs of West German and European Capitalist Crisis and Revival, 1972–1988." PhD dissertation, Harvard University, 2022.

Soysal, Levent. "The Migration Story of Turks in Germany: From the Beginning to the End." In *Turkey in the World,* Vol. 4 of *The Cambridge History of Turkey,* edited by Reşat Kasaba, 199–225. Cambridge, UK: Cambridge University Press, 2008.

Soysal, Levent. "Rap, HipHop, Kreuzberg: Scripts of/for Migrant Youth Culture in the WorldCity Berlin." *New German Critique* 92 (2004): 62–81.

Sosyal, Yasemin Nuhoğlu. *Limits of Citizenship: Migrants and Postnational Membership in Europe.* Chicago: University of Chicago Press, 1994.

Sökefeld, Martin. *Struggling for Recognition: The Alevi Movement in Germany and in Transnational Space.* New York: Berghahn Books, 2008.

Starr, June. "The Role of Turkish Secular Law in Changing the Lives of Rural Muslim Women, 1950–1970." *Law and Society Review* 23, no. 3 (1989): 497–523.

Steege, Paul. *Black Market, Cold War: Everyday Life in Berlin, 1946–1949.* Cambridge, UK: Cambridge University Press, 2007.

Steinhardt, Max Friedrich. "Does Citizenship Matter? The Economic Impact of Naturalizations in Germany." *Labour Economics* 19, no. 6 (December 2012): 813–23.

Stokes, Lauren. *Fear of the Family: Guest Workers and Family Migration in the Federal Republic of Germany.* Oxford: Oxford University Press, 2022.

Stokes, Lauren. "'An Invasion of Guest Worker Children': Welfare Reform and the Stigmatisation of Family Migration in West Germany." *Contemporary European History* 28, no. 3 (2019): 372–89.

Stokes, Lauren. "The Permanent Refugee Crisis in the Federal Republic of Germany, 1949-." *Central European History* 52, no. 1 (2019): 19–44.

Strumpen, Sarina. *Ältere Pendelmigranten aus der Türkei. Alters- und Versorgungserwartungen im Kontext von Migration, Kultur und Religion.* Bielefeld: Transcript, 2018.

Su, Phi Hong. *The Border Within: Vietnamese Migrants Transforming Ethnic Nationalism in Berlin.* Stanford: Stanford University Press, 2022.

Sungu, Can. "'Wenn wir nicht aufstehen, endet unser Elend nicht.' Gesellschaftskritik im türkischen Migrationskino: Baba (1971), Almanya Acı Vatan (1979) und Kara Kafa (1979)." In *Deutsch-Türkische Filmkultur im Migrationskontext,* edited by Ömer Alkın, 73–91. Berlin: Springer, 2017.

Szatkowski, Tim. *Die Bundesrepublik Deutschland und die Türkei 1978–1983.* Berlin: De Gruyter, 2016.

Şahin, Levent, and Kadir Yıldırım. "On Dukuzuncu Yüzyıldan Günümüze Türkiye'de İşsizlikle Mücadele Politikalarının Gelişimi." *Çalışma ve Toplum* 45 (2015): 123–25.

Şen, Faruk. "Motor der Entwicklung? Die Rolle des Tourismus in der türkischen Volkswirtschaft." Lecture at the Zentrum für Türkeistudien, Essen, 1994.

Şen, Faruk. *Türkische Arbeitnehmergesellschaften. Gründung, Struktur und wirtschaftliche Funktion der türkischen Arbeitnehmergesellschaften in der Bundesrepublik Deutschland für die sozioökonomische Lage der Türkei.* Frankfurt am Main: Peter D. Lang, 1980.

Tachau, Frank, and Metin Heper. "The State, Politics, and the Military in Turkey." *Comparative Politics* 16, no. 1 (October 1983): 17–33.

Tertilt, Hermann. *Turkish Power Boys: Ethnographie einer Jugendbande.* Frankfurt am Main: Suhrkamp, 1996.

Ther, Philipp. *Europe since 1989: A History.* Translated by Charlotte Hughes-Kreutzmiller. Princeton: Princeton University Press, 2016 [2014].

Ther, Philipp. *The Outsiders: Refugees in Europe since 1492.* Princeton: Princeton University Press, 2019.

Tibi, Bassam. *Europa ohne Identität: Die Krise der multikulturellen Gesellschaft.* Munich: Bertelsmannm, 1998.

Todorova, Maria. *Imagining the Balkans.* Oxford: Oxford University Press, 1996.

Treber, Leonie. *Mythos Trümmerfrauen: Vor der Trümmerbeseitigung in der Kriegs- und Nachkriegszeit und der Entstehung eines deutschen Erinnerungsortes.* Essen: Klartext, 2014.

Trede, Oliver. *Zwischen Misstrauen, Regulation und Integration: Gewerkschaften und Arbeitsmigration in der Bundesrepublik und Großbritannien in den 1960er und 70er Jahren.* Paderborn: Schöningh, 2015.

Tremblay, Sébastian. *A Badge of Injury: The Pink Triangle as Global Symbol of Memory.* Berlin: De Gruyter, 2023.

Triadafilopoulos, Triadafilos, and Karen Schönwälder. "How the Federal Republic Became an Immigration Country: Norms, Politics, and the Failure of West Germany's Guest Worker System." *German Politics and Society* 24, no. 3 (2006): 1–19.

Tschoepe, Aylın Yıldırım. "Locating the German-Turks: Transnational Migration to Turkey and Constructions of Identity and Space." In *Contemporary Turkey at a Glance II: Turkey Transformed? Power, History, Culture*, edited by M. Ersoy and E. Özyürek, 113–30. Wiesbaden: Springer VS, 2017.

Tsuda, Takeyuki, ed. *Diasporic Homecomings: Ethnic Return Migration in Comparative Perspective.* Stanford: Stanford University Press, 2009.

Van der Heyden, Ulrich, Wolfgang Semmel, and Ralf Straßburg, eds. *Mosambikanische Vertragsarbeiter in der DDR-Wirtschaft: Hintergrund – Vorlauf – Folgen.* Berlin: Lit Verlag, 2014.

Van Hear, Nicholas, Rebecca Brubaker, and Thais Bessa. "Managing Mobility for Human Development: The Growing Salience of Mixed Migration." MRPA paper, no. 19202. Oxford: United Nations Development Reports, 2009.

Van Schaaik, Gerjan. *The Oxford Turkish Grammar.* Oxford: Oxford University Press, 2020.

Van Wyck, Brian. "Guest Workers in the School? Turkish Teachers and the Production of Migrant Knowledge in West German Schools, 1971–1989." *Geschichte und Gesellschaft: Zeitschrift für historische Sozialwissenschaft* 3, no. 43 (2017): 466–91.

Van Wyck, Brian. "Turkish Teachers and Imams and the Making of Turkish German Difference." PhD dissertation, Michigan State University, 2019.

Vassaf, Gündüz. *Daha Sesimizi Duyurmadık: Avrupa'da Türk İşçi Çocukları.* 2nd ed. Istanbul: Istanbul Bilgi Üniversitesi Yayınları, 2010[1983].

Vierra, Sarah Thomsen. *Turkish Germans in the Federal Republic of Germany: Immigration, Space, and Belonging, 1961–1990.* Cambridge, UK: Cambridge University Press, 2018.

Von Oswald, Anne, and Barbara Schmidt. "'Nach Schichtende sind sie immer in ihr Lager zurückgekehrt....' Leben in 'Gastarbeiter'-Unterkünften in den sechziger und siebziger Jahren." In *50 Jahre Bundesrepublik – 50 Jahre Einwanderung. Nachkriegsgeschichte als Migrationsgeschichte,* edited by Jan Motte, Rainer Ohliger, and Anne von Oswald, 184–214. Frankfurt am Main: Campus, 1999.

Von Plato, Alexander, Almut Leh, and Christoph Thonfeld, eds. *Hitler's Slaves: Life Stories of Forced Labourers in Nazi-Occupied Europe.* New York: Berghahn Books, 2010.

Vukadinović, Vojin Saša, ed. *Rassismus: Von der frühen Bundesrepublik bis zur Gegenwart.* Berlin: De Gruyter, 2022.

Waldorf, B. S., A. Esparza, and J. O. Huff. "A Behavioral Model of International Labor and Nonlabor Migration: The Case of Turkish Movements to West Germany, 1960–1986." *Environment and Planning* 22 (1989): 961–73.

Wallace, Claire. "The New Migration Space as a Buffer Zone." In *Patterns of Migration in Central Europe,* edited by Claire Wallace and Dariusz Stola, 72–83. London: Palgrave, 2001.

Wallace, Claire, et al. "The Eastern Frontier of Western Europe: Mobility in the Buffer Zone." *Journal of Ethnic and Migration Studies* 22 (1996): 259–86.

Watson, Wallace Steadman. *Understanding Rainer Werner Fassbinder: Film as Private and Public Art.* Columbia: University of South Carolina Press, 1996.

Weber, Barbara M. *Violence and Gender in the "New" Europe: Islam in German Culture.* New York: Palgrave Macmillan, 2013.

Weiss, Karin, and Mike Dennis, eds. *Erfolg in der Nische? Die Vietnamesen in der DDR und in Ostdeutschland.* Münster: Lit Verlag, 2005.

Wildenthal, Lora. *The Language of Human Rights in West Germany.* Philadelphia: University of Pennsylvania Press, 2012.

Wilhelm, Cornelia, ed. *Migration, Memory, and Diversity: Germany from 1945 to the Present.* New York: Berghahn, 2017.

Wilhelm, Gülçin. *Generation Koffer. Die zurückgelassenen Kinder.* Berlin: Orlanda, 2011.

Wills, Clair. *Lovers and Strangers: An Immigrant History of Post-War Britain.* London: Penguin UK, 2017.

Winter, Elke, Annkathrin Diehl, and Anke Patzelt. "Ethnic Nation No More? Making Sense of Germany's New Stance on Dual Citizenship by Birth." *Review of European and Russian Affairs* 9, no. 1 (Spring 2015): 1–19.

Woesthoff, Julia. "Ambiguities of Anti-Racism: Representations of Foreign Laborers and the West German Media." PhD dissertation, Michigan State University, 2004.

Woesthoff, Julia. "'Foreigners and Women Have the Same Problems': Binational Marriages, Women's Grassroots Organizing, and the Quest for Legal Equality in Post-1968 Germany." *Journal of Family History* 38, no. 4 (October 2013): 422–42.

Wokoeck, Ursula. *German Orientalism: The Study of the Middle East and Islam from 1800 to 1945.* London: Routledge, 2009.

Wolbert, Barbara. *Der getötete Paß. Rückkehr in die Türkei. Eine ethnologische Migrationsstudie.* Berlin: Akademie Verlag, 1995.

Wyman, Mark. *Round-Trip to America: The Immigrants Return to Europe, 1880–1930.* Ithaca: Cornell University Press, 1993.

Yaman, Yunus Şaban, and Engin Başçı. "'Katma Değer Şaban' ve 'Orta Direk Şaban' Filmlerinde 1980'ler Türkiye'sinin Ekonomi Politikalarının Eleştirisi." *İletişim Çalışmaları Dergisi* 6, no. 2 (2020): 223–43.

Yardımcı, Deniz Güneş. "The Representation of Turkish Immigration to Germany in German, Turkish German and Turkish Cinema." PhD dissertation, Royal Holloway, University of London, 2017.

Yavuz, M. Hakan, and Ahmet Erdi Öztürk. *Erdoğan's Turkey: Islamism, Identity, and Memory.* New York: Routledge, 2022.

Yaycıoğlu, Ali. *Partners of the Empire: The Crisis of the Ottoman Order in the Age of Revolutions.* Stanford: Stanford University Press, 2016.

Yıldırım, Duygu. "The Age of the Perplexed: Translating Nature and Bodies between the Ottoman Empire and Europe, 1650–1730." PhD dissertation, Stanford University, 2021.

Yılmaz, Aytaç, and Mathilde Jamin, eds. *Fremde Heimat. Yaban, Sılan olur. Eine Geschichte der Einwanderung aus der Türkei. Ausstellungskatalog des Essener Ruhrmuseums und des DOMiT.* Essen: Klartext, 1998.

Yurdakul, Gökçe. *From Guest Workers into Muslims: The Transformation of Turkish Immigrant Associations in Germany.* Newcastle upon Tyne: Cambridge Scholars Publishing, 2009.

Yurdakul, Gökçe. "'We Don't Want To Be the Jews of Tomorrow': Jews and Turks in Germany after 9/11." *German Politics and Society* 24, no. 2 (2006): 44–67.

Zahra, Tara. *The Great Departure: Mass Migration from Eastern Europe and the Making of the Free World.* New York: W. W. Norton, 2017.

Zahra, Tara. "Migration, Mobility, and the Making of a Global Europe." *Contemporary European History* 31 (2022): 142–54.

Zaimoğlu, Feridun. *Kanak Sprak: 24 Mißtöne vom Rande der Gesellschaft.* Berlin: Rotbuch, 2013.

Zandi-Sayek, Sibel. *Ottoman Izmir: The Rise of a Cosmopolitan Port, 1840–1880.* Minneapolis: University of Minnesota Press, 2011.

Zentrum für Türkeistudien. "Türkische Remigranten." Essen: Zentrum für Türkeistudien, 1992.

Zeppenfeld, Stefan. *Vom Gast zum Gastwirt? Türkische Arbeitswelten in West-Berlin.* Göttingen: Wallstein, 2021.

Zimmerer, Jürgen. *Von Windhuk nach Auschwitz?: Beiträge zum Verhältnis von Kolonialismus und Holocaust.* Münster: Lit Verlag, 2011.

Zürcher, Erik J. *Turkey: A Modern History.* London: I. B. Tauris, 1993.

Index

www.ingramcontent.com/pod-product-compliance
Lightning Source LLC
Chambersburg PA
CBHW072351240225
22504CB00004B/288